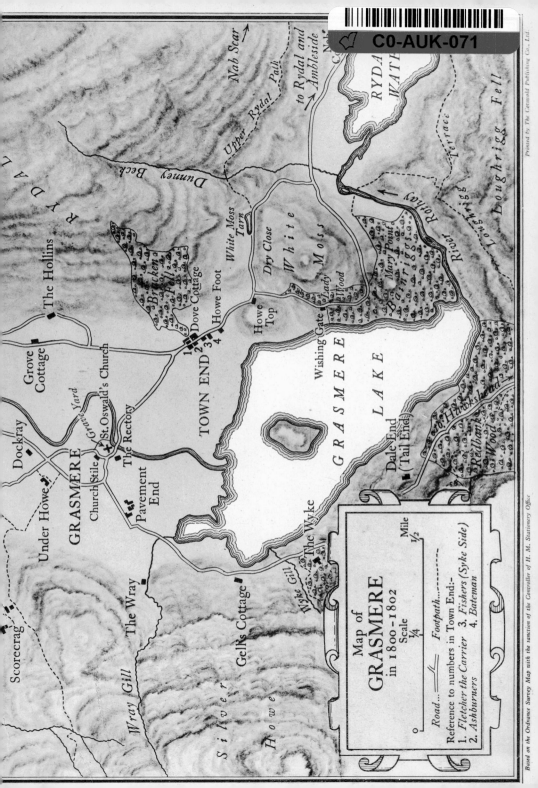

Printed by The Cotswold Publishing Co., Ltd.

RYDAL

Nab Scar →

to Rydal and Ambleside

Upper Rydal Path

RYDAL WATER

Dunney Beck

Loughrigg Terrace

River Rothay

Loughrigg Fell

The Hollins

White Moss Tarn

Dry Close

White Moss

Birrigs

Bracken Fell

Dove Cottage

Howe Foot

Lady Wood

Mary Point

Grove Cottage

Howe Top

Wishing Gate

TOWN END

St. Oswald's Church

Grave Yard

The Rectory

GRASMERE LAKE

Dockray

Under Howe

GRASMERE

Church Stile

Pavement End

Dale End (Tail End)

to Hawkshead

Redbank Wood

Scorecrag

The Wray

Gell's Cottage

The Wyke

Wyke Gill

Silver Howe

Wray Gill

Map of GRASMERE in 1800-1802
Scale ¼

0 ¼ ½ Mile

Road...——
Footpath...----
Reference to numbers in Town End:-
1. Fletcher the Carrier   3. Fishers (Syke Side)
2. Ashburners   4. Bateman

Based on the Ordnance Survey Map with the sanction of the Controller of H. M. Stationery Office

JOURNALS OF DOROTHY WORDSWORTH

Dove Cottage

From a water-colour by Dora Wordsworth

JOURNALS OF
DOROTHY
WORDSWORTH

Edited by
E. DE SELINCOURT

VOLUME I

LONDON
MACMILLAN & CO. LTD
1959

This book is copyright in all countries which
are signatories to the Berne Convention

First Edition 1941
Reprinted 1952
Reprinted 1959

PRINTED IN GREAT BRITAIN
BY LOWE & BRYDONE PRINTERS LTD., LONDON N.W.10

PREFACE

DOROTHY WORDSWORTH is probably the most remarkable and the most distinguished of English writers who never wrote a line for the general public. " I should detest ", she said, " the idea of setting myself up as an author " ; and throughout her life, though a pen was often in her hand, and her unique literary gift was fully recognised by a wide circle of friends, among them the finest critics of the age, her only compositions to be printed were short extracts from her journals and letters which her brother quoted in notes to his poems, or rehandled for insertion in his *Guide to the Lakes*. Her *Recollections of a Tour made in Scotland* (1803) remained in manuscript for seventy years after she wrote it, and it was not till 1897 that Professor Knight's well-known selection from her *Journals* made its appearance. Since that time interest has steadily grown in her fascinating personality and in the writings that so faithfully reflect it, and she has to-day countless enthusiastic admirers who would gladly possess a greater body of her work than has hitherto been available. To meet that desire these volumes have been prepared.

Their contents, with the exception of the *Journal* written at Alfoxden, which is given from the text of Professor Knight, are printed from the manuscripts formerly in the possession of Mr. Gordon Wordsworth,[1] and presented by him, shortly before his death, to the Wordsworth Museum at Grasmere. The manuscript of the *Alfoxden Journal* has been entirely lost sight of, and all attempts to trace its whereabouts have so far proved unavailing. This is peculiarly unfortunate, for though the passages omitted from the published text may be comparatively unimportant, it covers a vital epoch in the lives of the poet, his sister, and Coleridge, of which we would welcome the fullest details.

---

[1] The only exception to this is MS. B of *Recollections of a Tour made in Scotland*, which was given by the author to her nephew John and by him to his daughter Dorothy, who, in her turn, presented it to the Wordsworth Museum.

The *Journals* kept by Dorothy in Germany (1798) and at Grasmere (1800–1803) are now for the first time given in their entirety. They are preserved in four small notebooks, some pages of which have been utilised for other purposes, — for accounts, lists of books and miscellaneous memoranda, rough drafts of fragments of verse, etc., and anyone who is acquainted with the neat and often beautiful hand in which Dorothy copied her brother's poems would hardly recognise as hers the untidy scrawl in which she made these hurried daily entries, though unquestionably they reflect more truly her naturally impetuous temper. In my text I have retained her characteristic spellings and her capricious use of capitals : trivial *lapsus calami*, accidental droppings of letters, and misspellings due to haste have been corrected. Similarly, I have not scrupled to alter the punctuation when it distorts the sense ; and I have not everywhere kept the dash, which a rapid writer, and especially, perhaps, a diarist, tends to employ not only according to correct literary usage, but as a substitute alike for comma, semicolon, full stop, or often, as a space-saving device, to indicate a fresh paragraph. In these matters I have been actuated by the desire to present a readable document, and at the same time to retain all that is personally significant.

The *Grasmere Journal*, in particular, can only be justly appreciated when its private, intimate character is borne in mind. Here, indeed, lies much of its undying charm. Written at her brother's instigation, and, as she says, " because I shall give him pleasure by it ", it was meant for no eyes but his and her own. Thus it makes no pretension to continuous literary form, — it was set down from day to day, as the mood struck her ; and side by side with acute perception, and quick sympathetic response to all that surrounded her in the worlds of man and nature, expressed often with a delicate imaginative insight, and everywhere with a moving simplicity, are the homeliest details of household management and of the goings-on of every day. A more beautiful book might doubtless be made by rigorous selection from its contents. Yet this juxtaposition of entries on such widely different emotional levels, with its inevitable inconsequence, stamps the whole as a veritable transcript of real life ; and the greater moments are thrown into a stronger relief by their work-a-day setting. The result is a precious human document.

The greatest value of this *Journal* lies, unquestionably, in its revelation of Dorothy herself, with that genius for life in all its moods and aspects which was her supreme quality, and in particular in its record of her daily companionship with her beloved brother at the time when she had most to give him and gave it unstintingly ; but it has a further interest as a vivid picture of the life and people of a typical village community at the beginning of the last century. In elucidation of this I am fortunate in being able to draw upon the valuable notes compiled by the late Mr. Gordon Wordsworth. Mr. Wordsworth had an unrivalled knowledge of local history, and his exhaustive investigation of parish registers and local records brought to light much interesting information concerning persons and places mentioned in the *Journal*. I have distinguished his notes by affixing to them his initials, G. G. W.

The *Recollections of a Tour made in Scotland* (1803) has not, like the *Grasmere Journal*, the character of a purely private diary. It was written expressly for " the sake of a few friends, who, it seemed, ought to have been with us " ; hence it was carefully composed throughout ; and, further, it was not jotted down, like a diary, from day to day, but written at leisure after her return, while the events recorded were still vivid in her memory, and when she could see the whole tour in something of artistic perspective. Dorothy insists upon this in several of her letters. " I am writing ", she says, " not a Journal, *for we took no notes*, but *recollections* of our tour in the form of a Journal." The result is one of the most delightful of all books of travel, and it is, undoubtedly, her masterpiece. The friends for whom she wrote it recognised at once its value, and gave it a wide circulation in manuscript. The poet Rogers was among those who were anxious to see it in print, and he offered his services to secure terms for her with a publisher. But for some reason or other the negotiations fell through.

Fifteen years later, when her health had already given way, the matter was raised again. Her brother had hoped that " the business of taking it through the press might act as a profitable stirring of her mind ", but after much hesitation he decided that she was not equal to the task ; he was, moreover, acutely sensitive to the painful nature of her illness, and felt that " there would be some indelicacy in drawing public attention to her in her present melancholy state ".

The supreme place held by the *Recollections* among Dorothy's writings is emphasised by the existence of no less than five manuscripts ; [1] and a brief account of them will throw some light upon the composition and progress of the work.

MS. A, the first of these manuscripts, is in the hand of Dorothy's friend Catherine Clarkson, and is headed " Recollections of a Tour in Scotland by Dorothy Wordsworth. Addressed to her Friends." Appended is the following note : " This copy of my beloved friend's Journal was begun at Grasmere the beginning of September and finished at Patterdale this day (the 1st of November 1805). When I began the work I scarcely indulged the hope of finishing it myself, my health being so indifferent that every little exertion of mind or body fatigued me exceedingly ; but instead of a difficult task I have found it the easiest and pleasantest employment that I ever engaged in ; and though the possession of such a treasure makes me very happy, yet I am sincerely sorry that my work is ended. The whole (except a very few pages, the writing of which was the only toilsome part of the undertaking) was written in bed, and the whole by myself, except the title-pages and the divisions of the work which were written by George Hutchinson, brother of my two dear friends Mrs. Wordsworth and Sara Hutchinson, and the title on the first page of the work, which my Husband had the kindness to interrupt himself, when he was exceedingly busy in his own work, to write for me. — C. C."

---

[1] In my account of the manuscripts of the *Recollections* I have drawn largely upon the Appendix to my *Life of Dorothy Wordsworth* (Oxford, 1933). For permission to do this I am deeply indebted to the Delegates of the Oxford University Press.

As Dorothy's copy from which Mrs. Clarkson transcribed is no longer traceable, this MS. represents the first version of the book; it is divided into three parts: Part I, August 14–25; Part II, August 26–September 5; Part III, September 6–25.

Notes inserted in the manuscript [1] give detailed information as to the date at which different parts of the *Recollections* were composed. Beginning soon after her return from Scotland in September 1803, she worked steadily into December; but on December 20 she was interrupted by the arrival of Coleridge to pay them a farewell visit on his way to Malta. She had then brought her record down to the entry for September 2. She resumed work on February 2, but a few days later she laid it aside in order to make a copy of William's poems for Coleridge to take abroad with him; and though she took it up again towards the end of March, she seems to have found it difficult to recover the mood for composition. In June, and again in July, she made fruitless efforts to continue, but it was not until the following April that she completed her task, urged on by William, who thought that it might prove some distraction to her from her grief at the loss of her brother John, who had been drowned in the previous February. At the end of the manuscript is written the note: " Finished copying this Journal May 31st, 1805, in the Moss hut at the top of the Orchard. — D. W."

MS. B is Dorothy's own second copy, written in the clear, beautiful handwriting in which she had just transcribed *The Prelude*. It is a quarto volume, written on both sides of the paper and divided, like MS. A, into three parts. On the last page is the note: " This transcript finished Friday, February 21st, 1806 ". It must have been begun sometime after November 1, 1805, when Mrs. Clarkson had finished her transcript, and there is good reason to suppose that it is almost entirely the work of the months of January and February 1806 (*v. infra*). In the main, MS. B follows A; but, as she copied, Dorothy added some passages of importance, and introduced a large number of minor changes.

---

[1] The notes are reproduced in MS. B, and will be found on pp. 439 and 344 *infra*.

A complete collation of the two texts is hardly necessary, but the general character of the alterations made in MS. B is worth illustrating, for they were obviously aimed at rendering the style less colloquial. Thus the phrase " by the bye " is three times cut out, " I dare say " altered to " I believe ", " out of the way " to " lonely ", " seemed " continually to " appeared ", " guessed " to " conjectured ", and " about " to " respecting " or " concerning " ; while the adverb " very ", far too often occurring in A, is frequently removed. Some changes in the direction of a more literary style are not for the better, *e.g.* " struck me with a sort of stupid wonder " to " struck me with astonishment ", " I thought less of the Trossachs " to " I was less occupied with the remembrance of the Trossachs ", " how late it was " to " how far the evening was advanced ", " mistaken " to " erroneous ", " virtues " to " excellent qualities ", " lie " to " untruth ", and so on. And one must regret, too, the loss of a few personal touches, of which, when Dorothy is the writer, we can hardly have too many : the best of these I have recorded in footnotes to my text.[1] But the additions made to MS. B amply compensate for the loss. It was in re-copying that Dorothy added to the entry for August 18 the passage which begins with a reference to Drayton and ends with four stanzas addressed by her brother to the Sons of Burns ; that she added to September 3 the apt quotation of the poem *Brook and Road* ; to September 8 the reference to the battle of Killiecrankie ; to September 12 the poem on Rob Roy ; to September 13 *The Solitary Reaper*. MS. B unquestionably preserves the best text of the *Recollections*, and I have printed from it.

This was the copy used by Principal Shairp for his edition of 1874. Shairp made a few modifications of punctuation, corrected the reference to the " Haymarket " in Edinburgh to the " Grassmarket ", and improved the spelling of some of the place-names. This Dorothy herself would have admitted to be necessary. " Do not wonder ", she wrote to Lady Beaumont, " if you or Sir George should detect some in-

[1] To these notes are affixed the letters C. C.

accuracies, often misspelt and even miscalled, for I never looked into a book, and only bore in mind my own remembrance of the sounds as they were pronounced to us." Shairp made a few errors in transcription, and he substituted, for Dorothy's division of her book into three parts, a division into weeks. Some of Shairp's notes I have reproduced, placing after them his initials, J. C. S.

Professor Knight (1897) printed from Shairp, only making some changes in punctuation, and without reference to any manuscript. He states, indeed, in his Preface that he has seen the transcript made by Dorothy for Mrs. Clarkson, by which we must suppose him to mean Mrs. Clarkson's transcript from Dorothy's MS., but it is clear that he made no use of it, for he remarks, " It is difficult to know what the Author meant by the first, second, and third Parts of her Journal, as it is divided into separate weeks throughout ". But this, as we have seen, was first done by Shairp, and has no MS. authority. Knight also faithfully reproduces all Shairp's misprints.

MSS. Ci and Cii are in the exquisite handwriting of Sara Hutchinson, and though not of great importance in a study of the text, one of them, at least, has a great personal interest. For on the title-page is written " S. T. Coleridge. Oct. 24th, 1806." This was the day on which William, Mary, and Dorothy, together with Sara Hutchinson, first met Coleridge after his return from Malta. This copy was therefore prepared for Coleridge in his absence, and is the one referred to by Dorothy in her letter to Mrs. Clarkson of March 2, 1806 : " We have been engaged in making fair copies of W.'s poems, and I also in re-copying my Journal in a fair hand to be bequeathed to my niece and namesake. These works are finished, and also Sara's copy for Coleridge."

MSS. C represent a stage in the text intermediary between MSS. A and B. They contain most of the passages which Dorothy added to B, but few of the alterations and corrections which she introduced into the B text. The most natural explanation of this would be that when Mrs. Clarkson returned Dorothy's MS. of the *Recollections*, both she and Sara were already at work making copies of William's poems, and that, as both of them could not copy at the same time from the same MS., Dorothy, after adding the new passages to the *Journal*, handed it over to Sara, and addressed herself to the poems. Then, when Sara had copied the *Journal*, Dorothy, who had now finished the poems, took over her *Journal*, and, as she wrote MS. B, made the verbal changes already referred to. For Sara would hardly have copied the earlier version if B had already been in existence.

MS. D is a copy made in 1822–3 when the book was being prepared for the press ; some corrections may have been made to the MS. in 1832, when, as we have seen, the idea of publication was again mooted, but it is not likely that much was done at that time. This MS. is written on quarto sheets, with watermark 1820, roughly stitched together into four booklets. No. 1 goes down to the entry August 25 and is in Dorothy's writing ; No. 2, in a hand now unidentifiable, to the middle of the entry for September 1 ; No. 3, the first twenty pages in the hand of John Carter, the poet's clerk, and the rest in Dorothy's, takes the *Journal* to September 4 ; No. 4, which completes the book, is written by Dorothy, but the poems inserted in it are in the unknown hand. This copy differs widely from previous MSS. ; it is much corrected, and in places new versions are stuck with wafers over the older text. We can hardly be too grateful that the proposals for the publication of the book fell through, for in preparing it for press Dorothy submitted it to far too drastic a revision. In her desire to make it, as she thought, more suitable for the general public, she removed from it many of those intimate personal touches to which it owes so much of its value, whilst at the same time she " wrote it up ", giving it here and there a pomposity of phrasing which is a poor exchange for the simplicity and directness of the earlier text. For example, " the point where we had set off " becomes " the point where we had commenced our circuit ", " we were unwilling to leave this sweet spot " becomes " we reluctantly wheeled away from the scene ", " such a cruel woman " becomes " a woman who appeared to be destitute of common humanity ", and " I would willingly have given twenty pounds to ", " happy should I have been to"; similarly "showed us up" is altered to "conducted us", "hunted out" to "set ourselves to discover", "walked on" to "proceeded", "close" to "adjoining", "building" to "edifice", "called out" to "exclaimed", and "works of God" to "works of the Creator".

Naturally enough, when the audience for whom she destined her *Journal* was widened, she severely reduced its *personalia*. Familiar details, which a few personal friends might welcome, appeared to her wholly unsuited for the world at large. Authors in her day were for the most part reticent of their own and their friends' private lives. She had herself an abnormal shrinking from publicity, and she was anxious, too, in speaking of her fellow-travellers, men already famous and the subject of irritating and sometimes malicious gossip, not to overstep what she felt to be the bounds of a proper decorum. Accordingly William and Coleridge are often referred to simply as ".my companions", William's awkwardness in unharnessing the horse is cut out, "poor C. being unwell" becomes "our companion, not in strong health", and many references to his ailments are omitted, as well as the account of how they divided their purse with him at parting, and how, when he had left them, "their thoughts were full of him". So, too, the name of Scott, who so largely added to the joys of the last week of their tour, is never mentioned; he is spoken of simply as "our friend", and, inevitably, many delightful details of the time they spent with him — such as their arrival at his house before he was up, their extravagant indulgence in a bottle of wine in his honour, and his recitation to them of his new poem, *The Lay of the Last Minstrel*—find no place. Of herself, also, Dorothy is less communicative; if she tells that she tried in vain to buy a silver thimble at Dumfries, she omits to add that she actually bought a halfpenny brass one, and the world was not to know of occasional headaches, stiffness, or fatigue, or how at the inn she lay stretched at her ease upon the carriage cushions and three chairs. In compensation she now introduced such historical or legendary information as a literary guide-book was expected to supply. Thus, of Bothwell Bridge she tells (August 22) that it is "memorable for the discomfiture of the Covenanters by the Duke of Monmouth, who showed on that occasion, if we may credit Burnet, a clemency which was ill relished by Charles and his brother " ; and of Stirling Castle (September 14) that it is " so famous in Scottish history — the overlooker of many a bloody battle — and with the field of Bannockburn lying almost at its base. Stirling Castle was, in latter times, a favourite residence of some of the kings of Scotland on account of its delightful situation, and the salubrity, as it was supposed, of the air ; but being almost at a central point between the two coasts, it must be exposed to dreadful storms from the meeting of winds that blow from both quarters." To her account of Roslin Chapel (September 7) she adds, " One of the pillars of this beautiful little Gothic edifice is singularly elaborate, a twisted column, of which they tell a story at Roslin, that the master slew his apprentice, who performed the work, through envy in being surpassed by him in his own art ". The more interesting of the additions which Dorothy made to the latest text I have given in an Appendix, and also the revised version of her first day's travel, which illustrates better, perhaps, than any other passage, the general character of her revision.

The *Excursion on the Banks of Ullswater* (1805), of which Professor Knight printed an abbreviated version, is here given complete from Dorothy's manuscript, where it has no title, but is merely headed " November 1805 ". In the fourth edition of his *Guide to the Lakes* (1823) her brother included a much altered version of it, together with the next item in this volume, under the title of *Excursions to the Top of Scawfell and on the Banks of Ullswater*.[1] The account was written, he says, " for one acquainted with the general features of the country ", and it seems highly probable that his reference is to Lady Beaumont, for at this period Dorothy was in constant and intimate correspondence with her. In a letter dated November 7 she wrote : " I rode upon my little pony, and William walked by my side. We came over Kirkstone . . . we were

---

[1] *v.* my edition of Wordsworth's *Guide to the Lakes*, 1906, pp. 118-28 ; the account occupies pp. 112-16. It is interesting to compare Wordsworth's versions of both excursions with his sister's originals.

very anxious to visit some of the vales tributary to Ullswater, where we have never been before, while yet the brown leaves are upon some of the trees. . . . This is a wonderful country, the more wonderful the more we know of it. . . . Yesterday we had visions of things, imperfectly seen as we passed along, that might have employed our fancy happily for hours, if they had not been in the next moment replaced by others as beautiful." Again, in a letter of November 29, she makes allusion to the trip, and we can well believe that the *Journal* was compiled to satisfy her friend's entreaty for fuller details of it.

The *Excursion up Scawfell Pike*, not included in Knight's edition of the *Journals*, is an account of the ascent made by Dorothy in October 1818 with her friend Miss Barker. Originally it formed part of a letter to the Rev. William Johnson, who had become intimate with the Wordsworths during his curacy at Grasmere in 1811–12, and was at this time headmaster of the Central School, London. Wordsworth included an abridged and much altered version of it in the third edition (1822) of his *Guide to the Lakes*, where he speaks of it as " from a letter to a Friend " ; in the fourth edition, as stated above, it was joined to the *Excursion on the Banks of Ullswater*, and with it formed a kind of Appendix to his *Guide*.

The *Journal of a Tour on the Continent* tells the tale of a journey through France, Belgium, Germany, Switzerland, and Italy in July to October 1820. The party consisted of William, Mary, and Dorothy Wordsworth, Thomas Monkhouse (Mary's cousin) and his wife, then on their honeymoon, Miss Horrocks (Mrs. Monkhouse's sister), and her maid Jane. At Lucerne they were joined by Crabb Robinson. All the party except the poet and Monkhouse, we are told, kept some sort of record of their adventures, but Dorothy's was far the most elaborate.[1] She began to read it over with a view to connected composition soon after her return to Rydal in February 1821, but in March she could only report little progress, and it was not till April that she set to work in good earnest ; in May she was often

---

[1] It is two and a half times as long as Mary Wordsworth's.

sitting at her desk in her bedroom window from ten in the morning until four in the afternoon ; [1] and on August 25 her rough copy was finished, but, she wrote, " it is not fit to be read by others — I write so carelessly ".[2] In October she re-copied it " in plain hand ".

Unlike the *Recollections of a Tour made in Scotland*, the Continental *Journal* was, as we have seen, compiled from full notes taken at the time, and this method, though doubtless it was justified both by the greater length of the tour and by the fact that Dorothy could not trust her memory as surely as when she was some twenty years younger, did not produce so good a result. She was hampered by the very copiousness of her material, and, as she re-wrote, she became more and more painfully conscious that she had adopted far too elaborate a scale of treatment. " Had not my brother ", she tells Mrs. Clarkson, " so very much wished me to do my best I am sure I should never have had the resolution to go further than just re-copy what I did by snatches and very irregularly at the time ; but to please him I have amplified and arranged, and a long affair will come out of it ; which I cannot think any person can possibly have the patience to read through, but which through sympathy and a desire to revive distant recollections may in patches be interesting to a few others " ; [3] and later she referred to it as " that enormous journal which I can never expect anyone (except a few idle folks who have nothing else to do) ever to read through ". With characteristic modesty she even doubted whether it had any intrinsic worth. " It is ", she said, " utterly unsatisfactory to myself as a description of Switzerland ; a land where height, depth, bulk, nay immensity, — profusion — silence — solitude make up the grandest of our feelings, — where it is utterly impossible to describe the objects except by their effects on the mind." [4] And those for whom she wrote, though they estimated it far higher than she did, were forced to recognise that there was too much of it. Her brother, in a note dictated to Miss Fenwick in 1843, expressed the wish that " somebody would put

---

[1] *v. L.Y.* p. 37.
[3] *v. L.Y.* pp. 37, 38.
[2] *v. L.Y.* p. 47.
[4] *v. L.Y.* p. 31.

together, as in one work, the notions contained in [his sister's and his wife's journals] omitting particulars that were written down merely to aid our memory, and bringing the whole into as small a compass as is consistent with the general interest belonging to the scenes, circumstances, and spots touched upon by each writer ". And in 1824 Crabb Robinson, while he was anxious to see the *Journal* in print, urged her to compress it throughout, and to omit considerable portions of the descriptions. To which she replied : " Your advice is, I am sure, very good, provided it were worth while to make a Book of it, — provided I *could* do so, and provided it were my wish : but it is not. ' Far better ', I say, ' make another Tour and write the journal on a different plan ! ' . . . But, observe, my object is *not* to make a book, but to leave to my Niece a neatly penned Memorial of those few interesting months of our lives." [1]

It was with this end in view that she employed " a young friend " (whose identity is not now discoverable) to make a copy of the *Journal*. Before she handed over the manuscript to her copyist she gave it a hasty reading-over, but she had neither time nor patience to revise it drastically ; she was content with cutting out a " few passages, sometimes pretty long ones ". Yet despite these omissions the transcript made by the " young friend " runs to 745 closely written quarto pages.

This copy is the only manuscript known to exist, for Dorothy's notes, together with her own rough and fair copies, have all disappeared ; it was begun in November 1825 and progressed slowly ; the date of its completion is not recorded, but a note on page 389 states that it was copied in 1828, and it was in June 1830 that Dorothy herself added a Table of Contents. It is embellished with a few engravings, and with a set of coloured prints illustrating the costumes of the Swiss peasantry which Crabb Robinson had procured at Dorothy's request. Crabb Robinson also made some minor corrections and added a few notes. My text follows this copy, but out of regard to the views expressed by the author, her brother, and

---

[1] *Correspondence of H. C. R. with the W. Circle*, ed. by E. J. Morley (2 vols., Oxford, 1827), p. 127.

Crabb Robinson, as well as to the patience of subsequent readers, I have reduced its bulk by rather less than a quarter: even so I have given about four times as much as has been previously printed. My principle has been to present a continuous record of the Tour, only omitting some trivial details, and such descriptions of scenery as were repetitive or of little interest. But I have scrupulously retained what seemed typical of the author, all *personalia*, and all that throws light upon the poet and his work. Even so shortened, some readers may find parts of the *Journal* a little tedious; but those who revisit the scenes she describes could hardly take with them a better companion volume to their *Baedeker* or *Blue Guide*, noting how the country, both in its changed and its unchanging features, impressed an alert and sensitive traveller more than a century ago. I have reproduced in my text Dorothy's more characteristic spellings, except in the case of place-names, in which she is even more erratic than in her *Recollections of a Tour made in Scotland*; to these I have given the current forms.

The *Journal of my Second Tour in Scotland* recounts a journey made in 1822 with Joanna Hutchinson, Mary Wordsworth's youngest sister. It was written soon after her return, from notes which, said her brother, " are very amusing, particularly as a contrast to the loneliness of her former mode of travelling ".[1] Dorothy could not have given much time to its composition, for she was then occupied in preparing the *Recollections* of her previous tour for its projected publication; but, if we may judge by her rehandling of the *Recollections*, it is probably all the better for not having undergone revision, and as it stands it contains some vivid and characteristic writing. I have printed it from the manuscript with a few unimportant omissions.

The *Journal of a Tour in the Isle of Man* is taken from a series of rough diaries which Dorothy kept fitfully during the period from December 1824 to 1833; these are preserved in eleven shabby little notebooks. For the most part they consist

---

[1] W. W. to Richard Sharp (*L.Y.* p. 92).

of the briefest entries, simply recording the weather, the comings and goings of the family at Rydal and their guests, the books she was reading, and, in the last few years, painful details of the symptoms of her illness. The only portion written in consecutive style, as a journal rather than a mere diary, is that which treats of her visit to Joanna and Henry Hutchinson, who were now living in the Isle of Man : this fills the major part of two of the notebooks. Professor Knight printed extracts from the first of these, but apparently never saw the second. I have printed the whole account of her visit. It has a special interest as the record of her last tour before her health broke up ; and it shows her interest unabated in the life about her, while her gift for delineating it has much of its old distinctive charm.

For permission to reproduce the water-colours of Dove Cottage by Dora Wordsworth and of Town End by T. M. Richardson I am indebted to the Trustees of Dove Cottage ; for the two pencil drawings of the old road over White Moss Common by T. L. Aspland, to the Trustees of the Armitt Library, Ambleside. The drawing of old Grasmere I owe to the kindness of Mrs. Stewart and Miss Hilda Austin, granddaughters of the artist; the portrait of Wordsworth by Edridge, and the drawing of Grasmere Church and Bridge by J. Flower, to the kindness of Mrs. Rawnsley; the drawing of Rydal Mount by William Green, to Mr. Herbert Bell. The maps which illustrate the several Tours have been specially drawn for me by Messrs. Emery Walker, Ltd.

E. DE S.

GRASMERE
August 1940

CONTENTS

VOLUME I

ILLUSTRATIONS

MAPS

xxiii

ABBREVIATIONS, ETC., USED IN TEXT AND NOTES

D. W.   = Dorothy Wordsworth.

W., Wm., or W. W. = William Wordsworth.

C. C.   = The manuscript of *Recollections of a Tour made in Scotland*, written by Catherine Clarkson (MS. A).

I. F. note = One of the notes dictated by W. to Isabella Fenwick in 1843.

W. K.   = Professor William Knight, editor of D. W.'s *Journals* (1897).

J. C. S. = Principal Shairp, editor of *Recollections of a Tour made in Scotland*, 1874.

G. G. W. = Gordon Graham Wordsworth.

E.L.   = *The Early Letters of W. and D. W.*   Oxford, 1935.

M.Y.   = *The Letters of W. and D. W. : The Middle Years.*   2 vols. Oxford, 1937.

L.Y.   = *The Letters of W. and D. W. : The Later Years.*   3 vols. Oxford, 1939.

Memorials, etc. = *Memorials of a Tour on the Continent*, 1820, by W. W.

[   ] = word or words missing in manuscript.

[?   ] = word or words illegible in manuscript.

Words included in square brackets are editorial conjectures.

I

THE ALFOXDEN JOURNAL
1798

Alfoxden

From an engraving

DOROTHY WORDSWORTH'S JOURNAL, WRITTEN AT ALFOXDEN IN 1798

ALFOXDEN, *January* 20*th*, 1798. The green paths down the hill-sides are channels for streams. The young wheat is streaked by silver lines of water running between the ridges, the sheep are gathered together on the slopes. After the wet dark days, the country seems more populous. It peoples itself in the sunbeams. The garden, mimic of spring, is gay with flowers. The purple-starred hepatica spreads itself in the sun, and the clustering snow-drops put forth their white heads, at first upright, ribbed with green, and like a rosebud when completely opened, hanging their heads downwards, but slowly lengthening their slender stems. The slanting woods of an unvarying brown, showing the light through the thin net-work of their upper boughs. Upon the highest ridge of that round hill covered with planted oaks, the shafts of the trees show in the light like the columns of a ruin.

January 21*st*. Walked on the hill-tops — a warm day. Sate under the firs in the park. The tops of the beeches of a brown-red, or crimson. Those oaks, fanned by the sea breeze, thick with feathery sea-green moss, as a grove not stripped of its leaves. Moss cups more proper than acorns for fairy goblets.

January 22*nd*. Walked through the wood to Holford. The ivy twisting round the oaks like bristled serpents. The day cold — a warm shelter in the hollies, capriciously bearing berries. Query : Are the male and female flowers on separate trees ?

January 23*rd*. Bright sunshine, went out at 3 o'clock. The sea perfectly calm blue, streaked with deeper colour by the clouds, and tongues or points of sand ; on our return of a gloomy red. The sun gone down. The crescent moon, Jupiter, and Venus. The sound of the sea distinctly heard on the tops

3

of the hills, which we could never hear in summer. We attribute this partly to the bareness of the trees, but chiefly to the absence of the singing of birds, the hum of insects, that noiseless noise which lives in the summer air. The villages marked out by beautiful beds of smoke. The turf fading into the mountain road. The scarlet flowers of the moss.

January 24th. Walked between half-past three and half-past five. The evening cold and clear. The sea of a sober grey, streaked by the deeper grey clouds. The half dead sound of the near sheep-bell, in the hollow of the sloping coombe, exquisitely soothing.

January 25th. Went to Poole's after tea. The sky spread over with one continuous cloud, whitened by the light of the moon, which, though her dim shape was seen, did not throw forth so strong a light as to chequer the earth with shadows. At once the clouds seemed to cleave asunder, and left her in the centre of a black-blue vault. She sailed along, followed by multitudes of stars, small, and bright, and sharp. Their brightness seemed concentrated (half-moon).

January 26th. Walked upon the hill-tops; followed the sheep tracks till we overlooked the larger coombe. Sat in the sunshine. The distant sheep-bells, the sound of the stream; the woodman winding along the half-marked road with his laden pony; locks of wool still spangled with the dewdrops; the blue-grey sea, shaded with immense masses of cloud, not streaked; the sheep glittering in the sunshine. Returned through the wood. The trees skirting the wood, being exposed more directly to the action of the sea breeze, stripped of the net-work of their upper boughs, which are stiff and erect, like black skeletons; the ground strewed with the red berries of the holly. Set forward before two o'clock. Returned a little after four.

January 27th. Walked from seven o'clock till half-past eight. Upon the whole an uninteresting evening. Only once while we were in the wood the moon burst through the invisible veil which enveloped her, the shadows of the oaks blackened, and their lines became more strongly marked. The withered leaves were coloured with a deeper yellow, a brighter gloss

4

spotted the hollies ; again her form became dimmer ; the sky flat, unmarked by distances, a white thin cloud. The manufacturer's dog makes a strange, uncouth howl, which it continues many minutes after there is no noise near it but that of the brook. It howls at the murmur of the village stream.

January 28th. Walked only to the mill.

January 29th. A very stormy day. William walked to the top of the hill to see the sea. Nothing distinguishable but a heavy blackness. An immense bough riven from one of the fir trees.

January 30th. William called me into the garden to observe a singular appearance about the moon. A perfect rainbow, within the bow one star, only of colours more vivid. The semicircle soon became a complete circle, and in the course of three or four minutes the whole faded away. Walked to the blacksmith's and the baker's ; an uninteresting evening.

January 31st. Set forward to Stowey at half-past five. A violent storm in the wood ; sheltered under the hollies. When we left home the moon immensely large, the sky scattered over with clouds. These soon closed in, contracting the dimensions of the moon without concealing her.[1] The sound of the pattering shower, and the gusts of wind, very grand. Left the wood when nothing remained of the storm but the driving wind, and a few scattering drops of rain. Presently all clear, Venus first showing herself between the struggling clouds; afterwards Jupiter appeared. The hawthorn hedges, black and pointed, glittering with millions of diamond drops ; the hollies shining with broader patches of light. The road to the village of Holford glittered like another stream. On our return, the wind high — a violent storm of hail and rain at the Castle of Comfort. All the Heavens seemed in one perpetual motion when the rain ceased ; the moon appearing, now half veiled, and now retired behind heavy clouds, the stars still moving, the roads very dirty.

---

[1] Cf. *Christabel*, ll. 16-20 :

The thin gray cloud is spread on high,
It covers but not hides the sky.
The moon is behind, and at the full ;
And yet she looks both small and dull.
The night is chill, the cloud is gray.

February 1st. About two hours before dinner, set forward towards Mr. Bartholemew's.[1] The wind blew so keen in our faces that we felt ourselves inclined to seek the covert of the wood. There we had a warm shelter, gathered a burthen of large rotten boughs blown down by the wind of the preceding night. The sun shone clear, but all at once a heavy blackness hung over the sea. The trees almost *roared*, and the ground seemed in motion with the multitudes of dancing leaves, which made a rustling sound, distinct from that of the trees. Still the asses pastured in quietness under the hollies, undisturbed by these forerunners of the storm. The wind beat furiously against us as we returned. Full moon. She rose in uncommon majesty over the sea, slowly ascending through the clouds. Sat with the window open an hour in the moonlight.

February 2nd. Walked through the wood, and on to the Downs before dinner ; a warm pleasant air. The sun shone, but was often obscured by straggling clouds. The redbreasts made a ceaseless song in the woods. The wind rose very high in the evening. The room smoked so that we were obliged to quit it. Young lambs in a green pasture in the Coombe, thick legs, large heads, black staring eyes.

February 3rd. A mild morning, the windows open at breakfast, the redbreasts singing in the garden. Walked with Coleridge over the hills. The sea at first obscured by vapour ; that vapour afterwards slid in one mighty mass along the sea-shore ; the islands and one point of land clear beyond it. The distant country (which was purple in the clear dull air), overhung by straggling clouds that sailed over it, appeared like the darker clouds, which are often seen at a great distance apparently motionless, while the nearer ones pass quickly over them, driven by the lower winds. I never saw such a union of earth, sky, and sea. The clouds beneath our feet spread themselves to the water, and the clouds of the sky almost joined them. Gathered sticks in the wood ; a perfect stillness. The redbreasts sang upon the leafless boughs. Of a great number of sheep in the field, only one standing. Returned to dinner

---

[1] Mr. Bartholemew rented Alfoxden, and sub-let the house to Wordsworth.
—W. K.

at five o'clock. The moonlight still and warm as a summer's night at nine o'clock.

February 4th. Walked a great part of the way to Stowey with Coleridge. The morning warm and sunny. The young lasses seen on the hill-tops, in the villages and roads, in their summer holiday clothes — pink petticoats and blue. Mothers with their children in arms, and the little ones that could just walk, tottering by their side. Midges or small flies spinning in the sunshine ; the songs of the lark and redbreast ; daisies upon the turf ; the hazels in blossom ; honeysuckles budding. I saw one solitary strawberry flower under a hedge. The furze gay with blossom. The moss rubbed from the pailings by the sheep, that leave locks of wool, and the red marks with which they are spotted, upon the wood.

February 5th. Walked to Stowey with Coleridge, returned by Woodlands ; a very warm day. In the continued singing of birds distinguished the notes of a blackbird or thrush. The sea overshadowed by a thick dark mist, the land in sunshine. The sheltered oaks and beeches still retaining their brown leaves. Observed some trees putting out red shoots. Query : What trees are they ?

February 6th. Walked to Stowey over the hills, returned to tea, a cold and clear evening, the roads in some parts frozen hard. The sea hid by mist all the day.

February 7th. Turned towards Potsham, but finding the way dirty, changed our course. Cottage gardens the object of our walk. Went up the smaller Coombe to Woodlands, to the blacksmith's, the baker's, and through the village of Holford. Still misty over the sea. The air very delightful. We saw nothing very new, or interesting.

February 8th. Went up the Park, and over the tops of the hills, till we came to a new and very delicious pathway, which conducted us to the Coombe. Sat a considerable time upon the heath. Its surface restless and glittering with the motion of the scattered piles of withered grass, and the waving of the spiders' threads. On our return the mist still hanging over the sea, but the opposite coast clear, and the rocky cliffs distinguishable. In the deep Coombe, as we stood upon the sunless hill, we saw miles of grass, light and glittering, and the insects passing.

February 9th. William gathered sticks. . . .

February 10th. Walked to Woodlands, and to the waterfall. The adder's-tongue and the ferns green in the low damp dell. These plants now in perpetual motion from the current of the air ; in summer only moved by the drippings of the rocks. A cloudy day.

February 11th. Walked with Coleridge near to Stowey. The day pleasant, but cloudy.

February 12th. Walked alone to Stowey. Returned in the evening with Coleridge. A mild, pleasant, cloudy day.

February 13th. Walked with Coleridge through the wood. A mild and pleasant morning, the near prospect clear. The ridges of the hills fringed with wood, showing the sea through them like the white sky, and still beyond the dim horizon of the distant hills, hanging as it were in one undetermined line between sea and sky.

February 14th. Gathered sticks with William in the wood, he being unwell and not able to go further. The young birch trees of a bright red, through which gleams a shade of purple. Sat down in a thick part of the wood. The near trees still, even to their topmost boughs, but a perpetual motion in those that skirt the wood. The breeze rose gently ; its path distinctly marked, till it came to the very spot where we were.

February 15th. Gathered sticks in the further wood. The dell green with moss and brambles, and the tall and slender pillars of the unbranching oaks. I crossed the water with letters ; returned to Wm. and Basil.[1] A shower met us in the wood, and a ruffling breeze.

February 16th. Went for eggs into the Coombe, and to the baker's ; a hail shower ; brought home large burthens of sticks, a starlight evening, the sky closed in, and the ground white with snow before we went to bed.

February 17th. A deep snow upon the ground. Wm. and Coleridge walked to Mr. Bartholemew's, and to Stowey. Wm. returned, and we walked through the wood into the Coombe to

---

[1] The five-year-old son of W.'s friend Montagu (*v. E.L.* p. 138).

fetch some eggs. The sun shone bright and clear. A deep stillness in the thickest part of the wood, undisturbed except by the occasional dropping of the snow from the holly boughs ; no other sound but that of the water, and the slender notes of a redbreast, which sang at intervals on the outskirts of the southern side of the wood. There the bright green moss was bare at the roots of the trees, and the little birds were upon it. The whole appearance of the wood was enchanting ; and each tree, taken singly, was beautiful. The branches of the hollies pendent with their white burden, but still showing their bright red berries, and their glossy green leaves. The bare branches of the oaks thickened by the snow.

February 18th. Walked after dinner beyond Woodlands.[1] A sharp and very cold evening ; first observed the crescent moon, a silvery line, a thready bow, attended by Jupiter and Venus in their palest hues.

February 19th. I walked to Stowey before dinner ; Wm. unable to go all the way. Returned alone ; a fine sunny, clear, frosty day. The sea still, and blue, and broad, and smooth.

February 20th. Walked after dinner towards Woodlands.

February 21st. Coleridge came in the morning, which prevented our walking. Wm. went through the wood with him towards Stowey ; a very stormy night.

February 22nd. Coleridge came in the morning to dinner. Wm. and I walked after dinner to Woodlands ; the moon and two planets ; sharp and frosty. Met a razor-grinder with a soldier's jacket on, a knapsack upon his back, and a boy to drag his wheel. The sea very black, and making a loud noise as we came through the wood, loud as if disturbed, and the wind was silent.

February 23rd. William walked with Coleridge in the morning. I did not go out.

February 24th. Went to the hill-top. Sat a considerable time overlooking the country towards the sea. The air blew pleasantly round us. The landscape mildly interesting. The

---

[1] This house was afterwards John Kenyon's,—to whom *Aurora Leigh* is dedicated,—and was subsequently the residence of the Rev. William Nichols, author of *The Quantocks and their Associations*.—W. K.

Welsh hills capped by a huge range of tumultuous white clouds. The sea, spotted with white, of a bluish grey in general, and streaked with darker lines. The near shores clear; scattered farm houses, half-concealed by green mossy orchards, fresh straw lying at the doors; hay-stacks in the fields. Brown fallows, the springing wheat, like a shade of green over the brown earth, and the choice meadow plots, full of sheep and lambs, of a soft and vivid green; a few wreaths of blue smoke, spreading along the ground; the oaks and beeches in the hedges retaining their yellow leaves; the distant prospect on the land side, islanded with sunshine; the sea, like a basin full to the margin; the dark fresh-ploughed fields; the turnips of a lively rough green. Returned through the wood.

February 25th. I lay down in the morning, though the whole day was very pleasant, and the evening fine. We did not walk.

February 26th. Coleridge came in the morning, and Mr. and Mrs. Cruikshank; [1] walked with Coleridge nearly to Stowey after dinner. A very clear afternoon. We lay sidelong upon the turf, and gazed on the landscape till it melted into more than natural loveliness. The sea very uniform, of a pale greyish blue, only one distant bay, bright and blue as a sky; had there been a vessel sailing up it, a perfect image of delight. Walked to the top of a high hill to see a fortification. Again sat down to feed upon the prospect; a magnificent scene, *curiously* spread out for even minute inspection, though so extensive that the mind is afraid to calculate its bounds. A winter prospect shows every cottage, every farm, and the forms of distant trees, such as in summer have no distinguishing mark. On our return, Jupiter and Venus before us. While the twilight still overpowered the light of the moon, we were reminded that she was shining bright above our heads, by our faint shadows going before us. We had seen her on the tops of the hills, melting into the blue sky. Poole called while we were absent.

February 27th. I walked to Stowey in the evening. Wm.

---

[1] Of Nether-Stowey, the agent of the Earl of Egmont.—W. K.

and Basil went with me through the wood. The prospect bright, yet *mildly* beautiful. The sea big and white, swelled to the very shores, but round and high in the middle. Coleridge returned with me, as far as the wood. A very bright moonlight night. Venus almost like another moon. Lost to us at Alfoxden long before she goes down the large white sea.

  · · · · · · · ·

March 1st. We rose early. A thick fog obscured the distant prospect entirely, but the shapes of the nearer trees and the dome of the wood dimly seen and dilated. It cleared away between ten and eleven. The shapes of the mist, slowly moving along, exquisitely beautiful ; passing over the sheep they almost seemed to have more of life than those quiet creatures. The unseen birds singing in the mist.

March 2nd. Went a part of the way home with Coleridge in the morning. Gathered fir-apples afterwards under the trees.

March 3rd. I went to the shoemaker's. William lay under the trees till my return. Afterwards went to the secluded farm house in search of eggs, and returned over the hill. A very mild, cloudy evening. The rose trees in the hedges and the elders budding.

March 4th. Walked to Woodlands after dinner, a pleasant evening.

March 5th. Gathered fir-apples. A thick fog came on. Walked to the baker's and the shoemaker's, and through the fields towards Woodlands. On our return, found Tom Poole in the parlour. He drank tea with us.

March 6th. A pleasant morning, the sea white and bright, and full to the brim. I walked to see Coleridge in the evening. William went with me to the wood. Coleridge very ill. It was a mild, pleasant afternoon, but the evening became very foggy ; when I was near Woodlands, the fog overhead became thin, and I saw the shapes of the Central Stars. Again it closed, and the whole sky was the same.

March 7th. William and I drank tea at Coleridge's. A cloudy sky. Observed nothing particularly interesting — the distant prospect obscured. One only leaf upon the top of a tree — the sole remaining leaf — danced round and round like a rag blown by the wind.[1]

March 8th. Walked in the Park in the morning. I sate under the fir trees. Coleridge came after dinner, so we did not walk again. A foggy morning, but a clear sunny day.

March 9th. A clear sunny morning, went to meet Mr. and Mrs. Coleridge. The day very warm.

March 10th. Coleridge, Wm., and I walked in the evening to the top of the hill. We all passed the morning in sauntering about the park and gardens, the children playing about, the old man at the top of the hill gathering furze ; interesting groups of human creatures, the young frisking and dancing in the sun, the elder quietly drinking in the life and soul of the sun and air.

March 11th. A cold day. The children went down towards the sea. William and I walked to the top of the hills above Holford. Met the blacksmith. Pleasant to see the labourer on Sunday jump with the friskiness of a cow upon a sunny day.

March 12th. Tom Poole returned with Coleridge to dinner, a brisk, cold, sunny day ; did not walk.

March 13th. Poole dined with us. William and I strolled into the wood. Coleridge called us into the house.

. . . .

March 15th. I have neglected to set down the occurrences of this week, so I do not recollect how we disposed of ourselves to-day.

March 16th. William, and Coleridge, and I walked in the Park a short time. I wrote to ——. William very ill, better in the evening ; and we called round by Potsham.

March 17th. I do not remember this day.

March 18th. The Coleridges left us. A cold, windy morning. Walked with them half way. On our return, sheltered under the hollies, during a hail-shower. The withered leaves danced

---

[1] Cf. *Christabel*, 49-52 :
> *The one red leaf, the last of its clan,*
> *That dances as often as dance it can,*
> *Hanging so light, and hanging so high,*
> *On the topmost twig that looks up at the sky.*

with the hailstones. William wrote a description of the storm.[1]

March 19th. Wm. and Basil and I walked to the hill-tops, a very cold bleak day. We were met on our return by a severe hailstorm. William wrote some lines describing a stunted thorn.[2]

March 20th. Coleridge dined with us. We went more than half way home with him in the evening. A very cold evening, but clear. The spring seemingly very little advanced. No green trees, only the hedges are budding, and looking very lovely.

March 21st. We drank tea at Coleridge's. A quiet shower of snow was in the air during more than half our walk. At our return the sky partially shaded with clouds. The horned moon was set. Startled two night birds from the great elm tree.

March 22nd. I spent the morning in starching and hanging out linen ; walked *through* the wood in the evening, very cold.

March 23rd. Coleridge dined with us. He brought his ballad finished.[3] We walked with him to the Miner's house. A beautiful evening, very starry, the horned moon.

March 24th. Coleridge, the Chesters, and Ellen Cruikshank called. We walked with them through the wood. Went in the evening into the Coombe to get eggs ; returned through the wood, and walked in the park. A duller night than last night : a sort of white shade over the blue sky. The stars dim. The spring continues to advance very slowly, no green trees, the hedges leafless ; nothing green but the brambles that still retain their old leaves, the evergreens, and the palms, which indeed are not absolutely green. Some brambles I observed to-day budding afresh, and those have shed their old leaves. The crooked arm of the old oak tree points upwards to the moon.

March 25th. Walked to Coleridge's after tea. Arrived at home at one o'clock. The night cloudy but not dark.

March 26th. Went to meet Wedgwood at Coleridge's after dinner. Reached home at half-past twelve, a fine moonlight night ; half moon.

---

[1] " A whirl-blast from behind the hill."

[2] *The Thorn.*   [3] *The Rime of the Ancyent Marinere.*

March 27th. Dined at Poole's. Arrived at home a little after twelve, a partially cloudy, but light night, very cold.

March 28th. Hung out the linen.

March 29th. Coleridge dined with us.

March 30th. Walked I know not where.

March 31st. Walked.

April 1st. Walked by moonlight.

April 2nd. A very high wind. Coleridge came to avoid the smoke ; stayed all night. We walked in the wood, and sat under the trees. The half of the wood perfectly still, while the wind was making a loud noise behind us. The still trees only gently bowed their heads, as if listening to the wind. The hollies in the thick wood unshaken by the blast ; only, when it came with a greater force, shaken by the rain drops falling from the bare oaks above.

April 3rd. Walked to Crookham, with Coleridge and Wm., to make the appeal. Left Wm. there, and parted with Coleridge at the top of the hill. A very stormy afternoon. . . .

April 4th. Walked to the sea-side in the afternoon. A great commotion in the air, but the sea neither grand nor beautiful. A violent shower in returning. Sheltered under some fir trees at Potsham.

April 5th. Coleridge came to dinner. William and I walked in the wood in the morning. I fetched eggs from the Coombe.

April 6th. Went a part of the way home with Coleridge. A pleasant warm morning, but a showery day. Walked a short distance up the lesser Coombe, with an intention of going to the source of the brook, but the evening closing in, cold prevented us. The Spring still advancing very slowly. The horse-chestnuts budding, and the hedgerows beginning to look green, but nothing fully expanded.

April 7th. Walked before dinner up the Coombe, to the source of the brook, and came home by the tops of the hills ; a showery morning, at the hill-tops ; the view opened upon us very grand.

April 8th. Easter Sunday. Walked in the morning in the wood, and half way to Stowey ; found the air at first oppressively warm, afterwards very pleasant.

April 9th. Walked to Stowey, a fine air in going, but very hot in returning. The sloe in blossom, the hawthorns green, the larches in the park changed from black to green in two or three days. Met Coleridge in returning.

April 10th. I was hanging out linen in the evening. We walked to Holford. I turned off to the baker's, and walked beyond Woodlands, expecting to meet William, met him on the hill ; a close warm evening . . . in bloom.

April 11th. In the wood in the morning, walked to the top of the hill, then I went down into the wood. A pleasant evening, a fine air, the grass in the park becoming green, many trees green in the dell.

April 12th. Walked in the morning in the wood. In the evening up the Coombe, fine walk. The Spring advances rapidly, multitudes of primroses, dog-violets, periwinkles, stitchwort.

April 13th. Walked in the wood in the morning. In the evening went to Stowey. I staid with Mr. Coleridge. Wm. went to Poole's. Supped with Mr. Coleridge.

April 14th. Walked in the wood in the morning. The evening very stormy, so we staid within doors. Mary Wollstonecraft's life, etc., came.

April 15th. Set forward after breakfast to Crookham, and returned to dinner at three o'clock. A fine cloudy morning. Walked about the squire's grounds. Quaint waterfalls about, about which Nature was very successfully striving to make beautiful what art had deformed — ruins, hermitages, etc. etc. In spite of all these things, the dell romantic and beautiful, though everywhere planted with unnaturalised trees. Happily we cannot shape the huge hills, or carve out the valleys according to our fancy.

April 16th. New moon. William walked in the wood in the morning. I neglected to follow him. We walked in the park in the evening. . . .

April 17th. Walked in the wood in the morning. In the evening upon the hill. Cowslips plentiful.

April 18th. Walked in the wood, a fine sunny morning, met Coleridge returned from his brother's. He dined with us.

We drank tea, and then walked with him nearly to Stowey. . . .

April 20th. Walked in the evening up the hill dividing the Coombes. Came home the Crookham way, by the thorn, and the " little muddy pond." Nine o'clock at our return. William all the morning engaged in wearisome composition. The moon crescent. *Peter Bell* begun. . . .

April 24th. Walked a considerable time in the wood. Sat under the trees, in the evening walked on the top of the hill, found Coleridge on our return and walked with him towards Stowey.

April 25th. Coleridge drank tea, walked with him to Stowey.

April 26th. William went to have his picture taken.[1] I walked with him. Dined at home. Coleridge and he drank tea.

April 27th. Coleridge breakfasted and drank tea, strolled in the wood in the morning, went with him in the evening through the wood, afterwards walked on the hills : the moon, a many-coloured sea and sky.

April 28th, Saturday. A very fine morning, warm weather all the week.

May 6th, Sunday. Expected the painter, and Coleridge. A rainy morning — very pleasant in the evening. Met Coleridge as we were walking out. Went with him to Stowey ; heard the nightingale ; saw a glow-worm.

May 7th. Walked in the wood in the morning. In the evening, to Stowey with Coleridge who called.

May 8th. Coleridge dined, went in the afternoon to tea at Stowey. A pleasant walk home.

May 9th. . . . Wrote to Coleridge.

Wednesday, May 16th. Coleridge, William, and myself set forward to the Chedder rocks ; slept at Bridgewater.

May 22nd, Thursday.[2] Walked to Chedder. Slept at Cross.

---

[1] This was the earliest known portrait of Wordsworth, by W. Shuter.

[2] So MS., but May 22, 1798, was a *Tuesday.* D. W. was not exact as to dates.—W. K.

William Wordsworth,
after W. Shuter, 1798.

II

Journal of
VISIT TO HAMBURGH
and of Journey from
HAMBURGH TO GOSLAR
1798

JOURNAL OF VISIT TO HAMBURGH AND OF JOURNEY FROM HAMBURGH TO GOSLAR (1798)

QUITTED London, Friday, 14th September 1798. Arrived at Yarmouth on Saturday noon, and sailed on Sunday morning at eleven o'clock. Before we heaved the anchor I was consigned to the cabin, which I did not quit till we were in still water at the mouth of the Elbe on Tuesday morning at 10 o'clock. I was surprized to find, when I came upon deck, that we could not see the shores, though we were in the river. It was to my eyes a still sea, but oh! the gentle breezes and the gentle motion! I thought of returning to the cabin in the evening with a mingled sensation of shuddering and sickness. As we advanced towards Cuxhaven the shores appeared low and flat, and thinly peopled; here and there a farm-house, cattle feeding, hay-stacks, a cottage, a windmill. Some vessels were at anchor at Cuxhaven, an ugly, black-looking place; dismissed a part of our crew, and proceeded in the packet-boat up the river.

We cast anchor between 6 and 7 o'clock. The moon shone upon the waters. The shores were visible with here and there a light from the houses. Ships lying at anchor not far from us. We [1] drank tea upon deck by the light of the moon. I enjoyed solitude and quietness, and many a recollected pleasure, hearing still the unintelligible jargon of the many tongues that gabbled in the cabin. Went to bed between ten and eleven. The party playing at cards, but they were silent, and suffered us to go to sleep. At four o'clock in the morning we were awakened by the heaving of the anchor, and till seven, in the intervals of sleep,

---

[1] *i.e.* William and Dorothy Wordsworth, Coleridge, and Chester, a friend and disciple of Coleridge.

I enjoyed the thought that we were advancing towards Hamburgh ; but what was our mortification on being told that there was a thick fog, and that we could not sail till it was dispersed. I went on to the deck. The air was cold and wet, the decks streaming, the shores invisible, no hope of clear weather. At ten, however, the sun appeared, and we saw the green shores ; all became clear, and we set sail. Churches very frequent on the right, with spires ; red, blue, sometimes green houses, thatched or tiled, and generally surrounded with low trees. A beautiful low green island, houses, and wood. As we advanced, the left bank of the river became more interesting. Danish Yalstein.[1] The houses warm and comfortable, sheltered with trees, and neatly painted. Blankenese, a village or town scattered over the sides of three hills, woody where the houses lie and steep scars below ; the houses half-concealed by, and half-obtruding themselves from, the low trees. Naked boats with masts lying at the bare feet of the Blankenese hills. Houses more and more frequent as we approach Hamburgh, the banks of the Elbe more steep. Some gentlemen's seats after the English fashion. The spires of Altona and Hamburgh visible a considerable time. At Altona we took a boat, and rowed through the narrow passages of the Elbe, crowded with vessels of all nations. Landed at the Boom House, where we were received by porters, ready to carry our luggage to any part of the town. William went to seek lodgings, and the rest of the party guarded the luggage. Two boats were about to depart. An elegant English carriage was placed in one, and presently a very pretty woman, conducted by a gentleman, seated herself in it, and they rowed off. The other contained a medley crew of all ages. There was an old woman, with a blue cap trimmed with broad silver lace, and tied under her chin. She had a short coloured cloak, etc. While we stood in the street, which was open on one side to the Elbe, I was much amused by the various employments and dresses of the people who passed before us. There were Dutch women with immense straw bonnets, with flat crowns and rims in the shape of oyster

---

[1] So MS.

shells, without trimming, or with only a plain ribband round the crown, and literally as large as a small-sized umbrella. Hamburgher girls with white caps, with broad overhanging borders, crimped and stiff, and long lappets of ribband. Hanoverians with round borders, showing all the face, and standing upright, a profusion of ribband. Fruit-women, with large straw hats in the shape of an inverted bowl, or white handkerchiefs tyed round the head like a bishop's mitre. Jackets the most common ; often the petticoat and jacket of different colours. The ladies without hats, in dresses of all fashions. Soldiers with dull-looking red coats, and immense cocked hats. The men little differing from the English, except that they have generally a pipe in their mouths. After waiting about an hour we saw Wm. re-appear. Two porters carried our luggage upon a sort of wheelbarrow, and we were conducted through narrow dirty ill-paved stinking streets to an inn, where, with great difficulty, and after long seeking, lodgings had been procured for us.

The first impression that an Englishman receives on entering a Hamburgh inn is that of filth and filthy smells. I sate down for a few moments while the company went to look at the apartments. The landlord, landlady, and a party of waiters were preparing plumbs for preserving or bottling. He looked like an English landlord living on the good things of the house. She, about forty, had her hair full-dressed, spread out and powdered, without cap. We were conducted into Monsr. de Loutre's apartment. On enquiry we found we could have no dinner, for dinner was over. I went upstairs to dress, a *man*-servant brought up napkin, water etc. My room, at the top of the house, containing a small bed, a chest of drawers, a table, four chairs and a stove at one corner ; the floor just washed, but I could see that the process had spread or plastered the coating of dirt ; — no carpet — floor painted brown — a large looking glass — 4 marks (a mark is sixteenpence) the price of this room, and Chester's and Coleridge's. When I returned below I found the party eating cold beef — no cloth spread — no vegetables, but some bad cucumbers pickled without vinegar. Very good wine at one mark 4 sous the bottle. We

THE HAMBURGH JOURNAL (1798)

had afterwards tea and coffee ; the bread good, halfpenny rolls, butter not fresh.

[*September 20th,*] *Thursday Morning.* Rouzed by the noises of the market. I could not but observe, notwithstanding the dirt of the houses, that the lower orders of women seemed in general much cleaner in their persons than the same rank in England. This appeared to me on the first view and all the observation I have since made has confirmed me in this opinion. The market well supplied with eggs, fowls, and vegetables. Turkeys and geese, *driven* to market. Chickens 6d. or 7d. apiece, a small carp two marks, perhaps a Hamburgher would have got it for one and a half, but fish is very dear at this season. Beef 4d. or 5d. a pound, mutton 4d. or 5d., veal 8d., Butter 10d., eggs a halfpenny each, a turkey 6 marks, a goose 3 marks, coffee 1/8d. a pound, tea 6/- or 8/-. Sugar, fine, 1/8d, candles 6d., soap 6d, Fish [1] very dear, turf universally burnt.

Breakfasted with Mons. de Loutre. Chester and I went to the promenade. People of all ranks, and in various dresses, walking backwards and forwards. Ladies with small baskets hanging on their arms, some without handkerchiefs and their necks entirely exposed, long shawls of various colours thrown over their shoulders. The women of the lower order dressed with great modesty. Fruit and cakes of all kinds to be sold. English hardware — we asked the price of a plain leather ink-stand. It was three marks. After spending two hours very pleasantly we returned home.

The houses immensely large and very high — I counted one eight storeys from the ground — a great loss of room on account of the bad contrivance within, sometimes more than half covered with windows. The shops very dull, and arranged without order or elegance. We dined at a French hotel and were charged more than we ought to have paid for dinner and were cheated more than one half in the wine. Went to the French theatre in the evening. The piece a mixture of dull declamation and unmeaning rant. The ballet unintelligible to us, as the story was carried on in singing. The body of the

---

[1] Fish: so MS., but did D. W. mean to write " Fuel " here ?

house was imperfectly lighted, which has a good effect in bringing out the stage, but as the acting was not very amusing, I should have been glad to have had a better view of the audience. We returned home in the 2nd Act of the Ballet.

[*September 21st,*] *Friday*. Dined at the ordinary. The price a mark. About twenty at each table. Every man has his half or quarter pint of wine at 10d. the bottle, or a bottle of beer or porter — a napkin and a glass. Soup, boiled meat and stewed vegetables, roasted meat or fowls, sallad, fowls with stewed plumbs, veal with stewed pears, beef with apple sauce.

[*September 23rd,*] *Sunday*. I was unable to go to the Churches, being unwell. We dined at the ordinary at 12 o'clock. An addition of plumb tart, I suppose because it was Sunday. William went in the boat to Harburgh at ½ past 3 ; fare 4d. In our road to the boat we looked into one of the large churches. Service was just ended. The audience appeared to be simply composed of singing boys dressed in large cocked hats, and a few old women who sat in the aisles. The inferior shops open, women sitting at their doors knitting and sewing, and I saw one woman ironing. Met many bright-looking girls with white caps, carrying black prayer-books in their hands, old men with wigs, one in full dress with a bag and a chapeau de bras — old ladies in the London fashions of the years '80 or '82 and 3 — artificial flowers very common in their frizzled heads. Coleridge went to Ratzeberg at five o'clock in the diligence. Chester accompanied me towards Altona. The streets wide and pleasant in that quarter of the town. Immense crowds of people walking for pleasure, and many pleasure-waggons passing and repassing. Passed through a nest of Jews, were invited to view an exhibition of waxwork. The theatres open, and the billiard-tables attended. The walks very pleasing between Hamburgh and Altona, a large piece of ground planted with trees, and intersected by gravel walks. Music, cakes, fruit, carriages, and foot-passengers of all descriptions. A very good view of the shipping, and of Altona and the town and spires of Hamburgh. I could not but remark how much the prospect would have suffered by one of our English canopies of coal smoke. The ground on the opposite side of the Elbe appears marshy, there are many little canals or lines of water. While the sun was yet shining pleasantly, we were obliged to think perpetually to turn our eyes to the church clock. The gates are shut at ½ past six o'clock, and there is no admittance into the city after that time. This idea deducts much from the pleasure of an evening walk. You are haunted by it long before the time is elapsed. We returned by the ramparts. Many people still walking there and on the promenade.

[*September 24th,*] *Monday Morning.* William returned. The carriage, though very cheap, far too heavy. They could not take us without four horses. Wm.'s expenses for bed, a miserable supper and breakfast 3 marks.

[*September 25th,*] *Tuesday.* Went to see some French pictures with Monsr. De Loutre. The painter's lady very warm in her vindication of her husband's style of painting. She had been handsome, but her manners were to me harsh and unpleasant. A very nice chearful looking fille de chambre seemed very glad to see Monsr. de Loutre.

[*September 26th,*] *Wednesday.* Dined with Mr. Klopstock. Had the pleasure of meeting his brother the poet, a venerable old man, retaining the liveliness and alertness of youth, though his legs are swelled immensely and he evidently cannot be very far from the grave. His second wife much younger than he, a fine fresh-looking woman, but with an unpleasant expression of countenance, vain, and not pleasing in her manners. Mr. Klopstock, the merchant, very polite and kind ; his wife, who cannot speak a word of either English or French, appears a very interesting woman ; they have a little girl of 7 years old. She was dressed in a coloured frock, and her neck covered up with a thick handkerchief. (N.B. Mrs. Klopstock, the poet's lady, much exposed.) The child seemed indulged. The teeth of all the family very bad, their complexions fair. The rest of the party consisted of a young German who spoke a little English, a niece of Mr. Klopstock, Wm. and myself. We were conducted through the warehouse and counting house into a large low room with two windows at the end, and a glass door opening upon a balcony, which overlooks a part of the Elbe.

The room hung with gilt leather, a picture of Lessing, and some other portraits, a bust of his brother in one corner ; floor painted brown, no carpet, mahogany tables, desks, chairs etc. We had scarcely sate 5 minutes before we were called to dinner in the next room to which we were led by folding doors. We sate round the table without order ; Mrs. Klopstock on one side, her husband at the foot of the table. Mrs. K. distributed all the dishes in succession. Soup 1st, 2nd, stewed veal without vegetables, 3rd sausages with cabbage, 4th oysters with spinnach, 5th fowls with sallad and currant jelly, dessert — grapes, biscuits, pears, plumbs, walnuts ; afterwards coffee. A woman servant in the Hanoverian cap waited at table. She seemed more at her ease and more familiar than an English servant, she laughed and talked with the little girl. We withdrew into the next room and had tea. Mr. K's niece brought in the candles and washed up the tea things in a sort of passage or lobby. The party talked with much interest of the French comedy, and seemed fond of music. The poet and his lady were obliged to depart soon after six. He sustained an animated conversation with William during the whole afternoon. Poor old man ! I could not look upon him, the benefactor of his country, the father of German poetry, without the most sensible emotion. We returned home at a little after seven. I had a bad headach, and went to bed at 9.

During my residence in Hamburgh I have never seen anything like a quarrel in the streets but once, and that was so trifling that it would scarcely have been noticed in England. I have never seen a drunken man, nor a woman of the lower orders who was not perfectly decent and modest in her appearance and manners. In the shops (except the established booksellers and stationers) I have constantly observed a disposition to cheat, and take advantage of our ignorance of the language and money. A man asked 12 marks for a pair of silk stockings, which were no better than a pair for which he only demanded 5 when he found we would not be imposed upon.

September 27th, Thursday. A bad headach. William and I set forward at 12 o'clock to Altona. I asked the price of a portmanteau, 7 marks. At several other shops they demanded from 10 to 14 marks for what were neither larger nor better. The honest shopkeeper a Jewess. The entrance of the town of Altona is very pleasant, the street is only built on one side and overlooks the Elbe ; afterwards it becomes narrow and crowded. The walk between Hamburgh and Altona very pleasant, sandy and dry. The view towards Hamburgh pleasing, a large branch of the Elbe winding through a flat country, the spire of Hamburgh and gently rising grounds behind. The Elbe in the vicinity of Hamburgh is so divided and spread out, that the country looks more like a plain overflowed by heavy rains than the bed of a great river. We went about a mile and a half beyond Altona : the roads dry and sandy, and a causeway for foot-passengers. The country in general immediately around us not rich nor highly cultivated. The peasants were taking up their potatoes which appeared to have been ill-managed, they were very small. The houses on the banks of the Elbe, chiefly of brick, seemed very warm and well built. Some gentlemen's houses are of white stone and built after the English fashion. The small cottage houses seemed to have little gardens, and all the gentlemen's houses were surrounded by gardens quaintly disposed in beds and curious knots, with ever-twisting gravel walks and bending poplars. The view of the Elbe and the spreading country must be very interesting in a fine sunset. There is a want of some atmospherical irradiation to give a richness to the scene. We met a drunken man on returning home, and we were accosted by the first beggar whom we have seen since our arrival at Hamburgh. He was an old man, a woman who seemed connected with him sate near under a hedge, but did not make any petition. We got some cakes at a French pastry-cook's and after going nearly as far as the French theatre bought some bread. I lay down till Coleridge's return from Ratzeberg, a beautiful place, but very dear.

[*September 28th,*] *Friday.* Settled the account with Monsr. de Loutre. Still a bad headach. Sought Coleridge at the bookseller's, and went to the Promenade. Dined at the Ordinary. All the Hamburghers full of Admiral Nelson's victory. Our Landlord no very pleasing object to us while he sat with his greasy face at the head of the table, laughing with landlord-like vulgarity and complaisance at the jokes of his guests, or while he exercised the force of his mind in deliberating upon the best way of cutting the beef. He had cheated us in our bill of not less than 4 guineas. Yesterday [1] saw a man of about fifty years of age beating a woman decently dressed and about 37 years of age. He struck her on the breast several times, and beat her also with his stick. The expressions in her face and attitude were half of anger and half of a spirit of resistance. What her offence had been we could not learn. It was in the public street. He was better dressed than she was, and evidently a stranger, and this brutal treatment did not excite the smallest indignation in the breast of the spectators. They seemed rather inclined to take the man's part. Called at a Baker's shop. Put two shillings into the baker's hands, for which I was to have had four small rolls. He gave me two and I let him understand that I was to have four, and with this view I took one shilling from him, pointed to it and to two loaves, and at the same time offering it to him, again I took up two others. In a savage manner he half knocked the rolls out of my hand, and when I asked him for the other shilling he refused to return it, and would neither suffer me to take bread, nor give me back my money, and on these terms I quitted the shop. I am informed that it is the boast and glory of these people to cheat strangers, that when a feat of this kind is successfully performed the man goes from the shop into his house, and triumphantly relates it to his wife and family. The Hamburgh shopkeepers have three sorts of weights, and a great part of their skill, as shopkeepers, consists in calculating upon the knowledge of the buyer, and suiting him with scales accordingly.

September 29th, Saturday. The grand festival of the Hamburghers, dedicated to Saint Michael, observed with greater solemnity than Sunday, but little of festivity. Perhaps this might be partly owing to the raininess of the evening. In the

---

[1] From " yesterday " to the end of this day's entry the handwriting is W. W.'s. The coin which he calls here a shilling, and in his letter describing the incident (*v. E.L.* p. 199) " a piece of money ", had the value of a penny : *v.* p. 28, *infra.*

morning the churches were opened very early. St. Christopher's was quite full between 8 and 9 o'clock. It is a large heavy-looking building, immense without either grandeur or beauty; built of brick, and with few windows. It is adorned with a number of images within, which looked to me paltry and gaudy; there are some pictures, which I should think were ill-painted. There is one of the Saint fording the river with Christ upon his back, a giant figure, which amused me not a little. It seems that there is no churchyard belonging to this church, but there are many vaults within, as I judged by the iron rings which are fixed to huge flags evidently for the purpose of taking them up. Walked with Coleridge and Chester upon the promenade. Dined at the ordinary at ½ past 12, a cake after dinner in honour of the Saint. The ordinary ill attended. Drank tea. The price without bread 6d., the price of coffee 8d.

We took places in the morning in the Brunswick coach for Wednesday. The fare 12 marks. We had two small trunks which we wished to have conveyed to the post, the distance about 3 hundred yards. A porter had the audacity to demand 20d. for carrying them, and was very insolent when William refused to give it him. He offered him 8d., which was more than a London porter would have expected. William carried them himself through a very heavy shower of rain.

[*September* 30th,] *Sunday*. Coleridge and Chester went to Ratzeberg at 7 o'clock in the morning. C. had a violent contest with the postilion who insisted upon his paying 20d. a mile for each horse, instead of a mark the established fare. He was obliged to yield, but whether he can get redress or not I know not. Breakfasted upon tea. The price of tea with two rolls and butter 10d. William called at Monsr. de Loutre's from whom he learnt that the price of 10 small loaves was 4d. The day before a baker had refused to give him more than two for twopence ! The bread was baked this morning ; yesterday we had *old* bread, I suppose that yesterday there was no baking in honour of the Saint. It seems there is no imposition of either law or custom which prevents people from making Sunday as much a day of labour as any other if their avarice, or it may be their industry, but alas ! I fear the former motive is the

Samuel Taylor Coleridge

From a painting by Peter Vandyke

moving spring of the Hamburgher's mind ! gets the better of
their love of pleasure. I saw a cobbler at work and a carpenter
carrying his tools. It seems however the more general practice
to make Sunday a day of ease. The more wealthy citizens go
out in carriages or on horseback, the rest walk, all are clean
and well dressed. The men cannot look either chearful or
pleasant, but the women are often very pleasing in their
appearance. William and I set forward at ½-past 11 with an
intention of going to Blankenese. It was a fine morning but
very windy. When we had got nearly through the town we
saw a surly-looking German driving a poor Jew forward with
foul language, and making frequent use of a stick which he
had in his hand. The countenance of the Jew expressed neither
anger nor surprise nor agitation ; he spoke, but with meekness, and unresisting pursued his way, followed by his inhuman
driver, whose insolence we found was supported by law : the
Jew had no right to *reign* in the city of Hamburgh, as a German
told us in broken English. The soldiers who are stationed at
the drawbridge looked very surly at him, and the countenances
of the by-standers expressed cold unfeeling cruelty. We pass
many gentlemen's houses on the road to Blankenese. The
buildings all seem solid and warm in themselves, but still they
look cold from their nakedness of trees. They are generally
newly built, and placed in gardens, which are planted in front
with poplars and low shrubs, but the possessors seem to have
no prospective view to a shelter for their children ; they do
not plant behind their houses. All the buildings of this
character are near the road, which runs at different distances
from the edge of the bank which rises from the river. This
bank is generally steep, scattered over with trees which are
either not of ancient growth, or from some cause do not thrive,
but serve very well to shelter and often conceal the more
humble dwellings, which are close to the sandy bank of the
river. Many young men on horseback passed us, trotting as
fast as they could, dressed in the English fashion and so like
Englishmen that we could have imagined ourselves only 3 miles
from London. We saw many carriages. In one of them was
Klopstock, the poet. There are many inns and eating-houses

by the roadside. We went to a pretty village, or nest of houses about a league from Blankenese, and beyond to a large open field, enclosed on one side with oak trees, through which winds a pleasant gravel walk. On the other it is open to the river. We dined under these trees and then shaped our course homewards. When we were within about a mile and a half or two miles of Altona, we turned out of the road to go down to the river, and pursued our way along the path that leads from house to house. These houses are low, never more than two storeys high, built of brick, or a mixture of brick and wood, and thatched or tiled. They have all window-shutters, which are painted frequently a gay light green, but always painted. We were astonished at the excessive neatness which we observed in the arrangement of everything within these houses. They have all window curtains as white as snow ; the floors of all that we saw were perfectly clean, and the brass vessels as bright as a mirror. We asked for a glass of water at a house which invited our curiosity, the door being open ; a very clean-looking woman spoke to us, but instead of giving us the water told us that we should find some if we went a little further on. We went a considerable way, but found no water. We then turned to a cottage which was open, and a neat-looking young woman presented us with a mug which she brought upon a white plate. The man of the house who was a pilot spoke English and offered us brandy from a bottle. We sate at the door upon a bench under the shade of a row of trees cut out in the piazza or cloister form. The inside of the house would have done credit to the industry of any old English dame forty years ago when chests were rubbed as bright as looking glasses. There is a manufactory of glue carried on close to the Elbe, but I imagine these houses are chiefly inhabited by sailors, pilots, boat-makers, and others whose business is upon the water. I am sorry to add that notwithstanding the general view is so pleasing to the eye without, and all is so neat and clean within, there is such a constant succession of hateful smells, that it is quite disgusting to pass near the houses. We turned down nearer the river and walked along the sand till we came to Altona. Many people walking and riding between

Altona and Hamburgh. An exhibition of horsemanship. A little girl about 8 years old, well-dressed, took up her petticoats in full view of the crowd and upon the green where people walk, and sat undisturbed till she had finished her business. The smells which are everywhere met with in consequence of this practice are horrible. Saw some soldiers in grey coats of the second mourning colour, and several officers whom we supposed to be Prussians with long coat laps and yellow belts round their waists which pinch in the body and make them look like women. A boy offered us a cane for which he asked 8 schillings — Wm. offered him two — I have a lively recollection of the amusing dissatisfaction of the boy's countenance ; he said " What ! English schillings ! ! " We reached home between 5 and 6 — William lay down and had a long sleep. We passed a gentleman's house which has just been erected and is not yet quite finished about 2 miles from Altona. It is of wood cut in imitation of stone with a portico and large wooden pillars ; on the whole it has a paltry appearance, yet it looks warm and strong, it is painted stone colour with pink ornaments ; a large piece of ground near it is laid out in gardens and walks. We supped at the ordinary, price 10d., stewed haricos with forced meat and smoked sausages — a leg of mutton, roasted, with excellent apple sauce, Bread, butter and cheese.

[*October 1st,*] *Monday.* I breakfasted in my own room. William called at Klopstock's to inquire the road into Saxony. Bought Burgher's poems, the price 6 marks. Sate an hour at Remnant's. Bought Percy's ancient poetry, 14 marks. Walked on the ramparts ; a very fine morning. Dined at the ordinary, only 18 people at table — veal and stewed peas. The afternoon became very stormy which prevented our going out again ; drank tea.

We quitted Hamburgh on Wednesday evening, October 3, at 5 o'clock, reached Luneburg at breakfast on Thursday, and arrived at Brunswick between 3 and 4 o'clock on Friday evening. Our carriage was more than half-covered and lined with leather within, luxuries which I have since found are not often to be met with in a German diligence, though when I entered it I

E

was much more inclined to observe the wretched crazy appearance of the whole, the crevices in the upper part (which was made of wood), the basket work below, and the great space all round for the winds to blow through on every side, than to congratulate myself upon our good luck. Before we had got 4 miles from Hamburgh the shaking of the carriage gave me a violent pain in my bowels, which was followed by sickness. It was a very fine evening when we passed through the city gates, and the ramparts and spires looked gay and beautiful. There are fine shady walks which *seemed* to extend to the distance of at least two miles from the city, but I was probably not very accurate in my computation, I was in a German diligence where every mile seems doubled. We passed many gentlemen's houses with gardens ; some had jet-d'eaus and images. We crossed the Elbe at one o'clock. The same moon that shone when we crossed the channel, now in its wane, lighted the waters of the Elbe ; and it was of great use to us during the whole of our journey. Before we reached the river we had stopped at an inn where William and the rest of the party had coffee — I took some wine and water. We were shown into a room with a great number of people all smoking but the women ; amongst the rest were the Coachman and the Conductor, as he is called, a man who attends to take care of the luggage. Our carriage had 7 passengers (4 within, 2 half in, and one on the outside) and we were attended by two waggons called by-waggons, which contained luggage, and those passengers which ours would not admit. These waggons are entirely uncovered and only differ from an English dung-cart in being longer and narrower, and not so well made or painted. All the passengers pay the same price, 12 marks from Hamburgh to Brunswick, and at each station 2 schillings to the waggonmaster, and 2 schillings to the postilion when he is changed, but the same postilion sometimes drives 2 stations.

When we had crossed the Elbe we stopped at least an hour at another wretched publick house. We emptied our bottle of wine and got it filled with hot water, which I found a great comfort. We went on during the rest of the night without being able to sleep, and at $\frac{1}{2}$ past 5 arrived at the next station.

32

We were now in the Hanoverian dominions, and the inns were
more strange and more miserable. The first we came to was a
very large house without any partition. At the entrance was
the kitchen where was the fire etc., further up were the beds,
and still beyond stalls for the cattle, and straw spread upon the
ground. Fowls, geese and cats in abundance. The country
through which we passed to Luneburg very barren, and Luneburg a wretched miserable place. There was a fair held when
we passed through, but all seemed lifeless and dead. We
breakfasted here, the bread bad, but the butter very good.
We paid an English shilling for our breakfast. The roads
miserably bad ; within a mile of Luneburg they branch out
upon an immense sandy plain, into numberless courses or rather
wheel-tracks. The country becomes occasionally rather interesting from its strangeness. There are woods scattered
about at different distances, but even they look barren, though
the trees flourish. I saw very few cattle of any kind, there
were a few flocks of sheep, and here and there some cows, but
no wild colts, no asses, no cottages ; all lifeless. After travelling
till 4 o'clock we dined at a pretty little town, enquired for
something to eat at the post-house, but were told it was no
inn, that we must go to the White Horse. We could get no
meat, but had eggs and butter and milk and water soup made
with flour, water, milk, lemon-skin and sugar. They charged
us 4 bon gros each for our dinner. We arrived at Brunswick
the next day, Friday, at between 3 and 4 o'clock in the afternoon. This City stands upon a sandy plain at a little distance
from the town, seemingly incapable of cultivation, but the
numerous gardens, and potato cabbage and turnip fields, which
are near the city, shew strongly the good effects of human
industry. The road on the Hamburgh side of Brunswick is so
sandy that it is only marked by the irregular tracks of cart
wheels, and it is at the mercy of the winds to carry it where
they please. After waiting a considerable time to arrange our
baggage we sallied forth in search of an inn. The English
Arms or the King of England was not far distant, and there
we were taken in. As in all German houses that I have seen,
the best part of it was lost in the entrance, a huge place fit for

a senate or a council chamber. We were shewn into a parlour ; not so neat as the parlour of an English inn, though much more in the English style than at Hamburgh. After waiting a considerable time hungry and faint we sate down to dinner. We had very good soup, mutton chops and potatoes after the English fashion, fowls, veal and sallad, and some excellent pears. Our party was of six, we had two bottles of wine and a bottle of beer. The beds were excellent with blankets etc. as in England. Our share of the expenses amounted to half a Louis.

We had taken places in the Goslar diligence, and were to set off at 8 o'clock in the morning, so we rose at a little after seven. I ought to have mentioned that we walked about the City of Brunswick after we had dined. It is an old, silent, dull looking place, but has some good houses in it. We saw none of the bustle or gaiety of Hamburgh, there were few ladies to be seen, and they looked dismal from their manner of dressing. The ramparts are like those of Hamburgh only much less considerable. The Duke's palace is a large white building. There is nothing of elegance in its external appearance, but the gardens seemed as if they would be very pleasant. We peeped through a gateway, but were told it was too late to enter. When we left our inn Wm. carried the portmanteau, and I the small parcel. He left them under my charge and went in search of a baker's shop. He brought me his pockets full of apples, for which he paid two bon gros, and some excellent bread. Upon these I breakfasted and carried *Kubla*[1] to a fountain in the neighbouring market-place, where I drank some excellent water. It was on Saturday the 6th of October when we arrived at Goslar at between 5 and 6 in the evening.

---

[1] Presumably a MS. copy of Coleridge's *Kubla Khan*.

III

THE GRASMERE JOURNAL
1800–1803

See End-paper Maps

Town End, Grasmere

From a water-colour by T. M. Richardson

I. May 14th to December 22nd, 1800

May 14th, 1800 [*Wednesday*]. Wm. and John set off into Yorkshire after dinner at ½ past 2 o'clock, cold pork in their pockets. I left them at the turning of the Lowwood bay under the trees. My heart was so full that I could hardly speak to W. when I gave him a farewell kiss. I sate a long time upon a stone at the margin of the lake, and after a flood of tears my heart was easier. The lake looked to me, I knew not why, dull and melancholy, and the weltering on the shores seemed a heavy sound. I walked as long as I could amongst the stones of the shore. The wood rich in flowers ; a beautiful yellow, palish yellow, flower, that looked thick, round, and double, and smelt very sweet — I supposed it was a ranunculus. Crowfoot, the grassy-leaved rabbit-toothed white flower, strawberries, geranium, scentless violets, anemones two kinds, orchises, primroses. The heckberry very beautiful, the crab coming out as a low shrub. Met a blind man, driving a very large beautiful Bull, and a cow — he walked with two sticks. Came home by Clappersgate. The valley very green ; many sweet views up to Rydale head, when I could juggle away the fine houses ; but they disturbed me, even more than when I have been happier ; one beautiful view of the Bridge, without Sir Michael's.[1] Sate down very often, though it was cold. I resolved to write a journal of the time till W. and J. return, and I set about keeping my resolve, because I will not quarrel with myself, and because I shall give Wm. pleasure by it when he comes home again. At Rydale, a woman of the village, stout and well dressed, begged a half-penny ; she had never she said done it before, but these hard times ! Arrived at home with a bad headach, set some slips of privett, the evening cold,

---

[1] *i.e.* Rydal Hall, the seat of Sir Michael le Fleming.

had a fire, my face now flame-coloured. It is nine o'clock. I shall soon go to bed. A young woman begged at the door — she had come from Manchester on Sunday morn. with two shillings and a slip of paper which she supposed a Bank note — it was a cheat. She had buried her husband and three children within a year and a half — all in one grave — burying very dear — paupers all put in one place — 20 shillings paid for as much ground as will bury a man — a stone to be put over it or the right will be lost — 11/6 each time the ground is opened. Oh! that I had a letter from William!

May 15th, Thursday. A coldish dull morning — hoed the first row of peas, weeded etc. etc., sat hard to mending till evening. The rain which had threatened all day came on just when I was going to walk.

[*May 16th,*] *Friday morning*. Warm and mild, after a fine night of rain. Transplanted radishes after breakfast, walked to Mr. Gell's[1] with the books, gathered mosses and plants. The woods extremely beautiful with all autumnal variety and softness. I carried a basket for mosses, and gathered some wild plants. Oh! that we had a book of botany. All flowers now are gay and deliciously sweet. The primrose still pre-eminent among the later flowers of the spring. Foxgloves very tall, with their heads budding. I went forward round the lake at the foot of Loughrigg Fell. I was much amused with the business of a pair of stone-chats ; their restless voices as they skimmed along the water following each other, their shadows under them, and their returning back to the stones on the shore, chirping with the same unwearied voice. Could not cross the water, so I went round by the stepping-stones. The morning clear but cloudy, that is the hills were not overhung by mists. After dinner Aggy[2] weeded onions and carrots. I helped for a little — wrote to Mary Hutchinson — washed my head — worked. After tea went to Ambleside — a pleasant cool but not cold evening. Rydale was very beautiful, with spear-shaped streaks of polished steel. No letters ! — only one

---

[1] Mr. Gell occupied a cottage on the site of the house now called Silver How.—G. G. W.

[2] For Aggy, Molly and John Fisher, *v.* Fishers in Appendix, p. 434.

newspaper. I returned by Clappersgate. Grasmere was very solemn in the last glimpse of twilight ; it calls home the heart to quietness. I had been very melancholy in my walk back. I had many of my saddest thoughts, and I could not keep the tears within me. But when I came to Grasmere I felt that it did me good. I finished my letter to M. H. Ate hasty pudding and went to bed. As I was going out in the morning I met a half crazy old man. He shewed me a pincushion and begged a pin, afterwards a half-penny. He began in a kind of indistinct voice in this manner : " Matthew Jobson's lost a cow. Tom Nichol has two good horses strayed. Jim Jones's cow's brokken her horn, etc. etc." He went into Aggy's and persuaded her to give him some whey, and let him boil some porridge. She declares he ate two quarts.

[*May 17th*,] *Saturday*. Incessant rain from morning till night. T. Ashburner [1] brought us coals. Worked hard, and read *Midsummer Night's Dream*, [and] Ballads — sauntered a little in the garden. The Skobby [2] sate quietly in its nest, rocked by the wind, and beaten by the rain.

[*May*] 18*th*, *Sunday*. Went to church, slight showers, a cold air. The mountains from this window look much greener, and I think the valley is more green than ever. The corn begins to shew itself. The ashes are still bare, went part of the way home with Miss Simpson. A little girl from Coniston came to beg. She had lain out all night — her step-mother had turned her out of doors. Her father could not stay at home " she flights so ". Walked to Ambleside in the evening round the lake, the prospect exceedingly beautiful from Loughrigg Fell. It was so green that no eye could be weary of reposing upon it. The most beautiful situation for a house in the field next to Mr. Benson's. [3] It threatened rain all the evening but was mild and pleasant. I was overtaken by 2 Cumberland people on the other side of Rydale who complimented me upon my walking. They were going to sell cloth, and odd things which they make themselves, in Hawkshead and the neighbourhood. The post

---

[1] Ashburner, *v.* Appendix, p. 433.   [2] Skobby, dialect for chaffinch.
[3] The Bensons lived at Tail End, and were the owners of Dove Cottage (*v.* Jan. 31, 1802, *infra*).

was not arrived, so I walked thro' the town, past Mrs. Taylor's, and met him. Letters from Coleridge and Cottle. John Fisher overtook me on the other side of Rydale. He talked much about the alteration in the times, and observed that in a short time there would be only two ranks of people, the very rich and the very poor, " for those who have small estates ", says he, " are forced to sell, and all the land goes into one hand ". Did not reach home till 10 o'clock.

[*May 19th,*] *Monday.* Sauntered a good deal in the garden, bound carpets, mended old clothes. Read *Timon of Athens.* Dried linen. Molly weeded the turnips, John stuck the peas. We had not much sunshine or wind, but no rain till about 7 o'clock, when we had a slight shower just after I had set out upon my walk. I did not return but walked up into the Black Quarter.[1] I sauntered a long time among the rocks above the church. The most delightful situation possible for a cottage, commanding two distinct views of the vale and of the lake, is among those rocks. I strolled on, gathered mosses etc. The quietness and still seclusion of the valley affected me even to producing the deepest melancholy. I forced myself from it. The wind rose before I went to bed. No rain — Dodwell and Wilkinson called in my absence.

[*May 20th,*] *Tuesday Morning.* A fine mild rain. After breakfast the sky cleared and before the clouds passed from the hills I went to Ambleside. It was a sweet morning. Everything green and overflowing with life, and the streams making a perpetual song, with the thrushes and all little birds, not forgetting the stone-chats. The post was not come in. I walked as far as Windermere, and met him there. No letters ! no papers. Came home by Clappersgate. I was sadly tired, ate a hasty dinner and had a bad headach — went to bed and slept at least 2 hours. Rain came on in the evening — Molly washing.

[*May 21st,*] *Wednesday.* Went often to spread the linen which was bleaching — a rainy day and very wet night.

[*May 22nd,*] *Thursday.* A very fine day with showers —

---

[1] The Black Quarter, the name given by the W.s to Easedale, during their first year's residence at Grasmere. It does not appear in the *Journal* after Nov. 1800.—G. G. W.

dried the linen and starched. Drank tea at Mr. Simpson's.[1]
Brought down Batchelor's Buttons (Rock Ranunculus) and
other plants — went part of the way back, a showery mild
evening — all the peas up.

[May] 23rd, Friday. Ironing till tea time. So heavy a rain
that I could not go for letters — put by the linen, mended
stockings etc.

May 24th, Saturday. Walked in the morning to Ambleside.
I found a letter from Wm. and from Mary Hutchinson and
Douglas. Returned on the other side of the lakes — wrote to
William after dinner, nailed up the beds, worked in the garden,
sate in the evening under the trees. I went to bed soon with a
bad headach. A fine day.

[May 25th,] Sunday. A very fine warm day, had no fire.
Read Macbeth in the morning, sate under the trees after dinner.
Miss Simpson came just as I was going out and she sate with
me. I wrote to my brother Christopher, and sent John Fisher
to Ambleside after tea. Miss Simpson and I walked to the foot
of the lake — her Brother met us. I went with them nearly
home and on my return found a letter from Coleridge and from
Charles Lloyd,[2] and three papers.

May 26th, Monday. A very fine morning, worked in the
garden till after 10 when old Mr. Simpson came and talked to
me till after 12. Molly weeding — wrote letters to J. H.,[3]
Coleridge, C. Ll., and W. I walked towards Rydale, and turned
aside at my favorite field. The air and the lake were still —
one cottage light in the vale, and so much of day left that I
could distinguish objects, the woods, trees and houses. Two or
three different kinds of birds sang at intervals on the opposite
shore. I sate till I could hardly drag myself away, I grew so
sad. " When pleasant thoughts," etc. . . .[4]

---

[1] v. Appendix, p. 437.
[2] Charles Lloyd, the son of a Birmingham banker, had lived with Coleridge
at Nether Stowey in 1798. He settled in 1800 with his family at Old Brathay
near Clappersgate. His sister Priscilla was engaged to W.'s brother Christopher.
[3] J. H., i.e. Joanna Hutchinson.
[4] v. Lines Written in Early Spring :

> In that sweet mood when pleasant thoughts
> Bring sad thoughts to the mind.

[*May*] 27*th, Tuesday*. I walked to Ambleside with letters — met the post before I reached Mr. Partridge's, one paper, only a letter for Coleridge. I expected a letter from Wm. It was a sweet morning, the ashes in the valley nearly in full leaf, but still to be distinguished, quite bare on the higher ground. I was warm in returning, and becoming cold with sitting in the house I had a bad headach — went to bed after dinner, and lay till after 5. Not well after tea. I worked in the garden, but did not walk further. A delightful evening before the sun set, but afterwards it grew colder — mended stockings etc.

[*May* 28*th*,] *Wednesday*. In the morning walked up to the rocks above Jenny Dockeray's,[1] sate a long time upon the grass, the prospect divinely beautiful. If I had three hundred pounds, and could afford to have a bad interest for my money, I would buy that estate, and we would build a cottage there to end our days in. I went into her garden and got white and yellow lilies, periwinkle, etc., which I planted. Sate under the trees with my work. No fire in the morning. Worked till between 7 and 8, and then watered the garden, and was about to go up to Mr. Simpson's, when Miss S. and her visitors passed the door. I went home with them, a beautiful evening, the crescent moon hanging above Helm Crag.

[*May* 29*th*,] *Thursday*. In the morning worked in the garden a little, read *King John*. Miss Simpson, and Miss Falcon and Mr. S. came very early. Went to Mr. Gell's boat before tea. We fished upon the lake, and amongst us caught 13 Bass. Miss Simpson brought gooseberries *and cream*. Left the water at near nine o'clock, very cold. Went part of the way home with the party.

[*May* 30*th*,] *Friday*. In the morning went to Ambleside, forgetting that the post does not come till the evening. How was I grieved when I was so informed. I walked back, resolving to go again in the evening. It rained very mildly and sweetly in the morning as I came home, but came on a wet afternoon and

---

1 The two ancient farmsteads lying south of Butterlip How, and E. and W. of the road to Easedale, were called Dockray and Underhow respectively; both have been occupied by members of the Dockray family. Robert D. of Underhow was buried Jan. 30, 1792 ; Jenny D. was his wife or daughter.— G. G. W.

evening, but chilly. I caught Mr. Olliff's lad as he was going for letters, he brought me one from Wm. and 12 papers. I planted London Pride upon the well, and many things on the borders. John sodded the wall. As I came past Rydale in the morning, I saw a Heron swimming with only its neck out of water ; it beat and struggled amongst the water, when it flew away, and was long in getting loose.

[*May* 31*st*,] *Saturday*. A sweet mild rainy morning. Grundy the carpet man called. I paid him 1-10/-. Went to the blind man's [1] for plants. I got such a load that I was obliged to leave my basket in the road, and send Molly for it. Planted till after dinner when I was putting up vallances. Miss Simpson and her visitors called. I went with them to Brathay Bridge. We got Broom on returning, strawberries etc., came home by Ambleside. Grasmere looked divinely beautiful. Mr. and Miss Simpson and Tommy drank tea at 8 o'clock. I walked to the Potters with them.

June 1*st*, *Sunday*. Rain in the night — a sweet mild morning. Read Ballads ; went to church. Singers from Wytheburn, went part of the way home with Miss Simpson. Walked upon the hill above the house till dinner time — went again to church — Christening and singing which kept us very late. The pew-side came down with me. Walked with Mr. Simpson nearly home. After tea, went to Ambleside, round the lakes — a very fine warm evening. I lay upon the steep of Loughrigg, my heart dissolved in what I saw, when I was not startled but re-called from my reverie by a noise as of a child paddling without shoes. I looked up and saw a lamb close to me. It approached nearer and nearer, as if to examine me, and stood a long time. I did not move. At last it ran past me, and went bleating along the pathway, seeming to be seeking its mother. I saw a hare on the high road. The post was not come in ; waited in the road till John's apprentice came with a letter from Coleridge and 3 papers. The moon shone upon the water — reached home at 10 o'clock, went to bed immediately. Molly brought daisies etc. which we planted.

---

[1] Matthew Newton, referred to again on Jan. 6, 1803.—G. G. W.

[*June 2nd,*] *Monday.* A cold dry windy morning. I worked in the garden, and planted flowers, etc. Sate under the trees after dinner till tea time. John Fisher stuck the peas, Molly weeded and washed. I went to Ambleside after tea, crossed the stepping-stones at the foot of Grasmere, and pursued my way on the other side of Rydale and by Clappersgate. I sate a long time to watch the hurrying waves, and to hear the regularly irregular sound of the dashing waters. The waves round about the little Island seemed like a dance of spirits that rose out of the water, round its small circumference of shore. Inquired about lodgings for Coleridge, and was accompanied by Mrs. Nicholson [1] as far as Rydale. This was very kind, but God be thanked, I want not society by a moonlight lake. It was near 11 when I reached home. I wrote to Coleridge, and went late to bed.

[*June 3rd,*] *Tuesday.* I sent off my letter by the Butcher. A boisterous drying day. I worked in the garden before dinner. Read R[*ichar*]*d Second* — was not well after dinner and lay down. Mrs. Simpson's grandson brought me some gooseberries. I got up and walked with him part of the way home, afterwards went down rambling by the lake side — got Lockety [2] Goldings, strawberries etc., and planted. After tea the wind fell. I walked towards Mr. Simpson's, gave the newspapers to the Girl, reached home at 10. No letter, no William — a letter from R[ichar]d to John.

[*June 4th,*] *Wednesday.* A very fine day. I sate out of doors most of the day, wrote to Mr. Jackson. Ambleside Fair. I walked to the lake-side in the morning, took up plants, and sate upon a stone reading Ballads. In the evening I was watering plants when Mr. and Miss Simpson called. I accompanied them home, and we went to the waterfall at the head of the valley. It was very interesting in the Twilight. I brought home lemon thyme, and several other plants, and planted them by moonlight. I lingered out of doors in the hope of hearing my Brother's tread.

[*June 5th,*] *Thursday.* I sate out of doors great part of the

---

[1] The postmistress at Ambleside.
[2] Lockety : the globeflower (Cumberland and Westmorland dialect).

day and worked in the garden — had a letter from Mr. Jackson,[1] and wrote an answer to Coleridge. The little birds busy making love, and pecking the blossoms and bits of moss off the trees ; they flutter about and about, and thrid the trees as I lie under them. Molly went out to tea, I would not go far from home, expecting my Brothers. I rambled on the hill above the house, gathered wild thyme, and took up roots of wild columbine. Just as I was returning with my load, Mr. and Miss Simpson called. We went again upon the hill, got more plants, set them, and then went to the Blind Man's for London Pride for Miss Simpson. I went up with them as far as the Blacksmith's,[2] a fine lovely moonlight night.

[*June 6th,*] *Friday*. Sate out of doors reading the whole afternoon, but in the morning I wrote to my aunt Cookson. In the evening I went to Ambleside with Coleridge's letter — it was a lovely night as the day had been. I went by Loughrigg and Clappersgate and just met the post at the turnpike ; he told me there were two letters but none for me, so I was in no hurry and went round again by Clappersgate, crossed the stepping-stones and entered Ambleside at Matthew Harrison's. A letter from Jack Hutchinson, and one from Montagu, enclosing a 3£ note. No William ! I slackened my pace as I came near home, fearing to hear that he was not come. I listened till after one o'clock to every barking dog, cock-fighting, and other sports : it was Mr. Borwick's opening. Foxgloves just coming into blossom.

[*June 7th,*] *Saturday*. A very warm cloudy morning, threatening to rain. I walked up to Mr. Simpson's to gather gooseberries — it was a very fine afternoon. Little Tommy came down with me, ate gooseberry pudding and drank tea with me. We went up the hill, to gather sods and plants, and went down to the lake side, and took up orchises, etc. I watered the garden and weeded. I did not leave home, in the expectation of Wm. and John, and sitting at work till

---

[1] The owner of Greta Hall, Keswick, rented by Coleridge, and later by Southey. He was the employer of Benjamin the waggoner.

[2] John Watson, who lived at Winterseeds, and had his forge where Tongue Ghyll crosses the Keswick road.—G. G. W.

after 11 o'clock I heard a foot go to the front of the house, turn round, and open the gate. It was William! After our first joy was over, we got some tea. We did not go to bed till 4 o'clock in the morning, so he had an opportunity of seeing our improvements. The birds were singing, and all looked fresh, though not gay. There was a greyness on earth and sky. We did not rise till near 10 in the morning.[1] We were busy all day in writing letters to Coleridge, Montagu, Douglas, Richard. Mr. and Miss Simpson called in the evening, the little boy carried our letters to Ambleside. We walked with Mr. and Miss S. home, on their return. The evening was cold and I was afraid of the toothach for William. We met John on our return home.

[*June*] 9*th, Monday*. In the morning W. cut down the winter cherry tree. I sowed French beans and weeded. A coronetted Landau went by, when we were sitting upon the sodded wall. The ladies (evidently Tourists) turned an eye of interest upon our little garden and cottage. We went to R. Newton's [2] for pike floats and went round to Mr. Gell's boat, and on to the lake to fish. We caught nothing — it was extremely cold. The reeds and bullrushes or bullpipes of a tender soft green, making a plain whose surface moved with the wind. The reeds not yet tall. The lake clear to the bottom, but saw no fish. In the evening I stuck peas, watered the garden, and planted brocoli. Did not walk, for it was very cold. A poor girl called to beg, who had no work at home, and was going in search of it to Kendal. She slept in Mr. Benson's [?], and went off after breakfast in the morning with 7d. and a letter to the Mayor of Kendal.

[*June*] 10*th, Tuesday*. A cold, yet sunshiny morning. John carried letters to Ambleside. I made tarts, pies, etc. Wm. stuck peas. After dinner he lay down. John not at home. I stuck peas alone. Molly washing. Cold showers with hail and rain, but at half-past five, after a heavy rain, the lake became calm and very beautiful. Those parts of the water which were perfectly unruffled lay like green islands of various shapes.

---

[1] *i.e.* Sunday, June 8.   [2] *v.* note to Oct. 26, 1800.

W. and I walked to Ambleside to seek lodgings for C. No
letters. No papers. It was a very cold chearless evening. John
had been fishing in Langdale and was gone to bed.

On Tuesday, May 27th, a very tall woman,[1] tall much beyond
the measure of tall women, called at the door. She had on a
very long brown cloak and a very white cap, without bonnet ;
her face was excessively brown, but it had plainly once been
fair. She led a little bare-footed child about 2 years old by the
hand, and said her husband, who was a tinker, was gone before
with the other children. I gave her a piece of bread. Afterwards on my road to Ambleside, beside the bridge at Rydale,
I saw her husband sitting by the roadside, his two asses feeding
beside him, and the two young children at play upon the grass.
The man did not beg. I passed on and about $\frac{1}{4}$ of a mile further
I saw two boys before me, one about 10, the other about 8
years old, at play chasing a butterfly. They were wild figures,
not very ragged, but without shoes and stockings ; the hat of
the elder was wreathed round with yellow flowers, the younger
whose hat was only a rimless crown, had stuck it round with
laurel leaves. They continued at play till I drew very near,
and then they addressed me with the begging cant and the
whining voice of sorrow. I said " I served your mother this
morning ". (The Boys were so like the woman who had called
at the door that I could not be mistaken.) " O ! " says the
elder, " you could not serve my mother for she's dead, and my
father's on at the next town — he's a potter." I persisted in
my assertion, and that I would give them nothing. Says the
elder, " Come, let's away ", and away they flew like lightning.
They had however sauntered so long in their road that they did
not reach Ambleside before me, and I saw them go up to
Matthew Harrison's house with their wallet upon the elder's
shoulder, and creeping with a beggar's complaining foot. On
my return through Ambleside I met in the street the mother
driving her asses ; in the two panniers of one of which were the
two little children, whom she was chiding and threatening with
a wand which she used to drive on her asses, while the little

---

[1] *v.* W. W.'s poem *Beggars*.

things hung in wantonness over the pannier's edge. The woman had told me in the morning that she was of Scotland, which her accent fully proved, but that she had lived (I think) at Wigton, that they could not keep a house and so they travelled.

June 11th,[1] *Wednesday.* A very cold morning — we went on the lake to set pike floats with John's fish. W. and J. went first alone. Mr. Simpson called, and I accompanied him to the lake side. My Brothers and I again went upon the water, and returned to dinner. We landed upon the Island where I saw the whitest hawthorn I have seen this year, the generality of hawthorns are bloomless. I saw wild roses in the hedges. Went to bed in the afternoon and slept till after six — a threatening of the toothach. Wm. and John went to the pike floats — they brought in 2 pikes. I sowed kidney-beans and spinnach. A cold evening. Molly stuck the peas. I weeded a little. Did not walk.

June 12th, Thursday. William and I went upon the water to set pike floats. John fished under Loughrigg. We returned to dinner, 2 pikes boiled and roasted. A very cold air but warm sun. W. and I again went upon the water. We walked to Rydale after tea, and up to potter's. A cold night, but warmer.

June 13th, Friday. A rainy morning. W. and J. went upon the Lake. Very warm, and pleasant gleams of sunshine. Went upon the water after tea, caught a pike 7½ [lbs.]. Mr. Simpson trolling. Mr. Gell and his party came.

[*June 14th,*] *Saturday.* A fine morning but cloudy. W. and John went upon the lake. I staid at home. We drank tea at Mr. Simpson's. Stayed till after 10 o'clock.

[*June 15th,*] *Sunday.* John walked to Coniston. W. and I sauntered in the garden. Afterwards walked by the lake side — a cold air. We pushed through the wood. Walked behind the fir grove, and returned to dinner. W. lay down after dinner, Parker, the Tanner and the blacksmith from Hawkshead called.

[*June 16th,*] *Monday.* Wm. and I went to Brathay by Little

---

[1] This and the two following dates D. W. gives, incorrectly, as June 13, 14, and 15.

Langdale and Collath and Skelleth. It was a warm mild morning with threatening of rain. The vale of Little Langdale looked bare and unlovely. Collath was wild and interesting, from the peat carts and peat gatherers — the valley all perfumed with the gale and wild thyme. The woods about the waterfall veined with rich yellow Broom. A succession of delicious views from Skelleth to Brathay. We met near Skelleth a pretty little boy with a wallet over his shoulder. He came from Hawkshead and was going to " late a lock " [1] of meal. He spoke gently and without complaint. When I asked him if he got enough to eat, he looked surprized, and said " Nay ". He was 7 years old but seemed not more than 5. We drank tea at Mr. Ibbetson's, and returned by Ambleside. Lent 3 : 9 : 0 to the potter at Kendal. Met John on our return home at about 10 o'clock. Saw a primrose in blossom.

[*June 17th,*] *Tuesday.* We put the new window in. I ironed, and worked about a good deal in house and garden. In the evening we walked for letters. Found one for Coleridge at Rydale, and I returned much tired.

[*June 18th,*] *Wednesday.* We walked round the lake in the morning and in the evening to the lower waterfall at Rydale. It was a warm, dark, lowering evening.

[*June 19th,*] *Thursday.* A very hot morning. W. and I walked up to Mr. Simpson's. W. and old Mr. S. went to fish in Wytheburn water. I dined with John and lay under the trees. The afternoon changed from clear to cloudy, and to clear again. John and I walked up to the waterfall, and to Mr. Simpson's ; and with Miss Simpson met the fishers. W. caught a pike weighing 4¾ lbs. There was a gloom almost terrible over Grasmere water and vale. A few drops fell but not much rain. No Coleridge, whom we fully expected.

[*June 20th,*] *Friday.* I worked in the garden in the morning. Wm. prepared pea sticks. Threatening for rain, but yet it comes not. On Wednesday evening a poor man called, a potter — he had been long ill, but was now recovered, and his

---

[1] Late a lock of=beg a measure of (dialect).

wife was lying in of her 4th child. The parish would not help him, because he had implements of trade, etc. etc. We gave him 6d.

[*June 21st,*] *Saturday.* In the morning W. and I went to Ambleside to get his tooth drawn, and put in. A fine clear morning but cold. W.'s tooth drawn with very little pain — he slept till 3 o'clock. Young Mr. S. drank tea and supped with us. They fished in Rydale water and they caught 2 small fishes — W. no bite — John 3. Miss Simpson and 3 children called — I walked with them to Rydale. The evening cold and clear and frosty but the wind was falling as I returned — I staid at home about an hour and then walked up the hill to Rydale lake. Grasmere looked so beautiful that my heart was almost melted away. It was quite calm, only spotted with sparkles of light. The church visible. On our return all distant objects had faded away — all but the hills. The reflection of the light bright sky above Black Quarter was very solemn. Mr. S. did not go till 12 o'clock.

[*June 22nd,*] *Sunday.* In the morning W. and I walked towards Rydale and up into the wood but finding it not very pleasant we returned — sauntered in the garden — a showery day. In the evening I planted a honeysuckle round the yew tree. In the evening we walked for letters — no letters. No news of Coleridge. Jimmy Benson came home drunk beside us.

[*June 23rd,*] *Monday.* Mr. Simpson called in the morning. Tommy's Father dead. W. and I went into Langdale to fish. The morning was very cold. I sate at the foot of the lake, till my head ached with cold. The view exquisitely beautiful, through a gate, and under a sycamore tree beside the first house going into Loughrigg. Elter-water looked barren, and the view from the church less beautiful than in winter. When W. went down to the water to fish, I lay under the [? wind], my head pillowed upon a mossy rock, and slept about 10 minutes, which relieved my headach. We ate our dinner together, and parted again. Wm. was afraid he had lost his line and sought me. An old man saw me just after I had crossed the stepping stones and was going through a copse — " Ho, wherever were you going ? " " To Elterwater Bridge " —

" Why ", says he, " it's well I saw you ; ye were gane to Little
Langdale by Wrynose ", and several other places which he ran
over with a mixture of triumph, good-nature and wit — " It's
well I saw you or you'd ha' been lost." The [? evening] grew
very pleasant — We sate on the side of the hill looking to
Elterwater. I was much tired and returned home to tea. W.
went to fish for pike in Rydale. John came in when I had done
tea, and he and I carried a jug of tea to William. We met him
in the old road from Rydale. He drank his tea upon the turf.
The setting sun threw a red purple light upon the rocks, and
stone walls of Rydale, which gave them a most interesting and
beautiful appearance.

[*June 24th,*] *Tuesday.* W. went to Ambleside. John walked
out. I made tarts, etc. Mrs. B. Simpson called and asked us to
tea. I went to the view of Rydale, to meet William. John
went to him — I returned. W. and I drank tea at Mr. Simpson's.
Brought down lemon-thyme, greens, etc. The old woman was
very happy to see us, and we were so in the pleasure we gave.
She was an affecting picture of patient disappointment, suffering under no particular affliction.

[*June 25th,*] *Wednesday.* A very rainy day. I made a shoe.
Wm. and John went to fish in Langdale in the evening. I went
above the house, and gathered flowers, which I planted, foxgloves, etc. On Sunday [1] Mr. and Mrs. Coleridge and Hartley
came. The day was very warm. We sailed to the foot of
Loughrigg. They staid with us three weeks, and till the
Thursday following, *i.e.* till the 23rd of July.[2] On the Friday
preceding their departure we drank tea at the island. The
weather very delightful, and on the Sunday we made a great
fire, and drank tea in Bainriggs with the Simpsons. I accompanied Mrs. C. to Wytheburne, and returned with W. to tea at
Mr. Simpson's. It was excessively hot, but the day after,
Friday 24th July,[3] still hotter. All the morning I was engaged

---

[1] Coleridge arrived at Grasmere on Sunday, June 29.—W. K.
[2] The dates here given are confusing. S. T. C. says he was ill at Grasmere,
and stayed a fortnight. In a letter to Tom Poole he says he arrived at Keswick
on July 24, which was a Thursday.—W. K.
[3] That Friday was July 25. The two next dates were incorrectly entered by
Dorothy.—W. K.

in unpacking our Somersetshire goods and in making pies. The house was a hot oven, but yet we could not bake the pies. I was so weary, I could not walk : so I went and sate with Wm. in the orchard. We had a delightful half-hour in the warm still evening.

[*July*] 26*th, Saturday.* Still hotter. I sate with W. in the orchard all the morning, and made my shoes. In the afternoon from excessive heat I was ill in the headach and toothach and went to bed — I was refreshed with washing myself after I got up, but it was too hot to walk till near dark, and then I sate upon the wall finishing my shoes.

[*July*] 27*th, Sunday.* Very warm. Molly ill. John bathed in the lake. I wrote out *Ruth* in the afternoon. In the morning, I read Mr. Knight's *Landscape.*[1] After tea we rowed down to Loughrigg Fell, visited the white foxglove, gathered wild strawberries, and walked up to view Rydale. We lay a long time looking at the lake ; the shores all embrowned with the scorching sun. The ferns were turning yellow, that is, here and there one was quite turned. We walked round by Benson's wood home. The lake was now most still, and reflected the beautiful yellow and blue and purple and grey colours of the sky. We heard a strange sound in the Bainriggs wood, as we were floating on the water ; it *seemed* in the wood, but it must have been above it, for presently we saw a raven very high above us. It called out, and the dome of the sky seemed to echo the sound. It called again and again as it flew onwards, and the mountains gave back the sound, seeming as if from their center ; a musical bell-like answering to the bird's hoarse voice. We heard both the call of the bird, and the echo, after we could see him no longer.[2] We walked up to the top of the hill again in view of Rydale — met Mr. and Miss Simpson on horseback. The crescent moon which had shone upon the water was now gone down. Returned to supper at 10 o'clock.

[*July* 28*th,*] *Monday Morning.* Received a letter from Coleridge enclosing one from Mr. Davy about the *Lyrical*

---

[1] *The Landscape : a Didactic Poem in Three Books.* By Richard Payne Knight. 1794.—W. K.

[2] Cf. *The Excursion,* iv. 1185-95.

Ballads. Intensely hot. I made pies in the morning. William went into the wood, and altered his poems. In the evening it was so very warm that I was too much tired to walk.

[*July 29th,*] *Tuesday.* Still very hot. We gathered peas for dinner. We walked up in the evening to find out Hewetson's cottage but it was too dark. I was sick and weary.

[*July 30th,*] *Wednesday.* Gathered peas for Mrs. Simpson — John and I walked up with them — very hot — Wm. had intended going to Keswick. I was obliged to lie down after dinner from excessive heat and headach. The evening excessively beautiful — a rich reflection of the moon, the moonlight, clouds and the hills, and from the Rays gap [1] a huge rainbow pillar. We sailed upon the lake till it was 10 o'clock.

[*July 31st,*] *Thursday.* All the morning I was busy copying poems. Gathered peas, and in the afternoon Coleridge came, very hot ; he brought the 2nd volume of the Anthology. The men went to bathe, and we afterwards sailed down to Loughrigg. Read poems on the water, and let the boat take its own course. We walked a long time upon Loughrigg. I returned in the grey twilight. The moon just setting as we reached home.

August 1st, Friday. In the morning I copied *The Brothers.* Coleridge and Wm. went down to the lake. They returned, and we all went together to Mary Point,[2] where we sate in the breeze and the shade, and read Wm.'s poems. Altered *The Whirlblast,* etc. Mr. Simpson came to tea and Mr. B. Simpson afterwards. We drank tea in the orchard.

[*August*] *2nd, Saturday Morning.* Wm. and Coleridge went to Keswick. John went with them to Wytheburn, and staid all day fishing, and brought home 2 small pikes at night. I accompanied them to Lewthwaite's cottage,[3] and on my return

---

[1] *i.e.* Dunmail Raise, nearly always spelled " Rays " by D. W.

[2] One of the twin heath-clad rocks in Bainriggs, above the new road between Grasmere and Rydal.

[3] *i.e.* Grove Cottage, situated on the Keswick road between Town End and the Swan, midway between the Hollins and Forest Side. George Lewthwaite, whose wife had died in 1797, had four daughters. The Parish Register records the baptism of three of them, Jane, Mary, and Hannah, in 1783, 1786, and 1794. There is no mention of the baptism of Barbara (*v. The Pet Lamb*). Hannah L. was frequently taken into temporary service at Dove Cottage.— G. G. W.

papered Wm.'s room, I afterwards lay down till tea time and after tea worked at my shifts in the orchard. A grey evening. About 8 o'clock it gathered for rain, and I had the scatterings of a shower, but afterwards the lake became of a glassy calmness, and all was still. I sate till I could see no longer, and then continued my work in the house.

[*August*] 3*rd, Sunday Morning*. I made pies and stuffed the pike — baked a loaf. Headach after dinner — I lay down. A letter from Wm. roused me, desiring us to go to Keswick. After writing to Wm. we walked as far as Mrs. Simpson's and ate black cherries. A heavenly warm evening, with scattered clouds upon the hills. There was a vernal greenness upon the grass, from the rains of the morning and afternoon. Peas for dinner.

[*August*] 4*th, Monday*. Rain in the night. I tied up scarlet beans, nailed the honeysuckles, etc. etc. John was prepared to walk to Keswick all the morning. He seized a returned chaise and went after dinner. I pulled a large basket of peas and sent to Keswick by a returned chaise. A very cold evening. Assisted to spread out linen in the morning.

[*August*] 5*th, Tuesday*. Dried the linen in the morning. The air still cold. I pulled a bag full of peas for Mrs. Simpson. Miss Simpson drank tea with me, and supped, on her return from Ambleside. A very fine evening. I sate on the wall making my shifts till I could see no longer. Walked half-way home with Miss Simpson.

August 6*th, Wednesday*. A rainy morning. I ironed till dinner time — sewed till near dark — then pulled a basket of peas, and afterwards boiled and picked gooseberries. William came home from Keswick at 11 o'clock. A very fine night.

August 7*th, Thursday Morning*. Packed up the mattrass and sent to Keswick. Boiled gooseberries — N.B. 2 lbs. of sugar in the first panfull, 3 quarts all good measure — 3 lbs. in the 2nd 4 quarts — 2½ lbs. in the 3rd. A very fine day. William composing in the wood in the morning. In the evening we walked to Mary Point. A very fine sunset.

[*August* 8*th,*] *Friday Morning*. We intended going to Keswick, but were prevented by the excessive heat. Nailed up scarlet beans in the morning. Drank tea at Mr. Simpson's, and walked over the mountains by Wattendlath. Very fine gooseberries at Mr. S.'s. A most enchanting walk. Wattendlath a heavenly scene. Reached Coleridge's at eleven o'clock.

[*August 9th,*] *Saturday Morning.* I walked with Coleridge in the Windy Brow [1] woods.

[*August 10th,*] *Sunday.* Very hot. The C.'s went to church. We sailed upon Derwent in the evening.

[*August 11th,*] *Monday Afternoon.* Walked with C. to Windy Brow.

[*August 12th,*] *Tuesday.* Drank tea with the Cockins — Wm. and I walked along the Cockermouth road. He was altering his poems.

[*August 13th,*] *Wednesday.* Made the Windy Brow seat.

[*August 14th,*] *Thursday Morning.* Called at the Speddings. In the evening walked in the wood with W. Very very beautiful the moon.

[*August 15th.*] Friday morning W. in the wood — I went with Hartley to see the Cockins and to buy bacon. In the evening we walked to Water End — feasted on gooseberries at Silver Hill.

[*August 16th.*] Saturday morning worked for Mrs. C. — walked with Coleridge intending to gather raspberries — joined by Miss Spedding.

August 17th, Sunday. Came home. Dined in Borrowdale. A rainy morning, but a fine evening — saw the Bristol prison and Bassenthwaite at the same time — Wm. read us *The Seven Sisters* on a stone.

[*August 18th,*] *Monday.* Putting linen by and mending — walked with John to Mr. Simpson's and met Wm. in returning. A fine warm day.

[*August 19th,*] *Tuesday.* Mr. and Mrs. Simpson dined with us — Miss S. and Brother drank tea in the orchard.

[*August 20th,*] *Wednesday.* I worked in the morning. Cold

---

[1] Windy Brow was the Calverts' house where W. and D. W. stayed in 1794: *v. E.L.* 110-14. The Windy Brow seat is commemorated in an early poem of Wordsworth's.

in the evening and rainy. Did not walk.

[*August 21st,*] *Thursday.* Read *Wallenstein* [1] and sent it off — worked in the morning — walked with John round the two lakes — gathered white fox-glove seeds and found Wm. in Bainriggs at our return.

[*August*] *22nd, Friday.* Very cold. Baking in the morning, gathered pea seeds and took up — lighted a fire upstairs. Walked as far as Rydale with John intending to have gone on to Ambleside, but we found the papers at Rydale — Wm. walking in the wood all the time. John and he went out after our return — I mended stockings. Wind very high shaking the corn.

[*August*] *23rd, Saturday.* A very fine morning. Wm. was composing all the morning. I shelled peas, gathered beans, and worked in the garden till ½ past 12. Then walked with Wm. in the wood. The gleams of sunshine, and the stirring trees, and gleaming boughs, chearful lake, most delightful. After dinner we walked to Ambleside — showery — went to see Mr. Partridge's house. Came home by Clappersgate. We had intended going by Rydale woods, but it was cold — I was not well, and tired. Got tea immediately and had a fire. Did not reach home till 7 o'clock — mended stockings and Wm. read *Peter Bell*. He read us the poem of *Joanna*, beside the Rothay by the roadside.

[*August*] *24th, Sunday.* A fine cool pleasant breezy day — walked in the wood in the morning. Mr. Twining called. John walked up to Mr. Simpson's in the evening — I staid at home and wrote to Mrs. Rawson and my aunt Cookson — I was ill in the afternoon and lay down — got up restored by a sound sleep.

[*August 25th,*] *Monday.* A fine day — walked in the wood in the morning and to the firgrove — walked up to Mr. Simpson's in the evening.

[*August*] *26th, Tuesday.* We walked in the evening to Ambleside — Wm. not quite well. I bought sacking for the mattrass. A very fine solemn evening. The wind blew very

---

[1] *i.e.* in Coleridge's translation.

free from the islands at Rydale. We went on the other side of Rydale, and sate a long time looking at the mountains, which were all black at Grasmere, and very bright in Rydale ; Grasmere exceedingly dark, and Rydale of a light yellow green.

[*August*] 27*th*, *Wednesday*. In the morning Wm. walked [?]. We walked along the shore of the lake in the evening, went over into Langdale and down to Loughrigg Tarn — a very fine evening calm and still.

[*August* 28*th*,] *Thursday*. Still very fine weather. I baked bread and cakes. In the evening we walked round the Lake by Rydale. Mr. Simpson came to fish.

[*August* 29*th*,] *Friday Evening*. We walked to Rydale to inquire for letters. We walked over the hill by the firgrove. I sate upon a rock, and observed a flight of swallows gathering together high above my head. They flew towards Rydale. We walked through the wood over the stepping-stones. The lake of Rydale very beautiful, partly still. John and I left Wm. to compose an inscription — that about the path.[1] We had a very fine walk by the gloomy lake. There was a curious yellow reflection in the water, as of corn fields. There was no light in the clouds from which it appeared to come.

August 30*th*, *Saturday Morning*. I was baking bread, pies and dinner. It was very warm. William finished his Inscription of the Pathway, then walked in the wood ; and when John returned, he sought him, and they bathed together. I read a little of Boswell's *Life of Johnson*. I had a headach and went to lie down in the orchard. I was roused by a shout that Anthony Harrison was come. We sate in the orchard till tea time. Drank tea early, and rowed down the lake which was stirred by breezes. We looked at Rydale, which was soft, chearful, and beautiful. We then went to peep into Langdale. The Pikes were very grand. We walked back to the view of Rydale, which was now a dark mirror. We rowed home over a lake still as glass, and then went to George Mackareth's[2] to hire a horse for John. A fine moonlight night. The beauty of the moon was startling, as it rose to us over Loughrigg Fell.

---

[1] *v.* note to Sept. 1, *infra*.
[2] For George Mackereth *v.* Appendix, p. 435.

We returned to supper at 10 o'clock. Thomas Ashburner brought us our 8th cart of coals since May 17th.

[*August*] 31*st*, *Sunday*. Anthony Harrison and John left us at ½ past seven — a very fine morning. A great deal of corn is cut in the vale, and the whole prospect, though not tinged with a general autumnal yellow, yet softened down into a mellowness of colouring, which seems to impart softness to the forms of hills and mountains. At 11 o'clock Coleridge came, when I was walking in the still clear moonshine in the garden. He came over Helvellyn. Wm. was gone to bed, and John also, worn out with his ride round Coniston. We sate and chatted till ½-past three, W. in his dressing gown. Coleridge read us a part of *Christabel*. Talked much about the mountains, etc. etc. Miss Thrale's [?] — Losh's [1] opinion of Southey — the first of poets.

September 1*st*, *Monday Morning*. We walked in the wood by the lake. W. read *Joanna*, and the *Firgrove*,[2] to Coleridge. They bathed. The morning was delightful, with somewhat of an autumnal freshness. After dinner, Coleridge discovered a rock-seat in the orchard. Cleared away the brambles. Coleridge obliged to go to bed after tea. John and I followed Wm. up the hill, and then returned to go to Mr. Simpson's. We borrowed some bottles for bottling rum. The evening somewhat frosty and grey, but very pleasant. I broiled Coleridge a mutton chop, which he ate in bed. Wm. was gone to bed. I chatted with John and Coleridge till near 12.

[*September*] 2*nd*, *Tuesday*. In the morning they all went to Stickle Tarn. A very fine, warm, sunny, beautiful morning. I baked a pie etc. for dinner — Little Sally was with me. The fair-day. Miss Simpson and Mr. came down to tea — we walked to the fair. There seemed very few people and very few stalls, yet I believe there were many cakes and much beer sold. My brothers came home to dinner at 6 o'clock. We

---

[1] James Losh, of Woodside, near Carlisle, an early friend of W.'s: *v. L.Y.* p. 56.
[2] *The Firgrove*, probably an early draft of ll. 1-83 of *When, to the attractions of the busy world*. The Firgrove, a favourite walk of D. and W., and afterwards sacred to the memory of John W., was situated in that part of Ladywood immediately above the Wishing Gate.

Grasmere Church and Bridge
From a drawing by J. Flower

drank tea immediately after by candlelight. It was a lovely moonlight night. We talked much about a house on Helvellyn. The moonlight shone only upon the village. It did not eclipse the village lights, and the sound of dancing and merriment came along the still air. I walked with Coleridge and Wm. up the lane and by the church, and then lingered with Coleridge in the garden. John and Wm. were both gone to bed, and all the lights out.

September 3rd, Wednesday. Coleridge, Wm., and John went from home, to go upon Helvellyn with Mr. Simpson. They set out after breakfast. I accompanied them up near the blacksmith's. A fine coolish morning. I ironed till ½ past 3 — now very hot — I then went to a funeral at John Dawson's.[1] About 10 men and 4 women. Bread, cheese, and ale. They talked sensibly and chearfully about common things. The dead person, 56 years of age, buried by the parish. The coffin was neatly lettered and painted black, and covered with a decent cloth. They set the corpse down at the door ; and, while we stood within the threshold, the men with their hats off sang with decent and solemn countenances a verse of a funeral psalm. The corpse was then borne down the hill, and they sang till they had passed the Town-End. I was affected to tears while we stood in the house, the coffin lying before me. There were no near kindred, no children. When we got out of the dark house the sun was shining, and the prospect looked so divinely beautiful as I never saw it. It seemed more sacred than I had ever seen it, and yet more allied to human life. The green fields, neighbours of the churchyard, were as green as possible ; and, with the brightness of the sunshine, looked quite gay. I thought she was going to a quiet spot, and I could not help weeping very much. When we came to the bridge, they began to sing again, and stopped during four lines before they entered the churchyard. The priest met us — he did not look as a man ought to do on such an occasion — I

---

[1] John Dawson lived at How Top, between Dove Cottage and White Moss Common, near the Firgrove (*v.* Sept. 9). The funeral must have been that of " Susan Shaelock, a pauper " (Grasmere Register for Sept. 3). W. W. drew upon this entry in D. W.'s Journal in *Excursion*, II, 370-402, 548-66.—G. G. W.

had seen him half-drunk the day before in a pot-house. Before we came with the corpse one of the company observed he wondered what sort of cue our Parson would be in! N.B. It was the day after the Fair. I had not finished ironing till 7 o'clock. The wind was now high and I did not walk — writing my journal now at 8 o'clock. Wm. and John came home at 10 o'clock.

September 4th, Thursday. A fine warm day. I was busy all the morning making a mattrass. Mr. Simpson called in the afternoon. Wm. walked in the wood in the morning, and in the evening as we set forward to walk — a letter from Mrs. Clarkson.[1] We walked into the black quarter. The patches of corn very interesting.

[*September 5th,*] *Friday Morning.* Finished the mattrass, ironed the white bed in the afternoon — when I was putting it up Mr. and Mrs. Losh arrived while Wm. and John were walking.

[*September 6th,*] *Saturday Morning.* Breakfasted with the Loshes — very warm — returned through Rydale woods. The Clarksons dined. After tea we walked round Rydale — a little rain.

[*September*] *7th, Sunday Morning.* Rainy. Walked before dinner over the stepping-stones to Langdale and home on the other side of the lake. I lay down after dinner. Wm. poorly. Walked into the Black Quarter.

September 8th, Monday. Morning very rainy. The Clarksons left us after dinner — still rainy. We walked towards Rydale, and then to Mr. Olliff's gate [2] — a fine evening.

[*September*] *9th, Tuesday Morning.* Mr. Marshall [3] came — he dined with us. My Brothers walked with him round the lakes after dinner — windy — we went to the island. W. and I after to tea. John and I went to the B. quarter, before supper went to seek a horse at Dawson's, Firgrove. After supper, talked of Wm.'s poems.

---

[1] Catherine Clarkson, soon to become D. W.'s most intimate friend, the wife of Thomas Clarkson, the slave-abolitionist. The Clarksons were now living at Eusemere, near the foot of Ullswater.

[2] Mr. Olliff *v.* Appendix, p. 436.

[3] John Marshall, of Leeds, husband of Jane Pollard, D. W.'s greatest friend in her youth at Halifax. (*v. E.L. passim.*)

Sept[ember] 10th, Wednesday. After breakfast Mr. Marshall, Wm. and John went on horseback to Keswick — I wrote to Mrs. Marshall — a fine autumn day. I had a fire. Paid Mr. Bonsfield 8 : 2 : 11. After tea walked with French Beans to Mr. Simpson's — went up to the Forest side above a deserted house — sat till twilight came on. Mr. and Miss S. came down with me and supped.

[September] 11th, Thursday. All the morning mending white gown — washed my head — Molly washing. Drank tea at Mr. Simpson's. Found Wm. at home at my return — he was unable to go on with Mr. Marshall and parted from him in Borrowdale. Made tea after my return.

Sept[ember] 12th, Friday. I worked in the morning. Cut my thumb. Walked in the Firgrove before dinner — after dinner sate under the trees in the orchard — a rainy morning, but very fine afternoon. Miss Simpson called for my packing needle. The Fern of the mountains now spreads yellow veins among the trees ; the coppice wood turns brown. William observed some affecting little things in Borrowdale. A decayed house with this inscription [*blank space in MS.*] in the Church yard, the tall silent rocks seen thro' the broken windows. A kind of rough column put upon the gavel end of a house, with a ball stone, smooth from the river placed upon it for ornament. Near it one stone like it upon an old mansion, carefully hewn.

September 13th, Saturday Morning. William writing his Preface [1] — did not walk. Jones,[2] and Mr. Palmer came to tea. We walked with them to Borricks — a lovely evening, but the air frosty — worked when I returned home. Wm. walked out. John came home from Mr. Marshall. Sent back word [3] to Mrs. Clarkson.

[September] 14th, Sunday Morning. Made bread. A sore thumb from a cut. A lovely day. Read Boswell in the house in the morning, and after dinner under the bright yellow leaves

---

[1] The Preface to the second edition of *Lyrical Ballads.*—W. K.
[2] Rev. Robert Jones, W.'s College friend, who accompanied him on his continental tour in 1790.
[3] back word : *written in MS.* backward.

of the orchard. The pear trees a bright yellow. The apple trees green still. A sweet lovely afternoon.

Here I have long neglected my Journal. John came home in the evening, after Jones left us. Jones returned again on the Friday, the 19th September. Jones stayed with us till Friday, 26th September. Coleridge came on Tuesday 23rd and went home with Jones. Charles Lloyd called on Tuesday, 23rd, and on Sunday 28th we drank tea and supped with him and on that day heard of the Abergavenny's arrival. While Jones was with us we had much rainy weather. On Sunday 21st Tom Myers [1] and Father called, and on the 28th Mr. and Miss Smith.

[September] 29th, on Monday. John left us. Wm. and I parted with him in sight of Ulswater.[2] It was a fine day, showery, but with sunshine and fine clouds. Poor fellow, my heart was right sad. I could not help thinking we should see him again, because he was only going to Penrith.

September 30th, on Tuesday. Charles Lloyd dined with us. We walked homewards with him after dinner. It rained very hard. Rydale was extremely wild, and we had a fine walk. We sate quietly and comfortably by the fire. I wrote the last sheet of Notes and Preface.[3] Went to bed at twelve o'clock.

October 1st, Wednesday. A fine morning, a showery night. The lake still in the morning; in the forenoon flashing light from the beams of the sun, as it was ruffled by the wind. We corrected the last sheet.[3]

October 2nd, Thursday. A very rainy morning. We walked after dinner to observe the torrents. I followed Wm. to Rydale, he afterwards went to Butterlip How. I came home to receive the Lloyds. They walked with us to see Churnmilk force [4] and the Black quarter. The Black Quarter looked marshy, and the general prospect was cold, but the Force was very grand. The Lichens are now coming out afresh, I carried home a collection in the afternoon. We had a pleasant conversation

---

[1] W.'s cousin ; his father, the Rev. Thos. Myers, had married W.'s aunt, Anne W.

[2] For a description of their parting *v. Elegiac Verses in Memory of my Brother*, etc. (" The Sheep-boy whistled loud . . .").

[3] *i.e.* of the Notes and Preface to the second edition of *Lyrical Ballads.*— W. K.   [4] Now known as Sour Milk Ghyll.

about the manners of the rich — avarice, inordinate desires, and the effeminacy, unnaturalness, and the unworthy objects of education. After the Lloyds were gone we walked — a showery evening. The moonlight lay upon the hills like snow.

October 3rd, Friday. Very rainy all the morning. Little Sally learning to mark. Wm. walked to Ambleside after dinner, I went with him part of the way. He talked much about the object of his essay for the second volume of " L. B." I returned expecting the Simpsons — they did not come. I should have met Wm. but my teeth ached and it was showery and late — he returned after 10. Amos Cottle's death in the *Morning Post.* Wrote to S. Lowthian.

N.B. When William and I returned from accompanying Jones, we met an old man almost double. He had on a coat, thrown over his shoulders, above his waistcoat and coat. Under this he carried a bundle, and had an apron on and a night-cap. His face was interesting. He had dark eyes and a long nose. John, who afterwards met him at Wytheburn, took him for a Jew. He was of Scotch parents, but had been born in the army. He had had a wife, and " a good woman, and it pleased God to bless us with ten children ". All these were dead but one, of whom he had not heard for many years, a sailor. His trade was to gather leeches, but now leeches are scarce, and he had not strength for it. He lived by begging, and was making his way to Carlisle, where he should buy a few godly books to sell. He said leeches were very scarce, partly owing to this dry season, but many years they have been scarce — he supposed it owing to their being much sought after, that they did not breed fast, and were of slow growth. Leeches were formerly 2s. 6d. [per] 100 ; they are now 30s. He had been hurt in driving a cart, his leg broke, his body driven over, his skull fractured. He felt no pain till he recovered from his first insensibility. It was then late in the evening, when the light was just going away.[1]

October 4th, 1800, *Saturday.* A very rainy, or rather showery

---

[1] Cf. *Resolution and Independence.*—W. K.

and gusty, morning ; for often the sun shines. Thomas Ash-burner could not go to Keswick. Read a part of Lamb's Play.[1] The language is often very beautiful, but too imitative in particular phrases, words, etc. The characters, except Margaret's, unintelligible, and, except Margaret's, do not show themselves in action. Coleridge came in while we were at dinner, very wet — we talked till 12 o'clock. He had sate up all the night before, writing Essays for the newspaper. His youngest child had been very ill in convulsion fits. Exceedingly delighted with the second part of *Christabel*.

October 5th, Sunday Morning. Coleridge read a 2nd time *Christabel* ; we had increasing pleasure. A delicious morning. Wm. and I were employed all the morning in writing an addition to the Preface. Wm. went to bed, very ill after working after dinner. Coleridge and I walked to Ambleside after dark with the letter. Returned to tea at 9 o'clock. Wm. still in bed, and very ill. Silver How in both lakes.

[*October 6th,*] *Monday.* A rainy day. Coleridge intending to go, but did not get off. We walked after dinner to Rydale. After tea read *The Pedlar*. Determined not to print *Christabel* with the L. B.

[*October 7th,*] *Tuesday.* Coleridge went off at eleven o'clock. I went as far as Mr. Simpson's. Returned with Mary. She drank tea here. I was very ill in the evening at the Simpsons — went to bed — supped there. Returned with Miss S. and Mrs. J. — heavy showers. Found Wm. at home. I was still weak and unwell — went to bed immediately.

[*October 8th,*] *Wednesday.* A threatening bad morning — We dried the linen. Frequent threatening of showers. Received a £5 note from Montagu. Wm. walked to Rydale. I copied a part of *The Beggar* in the morning. I was not quite well in the evening, therefore I did not walk — Wm. walked. A very mild moonlight night. Glow-worms everywhere.

[*October 9th,*] *Thursday.* I was ironing all the day till tea time. Very rainy. Wm. and I walked in the evening, intending to go to Lloyd's, but it came on so very rainy that we were

---

[1] *Pride's Cure.* The title was afterwards changed to *John Woodvill.*—W. K.

obliged to shelter at Fleming's. A grand Ball at Rydale. After sitting some time we went homewards and were again caught by a shower and sheltered under the sycamores at the boat-house — a very cold snowlike rain. A man called in a soldier's dress — he was thirty years old, of Cockermouth, had lost a leg and thigh in battle, was going to his home. He could earn more money in travelling with his ass than at home.

October 10th, Friday. In the morning when I arose the mists were hanging over the opposite hills, and the tops of the highest hills were covered with snow. There was a most lovely combination at the head of the vale of the yellow autumnal hills wrapped in sunshine, and overhung with partial mists, the green and yellow trees, and the distant snow-topped mountains. It was a most heavenly morning. The Cockermouth traveller came with thread, hardware, mustard, etc. She is very healthy; has travelled over the mountains these thirty years. She does not mind the storms, if she can keep her goods dry. Her husband will not travel with an ass, because it is the tramper's badge ; she would have one to relieve her from the weary load. She was going to Ulverston, and was to return to Ambleside Fair. After I had finished baking I went out with Wm., Mrs. Jameson and Miss Simpson towards Rydale — the fern among the rocks exquisitely beautiful. We turned home and walked to Mr. Gell's. After dinner Wm. went to bed — I read Southey's letter. Miss Simpson and Mrs. Jameson came to tea. After tea we went to Lloyd's — a fine evening as we went, but rained in returning — we were wet — found them not at home. I wrote to Mrs. Clarkson. Sent off *The Beggar*, etc., by Thomas Ashburner who went to fetch our 9th cart of coals. William sat up after me, writing *Point Rash Judgment*.[1]

[October] 11th, Saturday. A fine October morning. Sat in the house working all the morning. William composing. Sally Ashburner learning to mark. After dinner we walked up Greenhead Gill in search of a sheepfold. We went by Mr. Olliff's, and through his woods. It was a delightful day, and the views looked excessively chearful and beautiful, chiefly that

---

[1] *i.e. Poems on the Naming of Places*, iv.

from Mr. Olliff's field, where our house is to be built. The colours of the mountains soft and rich, with orange fern ; the cattle pasturing upon the hill-tops ; kites sailing in the sky above our heads ; sheep bleating and in lines and chains and patterns scattered over the mountains. They come down and feed on the little green islands in the beds of the torrents, and so may be swept away. The sheepfold is falling away. It is built nearly in the form of a heart unequally divided. Look down the brook, and see the drops rise upwards and sparkle in the air at the little falls, the higher sparkles the tallest. We walked along the turf of the mountain till we came to a cattle track, made by the cattle which come upon the hills. We drank tea at Mr. Simpson's, returned at about nine — a fine mild night.

October 12th, Sunday. Beautiful day. Sate in the house writing in the morning while Wm. went into the wood to compose. Wrote to John in the morning, copied poems for the L. B. ; in the evening wrote to Mrs. Rawson. Mary Jameson and Sally Ashburner dined. We pulled apples after dinner, a large basket full. We walked before tea by Bainriggs to observe the many-coloured foliage. The oaks dark green with yellow leaves, the birches generally still green, some near the water yellowish, the sycamore crimson and crimson-tufted, the mountain ash a deep orange, the common ash lemon-colour, but many ashes still fresh in their summer green. Those that were discoloured chiefly near the water. William composing in the evening. Went to bed at 12 o'clock.

October 13th, Monday. A grey day. Mists on the hills. We did not walk in the morning. I copied poems on the Naming of Places. A fair at Ambleside. Walked in the Black Quarter at night.

[*October*] 14th, *Tuesday.* Wm. lay down after dinner — I read Southey's Spain. The wind rose very high at evening. Wm. walked out just at bedtime — I went to bed early. We walked before dinner to Rydale.

[*October 15th,*] *Wednesday.* A very fine clear morning. After Wm. had composed a little, I persuaded him to go into the orchard. We walked backwards and forwards. The prospect

most divinely beautiful from the seat ; all colours, all melting
into each other. I went in to put bread in the oven, and we
both walked within view of Rydale. Wm. again composed at
the sheep-fold [1] after dinner. I walked with him to Wytheburn,
and he went on to Keswick. I drank tea, and supped at Mr.
Simpson's. A very cold frosty air and a spangled [2] sky in returning. Mr. and Miss S. came with me. Wytheburn looked very
wintry, but yet there was a foxglove blossoming by the road-
side.

October 16th, Thursday. A very fine morning — starched
and hung out linen — a very fine day. John Fisher, F. A.,
and S. A. and Molly working in the garden. Wrote to Miss
Nicholson. I walked as far as Rydale between 3 and 4 —
Ironed till six — got tea and wrote to Mr. Griffith. A letter
from Mr. Clarkson.

[October] 17th, Friday. A very fine grey morning. The
swan hunt. Sally working in the garden. I walked round the
lake between ¼ past 12 and ½ past one. Wrote to M. H. After
dinner I walked to Lloyd's — carried my letters to Miss N.
and M. H. The Lloyds not in — I waited for them — Charles
not well. Letters from M. H., Biggs [3] and John. In my walk
in the morning, I observed Benson's honeysuckles in flower,
and great beauty. It was a very fine mild evening. Ll.'s
servants came with me to Parke's. [4] I found Wm. at home,
where he had been almost ever since my departure. Coleridge
had done nothing for the L. B. Working hard for Stuart. [5]
Glow-worms in abundance.

[October 18th,] Saturday. A very fine October morning.
William worked all the morning at the sheepfold, but in vain.
He lay down in the afternoon till 7 o'clock, but could not sleep.
I slept, my head better — he unable to work. We did not
walk all day.

[October 19th,] Sunday Morning. We rose late, and walked
directly after breakfast. The tops of G[ras]mere mountains cut

---

[1] *i.e. Michael.*   [2] *Written* splangled.
[3] The Bristol printer of the 1800 *Lyrical Ballads.*
[4] Nab Cottage, on Rydal Lake, the house where, later, Hartley Coleridge
lodged. *v.* Simpson of the Nab in Appendix, p. 436.
[5] The Editor of the *Morning Post.*

off. Rydale was very, very beautiful. The surface of the water quite still, like a dim mirror. The colours of the large island exquisitely beautiful, and the trees still fresh and green were magnified by the mists. The prospects on the west side of the Lake were very beautiful. We sate at the " two points "[1] looking up to Park's. The lowing of the cattle was echoed by a hollow voice in Knab Scar. We went upon Loughrigg Fell and were disappointed with G[ras]mere — It did not look near so beautiful as Rydale. We returned home over the stepping-stones. Wm. got to work. We are not to dine till 4 o'clock.— Dined at ½ past 5 — Mr. Simpson dined and drank tea with us. We went to bed immediately after he left us.

[*October*] 20*th, Monday*. William worked in the morning at the sheepfold. After dinner we walked to Rydale, crossed the stepping-stones, and while we were walking under the tall oak trees the Lloyds called out to us. They went with us on the western side of Rydale. The lights were very grand upon the woody Rydale hills. Those behind dark and topp'd with clouds. The two lakes were divinely beautiful. Grasmere excessively solemn and the whole lake was calm, and dappled with soft grey ripples. The Lloyds staid with us till 8 o'clock. We then walked to the top of the hill at Rydale. Very mild and warm. About 6 glow-worms shining faintly. We went up as far as the grove. When we came home the fire was out. We ate our supper in the dark, and went to bed immediately. William was disturbed in the night by the rain coming into his room, for it was a very rainy night. The ash leaves lay across the road.

[*October*] 21*st, Tuesday*. We walked in the morning past Mr. Gell's — a very fine clear sharp sunny morning. We drank tea at the Lloyds. It was very cold in the evening, quite frosty and starlight. Wm. had been unsuccessful in the morning at the sheepfold. The reflection of the ash scattered, and the tree stripped.

[*October 22nd,*] *Wednesday Morning*. We walked to Mr. Gell's — a very fine morning. Wm. composed without much

---

[1] *v.* Aug. 7, 1800.

success at the sheepfold. Coleridge came in to dinner. He had done nothing. We were very merry. C. and I went to look at the prospect from his seat. In the evening Stoddart [1] came in when we were at tea, and after tea Mr. and Miss Simpson with large potatoes and plumbs. Wm. read after supper, *Ruth*, etc. ; Coleridge *Christabel*.

[*October*] 23*rd, Thursday*. Coleridge and Stoddart went to Keswick. We accompanied them to Wytheburn — a wintry grey morning from the top of the Raise. Grasmere looked like winter, and Wytheburn still more so. We called upon Mrs. Simpson and sate 10 minutes in returning. Wm. was not successful in composition in the evening.

[*October*] 24*th, Friday*. A very fine morning. We walked before Wm. began to work to the top of the Rydale hill. He was afterwards only partly successful in composition. After dinner we walked round Rydale lake, rich, calm, streaked, very beautiful. We went to the top of Loughrigg. Grasmere sadly inferior. We were much tired — Wm. went to bed till ½ past seven. The ash in our garden green, one close to it bare, the next nearly so.

[*October* 25*th,*] *Saturday*. A very rainy day. Wm. again unsuccessful. We could not walk, it was so very rainy. We read Rogers, Miss Seward, Cowper, etc.

[*October* 26*th,*] *Sunday*. Heavy rain all night, a fine morning after 10 o'clock. Wm. composed a good deal in the morning. The Lloyds came to dinner and were caught in a shower. Wm. read some of his poems after dinner. A terrible night. I went with Mrs. Lloyd to Newton's [2] to see for lodgings. Mr. Simpson in coming from Ambleside called in for a glass of rum just before we went to bed.

October 27*th, Monday*. Not a rainy morning. The Hill tops covered with snow. Charles Lloyd came for his wife's glass. I walked home with him past Rydale. When he came I met him as I was carrying some cold meat to Wm. in the Fir-grove,

---

[1] Sir John Stoddart (1773–1856), a prominent journalist, and from 1805 to 1807 King's Advocate at Malta. In 1808 Hazlitt married S.'s sister.

[2] Robert Newton was the proprietor of the village inn, now Church Stile (opposite the church). W. and Coleridge had stayed there Nov. 3–8, 1799.— G. G. W.

I had before walked with him there for some time. It was a fine shelter from the wind. The coppices now nearly of one brown. An oak tree in a sheltered place near John Fisher's, not having lost any of its leaves, was quite brown and dry. We did not walk after dinner. It was a fine wild moonlight night. Wm. could not compose much, fatigued himself with altering.

[*October*] 28*th, Tuesday*. A very rainy night. I was baking bread in the morning and made a giblet pie. We walked out before dinner to our favourite field. The mists sailed along the mountains, and rested upon them, enclosing the whole vale. In the evening the Lloyds came. We drank tea with them at Borwick's and played a rubber at whist — stayed supper. Wm. looked very well — A fine moonlight night when we came home.

[*October 29th,*] *Wednesday*. William working at his poem all the morning. After dinner, Mr. Clarkson called. We went down to Borwick's and he and the Lloyds and Priscilla came back to drink tea with us. We met Stoddart upon the bridge. Played at cards. The Lloyds etc. went home to supper — Mr. Clarkson slept here.

[*October 30th,*] *Thursday*. A rainy morning. Mr. C. went over Kirkstone. Wm. talked all day, and almost all night, with Stoddart. Mrs. and Miss Ll. called in the morning. I walked with them to Tail End,[1] a fine pleasant morning, but a very rainy afternoon. W. and I in the house all day.

[*October 31st,*] *Friday*. W. and I did not rise till 1 o'clock. W. very sick and very ill. S. and I drank tea at Lloyds and came home immediately after. A very fine moonlight night — The moon shone like herrings in the water.

[*November 1st,*] *Saturday*. William better. We met as we walked to Rydale a boy from Lloyd's, coming for *Don Quixote*. Talk in the evening. Tom Ashburner brought his 10th cart of coals.

[*November 2nd,*] *Sunday Morning*. We walked into the Black Quarter — a very fine morning — a succession of beauti-

---

[1] On the western side of Grasmere Lake.—W. K.

ful views, mists, etc. etc., much rain in the night. In the evening drank tea at Lloyds — found them all ill, in colds — came home to supper.

[*November 3rd,*] *Monday Morning.* Walked to Rydale — a cold day. Wm. and Stoddart still talking. Frequent showers in our walk. In the evening we talked merrily over the fire. The Speddings [1] stopped at the door.

[*November 4th,*] *Tuesday.* Stoddart left us — I walked a little way with W. and him. W. went to the Tarn,[2] afterwards to the top of Seat Sandal. He was obliged to lie down in the tremendous wind. The snow blew from Helvellyn horizontally like smoke — the spray of the unseen waterfall like smoke. Miss Lloyd called upon me — I walked with her past Rydale. Wm. sadly tired — threatenings of the piles.

[*November 5th,*] *Wednesday.* Wm. not well. A very fine clear beautiful winter's day. I walked after dinner to Lloyd's — drank tea and Mrs. and Miss Lloyd came to Rydale with me. The moon was rising but the sky all over cloud. I made tea for William.

November 6th, Thursday. A very rainy morning and night. I was baking bread, dinner, and parkins. Charles and P. Lloyd called. Wm. somewhat better. Read *Point Rash Judgment.* The lake calm and very beautiful — a very rainy afternoon and night.

November 7th, Friday. A cold rainy morning. Wm. still unwell. I working and reading *Amelia.* The Michaelmas daisy droops, the pansies are full of flowers, the ashes opposite are green all but one, but they have lost many of their leaves. The copses are quite brown. The poor woman and child from White-haven drank tea — nothing warm that day. A very rainy morning. It cleared up in the afternoon. We expected the Lloyds but they did not come. Wm. still unwell. A rainy night.

November 8th, Saturday. A rainy morning. A whirlwind came that tossed about the leaves, and tore off the still green

---

[1] The Speddings lived at Armathwaite, near Keswick. W. and D. W. had made their acquaintance when staying at Windy Brow in 1794.

[2] *i.e.* Grisedale Tarn.

leaves of the ashes. A fine afternoon — Wm. and I walked out at 4 o'clock. Went as far as Rothay Bridge. Met the Butcher's man with a l[ette]r from Monk Lewis. The country very wintry — some oaks quite bare — others more sheltered with a few green leaves — others with brown leaves, but the whole face of the country in a winter covering. We went early to bed.

[*November 9th,*] *Sunday*. Wm. slept tolerably — better this morning. It was a frosty night. We walked to Rydale after dinner, partly expecting to meet the Lloyds. Mr. Simpson brought newspapers but met Molly with them. W. [? burnt] the sheepfold. A rainy night.

[*November 10th,*] *Monday*. I baked bread. A fine clear frosty morning. We walked after dinner to Rydale village. Jupiter over the hilltops, the only star, like a sun, flashed out at intervals from behind a black cloud.

[*November 11th,*] *Tuesday Morning*. Walked to Rydale before dinner for letters. William had been working at the sheepfold. They were salving sheep. A rainy morning. The Lloyds drank tea with us. Played at cards — Priscilla not well. We walked after they left us to the top of the Rydale hill — then towards Mr. Olliff's and towards the village. A mild night, partly cloudy, partly starlight. The cottage lights, the mountains not very distinct.

[*November 12th,*] *Wednesday*. We sate in the house all the day. Mr. Simpson called and found us at dinner — a rainy evening — he staid the evening and supper. I lay down after dinner with a headach.

[*November 13th,*] *Thursday*. A stormy night. We sate in the house all the morning. Rainy weather. Old Mr. Simpson, Mrs. J. and Miss S. drank tea and supped, played at cards, found us at dinner. A poor woman from Hawkshead begged, a widow of Grasmere. A merry African from Longtown.

[*November 14th,*] *Friday*. I had a bad headach. Much wind, but a sweet mild morning. I nailed up trees. Sent Molly Ashburner to excuse us to Lloyds. Two letters from Coleridge, very ill. One from Sara H. One from S. Lowthian — I wrote to S. Hutchinson and received £3 from her.

[*November 15th,*] *Saturday Morning.* A terrible rain, so William prevented from going to Coleridge's. The afternoon fine and mild — I walked to the top of the hill for a headach. We both set forward at five o'clock after tea. A fine wild but not cold night. I walked with W. over the Raise. It was starlight. I parted with him very sad, unwilling not to go on. The hills, and the stars, and the white waters, with their ever varying yet ceaseless sound, were very impressive. I supped at the Simpsons'. Mr. P. walked home with me.

November 16th, Sunday. A very fine warm sunny morning. A letter from Coleridge, and one from Stoddart. Coleridge better. My head aching very much — I sent to excuse myself to Lloyds — then walked to the Cottage beyond Mr. Gell's. One beautiful ash tree sheltered, with yellow leaves, one low one quite green. Some low ashes green. A noise of boys in the rocks hunting some animal. Walked a little in the garden when I came home — very pleasant. Now rain came on. Mr. Jackson called in the evening when I was at tea, brought me a letter from C. and W. C. better.

[*November 17th,*] *Monday Morning.* A fine clear frosty morning with a sharp wind. I walked to Keswick. Set off at 5 minutes past 10, and arrived at ½ past 2. I found them all well.

On *Tuesday* morning W. and C. set off towards Penrith. Wm. met Sara Hutchinson at Threlkeld. They arrived at Keswick at tea time.

[*November 19th,*] *Wednesday.* We walked by the lake side and they went to Mr. Denton's. I called upon the Miss Cockyns.

[*November 20th,*] *Thursday.* We spent the morning in the town. Mr. Jackson and Mr. Peach dined with us.

[*November 21st,*] *Friday.* A very fine day. Went to Mrs. Greaves'. Mrs. C. and I called upon the Speddings. A beautiful crescent moon.

[*November 22nd,*] *Saturday Morning.* After visiting Mr. Peach's Chinese pictures we set off to Grasmere. A threatening and rather rainy morning. Arrived at G. very dirty and a little wet at the closing in of evening. Wm. not quite well.

[*November 23rd,*] *Sunday.* Wm. not well. I baked bread and pie for dinner. Sara and I walked after dinner and met

Mr. Gawthorpe, paid his bill and he drank tea with us — paid £5 for Mr. Bonsfield.

[*November 24th,*] *Monday.* A fine morning. Sara and I walked to Rydale. After dinner we went to Lloyd's, and drank tea, and supped. A sharp cold night, with sleet and snow. I had the tooth ach in the night. Took laudanum.

[*November 25th,*] *Tuesday.* Very ill — in bed all day — better in the evening — read *Tom Jones* — very sleepy — slept all night.

[*November 26th,*] *Wednesday.* Well in the morning. Wm. very well. We had a delightful walk up into Easedale. The tops of the mountains covered with snow, frosty and sunny, the roads slippery. A letter from Mary. The Lloyds drank tea. We walked with them near to Ambleside. A beautiful moonlight night. Sara and I walked before [? home]. William very well, and highly poetical.

November 27th, Thursday. Wrote to Tom Hutchinson to desire him to bring Mary with him from Stockton. A thaw, and the ground covered with snow. Sara and I walked before dinner.

[*November 28th,*] *Friday.* Coleridge walked over. Miss Simpson drank tea with us. William walked home with her. Coleridge was very unwell. He went to bed before Wm.'s return. Great boils upon his neck.

[*November 29th,*] *Saturday.* A fine day.

November 30th, Sunday. A very fine clear morning. Snow upon the ground everywhere. Sara and I walked towards Rydale by the upper road, and were obliged to return, because of the snow. Walked by moonlight.

[*December 1st,*] *Monday.* A thaw in the night, and the snow was entirely gone. Sara and I had a delightful walk by the upper Rydale Road and Mr. King's. Coleridge unable to go home for his health. We walked by moonlight.

December 2nd, Tuesday. A rainy morning. Coleridge was obliged to set off. Sara and I met C. Lloyd and P. — turned back with them. I walked round the 2 lakes with Charles, very pleasant passing lights — I was sadly wet when we came home and very cold. Priscilla drank tea with us. We all walked to Ambleside. A pleasant moonlight evening, but not clear. Supped upon a hare. It came on a terrible evening. Hail, and wind, and cold, and rain.

December 3rd, Wednesday. We lay in bed till 11 o'clock. Wrote to John, and M. H. William and Sara and I walked to Rydale after tea — a very fine frosty night. Sara and W. walked round the other side. I was tired and returned home. We went to bed early.

[December 4th,] Thursday. Coleridge came in just as we finished dinner. Pork from the Simpsons. Sara and I walked round the 2 lakes — a very fine morning. C. ate nothing, to cure his boils. We walked after tea by moonlight to look at Langdale covered with snow, the Pikes not grand, but the Old Man very impressive. Cold and slippery, but exceedingly pleasant. Sat up till half-past one.

[December 5th,] Friday Morning. Terribly cold and rainy. Coleridge and Wm. set forwards towards Keswick, but the wind in Coleridge's eyes made him turn back. Sara and I had a grand bread and cake baking. We were very merry in the evening, but grew sleepy soon, though we did not go to bed till twelve o'clock.

[December 6th,] Saturday. Wm. accompanied Coleridge to the foot of the Rays. A very pleasant morning. Sara and I accompanied him half-way to Keswick. Thirlemere was very beautiful even more so than in summer. William was not well, had laboured unsuccessfully. Charles Lloyd had called. Sara and I drank tea with Mrs. Simpson. A sharp shower met us — it rained a little when we came home — Mr. B. S. accompanied us. Miss S. at Ambleside. Wm. tired and not well. A letter from M. H.

[December 7th,] Sunday. A fine morning. I read. Sara wrote to Hartley, Wm. to Mary, I to Mrs. C. We walked just before dinner to the lakeside, and found out a seat in a tree. Windy, but pleasant. Sara and Wm. walked to the waterfalls at Rydale. I was unwell and went to bed till 8 o'clock — a pleasant mild evening — went to bed at 12. Miss Simpson called.

December 8th, Monday. A sweet mild morning. I wrote to Mrs. Cookson, and Miss Griffith.

[*December*] 9*th, Tuesday*. I dined at Lloyd's. Wm. drank tea. Walked home. A pleasant starlight frosty evening. Reached home at one o'clock. Wm. finished his poem to-day.

[*December*] 10*th, Wednesday*. Walked to Keswick. Snow upon the ground. A very fine day. Ate bread and ale at John Stanley's.[1] Found Coleridge better. Stayed at Keswick till Sunday 14th December.

[*December* 15*th*,] *Monday*. Baking and starching.

[*December* 16*th*,] *Tuesday*. Ironing — the Lloyds called.

[*December* 17*th*,] *Wednesday*. A very fine day. Writing all the morning for William.

[*December* 18*th*,] *Thursday*. Mrs. Coleridge and Derwent came. Sweeping chimneys.

[*December* 19*th*,] *Friday*. Baking.

[*December* 20*th*,] *Saturday*. Coleridge came. Very ill, rheumatic, feverish. Rain incessantly.

[*December* 22*nd*,] *Monday*. S. and Wm. went to Lloyd's. Wm. dined. It rained very hard when he came home at . . .[2]

---

[1] John Stanley, the landlord of the King's Head at Thirlspot.—G. G. W.

[2] The fact that this volume of the Journal ends in the middle of a sentence points to the conclusion that another volume, now lost, continues the sentence, and contains also entries from Dec. 23 to Oct. 9, 1801.

II. *October 10th, 1801, to January 16th, 1803*

October 10th, Saturday. Coleridge went to Keswick, after we had built Sara's seat.

[October] 11th, Sunday. Mr and Miss Simpson came in after tea and supped with us.

[October] 12th, Monday. We drank tea at Mr. Simpson's.

[October] 13th, Tuesday. A thorough wet day.

[October] 15th, Thursday. Dined at Mr. Luff's.[1] A rainy morning. Coleridge came into Mr. Luff's while we were at dinner. Wm. and I walked up Loughrigg Fell, then by the waterside. I held my head under a spout — very sick and ill when I got home, went to bed in the sitting room — took laudanum.

[October] 16th, Friday. Tom Hutchinson came. It rained almost all day. Coleridge poorly.

[October] 17th, Saturday. We walked into Easedale. Coleridge poorly after dinner.

[October] 18th, Sunday. I have forgotten.

[October] 19th, Monday. Coleridge went home. Tom and William walked to Rydale — a very fine day. I was ill in bed all day. Mr. Simpson tea and supper.

[October] 20th, Tuesday. We went to the Langdales and Colleth — a very fine day ; a heavy shower in the afternoon in Langdale.

[October] 21st, Wednesday. Dined at Bowness, slept at Penny Bridge — in danger of being cast away on Windermere. A very fine day, but windy a little — a moonlight night.

[October] 22nd, Thursday. Breakfasted at Penny Bridge — dined at Coniston. A grand stormy day. Drank tea at home.

[October] 23rd, Friday. A sweet delightful morning. I

---

[1] Captain and Mrs. Luff were friends of the Clarksons, who lived at Patterdale (*v. E.L.* p. 38) ; at this time they were staying at Ambleside.

planted all sorts of plants, Tom helped me. He and W. then rode to Hawkeshead. I baked bread and pies. Tom brought me 2 shrubs from Mr. Curwen's nursery.

[*October*] *24th, Saturday*. Attempted Fairfield, but misty, and we went no further than Green Head Gill to the sheepfold ; mild, misty, beautiful, soft. Wm. and Tom put out the boat — brought the coat from Mr. Luff's. Mr. Simpson came in at dinner-time — drank tea with us and played at cards.

[*October*] *25th, Sunday*. Rode to Legberthwaite with Tom, expecting Mary — sweet day. Went upon Helvellyn, glorious glorious sights. The sea at Cartmel. The Scotch mountains beyond the sea to the right. Whiteside large, and round, and very soft, and green, behind us. Mists above and below, and close to us, with the Sun amongst them. They shot down to the coves. Left John Stanley's at 10 minutes past 12. Returned thither ¼ past 4, drank tea, ate heartily. Before we went on Helvellyn we got bread and cheese — Paid 4/- for the whole. Reached home at nine o'clock. A soft grey evening ; the light of the moon, but she did not shine on us.

October 26th, Monday. Omitted. They went to Butter-mere.[1]

October 27th, Tuesday. Omitted, drank tea at the Simpsons.

[*October*] *28th, Wednesday*. The Clarksons came.

[*October*] *29th, Thursday*. Rain all day.

[*October*] *30th, Friday*. Rain all day.

[*October*] *31st, Saturday*. We walked to Rydale — a soft and mild morning, but threatening for rain.

November 1st, Sunday. Very cold — we walked in the evening to Butterlip How.

[*November*] *2nd, Monday*. Very rainy.

[*November*] *3rd, Tuesday*. We dined at Lloyd's. Cold and clear day.

[*November*] *4th, Wednesday*. Mr. C. and Wm. rode out — very cold.

[*November 9th, Monday*]. . . . The mountains for ever varying, now hid in the clouds, and now with their tops visible

---

[1] Oct. 26 and 27. D. W. inserted these entries at some later date.

while perhaps they were half concealed below — Legberthwaite beautiful. We ate bread and cheese at John Stanley's, and reached Keswick without fatigue just before dark. We enjoyed ourselves in the study and were *at home*. Supped at Mr. Jackson's. Mary and I sate in C.'s room a while.

[*November*] 10*th*, *Tuesday*. Poor C. left us, and we came home together. We left Keswick at 2 o'clock and did not arrive at G. till 9 o'clock. Drank tea at John Stanley's very comfortably. I burnt myself with Coleridge's aquafortis. Mary's feet sore. C. had a sweet day for his ride. Every sight and every sound reminded me of him — dear, dear fellow, of his many walks to us by day and by night, of all dear things. I was melancholy, and could not talk, but at last I eased my heart by weeping — nervous blubbering, says William. It is not so. O! how many, many reasons have I to be anxious for him.

[*November*] 11*th*, *Wednesday*. Baked bread and giblet pie — put books in order — mended stockings. Put aside dearest C.'s letters, and now at about 7 o'clock we are all sitting by a nice fire. Wm. with his book and a candle, and Mary writing to Sara.

November 12*th*, *Thursday*. A beautiful still sunshiny morning. We rose very late. I put the rag-boxes into order. We walked out while the goose was roasting — we walked to the top of the hill. M. and I followed Wm. — he was walking upon the turf between John's Grove and the lane. It was a most sweet noon. We did not go into John's Grove, but we walked among the rocks and there we sate. Mr. Oliff passed Mary and me upon the road — Wm. still among the rocks. The lake beautiful from the orchard. Wm. and I walked out before tea — The crescent moon — we sate in the slate quarry — I sate there a long time alone. Wm. reached home before me — I found them at tea. There were a thousand stars in the sky.

[*November* 13*th*,] *Friday Morning*. Dullish, damp and cloudy — a day that promises not to dry our clothes. We spent a happy evening — went to bed late, and had a restless night — Wm. better than I expected.

[*November* 14*th*,] *Saturday Morning*. Still a cloudy dull day, very dark. I lay in bed all the day very unwell : they made me some broth and I rose better, after it was dark we spent a quiet evening by the fire.

[*November*] 15*th*, *Sunday*. I walked in the morning, to Churnmilk Force nearly, and went upon Heifer Crags. The valley of its winter yellow, but the bed of the brook still in some places almost *shaded* with leaves — the oaks brown in general, but one that might be almost called green — the whole prospect was very soft, and the distant view down the vale very impressive, a long vale down to Ambleside, the hills at Ambleside in mist and sunshine — all else grey. We sate by the fire and read Chaucer (Thomson, Mary read) and Bishop Hall. Letters from Sara and Mrs. Clarkson late at night.

November 16*th*, *Monday*. A very darkish misty wettish morning. Mary and Molly ironed all day. I made bread and called at Mr. Olliff's — Mrs. O. at home — the prospect soft from the windows. Mrs. O. observed that it was beautiful *even* in winter ! The Luffs passed us. We walked backwards and forwards in the Church field. Wm. somewhat weakish, but upon the whole pretty well ; he is now, at 7 o'clock, reading Spenser. Mary is writing beside me. The little syke [1] murmurs. We are quiet and happy, but poor Peggy Ashburner is very ill and in pain. She coughs, as if she would cough her life away. I am going to write to Coleridge and Sara. Poor C. ! I hope he was in London yesterday. Molly has been very witty with Mary all day. She says : " ye may say what ye will, but there's naething like a gay auld man for behaving weel to a young wife. Ye may laugh, but this wind blows no [?] and where there's no love there's no favour." On Sunday I lectured little John Dawson [2] for telling lies — I told him I had heard that he charged Jenny Baty falsely with having beaten him. Says Molly : " she says it's not so, that she never lifted hand till him, and she *should* speak truth you would think in her condition "— she is with child. Two Beggars to-day.

[*November*] 17*th*, *Tuesday*. A very rainy morning. We

---

[1] A Lake-country word for a rillet.—W. K.

[2] Probably the son of John Dawson of Howe Top (*v.* Sept. 3, 1800), baptized March 3, 1799, and thus a precocious little sinner.

walked into Easedale before dinner. Miss S. came in at dinner time — we went to Mr. Gell's cottage — then returned. The coppices a beautiful brown. The oaks many, a very fine leafy shade. We stood a long time to look at the corner birch tree. The wind was among the light thin twigs, and they yielded to it, this way and that. Drank tea and supped at the Simpsons — a moonlight wettish night. Dirty roads.

[*November*] 18*th, Wednesday.* We sate in the house in the morning reading Spenser. I was unwell and lay in bed all the afternoon. Wm. and Mary walked to Rydale. Very pleasant moonlight. The Lakes beautiful. The church an image of peace. Wm. wrote some lines upon it in bed when they came home. Mary and I walked as far as Sara's Gate before supper. We stood there a long time, the whole scene impressive, the mountains indistinct, the Lake calm and partly ruffled. Large Island, a sweet sound of water falling into the quiet Lake. A storm was gathering in Easedale, so we returned; but the moon came out, and opened to us the church and village. Helm Crag in shade, the larger mountains dappled like a sky. We stood long upon the bridge. Wished for Wm., he had stayed at home being sickish — found him better; we went to bed.

Nov[embe]r 19*th, Thursday.*—A beautiful sunny, frosty morning. We did not walk all day. Wm. said he would put it off till the fine moonlight night, and then it came on a heavy rain and wind. Charles and Olivia Lloyd called in the morning.

[*November*] 20*th, Friday.* We walked in the morning to Easedale. In the evening we had chearful letters from Coleridge and Sara.

[*November*] 21*st, Saturday.* We walked in the morning, and paid one pound and 4d. for letters. William out of spirits. We had a pleasant walk and spent a pleasant evening. There was a furious wind and cold at night. Mr. Simpson drank tea with us, and helped William out with the boat. Wm. and Mary walked to the Swan, homewards, with him. A keen clear frosty night. I went into the orchard while they were out.

[*November*] 22*nd, Sunday.*—We wrote to Coleridge and sent our letter by the boy. Mr. and Miss Simpson came in at tea time. We went with them to the Blacksmith's and returned by Butterlip How — a frost and wind with bright moonshine. The vale looked spacious and very beautiful — the level meadows seemed very large and some nearer us, unequal ground, heaving like sand, the Cottages beautiful and quiet, we passed one near which stood a cropped ash with upright forked branches like the Devil's horns frightening a guilty conscience. We were happy and chearful when we came home — we went early to bed.

Nov[ember] 23rd, Monday. A beautiful frosty morning. Mary was making William's woollen waistcoat. Wm. unwell, and did not walk. Mary and I sate in our cloaks upon the bench in the orchard. After dinner I went to bed unwell. Mary had a headach at night. We all went to bed soon.

[November] 24th, Tuesday. A rainy morning. We all were well except that my head ached a little, and I took my breakfast in bed. I read a little of Chaucer, prepared the goose for dinner, and then we all walked out. I was obliged to return for my fur tippet and spencer, it was so cold. We had intended going to Easedale, but we shaped our course to Mr. Gell's cottage. It was very windy, and we heard the wind everywhere about us as we went along the lane, but the walls sheltered us. John Green's house [1] looked pretty under Silver How. As we were going along we were stopped at once, at the distance perhaps of 50 yards from our favourite birch tree. It was yielding to the gusty wind with all its tender twigs, the sun shone upon it, and it glanced in the wind like a flying sunshiny shower. It was a tree in shape, with stem and branches, but it was like a Spirit of water. The sun went in, and it resumed its purplish appearance, the twigs still yielding to the wind, but not so visibly to us. The other birch trees that were near it looked bright and chearful, but it was a creature by its own self among them. We could not get into Mr. Gell's grounds— the old tree fallen from its undue exaltation above the gate. A shower came on when we were at Benson's. We went through the wood—it became fair. There was a rainbow which spanned

---

[1] *i.e.* Pavement End; *v.* also entry of May 12, 1802. The family of the Greens are described in *The Excursion*, vi, 632-94.—G. G. W.

the lake from the island-house to the foot of Bainriggs. The village looked populous and beautiful. Catkins are coming out ; palm trees budding ; the alder, with its plumb-coloured buds. We came home over the stepping-stones. The lake was foamy with white waves. I saw a solitary butter-flower in the wood. I found it not easy to get over the stepping stones.[1] Reached home at dinner time. Sent Peggy Ashburner some goose. She sent me some honey, with a thousand thanks. " Alas ! the gratitude of men has ", etc.[2] I went in to set her right about this, and sate a while with her. She talked about Thomas's having sold his land.[3] " Ay," says she, " I said many a time he's not come fra London to buy our land, how-ever." Then she told me with what pains and industry they had made up their taxes, interest, etc. etc., how they all got up at 5 o'clock in the morning to spin and Thomas carded, and that they had paid off a hundred pounds of the interest. She said she used to take such pleasure in the cattle and sheep. " O how pleased I used to be when they fetched them down, and when I had been a bit poorly I would gang out upon a hill and look ower 't fields and see them, and it used to do me so much good you cannot think." Molly said to me when I came in, " Poor body ! she's very ill, but one does not know how long she may last. Many a fair face may gang before her." We sate by the fire without work for some time, then Mary read a poem of Daniel upon Learning. After tea Wm. read Spenser, now and then a little aloud to us. We were making his waistcoat. We had a note from Mrs. C., with bad news from poor C.—very ill. William went to John's Grove. I went to meet him. Moonlight, but it rained. I met him before I had got as far as John Baty's [4] — he had been surprized and terrified by a sudden rushing of winds, which seemed to bring earth sky and lake together, as if the whole were going to enclose him in ; he was glad he was in a high road.

In speaking of our walk on Sunday evening, the 22nd

---

[1] At the head of Rydal Water, now superseded by Slater's Bridge.—G. G. W.
[2] *Simon Lee*, ll. 75-6.   [3] *v.* the poem *Repentance*.
[4] The Batys (colloquial for Bateman) lived at one of the four cottages just above Sykeside at right angles to the road.—G. G. W.

November, I forgot to notice one most impressive sight. It was the moon and the moonlight seen through hurrying driving clouds immediately behind the Stone-Man upon the top of the hill on the Forest Side. Every tooth and every edge of rock was visible, and the Man stood like a Giant watching from the roof of a lofty castle. The hill seemed perpendicular from the darkness below it. It was a sight that I could call to mind at any time, it was so distinct.

November 25th, Wednesday. It was a showery morning and threatened to be a wettish day, but the sun shone once or twice. We were engaged to the Lloyds and Wm. and Mary were determined to go that it might be over. I accompanied them to the thorn beside Rydale water. I parted from them first at the top of the hill, and they called me back. It rained a little, and rained afterwards all the afternoon. I baked pies and bread, and wrote to Sara Hutchinson and Coleridge. I passed a pleasant evening, but the wind roared so, and it was such a storm that I was afraid for them. They came in at nine o'clock, no worse for their walk, and chearful, blooming, and happy.

[November] 26th, Thursday. Mr. Olliff called before Wm. was up to say that they would drink tea with us this afternoon. We walked into Easedale, to gather mosses, and to fetch cream. I went for the cream, and they sate under a wall. It was piercing cold and a hailstorm came on in the afternoon. The Olliffs arrived at 5 o'clock. We played at cards and passed a decent evening. It was a very still night but piercing cold when they went away at 11 o'clock — a shower came on.

November 27th, Friday. Snow upon the ground thinly scattered. It snowed after we got up, and then the sun shone, and it was very warm though frosty—now the sun shines sweetly. A woman came who was travelling with her husband ; he had been wounded and was going with her to live at Whitehaven. She had been at Ambleside the night before, offered 4d at the Cock for a bed — they sent her to one Harrison's where she and her husband had slept upon the hearth and bought a pennyworth of chips for a fire. Her husband was gone before, very lame — " Aye " says she, " I was once an officer's wife, I, as you see me now. My first husband married me at Appleby ; I had 18£ a year for teaching a school, and because I had no fortune his father turned him out of doors. I have been in the West Indies. I lost the use of this finger just before he died ; he came to me and said he must bid farewell to his dear children and me. I had a muslin gown on like yours — I seized hold of his coat as he went from me, and slipped the joint of my finger. He was shot directly. I came to London and married this man. He was clerk to Judge Chambray, *that man*, that man that's going on the road now. If he, Judge Chambray, had been at Kendal he would [have] given us a guinea or two, and made nought of it, for he is very generous." Before dinner we set forward to walk intending to return to dinner, but as we had got as far as Rydale Wm. thought he would go on to Mr. Luff's. We accompanied him under Loughrigg, and parted near the stepping stones. It was very cold. Mary and I walked quick home. There was a fine gleam of sunshine upon the eastern side of Ambleside Vale. We came up the old road and turning round we were struck with the appearance. Mary wrote to her aunt. We expected the Simpsons. I was sleepy and weary and went to bed before tea. It came on wet in the evening and was very cold. We expected letters from C. and Sara — Sara's came by the boy, but none from C. — a sad disappointment. We did not go to meet Wm. as we had intended — Mary was at work at Wm.'s warm waistcoat.

November 28th, Saturday.—A very fine sunny morning. Soldiers still going by. I should have mentioned that yesterday when we went with Wm. to Mr. Luff's we met a soldier and his wife, he with a child in his arms, she carrying a bundle and his gun — we gave them some halfpence, it was such a pretty sight. William having slept ill lay in bed till after one o'clock. Mary and I walked up to Mr. Simpson's between 20 minutes before 2 and 20 minutes before 3 to desire them not to come. We drank tea and supped at Mr. Olliff's — a keen frost and sparkling stars when we came home at ½ past 11.

November 29th, Sunday. Baking bread, apple pies and giblet pie — a bad giblet pie. It was a most beautiful morning.

George Olliff brought Wm.'s stick. The sun shone all the day, but we never walked. In the evening we had intended going for letters, but the lad said he would go. We sate up till after one — no letters ! very cold — hard frost.

[*November*] 30*th, Monday.* A fine sharp morning. The lad brought us a letter from Montagu, and a short one from Coleridge. C. very well, promised to write to-morrow. We walked round the Lake, Wm. and Mary went first over the stepping stones — I remained after them and went into the prospect field above Benson's to sit — Mary joined me there. Clear and frosty without wind. William went before to look at Langdale. We saw the Pikes and then came home. They have cropped the tree which overshadowed the gate beside that cottage at the turning of the hill which used to make a frame for Loughrigg Tarn and Windermere. We came home and read — Mary wrote to Joanna — I wrote to Richard, and Mrs. Coleridge.

December 1st, 1801, *Tuesday.* A fine sunny and frosty morning. Mary and I walked to Rydale for letters. William was not well and staid at home reading after having lain long in bed. We found a letter from Coleridge, a short one — he was pretty well. We were overtaken by two soldiers on our return — one of them being very drunk we wished them to pass us, but they had too much liquor in them to go very fast so we contrived to pass them — they were very merry and very civil. They fought with the mountains with their sticks. " Aye " says one, " that will [? fall] upon us. One might stride over that etc." They never saw such a wild country, though one of them was a Scotchman. They were honest looking fellows. The Corporal said he was frightened to see the road before them. We met Wm. at Sara's gate — he went back intending to go round the lake, but having attempted to cross the water and not succeeding he came back. The Simpsons, Mr. and Miss, drank tea with us — Wm. was very poorly and out of spirits. They stayed supper.

[*December*] 2*nd, Wednesday.* A fine grey frosty morning. Wm. rose late. I read the Tale of Phœbus and the Crow,[1]

---

[1] *i.e.* Chaucer's *Maunciple's Tale.*

which he afterwards attempted to translate, and did translate a large part of it to-day. Mrs. Olliff brought us some yeast and made us promise to go there the next day to meet the Luffs. We were sitting by the fire in the evening when Charles and Olivia Lloyd came in. I had not been very well so I did not venture out with them when they went away — Mary and William went as far as Rydale village. It snowed after it was dark and there was a thin covering over the ground which made it light and soft. They looked fresh and well when they came in. I wrote part of a letter to Coleridge. After his return William went on a little with Chaucer.

December 3rd, 1801, *Thursday.* I was not well in the morning — we baked bread — after dinner I went to bed — Wm. walked into Easedale. Rain, hail and snow. I rose at ½ past 7, got tea, then went to sup at Mr. Olliff's — I had a glorious sleep and was quite well. A light night, roads very slippery. We spent a pleasant evening — Mr. and Mrs. Luff there — Mrs. L. poorly. I wrote a little bit of my letter to Coleridge before I went to Mr. O.'s. We went to bed immediately after our return — Molly gone.

[December] 4th, Friday. My head bad and I lay long. Mrs. Luff called — Mary went with her to the slate quarry. Mr. Simpson and Charles Lloyd called for the yeast receipt. William translating *The Prioress's Tale.* William and Mary walked after tea to Rydale. It snowed and rained and they came in wet. I finished the letter to Coleridge, and we received a letter from him and Sara. S.'s letter written in good spirits — C.'s also. A letter of Lamb's about George Dyer with it.

[December] 5th, Saturday. My head bad and I lay long. Mr. Luff called before I rose. We put off walking in the morning, dull and misty and grey — very rainy in the afternoon and we could not go out. Wm. finished *The Prioress's Tale*, and after tea Mary and he wrote it out. Wm. not well. No parcel from Mrs. Coleridge.

[December] 6th, Sunday. A very fine beautiful sunshiny morning. Wm. worked a while at Chaucer, then we set forward to walk into Easedale. We met Mr. and Mrs. Olliff who were going to call upon us ; they turned back with us and we parted

at the White Bridge. We went up into Easedale and walked backwards and forwards in that flat field, which makes the second circle of Easedale, with that beautiful rock in the field beside us, and all the rocks and the woods and the mountains enclosing us round. The sun was shining among them, the snow thinly scattered upon the tops of the mountains. In the afternoon we sate by the fire : I read Chaucer aloud, and Mary read the first canto of *The Fairy Queen*. After tea Mary and I walked to Ambleside for letters — reached home by 11 o'clock — we had a sweet walk. It was a sober starlight evening, the stars not shining as it were with all their brightness when they were visible, and sometimes hiding themselves behind small greyish clouds, that passed soberly along. We opened C.'s letter at Wilcock's door. We thought we saw that he wrote in good spirits, so we came happily homewards where we arrived 2 hours after we left home. It was a sad melancholy letter, and prevented us all from sleeping.

December 7th, Monday Morning. We rose by candlelight. A showery unpleasant morning, after a downright rainy night. We determined, however, to go to Keswick if possible, and we set off at a little after 9 o'clock. When we were upon the Rays, it snowed very much ; and the whole prospect closed in upon us, like a moorland valley, upon a moor very wild. But when we were at the top of the Rays we saw the mountains before us. The sun shone upon them, here and there ; and Wytheburn vale, though wild, looked soft. The [? day] went on chearfully and pleasantly. Now and then a hail shower attacked us ; but we kept up a good heart, for Mary is a famous jockey. We met Miss Barcroft — she had been unwell in the " *Liverpool* complaint ", and was riding out for the benefit of her health. She had not seen Mrs. C. " The weather had been such as to preclude all intercourse between neighbours ! " We reached Greta Hall at about one o'clock, met Mrs. C. in the field, Derwent in the cradle asleep — Hartley at his dinner — Derwent pale, the image of his Father. Hartley well. We wrote to C. Mrs. C. left us at ½ past 2. We drank tea by ourselves, the children playing about us. Mary said to Hartley, " Shall I take Derwent with me ? " " No," says H., " I cannot spare my little Brother," in the sweetest tone possible, " and he can't do without his mamma." " Well," says Mary, " why can't I be his mamma ? Can't he have more mammas than one ? " " No," says H. " What for ? " " Because they do not love, and mothers do." " What is the difference between mothers and mammas ? " Looking at his sleeves, " Mothers wear sleeves like this," (pulling his own tight down), " and mammas " (pulling them up, and making a bustle about his shoulders) " so". We parted from them at 4 o'clock. It was a little of the dusk when we set off. Cotton mills lighted up. The first star at Nadel Fell, but it was never dark. We rode very briskly. Snow upon the Rays. Reached home far sooner than we expected — at seven o'clock. William at work with Chaucer, *The God of Love.*[1] Sate latish. I wrote a letter to C.

December 8th, 1801, *Tuesday.* A dullish, rainyish morning. Wm. at work with Chaucer. I read Bruce's *Lochleven* and *Life.* Going to bake bread and pies. After dinner I felt myself unwell having not slept well in the night, so, after we had put up the Bookcases which Charles Lloyd sent us, I lay down — I did not sleep much but I rose refreshed. Mary and William walked to the boat house at Rydale while I[2] was in bed. It rained very hard all night. No company. Wm. worked at *The Cuckow and the Nightingale* till he was tired. Mary very sleepy and not quite well. We both slept sound. Letter from Richard with news of John, dated 7th August.

December 9th, Wednesday Morning. William slept well, but his tongue [? furred]. I read *Palamon and Arcite.* Mary read Bruce. William writing out his alteration of Chaucer's *Cuckow and Nightingale.* After dinner it was agreed that we should walk — when I had finished a letter to C. part of which I had written in the morning by the kitchen fire while the mutton was roasting. Wm. did not go with us but Mary and I walked into Easedale, and backwards and forwards in that large field under George Rawnson's[3] white cottage. We had intended gathering mosses, and for that purpose we turned into the

---

[1] *i.e. The Cuckow and the Nightingale.*   [2] *Written* he.
[3] D. W.'s spelling of Rowlandson. His cottage was on the site of the present " Lancrigg ".—G. G. W.

green lane, behind the tailor's, but it was too dark to see the mosses. The river came galloping past the Church, as fast as it could come ; and when we got into Easedale we saw Churn Milk Force, like a broad stream of snow. At the little foot-bridge we stopped to look at the company of rivers, which came hurrying down the vale this way and that ; it was a valley of streams and islands, with that great waterfall at the head, and lesser falls in different parts of the mountains, coming down to these rivers. We could hear the sound of those lesser falls, but we could not *see* them. We walked backwards and forwards till all distant objects, except the white shape of the waterfall and the lines of the mountains, were gone. We had the crescent moon when we went out, and at our return there were a few stars that shone dimly, but it was a grey cloudy night.

December 10*th, Thursday.* A very fine sunny morning — not frosty. We walked into Easedale to gather mosses, and then we went past to Aggy Fleming's[1] and up the Gill, beyond that little waterfall. It was a wild scene of crag and mountain. One craggy point rose above the rest irregular and rugged, and very impressive it was. We called at Aggy Fleming's — she told us about her miserable house — she looked shockingly with her head tied up. Her mother was there — the children looked healthy. We were very unsuccessful in our search after mosses. Just when the evening was closing in, Mr. Clarkson came to the door. It was a fine frosty evening. We played at cards.

[*December*] 11*th, Friday.* Baked pies and cakes. It was a stormy morning with hail showers. The Luffs dined with us — Mrs. L. came with Mrs. Olliff in the gig. We sate lazily round the fire after dinner. Mr. and Mrs. Olliff drank tea and supped with us — a hard frost when they came.

[*December*] 12*th, Saturday.* A fine frosty morning — Snow upon the ground. I made bread and pies. We walked with Mrs. Luff to Rydale and came home the other side of the Lake, met Townley with his dogs. All looked chearful and bright. Helm Crag rose very bold and craggy, a Being by itself, and

---

[1] Probably the Agnes Hird who married John Fleming, Nov. 27, 1784, and was buried Jan. 8, 1808, when she is described as " widow, of Gillside ".— G. G. W.

The Road over White Moss, looking South

From a pencil drawing by T. L. Aspland. 1849

behind it was the large ridge of mountain, smooth as marble and snow white. All the mountains looked like solid stone, on our left, going from Grasmere, *i.e.* White Moss and Nab Scar. The snow hid all the grass, and all signs of vegetation, and the rocks showed themselves boldly everywhere, and seemed more stony than rock or stone. The birches on the crags beautiful, red brown and glittering. The ashes glittering spears with their upright stems. The hips very beautiful, and so good ! ! and, dear Coleridge ! I ate twenty for thee, when I was by myself. I came home first — they walked too slow for me. Wm. went to look at Langdale Pikes. We had a sweet invigorating walk. Mr. Clarkson came in before tea. We played at cards — sate up late. The moon shone upon the water below Silver-How, and above it hung, combining with Silver-How on one side, a bowl-shaped moon, the curve downwards ; the white fields, glittering roof of Thomas Ashburner's house, the dark yew tree, the white fields gay and beautiful. Wm. lay with his curtains open that he might see it.

[December] 13*th, Sunday.* Mr. Clarkson left us, leading his horse. Went to Brathay and Luffs. We drank tea at Betty Dixon's. Very cold and frosty — a pleasant walk home. Wm. had been very unwell, but we found him better. The boy brought letters from Coleridge, and from Sara. Sara in bad spirits about C.

December 14*th, Monday.* Wm. and Mary walked to Ambleside in the morning to buy mouse-traps. Mary fell and hurt her wrist. I accompanied them to the top of the hill — clear and frosty. I wrote to Coleridge a very long letter while they were absent. Sate by the fire in the evening reading.

[December] 15*th, Tuesday.* Wm. and I walked to Rydale for letters — found one from Joanna. We had a pleasant walk but coldish — it thawed a little.

[December] 16*th, Wednesday.* A very keen frost, extremely slippery. After dinner Wm. and I walked twice up to the Swan and back again — met Miss Simpson. She came with us to Olliff's and we went back with her. Very cold.

[December] 17*th, Thursday.* Snow in the night and still snowing. We went to Mr. Luff's to dine — met Mrs. King.

Hard frost and as light as day — we had a delightful walk and reached home a little after twelve. Mrs. Luff ill. Ambleside looked excessively beautiful as we came out — like a village in another country ; and the light chearful mountains were seen in the long, long distance as bright and as clear as at midday with the blue sky above them. We heard waterfowl calling out by the lake side. Jupiter was very glorious above the Ambleside hills, and one large star hung over the coombe of the hills on the opposite side of Rydale water.

December 18th, 1801, *Friday.* Mary and Wm. walked round the two lakes. I staid at home to make bread, cakes and pies. I afterwards went to meet them, and I met Wm. near Benson's. Mary had gone to look at Langdale Pikes. It was a chearful glorious day. The birches and all trees beautiful, hips bright red, mosses green. I wrote to Coleridge for money.

[*December*] 19*th, Saturday.* I was not quite well and did not rise to breakfast. We walked by Brathay to Ambleside — called at the Lloyds — they were at Kendal. Dined with the Luffs and came home in the evening — the evening cloudy and promising snow. The day very beautiful — Brathay vale scattered and very chearful and interesting.

December 20th, Sunday. It snowed all day. In the evening we went to tea at Thomas Ashburner's. It was a very deep snow. The brooms were very beautiful, arched feathers with wiry stalks pointed to the end, smaller and smaller. They waved gently with the weight of the snow. We stayed at Thomas A.'s till after 9 o'clock — Peggy better. The lasses neat and clean and rosy.

Monday 21*st,* being the shortest day. Mary walked to Ambleside for letters. It was a wearisome walk, for the snow lay deep upon the roads and it was beginning to thaw. I stayed at home and clapped the small linen. Wm. sate beside me, and read *The Pedlar.*[1] He was in good spirits, and full of hope of what he should do with it. He went to meet Mary, and they brought 4 letters — 2 from Coleridge, one from Sara, and one from France. Coleridge's were melancholy letters, he

---

[1] *The Pedlar* : afterwards incorporated in *The Excursion. v. E.L.* p. 424.

had been very ill in his bowels. We were made very unhappy. Wm. wrote to him, and directed the letter into Somersetshire. I finished it after tea. In the afternoon Mary and I ironed, afterwards she packed her clothes up, and I mended Wm.'s stockings while he was reading *The Pedlar*. I then packed up for Mr. Clarkson's—we carried the boxes cross the road to Fletcher's [? peat] house,[1] after Mary had written to Sara and Joanna.

[December] 22nd, Tuesday. Still thaw. I washed my head. Wm. and I went to Rydale for letters, the road was covered with dirty snow, rough and rather slippery. We had a melancholy letter from C., for he had been very ill, though he was better when he wrote. We walked home almost without speaking. Wm. composed a few lines of *The Pedlar*. We talked about Lamb's tragedy as we went down the White Moss. We stopped a long time in going to watch a little bird with a salmon-coloured breast, a white cross or T upon its wings, and a brownish back with faint stripes. It was pecking the scattered dung upon the road. It began to peck at the distance of four yards from us, and advanced nearer and nearer till it came within the length of W.'s stick, without any apparent fear of us. As we came up the White Moss, we met an old man, who I saw was a beggar by his two bags hanging over his shoulder ; but, from a half laziness, half indifference, and a wanting to *try* him, if he would speak, I let him pass. He said nothing, and my heart smote me. I turned back, and said, " You are begging ? " " Ay ", says he. I gave him a halfpenny. William, judging from his appearance, joined in, " I suppose you were a sailor ? " " Ay ", he replied, " I have been 57 years at sea, 12 of them on board a man-of-war under Sir Hugh Palmer." " Why have you not a pension ? " " I have no pension, but I could have got into Greenwich hospital, but all my officers are dead." He was 75 years of age, had a freshish colour in his cheeks, grey hair, a decent hat with a binding round the edge, the hat worn brown and glossy, his shoes were small thin shoes low in the quarters, pretty good. They had belonged to a gentleman. His coat was blue, frock shaped, coming over his thighs, it had been

---

[1] *v.* note, p. 106.

joined up at the seams behind with paler blue, to let it out, and there were three bell-shaped patches of darker blue behind, where the buttons had been. His breeches were either of fustian, or grey cloth, with strings hanging down, whole and tight ; he had a checked shirt on, and a small coloured handkerchief tied round his neck. His bags were hung over each shoulder, and lay on each side of him, below his breast. One was brownish and of coarse stuff, the other was white with meal on the outside, and his blue waistcoat was whitened with meal. In the coarse bag I guess he put his scraps of meat etc. He walked with a slender stick — decently stout, but his legs bowed outwards.

We overtook old Fleming [1] at Rydale, leading his little Dutchman-like grandchild along the slippery road. The same pace seemed to be natural to them both, the old man and the little child, and they went hand in hand, the grandfather cautious, yet looking proud of his charge. He had two patches of new cloth at the shoulder-blades of his faded claret-coloured coat, like eyes at each shoulder not worn elsewhere. I found Mary at home in her riding-habit, all her clothes being put up. We were very sad about Coleridge. Wm. walked further. When he came home he cleared a path to the necessary, called me out to see it, but before we got there a whole housetopfull of snow had fallen from the roof upon the path and it echoed in the ground beneath like a dull beating upon it. We talked of going to Ambleside after dinner to borrow money of Luff, but we thought we would defer our visit to Eusemere a day. Half the seaman's nose was reddish as if he had been in his youth somewhat used to drinking, though he was not injured by it. We stopped to look at the stone seat at the top of the hill. There was a white cushion upon it, round at the edge like a cushion, and the rock behind looked soft as velvet, of a vivid green, and so tempting ! The snow too looked as soft as a down cushion. A young foxglove, like a star, in the centre. There were a few green lichens about it, and a few withered brackens of fern here and there upon the ground near, all else

---

[1] Thomas Fleming kept the Hare and Hounds Inn at Rydal : it had ceased to exist by 1806.—G. G. W.

was a thick snow ; no footmark to it, not the foot of a sheep. When we were at Thomas Ashburner's on Sunday Peggy talked about the Queen of Patterdale. She had been brought to drinking by her husband's unkindness and avarice. She was formerly a very nice tidy woman. She had taken to drinking but that was better than if she had taken to something worse (by this I suppose she meant killing herself). She said that her husband used to be out all night with other women and she used to *hear* him come in in the morning, for they never slept together — " Many a poor body, a wife like me, has had a working heart for her, as much stuff as she had ". We sate snugly round the fire. I read to them the Tale of Custance and the Syrian monarch, also some of the *Prologues*. It is the Man of Lawe's Tale. We went to bed early. It snowed and thawed.

[*December*] 23*rd, Wednesday*. A downright thaw, but the snow not gone off the ground except on the steep hillsides — it was a thick black heavy air. I baked pies and bread. Mary wrote out the Tales from Chaucer for Coleridge. William worked at *The Ruined Cottage* and made himself very ill. I went to bed without dinner — he went to the other bed — we both slept and Mary lay on the rug before the fire. A broken soldier came to beg in the morning. Afterwards a tall woman, dressed somewhat in a tawdry style, with a long checked muslin apron, a beaver hat, and throughout what are called good clothes. Her daughter had gone before, with a soldier and his wife. She had buried her husband at Whitehaven, and was going back into Cheshire.

[*December*] 24*th, Thursday*. Still a thaw. We walked to Rydale, Wm. Mary and I — left the patterns at Thomas Fleming's for Mrs. King. The roads uncomfortable and slippery. We sate comfortably round the fire in the evening, and read Chaucer. Thoughts of last year. I took out my old Journal.

[*December*] 25*th, Friday*. Christmas Day. A very bad day — we drank tea at John Fisher's — we were unable to walk. I went to bed after dinner. The roads very slippery. We received a letter from Coleridge while we were at John Fisher's — a terrible night — little John brought the letter. Coleridge poorly but better — his letter made us uneasy about him. I was glad I was not by myself when I received it.

[*December*] 26*th*, *Saturday*. My head ached and I lay long in bed and took my breakfast there — soon after I had breakfasted we went to call at Mr. Olliff's. They were not at home. It came on very wet. Mary went into the house, and Wm. and I went up to Tom Dawson's to speak about his Grandchild, the rain went off and we walked to Rydale. It was very pleasant — Grasmere Lake a beautiful image of stillness, clear as glass, reflecting all things, the wind was up, and the waters sounding. The lake of a rich purple, the fields a soft yellow, the island yellowish-green, the copses red-brown, the mountains purple. The Church and buildings, how quiet they were! Poor Coleridge, Sara, and dear little Derwent here last year at this time. After tea we sate by the fire comfortably. I read aloud *The Miller's Tale*. Wrote to Coleridge. The Olliffs passed in chaise and gig. Wm. wrote part of the poem to Coleridge.[1]

[*December*] 27*th*, *Sunday*. A fine soft beautiful, mild day, with gleams of sunshine. I lay in bed till 12 o'clock, Mr. Clarkson's man came — we wrote to him. We walked up within view of Rydale. William went to take in his Boat. I sate in John's Grove a little while. Mary came home. Mary wrote some lines of the third part of Wm.'s poem, which he brought to read to us, when we came home. Mr. Simpson came in at dinner time and stayed tea. They fetched in the boat. I lay down upon the bed in the meantime. A sweet evening.

December 28*th*, *Monday*. William, Mary, and I set off on foot to Keswick. We carried some cold mutton in our pockets, and dined at John Stanley's, where they were making Christmas pies. The sun shone, but it was coldish. We parted from Wm. upon the Rays. He joined us opposite Sara's rock.[2] He was busy in composition, and sate down upon the wall. We did not see him again till we arrived at John Stanley's. There we roasted apples in the oven. After we had left John Stanley's, Wm. discovered that he had lost his gloves. He turned back, but

---

[1] *i.e. The Prelude.*

[2] Usually referred to in the W. family as the Rock of Names; on which were carved the initials W. W., M. H., D. W., S. T. C., J. W., S. H. : it was on the road, now submerged, along Thirlmere, midway between Grasmere and Keswick. *v.* W.'s note to *The Waggoner*.

they were gone. We were tired and had bad headaches. We rested often. Once he left his Spenser, and Mary turned back for it, and found it upon the bank, where we had last rested. We reached Greta Hall at about ½ past 5 o'clock. The Children and Mrs. C. well. After tea, message came from Wilkinson,[1] who had passed us on the road, inviting Wm. to sup at the Oak. He went. Met a young man (a predestined Marquis) called Johnston. He spoke to him familiarly of the L. B. He had seen a copy presented by the Queen to Mrs. Harcourt. Said he saw them everywhere, and wondered they did not sell. We all went weary to bed — my bowels very bad.

December 29th, Tuesday. A fine morning. A thin fog upon the hills which soon disappeared. The sun shone. Wilkinson went with us to the top of the hill. We turned out of the road at the second mile stone, and passed a pretty cluster of houses at the foot of St. John's Vale. The houses were among tall trees, partly of Scotch fir, and some naked forest trees. We crossed a bridge just below these houses, and the river winded sweetly along the meadows. Our road soon led us along the sides of dreary bare hills, but we had a glorious prospect to the left of Saddleback, half-way covered with snow, and underneath the comfortable white houses and the village of Threlkeld. These houses and the village want trees about them. Skiddaw was behind us, and dear Coleridge's desert home. As we ascended the hills it grew very cold and slippery. Luckily, the wind was at our backs, and helped us on. A sharp hail-shower gathered at the head of Martindale, and the view upwards was very grand — the wild cottages, seen through the hurrying hail-shower. The wind drove and eddied about and about, and the hills looked large and swelling through the storm. We thought of Coleridge. O! the bonny nooks and windings and curlings of the beck, down at the bottom of the steep green mossy banks. We dined at the publick-house on porridge, with a second course of Christmas pies. We were well received by the Landlady, and her little Jewish daughters were glad to see us again. The husband a very handsome man. While we

---

[1] Thomas Wilkinson, the Quaker of Yanwath, between Penrith and Ullswater.

were eating our dinners a traveller came in. He had walked over Kirkstone that morning. We were much amused by the curiosity of the landlord and landlady to learn who he was, and by his mysterious manner of letting out a little bit of his errand, and yet telling nothing. He had business further up in the vale. He left them with this piece of information to work upon, and I doubt not they discovered who he was and all his business before the next day at that hour. The woman told us of the riches of a Mr. Walker, formerly of Grasmere. We said, " What, does he do nothing for his relations ? He has a sickly sister at Grasmere." " Why," said the man, " I daresay if they had any sons to put forward he would do it for them, but he has children of his own." N.B.—His fortune is above £60,000, and he has two children ! ! The landlord went about 1 mile and a ½ with us to put us in the right way. The road was often very slippery, the wind high, and it was nearly dark before we got into the right road. I was often obliged to crawl upon all fours, and Mary fell many a time. A stout young man whom we met on the hills, and who knew Mr. Clarkson, very kindly set us into the right road, and we inquired again near some houses, and were directed by a miserable, poverty-struck looking woman, who had been fetching water, to go down a nasty miry lane. We soon got into the main road and reached Mr. Clarkson's at tea time. Mary H. spent the next day with us, and we walked on Dunmallet before dinner, but it snowed a little. The day following, being New Year's Eve, we accompanied Mary to Stainton Bridge — met Mr. Clarkson with a calf's head in a basket — we turned with him and parted from Mary.

New Year's Day [1802]. We walked, Wm. and I, towards Martindale.

January 2nd, Saturday. It snowed all day. We walked near to Dalemain in the snow.

January 3rd, Sunday. Mary brought us letters from Sara and Coleridge, and we went with her homewards to Sockbridge.[1]

---

[1] Sockbridge in the parish of Barton, 3 m. S.S.W. of Penrith. Here W.'s grandfather settled when he came to Penrith : his property there descended, through W.'s father, to his eldest brother Richard.

Parted at the stile on the Pooley side. Thomas Wilkinson dined with us, and stayed supper.

I do not recollect how the rest of our time was spent exactly. We had a very sharp frost which broke on Friday the 15th January, or rather on the morning of Saturday 16th.

On Sunday the 17th we went to meet Mary. It was a mild gentle thaw. She stayed with us till Friday, 22nd January ; she was to have left on Thursday 21st but it was too stormy. On Thursday we dined at Mr. Myers's, and on Friday, 22nd, we parted from Mary. Before our parting we sate under a wall in the sun near a cottage above Stainton Bridge. The field in which we sate sloped downwards to a nearly level meadow, round which the Emont flowed in a small half-circle as at Sockburn.[1] The opposite bank is woody, steep as a wall, but not high, and above that bank the fields slope gently and irregularly down to it. These fields are surrounded by tall hedges, with trees among them, and there are clumps or grovelets of tall trees here and there. Sheep and cattle were in the fields. Dear Mary ! there we parted from her. I daresay, as often as she passes that road she will turn in at the gate to look at this sweet prospect. There was a barn and I think two or three cottages to be seen among the trees, and slips of lawn and irregular fields. During our stay at Mr. Clarkson's we walked every day, except that stormy Thursday, and then we dined at Mr. Myers's and I went after dinner on a double horse — Mrs. Clarkson was poorly all the time we were there. We dined at Thomas Wilkinson's on Friday the 15th, and walked to Penrith for Mary. The trees were covered with hoar-frost — grasses and trees and hedges beautiful ; a glorious sunset ; frost keener than ever. Next day thaw. Mrs. Clarkson amused us with many stories of her family and of persons whom she had known. I wish I had set them down as I heard them, when they were fresh in my memory. She had two old Aunts who lived at Norwich. The son of one of them (Mrs. Barnard) had had a large fortune left him. The other sister, rather

---

[1] Sockburn, the farm-house on the Tees where Mary and Sara Hutchinson had lived with their brother Thomas. W. and D. W. had visited them there in 1799.

piqued that her child had not got it, says to her : " Well, we have one Squire in the family however ". Mrs. Barnard replied with tears rushing out " Sister Harmer, Sister Harmer, there you sit. My son's no more a Squire than yours. I take it very unkindly of you, Sister Harmer." She used to say " Well, I wish it may do him any good ". When her son wished to send his carriage for her she said : " Nay I can walk to the Tabernacle and surely I may walk to see him " ! She kept two maids yet she whitewashed her kitchen herself — the two sisters lived together. She had a grand cleaning day twice a week and the sister had a fire made upstairs that all below might be thoroughly cleaned. She gave a great deal away in charity, visited the sick and was very pious. Mrs. Clarkson knew a clergyman and his wife who brought up ten children upon a curacy, sent two sons to college, and he left £1000 when he died. The wife was very generous, gave to all poor people victuals and drink. She had a passion for feeding animals. She killed a pig with feeding it over much. When it was dead she said, " To be sure it's a great loss, but I thank God it did not die *clemmed* " (the Cheshire word for starved). Her husband was very fond of playing Back-gammon, and used to play whenever he could get anybody to play with him. She had played much in her youth, and was an excellent player ; but her husband knew nothing of this, till one day she said to him, " You're fond of Back-gammon, come play with me ". He was surprised. She told him that she had kept it to herself, while she had a young family to attend to, but that now she would play with him ! So they began to play, and played afterwards every night. Mr. C. told us many pleasant stories. His journey from London to Wisbech on foot when a schoolboy, Irish murderer's knife and stick, postboy, etc., the white horse sleeping at the turnpike gate, snoring of the turnpike man, clock ticking, the burring story, the story of the mastiff, bull-baitings by men at Wisbech.

On Saturday, January 23rd, we left Eusemere at 10 o'clock in the morning, I behind Wm., Mr. Clarkson on his Galloway.[1]

---

[1] A Galloway pony.—W. K.

The morning not very promising, the wind cold. The mountains large and dark, but only thinly streaked with snow ; a strong wind. We dined in Grisdale on ham, bread, and milk. We parted from Mr. C. at one o'clock — it rained all the way home. We struggled with the wind, and often rested as we went along. A hail shower met us before we reached the Tarn, and the way often was difficult over the snow ; but at the Tarn the view closed in. We saw nothing but mists and snow : and at first the ice on the Tarn below us cracked and split, yet without water, a dull grey white. We lost our path, and could see the Tarn no longer. We made our way out with difficulty, guided by a heap of stones which we well remembered. We were afraid of being bewildered in the mists, till the darkness should overtake us. We were long before we knew that we were in the right track, but thanks to William's skill we knew it long before we could see our way before us. There was no footmark upon the snow either of man or beast. We saw 4 sheep before we had left the snow region. The Vale of Grasmere, when the mists broke away, looked soft and grave, of a yellow hue. It was dark before we reached home. We were not very much tired. My inside was sore with the cold — we had both of us been much heated upon the mountains but we caught no cold. O how comfortable and happy we felt ourselves, sitting by our own fire, when we had got off our wet clothes and had dressed ourselves fresh and clean. We found 5£ from Montagu and 20£ from Christopher. We talked about the Lake of Como, read in the *Descriptive Sketches*, looked about us, and felt that we were happy. We indulged dear thoughts about home — poor Mary ! we were sad to think of the contrast for her.

[*January*] 24*th, Sunday*. We went into the orchard as soon as breakfast was over. Laid out the situation for our new room, and sauntered a while. We had Mr. Clarkson's turkey for dinner ; the night before we had boiled the gizzard and some mutton, and made a nice piece of cookery for Wm.'s supper. Wm. walked in the morning, I wrote to Coleridge. After dinner I lay down till tea time — I rose refreshed and better. Wm. could not beat away sleep when I was gone. We went late to bed.

January 25*th, Monday*. We did not rise so soon as we

intended — I made bread and apple pies — we walked at dusk to Rydale — no letters ! it rained all the way. I wrote to Christopher and Mrs. Clarkson and Mrs. Coleridge, and sent off C.'s letter to Mary. Wm. tired with composition. We both went to bed at 10 o'clock.

[*January*] 26*th, Tuesday*. A dull morning. I have employed myself in writing this journal and reading newspapers till now ($\frac{1}{2}$ past 10 o'clock). We are going to walk, and I am ready, and waiting by the kitchen fire for Wm. We set forward intending to go into Easedale, but the wind being rather loudish, and blowing down Easedale, we turned under Silver How for a sheltered walk. We went a little beyond the Wyke ; then up to John's Grove, where the storm of Thursday has made sad ravages ; two of the finest trees are uprooted, one lying with the turf about its root, as if the whole together had been pared by a knife. The other is a larch. Several others are blown aside, one is snapped in two. We gathered together a faggot. William had tired himself with working — he resolved to do better. We received a letter from Mary by Fletcher with an account of C.'s arrival in London. I wrote to Mary before bedtime. We sate till we were both tired, for Wm. wrote out part of his poem, and endeavoured to alter it, and so made himself ill. I copied out the rest for him. We went late to bed. Wm. wrote to Annette.

[*January*] 27*th, Wednesday*. A beautiful mild morning — the sun shone, the lake was still, and all the shores reflected in it. I finished my letter to Mary, Wm. wrote to Stuart. I copied out sonnets for him. Mr. Olliff called and asked us to tea to-morrow. We stayed in the house till the sun shone more dimly and we thought the afternoon was closing in, but though the calmness of the Lake was gone with the bright sunshine, yet it was delightfully pleasant. We found no letter from Coleridge. One from Sara which we sate upon the wall to read — a sweet long letter, with a most interesting account of Mr. Patrick.[1] We had ate up the cold turkey before we walked

---

[1] David Patrick, husband of Sara H.'s cousin Margaret, with whom she lived as a child at Kendal, was known far and wide throughout the North Country. Sara said that " the best part of her education was gathered from

so we cooked no dinner. Sate a while by the fire, and then drank tea at Frank Baty's. As we went past the Nab [1] I was surprised to see the youngest child amongst the rest of them running about by itself, with a canny round fat face, and rosy cheeks. I called in. They gave me some nuts. Everybody surprised that we should come over Grisdale. Paid £1 : 3 : 3 for letters come since December 1st. Paid also about 8 shillings at Penrith. The bees were humming about the hive. William raked a few stones off the garden, his first garden labour this year ; I cut the shrubs. When we returned from Frank's, Wm. wasted his mind in the Magazines. I wrote to Coleridge, and Mrs. C., closed the letters up to [? Samson]. Then we sate by the fire, and were happy, only our tender thoughts became painful. Went to bed at ½ past 11.

January 28th, Thursday. A downright rain. A wet night. Wm. slept better — better this morning — he had [written an] [2] epitaph, and altered one that he wrote when he was a boy. It cleared up after dinner. We were both in miserable spirits, and very doubtful about keeping our engagement to the Olliffs. We walked first within view of Rydale, then to Lewthwaite's, then we went to Mr. Olliff's. We talked a while. Wm. was tired. We then played at cards. Came home in the rain. Very dark. Came with a lantern. Wm. out of spirits and tired. After we went to bed I heard him continually, he called at ¼ past 3 to know the hour.

January 29th, Friday. Wm. was very unwell. Worn out with his bad night's rest. He went to bed — I read to him, to endeavour to make him sleep. Then I came into the other room, and read the first book of *Paradise Lost*. After dinner we walked to Ambleside — found Lloyds at Luff's — we stayed and drank tea by ourselves. A heart-rending letter from Coleridge — we were sad as we could be. Wm. wrote to him. We talked about Wm.'s going to London. It was a mild afternoon — there was an unusual softness in the prospects as we went, a rich yellow upon the fields, and a soft grave purple

---

the stores of that good man's mind " ; and W. W. drew on her account of him for many touches in his portrait of the Wanderer in *The Excursion*.

[1] *v.* Simpson of the Nab in Appendix, p. 436.   [2] Words omitted in MS.

on the waters. When we returned many stars were out, the clouds were moveless, in the sky soft purple, the Lake of Rydale calm, Jupiter behind, Jupiter at least *we* call him, but William says we always call the largest star Jupiter. When we came home we both wrote to C. I was stupefied.

January 30*th, Saturday.* A cold dark morning. William chopped wood — I brought it in a basket. A cold wind. Wm. slept better, but he thinks he looks ill — he is shaving now. He asks me to set down the story of Barbara Wilkinson's turtle dove. Barbara is an old maid. She had two turtle doves. One of them died, the first year I think. The other bird continued to live alone in its cage for 9 years, but for one whole year it had a companion and daily visitor — a little mouse, that used to come and feed with it ; and the dove would caress it, and cower over it with its wings, and make a loving noise to it. The mouse, though it did not testify equal delight in the dove's company, yet it was at perfect ease. The poor mouse disappeared, and the dove was left solitary till its death. It died of a short sickness, and was buried under a tree with funeral ceremony by Barbara and her maidens, and one or two others.

On *Saturday,* 30*th,* Wm. worked at *The Pedlar* all the morning. He kept the dinner waiting till four o'clock. He was much tired. We were preparing to walk when a heavy rain came on.

[*January*] 31*st, Sunday.* Wm. had slept very ill — he was tired and had a bad headache. We walked round the two lakes. Grasmere was very soft, and Rydale was extremely beautiful from the western side. Nab Scar was just topped by a cloud which, cutting it off as high as it could be cut off, made the mountain look uncommonly lofty. We sate down a long time in different places. I always love to walk that way, because it is the way I first came to Rydale and Grasmere, and because our dear Coleridge did also. When I came with Wm., 6½ years ago, it was just at sunset. There was a rich yellow light on the waters, and the Islands were reflected there. To-day it was grave and soft, but not perfectly calm. William says it was much such a day [1] as when Coleridge came with

---

[1] Nov. 3, 1799 : *v. E.L.* p. 233.

him. The sun shone out before we reached Grasmere. We sate by the roadside at the foot of the Lake, close to Mary's dear name, which she had cut herself upon the stone. Wm. cut at it with his knife to make it plainer. We amused ourselves for a long time in watching the breezes, some as if they came from the bottom of the lake, spread in a circle, brushing along the surface of the water, and growing more delicate, as it were thinner, and of a *paler* colour till they died away. Others spread out like a peacock's tail, and some went right forward this way and that in all directions. The lake was still where these breezes were not, but they made it all alive. I found a strawberry blossom in a rock. The little slender flower had more courage than the green leaves, for *they* were but half expanded and half grown, but the blossom was spread full out. I uprooted it rashly, and I felt as if I had been committing an outrage, so I planted it again. It will have but a stormy life of it, but let it live if it can. We found Calvert [1] here. I brought a handkerchief full of mosses, which I placed on the chimneypiece when C. was gone. He dined with us, and carried away the encyclopaedias. After they were gone, I spent some time in trying to reconcile myself to the change, and in rummaging out and arranging some other books in their places. One good thing is this — there is a nice elbow place for William, and he may sit for the picture of John Bunyan any day. Mr. Simpson drank tea with us. We paid our rent to Benson. William's head was bad after Mr. S. was gone. I petted him on the carpet and began a letter to Sara.

February 1st, Monday. Wm. slept badly. I baked pies and bread. William worked hard at *The Pedlar*, and tired himself. He walked up with me towards Mr. Simpson's. There was a purplish light upon Mr. Olliff's house, which made me look to the other side of the vale, when I saw a strange stormy mist coming down the side of Silver How of a reddish purple colour. It soon came on a heavy rain. We parted presently — Wm. went to Rydale — I drank tea with Mrs. S., the two Mr.

---

[1] William Calvert, the friend with whom W. had spent part of the summer of 1793 on the Isle of Wight, and who had lent him Windy Brow in 1794. Brother of Raisley Calvert, to whose legacy W. owed his independence.

Simpsons both tipsy. I came home with Jenny as far as the Swan. A cold night, dry and windy — Jupiter above the Forest Side. Wm. pretty well but he worked a little. In the morning a box of clothes with books came from London. I sate by his bedside, and read in *The Pleasures of Hope* to him, which came in the box. He could not fall asleep, but I found in the morning that he had slept better than he expected. No letters.

February 2nd, Tuesday. A fine clear morning, but sharp and cold. Wm. went into the orchard after breakfast to chop wood. I walked backwards and forwards on the platform. Molly called me down to Charles Lloyd — he brought me flower seeds from his Brother. William not quite well. We walked into Easedale — were turned back in the open field by the sight of a cow — every horned cow puts me in terror. We walked as far as we could, having crossed the footbridge, but it was dirty, and we turned back — walked backwards and forwards between Goody Bridge and Butterlip How. William wished to break off composition, and was unable, and so did himself harm. The sun shone, but it was cold. After dinner William worked at *The Pedlar*. After tea I read aloud the eleventh book of *Paradise Lost*. We were much impressed, and also melted into tears. The papers came in soon after I had laid aside the book — a good thing for my Wm. I worked a little to-day at putting the linen into repair that came in the box. Molly washing.

[*February*] *3rd, Wednesday.* A rainy morning. We walked to Rydale for letters, found one from Mrs. Cookson and Mary H. It snowed upon the hills. We sate down on the wall at the foot of White Moss. Sate by the fire in the evening. Wm. tired, and did not compose. He went to bed soon, and could not sleep. I wrote to Mary H. Sent off the letter by Fletcher.[1] Wrote also to Coleridge. Read Wm. to sleep after dinner, and read to him in bed till $\frac{1}{2}$ past one.

---

[1] Fletcher, the Keswick carrier : he lived at Townhead, but seems to have kept his horses and cart in the peat-house adjoining the Ashburners' cottage. As he started early in the morning letters written the night before were sometimes pushed under the door of the peat-house. (*v.* Journal for Dec. 21, 1801 and Feb. 8 and 24, 1802, *infra* ; *E.L.* pp. 278, 352.)

[February] 4*th, Thursday.* I was very sick, bad headach and unwell — I lay in bed till 3 o'clock, that is I lay down as soon as breakfast was over. It was a terribly wet day. William sate in the house all day. Fletcher's boy did not come home. I worked at Montagu's shirts. Wm. thought a little about *The Pedlar.* I slept in the sitting room. Read Smollet's life.

[February] 5*th, Friday.* A cold snowy morning. Snow and hail showers. We did not walk. Wm. cut wood a little. I read the story of [?] in Warly [?]. Sara's parcel came with waistcoat. The Chaucer not only misbound, but a leaf or two wanting. I wrote about it to Mary and wrote to Soulby. We received the waistcoat, shoes and gloves from Sara by the waggon. William not well. Sate up late at *The Pedlar.*

February 6*th, Saturday.* William had slept badly. It snowed in the night, and was on Saturday, as Molly expressed it, a cauld clash. William went to Rydale for letters — he came home with two very affecting letters from Coleridge — resolved to try another climate. I was stopped in my writing, and made ill by the letters. William a bad headach ; he made up a bed on the floor, but could not sleep — I went to his bed and slept not — better when I rose — wrote again after tea, and translated two or three of Lessing's *Fables.*

[February] 7*th, Sunday.* A fine clear frosty morning. The eaves drop with the heat of the sun all day long. The ground thinly covered with snow. The road black, rocks bluish. Before night the Island was quite green ; the sun had melted all the snow upon it. Mr. Simpson called before Wm. had done shaving — William had had a bad night and was working at his poem. We sate by the fire, and did not walk, but read *The Pedlar,* thinking it done ; but lo ! though Wm. could find fault with no one part of it, it was uninteresting, and must be altered. Poor Wm. !

February 8*th,* 1802, *Monday Morning.* It was very windy and rained very hard all the morning. William worked at his poem and I read a little in Lessing and the grammar. A chaise came past to fetch Ellis the Carrier who had hurt his head.

After dinner (*i.e.* we set off at about ½ past 4) we went towards Rydale for letters. It was a cold " *cauld clash* ". The rain had been so cold that it hardly melted the snow. We stopped at Park's to get some straw in Wm.'s shoes. The young mother was sitting by a bright wood fire with her youngest child upon her lap, and the other two sate on each side of the chimney. The light of the fire made them a beautiful sight, with their innocent countenances, their rosy cheeks, and glossy curling hair. We sate and talked about poor Ellis, and our journey over the Hawes.[1] It had been reported that we came over in the night. Willy told us of 3 men who were once lost in crossing that way in the night ; they had carried a lantern with them ; the lantern went out at the Tarn, and they all perished. Willy had seen their cloaks drying at the public-house in Patterdale the day before their funeral. We walked on very wet through the clashy cold roads in bad spirits at the idea of having to go as far as Rydale, but before we had come again to the shore of the Lake, we met our patient bow-bent Friend, with his little wooden box at his back. " Where are you going ? " said he. " To Rydale for letters." " I have two for you in my box." We lifted up the lid, and there they lay. Poor fellow, he straddled and pushed on with all his might ; but we soon outstripped him far away when we had turned back with our letters. We were very thankful that we had not to go on, for we should have been sadly tired. In thinking of this I could not help comparing lots with him ! He goes at that slow pace every morning, and after having wrought a hard day's work returns at night, however weary he may be, takes it all quietly, and, though perhaps he neither feels thankfulness nor pleasure, when he eats his supper, and has no luxury to look forward to but falling asleep in bed, yet I daresay he neither murmurs nor thinks it hard. He seems mechanized to labour. We broke the seal of Coleridge's letter, and I had light enough just to see that he was not ill. I put it in my pocket, but at the top of the White Moss I took it to my bosom, a safer place for it. The night was wild. There was a strange mountain lightness, when we were at the top of the White Moss. I have often observed it there in the evenings, being between the two valleys. There

---

[1] *i.e.* Grisdale, *v.* Jan. 23, 1802.

is more of the sky there than any other place. It has a strange effect sometimes along with the obscurity of evening or night. It seems almost like a peculiar *sort* of light. There was not much wind till we came to John's Grove, then it roared right out of the grove ; all the trees were tossing about. C.'s letter somewhat damped us, it spoke with less confidence about France. Wm. wrote to him. The other letter was from Montagu, with £8. Wm. was very unwell, tired when he had written. He went to bed, and left me to write to M. H., Montagu, and Calvert, and Mrs. Coleridge. I had written in his letter to Coleridge. We wrote to Calvert to beg him not to fetch us on Sunday. Wm. left me with a *little* peat fire — it grew less. I wrote on, and was starved. At 2 o'clock I went to put my letters under Fletcher's door. I never felt such a cold night. There was a strong wind and it froze very hard. I collected together all the clothes I could find (for I durst not go into the pantry for fear of waking William). At first when I went to bed I seemed to be warm. I suppose because the cold air, which I had just left, no longer touched my body ; but I soon found that I was mistaken. I could not sleep from sheer cold. I had baked pies and bread in the morning. Coleridge's letter contained prescriptions.

N.B. The moon came out suddenly when we were at John's Grove, and a star or two besides.

[*February 9th,*] *Tuesday*. Wm. had slept better. He fell to work, and made himself unwell. We did not walk. A funeral came by of a poor woman who had drowned herself, some say because she was hardly treated by her husband ; others that he was a very decent respectable man, and *she* but an indifferent wife. However this was, she had only been married to him last Whitsuntide and had had very indifferent health ever since. She had got up in the night, and drowned herself in the pond. She had requested to be buried beside her mother, and so she was brought in a hearse. She was followed by several decent-looking men on horseback, her sister, Thomas Fleming's wife, in a chaise, and some others with her, and a cart full of women. Molly says folks thinks o' their mothers. Poor body, *she* has been little thought of by any body else. We did a little of Lessing. I attempted a fable, but my head ached ; my bones were sore with the cold of the day before, and I was downright stupid. We went to bed, but not till Wm. had tired himself.

[*February*] 10*th, Wednesday.* A very snowy morning. It cleared up a little however for a while but we did not walk. We sent for our letters by Fletcher and for some writing paper etc. He brought us word there were none. This was strange for I depended on Mary. While I was writing out the poem, as we hope for a final writing, a letter was brought me by John Dawson's daughter, the letter written at Eusemere. I paid Wm. Jackson's bill by John Fisher, sent off a letter to Montagu by Fletcher. After Molly went we read the first part of the poem and were delighted with it, but Wm. afterwards got to some ugly place, and went to bed tired out. A wild, moonlight night.

[*February*] 11*th, Thursday.* A very fine clear sunny frost, the ground white with snow — William rose before Molly was ready for him, I rose at a little after nine. William sadly tired and working still at *The Pedlar.* Miss Simpson called when he was worn out — he escaped and sate in his own room till she went. She was very faint and ill, had had a tooth drawn and had suffered greatly. I walked up with her past Gawain's.[1] The sun was very warm till we got past Lewthwaite's — then it had little power, and had not melted the roads. As I came back again I felt the vale like a different climate. The vale was bright and beautiful. Molly had linen hung out. We had pork to dinner sent us by Mrs. Simpson. William still poorly. We made up a good fire after dinner, and Wm. brought his mattress out, and lay down on the floor. I read to him the life of Ben Jonson, and some short poems of his, which were too *interesting* for him, and would not let him go to sleep. I had begun with Fletcher, but he was too *dull* for me. Fuller says, in his *Life of Jonson* (speaking of his plays), " If his latter be not so spriteful and vigorous as his first pieces, all that are old, and all who desire to be old, should excuse him therein ". He says he "*beheld*" wit-combats between Shakespeare and Jonson,

---

[1] Gawain, *v.* Mackereth in Appendix, p. 435.

and compares Shakespeare to an English man-of-war, Jonson to a Spanish great galleon. There is one affecting line in Jonson's epitaph on his first daughter —

> *Here lies to each her parents ruth,*
> Mary the daughter of their youth.
> *At six months' end she parted hence,*
> *In safety of her innocence.*

I have been writing this journal while Wm. has had a nice little sleep. Once he was waked by Charles Lloyd who had come to see about lodgings for his children in the hooping cough. It is now 7 o'clock — I have a nice coal fire — Wm. is still on his bed. Two beggars to-day. I continued to read to him. We were much delighted with the poem of *Penshurst.* Wm. rose better. I was chearful and happy. But he got to work again, and went to bed unwell.

[*February*] 12*th, Friday.* A very fine, bright, clear, hard frost. Wm. working again. I recopied *The Pedlar,* but poor Wm. all the time at work. Molly tells me " What ! little Sally's gone to visit at Mr. Simpson's. They say she's very smart, she's got on a new bed-gown that her Cousin gave her, it's a very bonny one, they tell me, but I've not seen it. Sally and me's in luck." In the afternoon a poor woman came, *she said*, to beg some rags for her husband's leg, which had been wounded by a slate from the roof in the great wind — but she has been used to go a-begging, for she has often come here. Her father lived to the age of 105. She is a woman of strong bones, with a complexion that has been beautiful, and remained very fresh last year, but now she looks broken, and her little boy — a pretty little fellow, and whom I have loved for the sake of Basil[1] — looks thin and pale. I observed this to her. " Ay," says she, " we have all been ill. Our house was un-roofed in the storm nearly, and so we lived in it so for more than a week." The child wears a ragged drab coat and a fur cap, poor little fellow, I think he seems scarcely at all grown since the first time I saw him. William was with me ; we met him in a lane going to Skelwith Bridge. He looked very pretty.

---

[1] Little Basil Montagu : *v. E.L.* p. 138.

He was walking lazily, in the deep narrow lane, overshadowed with the hedgerows, his meal poke hung over his shoulder. He said he " was going a laiting ". Poor creatures! He now wears the same coat he had on at that time. When the woman was gone, I could not help thinking that we are not half thankful enough that we are placed in that condition of life in which we are. We do not so often bless God for this, as we wish for this £50, that £100, etc. etc. We have not, however, to reproach ourselves with ever breathing a murmur. This woman's was but a *common* case. The snow still lies upon the ground. Just at the closing in of the day, I heard a cart pass the door, and at the same time the dismal sound of a crying infant. I went to the window, and had light enough to see that a man was driving a cart, which seemed not to be very full, and that a woman with an infant in her arms was following close behind and a dog close to her. It was a wild and melancholy sight. Wm. rubbed his table after candles were lighted, and we sate a long time with the windows unclosed; I almost finished writing *The Pedlar*; but poor Wm. wore himself and me out with labour. We had an affecting conversation. Went to bed at 12 o'clock.

February 13th, *Saturday*. It snowed a little this morning. Still at work at *The Pedlar*, altering and refitting. We did not walk, though it was a very fine day. We received a present of eggs and milk from Janet Dockeray,[1] and just before she went, the little boy from the Hill brought us a letter from Sara H., and one from the Frenchman in London. I wrote to Sara after tea, and Wm. took out his old newspapers, and the new ones came in soon after. We sate, after I had finished the letter, talking; and Wm. read parts of his *Recluse* aloud to me. We did not drink tea till ½ past 7.

February 14th, *Sunday*. A fine morning. The sun shines but it has been a hard frost in the night. There are some little snowdrops that are afraid to pop their white heads quite out, and a few blossoms of hepatica that are half-starved. Wm. left me at work altering some passages of *The Pedlar*, and

---

1 *v.* May 18, 1800.

went into the orchard. The fine day pushed him on to resolve ; and as soon as I had read a letter to him, which I had just received from Mrs. Clarkson, he said he would go to Penrith, so Molly was despatched for the horse. I worked hard, got the backs pasted, the writing finished, and all quite trim. I wrote to Mrs. Clarkson, and put up some letters for Mary H., and off he went in his blue spencer, and a pair of *new* pantaloons fresh from London. He turned back when he had got as far as Frank's [1] to ask if he had his letters safe, then for some apples, then fairly off. We had money to borrow for him. It was a pleasant afternoon. I ate a little bit of cold mutton without laying cloth and then sate over the fire, reading Ben Jonson's *Penshurst*, and other things. Before sunset I put on my shawl and walked out. The snow-covered mountains were spotted with rich sunlight, a palish buffish colour. The roads were very dirty for, though it was a keen frost, the sun had melted the snow and water upon them. I stood at Sara's gate,[2] and when I came in view of Rydale, I cast a long look upon the mountains beyond. They were very white, but I concluded that Wm. would have a very safe passage over Kirkstone, and I was quite easy about him. After dinner, a little before sunset, I walked out about 20 yards above Glow-worm Rock. I met a carman, a Highlander I suppose, with 4 carts, the first 3 belonging to himself, the last evidently to a man and his family who had joined company with him, and who I guessed to be potters. The carman was cheering his horses, and talking to a little lass about 10 years of age who seemed to make him her companion. She ran to the wall, and took up a large stone to support the wheel of one of his carts, and ran on before with it in her arms to be ready for him. She was a beautiful creature, and there was something uncommonly impressive in the lightness and joyousness of her manner. Her business seemed to be all pleasure — pleasure in her own motions, and the man looked at her as if he too was pleased, and spoke to her in the same tone in which he spoke to his horses. There was a wildness in her whole figure, not the wildness of a Mountain lass, but a *Road*

---

[1] *i.e.* Frank Batey.   [2] *i.e.* the Wishing Gate.

lass, a traveller from her birth, who had wanted neither food nor clothes. Her Mother followed the last cart with a lovely child, perhaps about a year old, at her back, and a good-looking girl, about 15 years old, walked beside her. All the children were like the mother. She had a very fresh complexion, but she was blown with fagging up the hill, with the steepness of the hill and the bairn that she carried. Her husband was helping the horse to drag the cart up by pushing it with his shoulder. I got tea when I reached home, and read German till about 9 o'clock. Then Molly went away and I wrote to Coleridge. Went to bed at about 12 o'clock. Slept in Wm.'s bed and I slept badly, for my thoughts were full of William.

February 15th, Monday. I was starching small linen all the morning. It snowed a good deal, and was terribly cold. After dinner it was fair, but I was obliged to run all the way to the foot of the White Moss, to get the least bit of warmth into me. I found a letter from C. — he was much better — this was very satisfactory, but his letter was not an answer to Wm.'s which I expected. A letter from Annette. I got tea when I reached home, and then set on to reading German. I wrote part of a letter to Coleridge, went late to bed and slept badly.

[*February*] 16*th, Tuesday.* A fine morning, but I had persuaded myself not to expect Wm.; I believe because I was afraid of being disappointed. I ironed all day. He came in just at tea time, had only seen Mary H. for a couple of hours between Eamont Bridge and Hartshorn Tree. Mrs. C. better. He had had a difficult journey over Kirkstone, and came home by Threlkeld — his mouth and breath were very cold when he kissed me. We spent a sweet evening. He was better, had altered *The Pedlar.* We went to bed pretty soon. Mr. Graham said he wished Wm. had been with him the other day — he was riding in a post-chaise and he heard a strange cry that he could not understand, the sound continued, and he called to the chaise driver to stop. It was a little girl that was crying as if her heart would burst. She had got up behind the chaise, and her cloak had been caught by the wheel, and was jammed in, and it hung there. She was crying after it. Poor thing. ' Mr. Graham took her into the chaise, and the cloak was released from the wheel, but the child's misery did not cease, for her cloak was torn to rags ; it had been a miserable cloak before, but she had no other, and it was the greatest sorrow that could befal her. Her name was Alice Fell.[1] She had no parents, and belonged to the next town. At the next town, Mr. G. left money with some respectable people in the town, to buy her a new cloak.'

[February] 17th, Wednesday. A miserable nasty snowy morning. We did not walk, but the old man from the hill brought us a short letter from Mary H. I copied the second part of Peter Bell. William pretty well.

[February] 18th, Thursday. A foggy morning, but it cleared up in the afternoon, and Wm. went to Mrs. Simpson's to tea. I went with him to Goan Mackereth's. Roads very dirty. I copied third part of Peter Bell in his absence, and began a letter to Coleridge. Wm. came in with a letter from Coleridge, that came by Keswick. We talked together till 11 o'clock, when Wm. got to work, and was the worse for it. Hard frost.

[February] 19th, Friday. Hard frost this morning, but it soon snowed, then thawed — a miserable afternoon. Williamson came and cut William's hair — I wrote to C. He carried the letter to Ambleside. Afterwards I wrote to Mary and Sara, tired and went early to bed.

[February] 20th, Saturday. A very rainy morning, but it cleared up a little — we walked to Rydale, there were no letters. The roads were very dirty. We met little Dawson on horseback and desired him to bring us paper from Mrs. Jameson's. After tea I wrote the first part of Peter Bell. William better.

[February] 21st, Sunday. A very wet morning. I wrote the 2nd prologue to Peter Bell, then went to Mrs. Olliff's. After dinner I wrote the 1st prologue. William walked to the Tailor's, while I was at Mrs. O.'s — it rained all the time. Snowdrops quite out, but cold and winterly ; yet, for all this, a thrush that lives in our orchard has shouted and sung its merriest all day long. In the evening I wrote to Mrs. Clarkson,

---

[1] v. Alice Fell ; for Mr. Graham v. I. F. note to the poem.

and my Br. Richard. Wm. went to bed exhausted.

[*February*] 22nd, *Monday*. A wet morning. I lay down, as soon as breakfast was over, very unwell. I slept. Wm. brought me 4 letters to bed — from Annette and Caroline, Mary and Sara, and Coleridge. C. had had another attack in his bowels ; otherwise mending — M. and S. both well. M. reached Middleham the Monday night before at 12 o'clock — Tom there. In the evening we walked to the top of the hill, then to the bridge, we hung over the wall, and looked at the deep stream below ; it came with a full, steady, yet very rapid flow down to the lake. The sykes made a sweet sound everywhere, and looked very interesting in the twilight. That little one above Mr. Olliff's house was very impressive. A ghostly white serpent line, it made a sound most distinctly heard of itself. The mountains were black and steep — the tops of some of them having yet snow visible, but it rained so hard last night much of it has been washed away. After tea I was just going to write to Coleridge when Mr. Simpson came in. Wm. began to read *Peter Bell* to him, so I carried my writing to the kitchen fire. Wm. called me upstairs to read the 3rd part. Mr. S. had brought his first engraving to let us see — he supped with us. Wm. was tired with reading and talking and went to bed in bad spirits.

[*February*] 23rd, *Tuesday*. A misty rainy morning — the lake calm. I baked bread and pies. Before dinner worked a little at Wm.'s waistcoat — after dinner read German Grammar. Before tea we walked into Easedale. We turned aside in the Parson's field, a pretty field with 3 pretty prospects. Then we went to the first large field, but such a cold wind met us that we turn'd again. The wind seemed warm when we came out of our own door. That dear thrush was singing upon the topmost of the smooth branches of the ash tree at the top of the orchard. How long it had been perched on that same tree I cannot tell, but we had heard its dear voice in the orchard the day through, along with a chearful undersong made by our winter friends, the robins. We came home by Goan's. I picked up a few mosses by the roadside, which I left at home. We then went to John's Grove, there we sate a little while looking at the fading landscape. The lake, though the objects on the shore were fading, seemed brighter than when it is perfect day, and the Island pushed itself upwards, distinct and large. All the shores marked. There was a sweet, sea-like sound in the trees above our heads. We walked backwards and forwards some time for dear John's sake, then walked to look at Rydale. Darkish when we reached home, and we got tea immediately with candles. William now reading in Bishop Hall — I going to read German. We have a nice singing fire, with one piece of wood. Fletcher's carts are arrived but no papers from Mrs. Coleridge.

[*February*] 24th, *Wednesday*. A rainy day — we were busy all day unripping William's coats for the tailor.[1] William wrote to Annette, to Coleridge and the Frenchman — I received a letter from Mrs. Clarkson, a very kind affecting letter, which I answered telling her I would go to Eusemere when William went to Keswick — I wrote a little bit to Coleridge. We sent off these letters by Fletcher. It was a tremendous night of wind and rain. Poor Coleridge ! a sad night for a traveller such as he. God be praised he was in safe quarters. Wm. went out, and put the letters under the door — he never felt a colder night.

[*February*] 25th, *Thursday*. A fine, mild, grey, beautiful morning. The tailor here. I worked at unripping. Wm. wrote to Montagu in the morning. After dinner he went to Lloyd's — I accompanied him to the gate in the corner or turning of the vale close to the riverside beyond Lenty Fleming's Cottage.[1] It was coldish and like for frost — a clear evening. I reached home just before dark, brought some mosses and ivy, then got tea, and fell to work at German. I read a good deal of Lessing's Essay. Wm. came home between 9 and 10 o'clock. We sate nicely together by the fire till bedtime. Wm. not very much tired.

[*February*] 26th, *Friday*. A grey morning till 10 o'clock, then the sun shone beautifully. Mrs. Lloyd's children and Mrs. Luff came in a chaise, were here at 11 o'clock, then went

---

[1] Lenty Fleming, the tailor, lived in the house under Loughrigg now known as The Stepping Stones.—G. G. W.

to Mrs. Olliff. Wm. and I accompanied them to the gate. I prepared dinner, sought out *Peter Bell*, gave Wm. some cold meat, and then we went to walk. We walked first to Butterlip How, where we sate and overlooked the vale ; no sign of spring but the red tints of the upper twigs of the woods and single trees. Sate in the sun. Met Charles Lloyd near the Bridge, got dinner — I lay down unwell — got up to tea. Mr. and Mrs. Luff walked home, the Lloyds stayed till 8 o'clock. We always get on better with conversation at home than elsewhere — discussion about Mrs. King and Mrs. Olliff. The chaise-driver brought us a letter from M. H., a short one from C. We were perplexed about Sara's coming. I wrote to Mary. Wm. closed his letter to Montagu, and wrote to Calvert and to Mrs. Coleridge. Birds sang divinely to-day. Bowels and head bad. Wm. better.

[*February*] *27th, Saturday.* We walked in the afternoon towards Rydale returning to tea. Mr. Barth Simpson called after supper, a little tipsy. Fletcher said he had had no papers. Wm. was not very well. I sate in the orchard after dinner — we walked in the evening towards Rydale.

February 28th, Sunday. Wm. very ill, employed with *The Pedlar.* We got papers in the morning. William shaved himself. I was obliged to go to bed after dinner, rose better — wrote to Sara H. and Mrs. Clarkson — no walk. Disaster Pedlar.[1]

[*March 1st,*] *Monday.* A fine pleasant day, we walked to Rydale. I went on before for the letters, brought 2 from M. and S. H. We climbed over the wall and read them under the shelter of a mossy rock. We met Mrs. Lloyd in going — Mrs. Olliff's child ill. The catkins are beautiful in the hedges, the ivy is very green. Robert Newton's paddock is greenish — that is all we see of Spring ; finished and sent off the letter to Sara, and wrote to Mary. Wrote again to Sara, and Wm. wrote to Coleridge. Mrs. Lloyd called when I was in bed.

[*March 2nd,*] *Tuesday.* A fine grey morning. I was baking bread and pies. After dinner I read German, and a little before

---

[1] Added in margin.

dinner Wm. also read. We walked on Butterlip How under
the wind. It rained all the while, but we had a pleasant walk.
The mountains of Easedale, black or covered with snow at the
tops, gave a peculiar softness to the valley, the clouds hid the
tops of some of them. The valley was populous and enlivened
with the streams. Mrs. Lloyd drove past without calling.

[*March 3rd,*] *Wednesday.* I was so unlucky as to propose
to rewrite *The Pedlar.* Wm. got to work, and was worn to
death. We did not walk. I wrote in the afternoon.

[*March 4th,*] *Thursday.* Before we had quite finished breakfast Calvert's man brought the horses for Wm. We had a
deal to do, to shave, pens to make, poems to put in order for
writing, to settle the dress, pack up etc., and the man came
before the pens were made, and he was obliged to leave me
with only two. Since he has left me at half-past 11 (it is now 2)
I have been putting the drawers into order, laid by his clothes
which we had thrown here and there and everywhere, filed
two months' newspapers and got my dinner, 2 boiled eggs and
2 apple tarts. I have set Molly on to clear the garden a little,
and I myself have helped. I transplanted some snowdrops —
the Bees are busy. Wm. has a nice bright day. It was hard
frost in the night. The Robins are singing sweetly. Now for
my walk. I *will* be busy. I *will* look well, and be well when
he comes back to me. O the Darling ! Here is one of his bitten
apples. I can hardly find in my heart to throw it into the fire.
I must wash myself, then off. I walked round the two Lakes,
crossed the stepping-stones at Rydale foot. Sate down where
we always sit. I was full of thoughts about my darling. Blessings on him. I came home at the foot of our own hill under
Loughrigg. They are making sad ravages in the woods.
Benson's wood is going, and the wood above the River. The
wind has blown down a small fir tree on the Rock that terminates
John's path — I suppose the wind of Wednesday night. I
read German after my return till tea time. I worked and read
the L. B., enchanted with the *Idiot Boy*. Wrote to Wm.,
then went to bed. It snowed when I went to bed.

[*March 5th,*] *Friday.* First walked in the garden and
orchard, a frosty sunny morning. After dinner I gathered

mosses in Easedale. I saw before me sitting in the open field upon his sack of rags the old Ragman that I know. His coat is of scarlet in a thousand patches. His breeches' knees were untied. The breeches have been given him by some one — he has a round hat, pretty good, small crowned but large rimmed. When I came to him, he said " Is there a brigg yonder that'll carry me ow'r t'watter ? " He seemed half stupid. When I came home Molly had shook the carpet and cleaned everything upstairs. When I see her so happy in her work, and exulting in her own importance, I often think of that affecting expression which she made use of to me one evening lately. Talking of her good luck in being in this house, " Aye, Mistress, them 'at's low laid would have been a proud creature could they but have [seen] where I is now, fra what they thought mud be my doom ". I was tired when I reached home. I sent Molly Ashburner to Rydale. No letters ! I was sadly mortified. I expected one fully from Coleridge. Wrote to William, read the L. B., got into sad thoughts, tried at German, but could not go on. Read L. B. Blessings on that Brother of mine ! Beautiful new moon over Silver How.

· [*March 6th*,] *Saturday Morning.* I awoke with a bad head-ache and partly on that account, partly for ease I lay in bed till one o'clock. At one I pulled off my nightcap — ½ past one sate down to breakfast. A very cold sunshiny frost. I wrote *The Pedlar*, and finished it before I went to Mr. Simpson's to drink tea. Miss S. at Keswick, but she came home. Mrs. Jameson came in — I stayed supper. Fletcher's carts went past and I let them go with William's letter. Mr. B. S. came nearly home with me. I found letters from Wm., Mary, and Coleridge. I wrote to C. Sate up late, and could not fall asleep when I went to bed.

[*March 7th*,] *Sunday Morning.* A very fine, clear frost. I stitched up *The Pedlar* ; wrote out *Ruth* ; read it with the alterations ; then wrote Mary H. Read a little German, got my dinner. Mrs. Lloyd called at the door, and in came William. I did not expect him till to-morrow. How glad I was. After we had talked about an hour, I gave him his dinner, a beef steak. We sate talking and happy. Mr. and Miss Simpson came in at tea time. William came home very well — he had been a little fatigued with reading his poems. He brought two new stanzas of *Ruth*. We went to bed pretty soon and slept well. A mild grey evening.

[*March 8th,*] *Monday Morning*. A soft rain and mist. We walked to Rydale for letters. The Vale looked very beautiful in excessive simplicity, yet, at the same time, in uncommon obscurity. The Church stood alone, no mountains behind. The meadows looked calm and rich, bordering on the still lake. Nothing else to be seen but lake and island. Found a very affecting letter from Montagu, also one from Mary. We read Montagu's in walking on — sate down to read Mary's. I came home with a bad headach and lay down — I slept, but rose little better. I have got tea and am now much relieved. On Friday evening the moon hung over the northern side of the highest point of Silver How, like a gold ring snapped in two, and shaven off at the ends, it was so narrow. Within this ring lay the circle of the round moon, as *distinctly* to be seen as ever the enlightened moon is. William had observed the same appearance at Keswick, perhaps at the very same moment, hanging over the Newland Fells. Sent off a letter to Mary H., also to Coleridge and Sara, and rewrote in the evening the alterations of *Ruth*, which we sent off at the same time.

[*March 9th,*] *Tuesday Morning*. William was reading in Ben Jonson — he read me a beautiful poem on Love. We then walked. The first part of our walk was melancholy — we went within view of Rydale — then we sate on Sara's seat — we walked afterwards into Easedale. It was cold when we returned. We met Sally Newton and her water dog. We sate by the fire in the evening, and read *The Pedlar* over. William worked a little, and altered it in a few places. I was not very well — mended stockings.

[*March 10th,*] *Wednesday*. A fine mildish morning, that is, not frost. Wm. read in Ben Jonson in the morning. I read a little German, altered various waistcoats. We then walked to Rydale. No letters ! They are slashing away in Benson's wood. We walked round by the Church, through Olliff's field when we returned, then home and went up into the orchard.

We sate on the seat, talked a little by the fire and then got our tea. William has since tea been talking about publishing the Yorkshire Wolds Poem with *The Pedlar*.

[*March 11th*,] *Thursday*. A fine morning. William worked at the poem of *The Singing Bird*.[1] Just as we were sitting down to dinner we heard Mr. Clarkson's voice. I ran down, William followed. He was so finely mounted that William was more intent upon the horse than the rider, an offence easily forgiven, for Mr. Clarkson was as proud of it himself as he well could be. We ate our dinner, then Mr. Clarkson came. We walked with him round by the White Bridge after dinner. The vale in mist, rather the mountains, big with the rain, soft and beautiful. Mr. C. was sleepy and went soon to bed.

[*March 12th*,] *Friday*. A very fine morning. We went to see Mr. Clarkson off. Then we went up towards Easedale but a shower drove us back. The sun shone while it rained, and the stones of the walls and the pebbles on the road glittered like silver. When William was at Keswick I saw Jane Ashburner driving the cow along the high road from the well where she had been watering it — she had a stick in her hand and came tripping along in the jig-step, as if she were dancing. Her presence was bold and graceful, her cheeks flushed with health, and her countenance was free and gay. William finished his poem of *The Singing Bird*. In the meantime I read the remainder of Lessing. In the evening after tea William wrote *Alice Fell* — he went to bed tired, with a wakeful mind and a weary body. A very sharp clear night.

[*March 13th*,] *Saturday Morning*. It was as cold as ever it has been all winter, very hard frost. I baked pies bread and seed cake for Mr. Simpson. William finished *Alice Fell*, and then he wrote the poem of *The Beggar Woman*, taken from a woman whom I had seen in May (now nearly 2 years ago) when John and he were at Gallow Hill. I sate with him at intervals all the morning, took down his stanzas, etc. After dinner we walked to Rydale for letters — it was terribly cold — we had 2 or 3 brisk hail showers — the hail stones looked clean

---

[1] First published in 1807, under the title *The Sailor's Mother*.

and pretty upon the dry clean road. Little Peggy Simpson was standing at the door catching the hail stones in her hand — she grows very like her mother. When she is sixteen years old I dare say that to her Grandmother's eye she will seem as like to what her mother was, as any rose in her garden is like the rose that grew there years before. No letters at Rydale. We drank tea as soon as we reached home. After tea I read to William that account of the little boy belonging to the tall woman, and an unlucky thing it was, for he could not escape from those very words, and so he could not write the poem. He left it unfinished, and went tired to bed. In our walk from Rydale he had got warmed with the subject, and had half cast the poem.

[*March 14th*,] *Sunday Morning*. William had slept badly — he got up at nine o'clock, but before he rose he had finished *The Beggar Boys*, and while we were at breakfast that is (for I had breakfasted) he, with his basin of broth before him untouched, and a little plate of bread and butter he wrote the Poem to a Butterfly! He ate not a morsel, nor put on his stockings, but sate with his shirt neck unbuttoned, and his waistcoat open while he did it. The thought first came upon him as we were talking about the pleasure we both always feel at the sight of a butterfly. I told him that I used to chase them a little, but that I was afraid of brushing the dust off their wings, and did not catch them. He told me how they used to kill all the white ones when he went to school because they were Frenchmen. Mr. Simpson came in just as he was finishing the Poem. After he was gone I wrote it down and the other poems, and I read them all over to him. We then called at Mr. Olliff's — Mr. O. walked with us to within sight of Rydale — the sun shone very pleasantly, yet it was extremely cold. We dined and then Wm. went to bed. I lay upon the fur gown before the fire, but I could not sleep — I lay there a long time. It is now halfpast 5 — I am going to write letters — I began to write to Mrs. Rawson. William rose without having slept — we sate comfortably by the fire till he began to try to alter *The Butterfly*, and tired himself — he went to bed tired.

[*March 15th*,] *Monday Morning*. We sate reading the poems,

and I read a little German. Mr. Luff came in at one o'clock.
He had a long talk with William — he went to Mr. Olliff's after
dinner and returned to us to tea. During his absence a sailor
who was travelling from Liverpool to Whitehaven called ;
he was faint and pale when he knocked at the door — a young
man very well dressed. We sate by the kitchen fire talking
with him for 2 hours. He told us interesting stories of his life.
His name was Isaac Chapel. He had been at sea since he was
15 years old. He was by trade a sail-maker. His last voyage
was to the coast of Guinea. He had been on board a slave
ship, the captain's name Maxwell, where one man had been
killed, a boy put to lodge with the pigs and was half eaten,
one boy set to watch in the hot sun till he dropped down
dead. He had been cast away in North America and had
travelled thirty days among the Indians, where he had been
well treated. He had twice swum from a King's ship in the
night and escaped. He said he would rather be in hell than be
pressed. He was now going to wait in England to appear
against Captain Maxwell. " O he's a Rascal, Sir, he ought to
be put in the papers ! " The poor man had not been in bed
since Friday night. He left Liverpool at 2 o'clock on Saturday
morning ; he had called at a farm house to beg victuals and
had been refused. The woman said she would give him nothing.
" Won't you ? Then I can't help it." He was excessively like
my brother John. A letter was brought us at tea time by
John Dawson from M. H. I wrote to her, to Sara about
Mr. Olliff's gig, and to Longman and Rees — I wrote to Mrs.
Clarkson by Mr. Luff.

[*March 16th,*] *Tuesday.* A very fine morning. Mrs. Luff
called — William went up into the orchard while she was here
and wrote a part of *The Emigrant Mother.* After dinner I read
him to sleep. I read Spenser while he leaned upon my shoulder.
We walked to look at Rydale. Then we walked towards
Goan's.[1] The moon was a good height above the mountains.
She seemed far and distant in the sky ; there were two stars
beside her, that twinkled in and out, and seemed almost like

---

[1] *i.e.* Goan Mackereth.

Helm Crag
from the old road to Grasmere

The Road over White Moss, looking North

From a pencil drawing by T. L. Aspland. 1849

butterflies in motion and lightness. They looked to be far nearer to us than the moon.

[*March 17th,*] *Wednesday.* William went up into the orchard and finished the Poem. Mrs. Luff and Mrs. Olliff called. I went with Mrs. O. to the top of the White Moss — Mr. O. met us and I went to their house — he offered me manure for the garden. I went and sate with W. and walked backwards and forwards in the orchard till dinner time. He read me his poem. I broiled beefsteaks. After dinner we made a pillow of my shoulder — I read to him and my Beloved slept. I afterwards got him the pillows, and he was lying with his head on the table when Miss Simpson came in. She stayed tea. I went with her to Rydale — no letters ! A sweet evening as it had been a sweet day, a grey evening, and I walked quietly along the side of Rydale Lake with quiet thoughts — the hills and the lake were still — the Owls had not begun to hoot, and the little birds had given over singing. I looked before me and I saw a red light upon Silver How as if coming out of the vale below,

> *There was a light of most strange birth,*
> *A light that came out of the earth,*
> *And spread along the dark hill-side.*

Thus I was going on when I saw the shape of my Beloved in the road at a little distance. We turned back to see the light but it was fading — almost gone. The owls hooted when we sate on the wall at the foot of White Moss ; the sky broke more and more, and we saw the moon now and then. John Green passed us with his cart — we sate on. When we came in sight of our own dear Grasmere, the vale looked fair and quiet in the moonshine, the Church was there and all the cottages. There were huge slow-travelling clouds in the sky, that threw large masses of shade upon some of the mountains. We walked backwards and forwards, between home and Olliff's, till I was tired. William kindled, and began to write the poem. We carried cloaks into the orchard, and sate a while there. I left him, and he nearly finished the poem. I was tired to death, and went to bed before him — he came down to me, and read the poem to me in bed. A sailor begged here to-day, going to Glasgow. He spoke chearfully in a sweet tone.

[*March 18th,*] *Thursday.* A very fine morning. The sun shone, but it was far colder than yesterday. I felt myself weak and William charged me not to go to Mrs. Lloyd's. I seemed indeed to myself unfit for it, but when he was gone I thought I would get the visit over if I could, so I ate a beefsteak thinking it would strengthen me ; so it did, and I went off. I had a very pleasant walk — Rydale vale was full of life and motion. The wind blew briskly, and the lake was covered all over with bright silver waves, that were there each the twinkling of an eye, then others rose up and took their place as fast as they went away. The rocks glittered in the sunshine, the crows and the ravens were busy, and the thrushes and little birds sang. I went through the fields, and sate ½ an hour afraid to pass a cow. The cow looked at me, and I looked at the cow, and whenever I stirred the cow gave over eating. I was not very much tired when I reached Lloyd's — I walked in the garden — Charles is all for agriculture — Mrs. L. in her kindest way. A parcel came in from Birmingham, with Lamb's play for us, and for C. They came with me as far as Rydale. As we came along Ambleside vale in the twilight it was a grave evening. There was something in the air that compelled me to serious thought — the hills were large, closed in by the sky. It was nearly dark when I parted from the Lloyds, that is night was come on, and the moon was overcast. But, as I climbed Moss,[1] the moon came out from behind a mountain mass of black clouds. O, the unutterable darkness of the sky, and the earth below the moon ! and the glorious brightness of the moon itself ! There was a vivid sparkling streak of light at this end of Rydale water, but the rest was very dark, and Loughrigg Fell and Silver How were white and bright, as if they were covered with hoar frost. The moon retired again, and appeared and disappeared several times before I reached home. Once there was no moonlight to be seen but upon the island-house and the promontory of the

---

[1] *i.e.* White Moss Common.

island where it stands. " That needs must be a holy place ",
etc. etc. I had many very exquisite feelings, and when I saw
this lowly Building in the waters, among the dark and lofty
hills, with that bright, soft light upon it, it made me more
than half a poet. I was tired when I reached home, and could
not sit down to reading, and tried to write verses, but alas !
I gave up expecting William, and went soon to bed. Fletcher's
carts came home late.

[*March* 19*th*,] *Friday*. A very rainy morning. I went up
into the lane to collect a few green mosses to make the chimney
gay against my darling's return. Poor C., I did not wish for,
or expect him, it rained so. Mr. Luff came in before my dinner.
We had a long talk. He left me before 4 o'clock, and about
half an hour after Coleridge came in — his eyes were a little
swollen with the wind. I was much affected with the sight of
him, he seemed half stupefied. William came in soon after.
Coleridge went to bed late, and William and I sate up till
four o'clock. A letter from Sara sent by Mary. They disputed
about Ben Jonson. My spirits were agitated very much.

[*March* 20*th*,] *Saturday*. A tolerably fine morning after
11 o'clock but when I awoke the whole vale was covered with
snow. William and Coleridge walked to Borwick's. I followed but did not find them — came home and they were here.
We had a little talk about going abroad. We sate pleasantly
enough. After tea William read *The Pedlar*. After supper we
talked about various things — christening the children, etc. etc.
Went to bed at 12 o'clock.

[*March* 21*st*,] *Sunday*. A showery day. Coleridge and
William lay long in bed. We sent up to Mackareth's for the
horse to go to Keswick, but we could not have it. Went with
C. to Borwick's where he left us. William was very unwell this
evening. We had a sweet and tender conversation. I wrote
to Mary and Sara.

[*March* 22*nd*,] *Monday*. A rainy day. William very
poorly. Mr. Luff came in after dinner and brought us 2 letters
from Sara H. and one from poor Annette. I read Sara's letters
while he was here, I finished my letters to M. and S. and wrote
to my brother Richard. We talked a good deal about C. and

L.

other interesting things. We resolved to see Annette, and that Wm. should go to Mary. Wm. wrote to Coleridge not to expect us till Thursday or Friday.

[*March 23rd,*] *Tuesday.* A mild morning. William worked at *The Cuckow* poem. I sewed beside him. After dinner he slept, I read German, and, at the closing-in of day, went to sit in the orchard — he came to me, and walked backwards and forwards. We talked about C. Wm. repeated the poem to me. I left him there, and in 20 minutes he came in, rather tired with attempting to write. He is now reading Ben Jonson. I am going to read German. It is about 10 o'clock, a quiet night. The fire flutters, and the watch ticks. I hear nothing else save the breathing of my Beloved, and he now and then pushes his book forward, and turns over a leaf. Fletcher is not come home. No letter from C.

[*March 24th,*] *Wednesday.* We walked to Rydale for letters. It was a beautiful spring morning — warm, and quiet with mists. We found a letter from M. H. I made a vow that we would not leave this country for G. Hill [1]— Sara and Tom not being going to the Wolds. I wrote to Mary in the evening. I went to bed after dinner. William walked out and wrote [to] Peggy Ashburner — I rose better. Wm. altered *The Butterfly* as we came from Rydale.

[*March 25th,*] *Thursday.* We did not walk though it was a fine day — [? old] Mrs. Simpson drank tea with us. No letter from Coleridge.

[*March 26th,*] *Friday.* A beautiful morning. William wrote to Annette, then worked at *The Cuckow*. I was ill and in bad spirits — After dinner I sate 2 hours in the orchard. William and I walked together after tea, first to the top of White Moss, then to Mr. Olliff's. I left Wm. and while he was absent wrote out poems. I grew alarmed, and went to seek him — I met him at Mr. Olliff's. He has been trying, without success, to alter a passage — in *Silver How* poem. He had written a conclusion just before he went out. While I was getting into bed, he wrote *The Rainbow*.[2]

---

[1] Gallow Hill, Yorkshire, where the Hutchinsons were then farming.
[2] *i.e.* " My heart leaps up ", etc.

[*March 27th,*] *Saturday.* A divine morning. At breakfast William wrote part of an ode. Mr. Olliff sent the dung and Wm. went to work in the garden. We sate all day in the orchard.

[*March 28th,*] *Sunday.* We went to Keswick. Arrived wet to skin. A letter from Mary. C. was not tired with walking to meet us. I lay down after dinner with a bad headach.

[*March 29th,*] *Monday.* A cold day. I went down to Miss Crosthwaite's to unpack the box — Wm. and C. went to Armathwaite — a letter from S. H.— had headach, I lay till after tea. Conversation with Mrs. Coleridge.

March 30th, Tuesday. We went to Calvert's. I was somewhat better though not well.

March 31st, Wednesday. Very unwell. We walked to Portinscale, lay upon the turf, and saw into the Vale of Newlands up to Borrowdale, and down to Keswick — a soft Venetian view. I returned better. Calvert and Wilkinsons dined with us. I walked with Mrs. W. to the Quaker's meeting, met Wm., and we walked in the field together.

April 1st, Thursday. Mrs. C., Wm., C. and I went to the How — a pleasant morning. We came home by Portinscale — sate for some time on the hill.

[*April*] *2nd, Friday.* Wm. and I sate all the morning in the field. I nursed Derwent. Drank tea with the Miss Cockins.

[*April*] *3rd, Saturday.* Wm. went on to Skiddaw with C. We dined at Calvert's. Fine day.

[*April*] *4th, Sunday.* We drove in the gig to Water End — I walked down to Coleridge's. Mrs. C.[1] came to Greta Bank to tea. Wm. walked down with Mrs. C. I repeated his verses to them. We sate pleasantly enough after supper.

[*April*] *5th, Monday.* We came to Eusemere. Coleridge walked with us to Threlkeld—reached Eusemere to tea. The schoolmistress at Dacre and her scholars. Mrs. C. at work in the garden — she met us.

April 6th, Tuesday. Mrs. C., Wm. and I walked to Waterside. Wm. and I walked together in the evening towards Dalemain — the moon and stars.

---

[1] *i.e.* Mrs. Calvert.

[*April*] *7th, Wednesday*. Wm.'s birthday. Wm. went to Middleham. I walked 6 miles with him. It rained a little, but a fine day. Broth to supper, and went soon to bed.

[*April*] *8th, Thursday*. Mrs. C. and I walked to Woodside. We slept after dinner on the sofa — sate up till ½ past 10. Mrs. C. tired. I wrote to M. H. in the morning, to Sara in the evening.

[*April*] *9th, Friday*. Mrs. C. planting. Sent off letters. A windy morning — rough lake — sun shines — very cold — a windy night. Walked in Dunmallet, marked our names on a tree.

[*April*] *10th, Saturday*. Very cold — a stormy night, wrote to C. A letter from Wm. and S. H.

[*April*] *11th, Sunday*. Very stormy and cold. I did not walk.

[*April*] *12th, Monday*. Had the mantua-maker. The ground covered with snow. Walked to T. Wilkinson's and sent for letters. The woman brought me one from William and Mary. It was a sharp, windy night. Thomas Wilkinson came with me to Barton, and questioned me like a catechizer all the way. Every question was like the snapping of a little thread about my heart — I was so full of thought of my half-read letter and other things. I was glad when he left me. Then I had time to look at the moon while I was thinking over my own thoughts. The moon travelled through the clouds, tinging them yellow as she passed along, with two stars near her, one larger than the other. These stars grew or diminished as they passed from, or went into, the clouds. At this time William, as I found the next day, was riding by himself between Middleham and Barnard Castle, having parted from Mary. I read over my letter when I got to the house. Mr. and Mrs. C. were playing at cards.

April 13th, Tuesday. I had slept ill and was not well and obliged to go to bed in the afternoon — Mrs. C. waked me from sleep with a letter from Coleridge. After tea I went down to see the bank and walked along the Lakeside to the field where Mr. Smith thought of building his house. The air was become still, the lake was of a bright slate colour, the hills darkening.

The bays shot into the low fading shores. Sheep resting. All things quiet. When I returned Jane met me — *William* was come. The surprise shot through me. He looked well, but he was tired and went soon to bed after a dish of tea.

April 14th, Wednesday. William did not rise till dinner time. I walked with Mrs. C. I was ill, out of spirits, disheartened. Wm. and I took a long walk in the rain.

[*April*] 15*th, Thursday.* It was a threatening, misty morning, but mild. We set off after dinner from Eusemere. Mrs. Clarkson went a short way with us, but turned back. The wind was furious, and we thought we must have returned. We first rested in the large boat-house, then under a furze bush opposite Mr. Clarkson's. Saw the plough going in the field. The wind seized our breath. The Lake was rough. There was a boat by itself floating in the middle of the bay below Water Millock. We rested again in the Water Millock Lane. The hawthorns are black and green, the birches here and there greenish, but there is yet more of purple to be seen on the twigs. We got over into a field to avoid some cows — people working. A few primroses by the roadside — woodsorrel flower, the anemone, scentless violets, strawberries, and that starry, yellow flower which Mrs. C. calls pile wort. When we were in the woods beyond Gowbarrow Park we saw a few daffodils [1] close to the water-side. We fancied that the lake had floated the seeds ashore, and that the little colony had so sprung up. But as we went along there were more and yet more ; and at last, under the boughs of the trees, we saw that there was a long belt of them along the shore, about the breadth of a country turnpike road. I never saw daffodils so beautiful. They grew among the mossy stones about and about them ; some rested their heads upon these stones as on a pillow for weariness ; and the rest tossed and reeled and danced, and seemed as if they verily laughed with the wind, that blew upon them over the lake ; they looked so gay, ever glancing, ever changing. This wind blew directly over the lake to them. There was here and there a little knot, and a few stragglers a

---

[1] Cf. W.'s poem, " I wandered lonely as a cloud ".

few yards higher up ; but they were so few as not to disturb the simplicity, unity, and life of that one busy highway. We rested again and again.' The bays were stormy, and we heard the waves at different distances, and in the middle of the water, like the sea. Rain came on — we were wet when we reached Luff's, but we called in. Luckily all was chearless and gloomy, so we faced the storm — we *must* have been wet if we 'had waited — put on dry clothes at Dobson's. I was very kindly treated by a young woman, the landlady looked sour, but it is her way. She gave us a goodish supper, excellent ham and potatoes. We paid 7/- when we came away. William was sitting by a bright fire when I came downstairs. He soon made his way to the library, piled up in a corner of the window. He brought out a volume of Enfield's *Speaker*, another miscellany, and an odd volume of Congreve's plays. We had a glass of warm rum and water. We enjoyed ourselves, and wished for Mary. It rained and blew, when we went to bed. N.B. Deer in Gowbarrow Park like skeletons.

April 16th, Friday (Good Friday). When I undrew my curtains in the morning, I was much affected by the beauty of the prospect, and the change. The sun shone, the wind had passed away, the hills looked chearful, the river was very bright as it flowed into the lake. The church rises up behind a little knot of rocks, the steeple not so high as an ordinary three-story house. Trees in a row in the garden under the wall. After Wm. had shaved we set forward ; the valley is at first broken by little rocky woody knolls that make retiring places, fairy valleys in the vale ; the river winds along under these hills, travelling, not in a bustle but not slowly, to the lake. We saw a fisherman in the flat meadow on the other side of the water. He came towards us, and threw his line over the two-arched bridge. It is a bridge of a heavy construction, almost bending inwards in the middle, but it is grey, and there is a look of ancientry in the architecture of it that pleased me. As we go on the vale opens out more into one vale, with some-what of a cradle bed. Cottages, with groups of trees, on the side of the hills. We passed a pair of twin Children, 2 years old. Sate on the next bridge which we crossed — a single arch. We rested again upon the turf, and looked at the same bridge. We observed arches in the water, occasioned by the large stones sending it down in two streams. A sheep came plunging through the river, stumbled up the bank, and passed close to us, it had been frightened by an insignificant little dog on the other side. Its fleece dropped a glittering shower under its belly. Primroses by the road-side, pile wort that shone like stars of gold in the sun, violets, strawberries, retired and half-buried among the grass. When we came to the foot of Brothers Water, I left William sitting on the bridge, and went along the path on the right side of the Lake through the wood. I was delighted with what I saw. The water under the boughs of the bare old trees, the simplicity of the mountains, and the exquisite beauty of the path. There was one grey cottage. I repeated *The Glow-worm*,[1] as I walked along. I hung over the gate, and thought I could have stayed for ever. When I returned, I found William writing a poem descriptive of the sights and sounds we saw and heard.[2] There was the gentle flowing of the stream, the glittering, lively lake, green fields without a living creature to be seen on them, behind us, a flat pasture with 42 cattle feeding ; to our left, the road leading to the hamlet. No smoke there, the sun shone on the bare roofs. The people were at work ploughing, harrowing, and sowing ; lasses spreading dung, a dog's barking now and then, cocks crowing, birds twittering, the snow in patches at the top of the highest hills, yellow palms, purple and green twigs on the birches, ashes with their glittering spikes quite bare. The hawthorn a bright green, with black stems under the oak. The moss of the oak glossy. We then went on, passed two sisters at work (*they first passed us*), one with two pitchforks in her hand, the other had a spade. We had some talk with them. They laughed aloud after we were gone, perhaps half in wantonness, half boldness. William finished his poem [2] before we got to the foot of Kirkstone. There we ate our dinner. There were hundreds of cattle in the vale. The walk up Kirkstone was very interesting. The becks among the rocks were all alive.

---

[1] *i.e.* " Among all lovely things my Love had been ".
[2] *The Cock is crowing.*

Wm. showed me the little mossy streamlet which he had before loved when he saw its bright green track in the snow. The view above Ambleside very beautiful. There we sate and looked down on the green vale. We watched the crows at a little distance from us become white as silver as they flew in the sunshine, and when they went still further, they looked like shapes of water passing over the green fields. The whitening of Ambleside church is a great deduction from the beauty of it, seen from this point. We called at the Luffs, the Boddingtons there. Did not go in, and went round by the fields. I pulled off my stockings, intending to wade the beck, but I was obliged to put them on, and we climbed over the wall at the bridge. The post passed us. No letters ! Rydale Lake was in its own evening brightness : the Islands and Points distinct. Jane Ashburner came up to us when we were sitting upon the wall. We rode in her cart to Tom Dawson's.[1] All well. The garden looked pretty in the half-moonlight, half-daylight. As we went up the vale of Brother's Water more and more cattle feeding, 100 of them.

April 17th, Saturday. A mild warm rain. We sate in the garden all the morning. William dug a little. I transplanted a honey-suckle. The lake was still. The sheep on the island, reflected in the water, like the grey deer we saw in Gowbarrow Park. We walked after tea by moonlight. I had been in bed in the afternoon, and William had slept in his chair. We walked towards Rydale first, then backwards and forwards below Mr. Olliff's. The village was beautiful in the moonlight. Helm Crag we observed very distinct. The dead hedge round Benson's field bound together at the top by an interlacing of ash sticks, which made a chain of silver when we faced the moon. A letter from C. and also from S. H. I saw a robin chacing a scarlet butterfly this morning.

[April] 18th, *Sunday.* I lay in bed late, again a mild grey morning, with rising vapours. We sate in the orchard. William wrote the poem on *The Robin and the Butterfly.* I went to drink tea at Luff's, but as we did not dine till 6 o'clock it was late.

---

[1] *i.e.* How Top.

It was mist and small rain all the way, but very pleasant. William met me at Rydale — Aggie [1] accompanied me thither. We sate up late. He met me with the conclusion of the poem of the Robin. I read it to him in bed. We left out some lines.

[*April*] 19*th, Monday*. A mild rain, very warm. Wm. worked in the garden — I made pies and bread. After dinner the mist cleared away and sun shone. Wm. walked to Luff's — I was not very well and went to bed. Wm. came home pale and tired. I could not rest when I got to bed.

April 20*th, Tuesday*. A beautiful morning. The sun shone. William wrote a conclusion to the poem of the Butterfly — " I've watched you now a full half-hour ". I was quite out of spirits, and went into the orchard. When I came in, he had finished the poem. We sate in the orchard after dinner — it was a beautiful afternoon. The sun shone upon the level fields, and they grew greener beneath the eye. Houses, village, all chearful — people at work. We sate in the orchard and repeated *The Glow-worm* and other poems. Just when William came to a well or a trough, which there is in Lord Darlington's park, he began to write that poem of *The Glow-worm*, not being able to ride upon the long trot — interrupted in going through the town of Staindrop, finished it about 2 miles and a half beyond Staindrop. He did not feel the jogging of the horse while he was writing ; but, when he had done, he felt the effect of it, and his fingers were cold with his gloves. His horse fell with him on the other side of St. Helen's, Auckland. So much for *The Glow-worm*. It was written coming from Middleham on Monday, 12th April 1802. On Tuesday 20th, when we were sitting after tea, Coleridge came to the door. I startled Wm. with my voice. C. came up palish, but I afterwards found he looked well. William was not well, and I was in low spirits.

April 21*st, Wednesday*. William and I sauntered a little in the garden. Coleridge came to us, and repeated the verses he

---

[1] Agnes Ashburner.

wrote to Sara.[1] I was affected with them, and was on the whole, not being well, in miserable spirits. The sunshine, the green fields, and the fair sky made me sadder ; even the little happy, sporting lambs seemed but sorrowful to me. The pile wort spread out on the grass a thousand shining stars. The primroses were there, and the remains of a few daffodils. The well, which we cleaned out last night, is still but a little muddy pond, though full of water. I went to bed after dinner, could not sleep, went to bed again. Read Ferguson's life and a poem or two — fell asleep for 5 minutes and awoke better. We got tea, sate comfortably in the evening. I went to bed early.

April 22nd, Thursday. A fine mild morning — we walked into Easedale. The sun shone. Coleridge talked of his plan of sowing the laburnum in the woods. The waters were high, for there had been a great quantity of rain in the night. I was tired and sate under the shade of a holly tree that grows upon a rock, I sate there and looked down the stream. I then went to the single holly behind that single rock in the field, and sate upon the grass till they came from the waterfall. I saw them there, and heard Wm. flinging stones into the river, whose roaring was loud even where I was. When they returned, William was repeating the poem : " I have thoughts that are fed by the sun ". It had been called to his mind by the dying away of the stunning of the waterfall when he came behind a stone. When we had got into the vale heavy rain came on. We saw a family of little children sheltering themselves under a wall before the rain came on ; they sat in a row making a canopy for each other of their clothes. The servant lass was planting potatoes near them. Coleridge changed his clothes — we were all wet. Wilkinson came in while we were at dinner. Coleridge and I after dinner drank black currants and water.

April 23rd, 1802, *Friday.* It being a beautiful morning we set off at 11 o'clock, intending to stay out of doors all the morning. We went towards Rydale, and before we got to

---

[1] The poem published later as *Dejection,* but with several personal stanzas not published till 1937. *v. Essays and Studies by Members of the English Association,* Oxford, 1937.

Tom Dawson's we determined to go under Nab Scar. Thither we went. The sun shone and we were lazy. Coleridge pitched upon several places to sit down upon, but we could not be all of one mind respecting sun and shade, so we pushed on to the foot of the Scar. It was very grand when we looked up, very stony, here and there a budding tree. William observed that the umbrella yew tree, that breasts the wind, had lost its character as a tree, and had become something like to solid wood. Coleridge and I pushed on before. We left William sitting on the stones, feasting with silence ; and C. and I sat down upon a rocky seat — a couch it might be under the bower of William's eglantine, Andrew's Broom. He was below us, and we could see him. He came to us, and repeated his poems [1] while we sate beside him upon the ground. He had made himself a seat in the crumbling ground. After we had lingered long, looking into the vales,—Ambleside vale, with the copses, the village under the hill, and the green fields — Rydale, with a lake all alive and glittering, yet but little stirred by breezes, and our own dear Grasmere, first making a little round lake of nature's own, with never a house, never a green field, but the copses and the bare hills enclosing it, and the river flowing out of it. Above rose the Coniston Fells, in their own shape and colour — not man's hills, but all for themselves, the sky and the clouds, and a few wild creatures. C. went to search for something new. We saw him climbing up towards a rock. He called us, and we found him in a bower — the sweetest that was ever seen. The rock on one side is very high, and all covered with ivy, which hung loosely about, and bore bunches of brown berries. On the other side it was higher than my head. We looked down upon the Ambleside vale, that seemed to wind away from us, the village *lying* under the hill. The fir-tree island was reflected beautifully. We now first saw that the trees are planted in rows. About this bower there is mountain-ash, common-ash, yew-tree, ivy, holly, haw-thorn, mosses, and flowers, and a carpet of moss. Above, at the top of the rock, there is another spot — it is scarce a bower,

---

[1] *The Waterfall and the Eglantine* and *The Oak and the Broom.*

a little parlour on[ly], not *enclosed* by walls, but shaped out for a resting-place by the rocks, and the ground rising about it. It had a sweet moss carpet. We resolved to go and plant flowers in both these places to-morrow. We wished for Mary and Sara. Dined late. After dinner Wm. and I worked in the garden. C. read letter from Sara.

[*April*] 24*th*, *Saturday*. A very wet day. William called me out to see a waterfall behind the barberry tree. We walked in the evening to Rydale. Coleridge and I lingered behind. C. stopped up the little runner by the road-side to make a lake. We all stood to look at Glow-worm Rock — a primrose that grew there, and just looked out on the road from its own sheltered bower.[1] The clouds moved, as William observed, in one regular body like a multitude in motion — a sky all clouds over, not one cloud.[2] On our return it broke a little out, and we saw here and there a star. One appeared but for a moment in a lake [of] pale blue sky.

April 25*th*, *Sunday*. After breakfast we set off with Coleridge towards Keswick. Wilkinson overtook us near the Potter's, and interrupted our discourse. C. got into a gig with Mr. Beck, and drove away from us. A shower came on, but it was soon over. We spent the morning in the orchard — read the *Prothalamium* of Spenser ; walked backwards and forwards. Mr. Simpson drank tea with us. I was not well before tea. Mr. S. sent us some quills by Molly Ashburner, and his brother's book. The Luffs called at the door.

[*April*] 26*th*, *Monday*. I copied Wm.'s poems for Coleridge. Letters from Peggy[3] and Mary H. — wrote to Peggy and Coleridge. A terrible rain and wind all day — went to bed at 12 o'clock.

[*April*] 27*th*, *Tuesday*. A fine morning. Mrs. Luff called. I walked with her to the boat-house. William met me at the top of the hill with his fishing-rod in his hand. I turned with him, and we sate on the hill looking to Rydale. I left him, intending to join him, but he came home, and said his lines would not stand the pulling — he had had several bites. He sate in the orchard, I made bread. Miss Simpson called, I

---

[1] *v. The Primrose of the Rock.* [2] *v. To the Clouds,* and I. F. note.
[3] *i.e.* Margaret Ashburner ; *v.* Appendix, p. 433.

walked with her to Goan's. When I came back I found that he and John Fisher had cleaned out the well ; John had sodded about the bee-stand. In the evening Wm. began to write *The Tinker*. We had a letter and verses from Coleridge.

April 28th, Wednesday. A fine sunny but coldish morning. I copied *The Prioress's Tale*. Wm. was in the orchard. I went to him ; he worked away at his poem though he was ill and tired. I happened to say that when I was a child I would not have pulled a strawberry blossom. I left him, and wrote out *The Manciple's Tale*. At dinner time he came in with the poem of *Children gathering Flowers*,[1] but it was not quite finished, and it kept him long off his dinner. It is now done. He is working at *The Tinker*. He promised me he would get his tea, and do no more, but I have got mine an hour and a quarter, and he has scarcely begun his. I am not quite well. We have let the bright sun go down without walking. Now a heavy shower comes on, and I guess we shall not walk at all. I wrote a few lines to Coleridge. Then we walked backwards and forwards between our house and Olliff's. We talked about T. Hutchinson, and Bell Addison. William left me sitting on a stone. When we came in we corrected the Chaucers, but I could not finish them to-night. Went to bed.

[April] 29th, Thursday. A beautiful morning — the sun shone and all was pleasant. We sent off our parcel to Coleridge by the waggon. Mr. Simpson heard the Cuckow to-day. Before we went out, after I had written down *The Tinker*, which William finished this morning, Luff called — he was very lame, limped into the kitchen. He came on a little pony. We then went to John's Grove, sate a while at first. Afterwards William lay, and I lay, in the trench under the fence — he with his eyes shut, and listening to the waterfalls and the birds. There was no one waterfall above another — it was a sound of waters in the air — the voice of the air. William heard me breathing and rustling now and then, but we both lay still, and unseen by one another ; he thought that it would be as sweet thus to lie so in the grave, to hear the *peaceful*

---

[1] *i.e. Foresight.*

sounds of the earth, and just to know that our dear friends were near. The lake was still ; there was a boat out. Silver How reflected with delicate purple and yellowish hues, as I have seen spar ; lambs on the island, and running races together by the half-dozen, in the round field near us. The copses greenish, hawthorns green. Came home to dinner, then went to Mr. Simpson — we rested a long time under a wall, sheep and lambs were in the field — cottages smoking. As I lay down on the grass, I observed the glittering silver line on the ridge of the backs of the sheep, owing to their situation respecting the sun, which made them look beautiful, but with something of strangeness, like animals of another kind, as if belonging to a more splendid world. Met old Mrs. S. at the door — Mrs. S. poorly. I got mullins and pansies. I was sick and ill and obliged to come home soon. We went to bed immediately — I slept upstairs. The air coldish, where it was felt — somewhat frosty.

April 30th, Friday. We came into the orchard directly after breakfast, and sate there. The lake was calm, the day cloudy. We saw two fishermen by the lake side. William began to write the poem of *The Celandine.* I wrote to Mary H. sitting on the fur-gown. Walked backwards and forwards with William — he repeated his poem to me, then he got to work again and could not give over. He had not finished his dinner till 5 o'clock. After dinner we took up the fur **gown** into the Hollins above. We found a sweet seat, and thither we will often go. We spread the gown, put on each a cloak, and there we lay. William fell asleep — he had a bad headache owing to his having been disturbed the night before, with reading C.'s letter which Fletcher had brought to the door. I did not sleep, but I lay with half-shut eyes looking at the prospect as in a vision almost, I was so resigned [1] to it. Loughrigg Fell was the most distant hill ; then came the lake, slipping in between the copses, and above the copse the round swelling field ; nearer to me, a wild intermixture of rocks, trees, and

---

[1] " Resigned " is curiously used in the Lake District. A woman there once told me that Mr. Ruskin was " very much resigned to his own company ".— W. K. Cf. *Peter Bell,* l. 572.

slacks [1] of grassy ground. When we turned the corner of our little shelter, we saw the church and the whole vale. It is a blessed place. The birds were about us on all sides — skobbies, robins, bull-finches. Crows now and then flew over our heads, as we were warned by the sound of the beating of the air above. We stayed till the light of day was going, and the little birds had begun to settle their singing. But there was a thrush not far off, that seemed to sing louder and clearer than the thrushes had sung when it was quite day. We came in at 8 o'clock, got tea, wrote to Coleridge, and I wrote to Mrs. Clarkson part of a letter. We went to bed at 20 minutes past 11, with prayers that William might sleep well.

May 1st, Saturday. Rose not till half-past 8, a heavenly morning. As soon as breakfast was over, we went into the garden, and sowed the scarlet beans about the house. It was a clear sky, a heavenly morning.

I sowed the flowers, William helped me. We then went and sate in the orchard till dinner time. It was very hot. William wrote *The Celandine.* We planned a shed, for the sun was too much for us. After dinner we went again to our old resting-place in the Hollins under the rock. We first lay under a holly, where we saw nothing but the holly tree, and a budding elm [?], and the sky above our heads. But that holly tree had a beauty about it more than its own, knowing as we did where we were. When the sun had got low enough, we went to the rock shade. Oh, the overwhelming beauty of the vale below, greener than green ! Two ravens flew high, high in the sky, and the sun shone upon their bellies and their wings, long after there was none of his light to be seen but a little space on the top of Loughrigg Fell. We went down to tea at 8 o'clock, had lost the poem, and returned after tea. The landscape was fading : sheep and lambs quiet among the rocks. We walked towards King's,[2] and backwards and forwards. The sky was perfectly cloudless. N.B. Is it often so ? Three solitary stars in the middle of the blue vault, one or two on

---

[1] Slack, dialect for a small hollow, especially in a hillside.

[2] *i.e.* the house until a month or two before this occupied by the Olliffs : *v.* Appendix, p. 436.

the points of the high hills. Wm. wrote *The Celandine*, 2nd part, to-night. Heard the cuckow to-day, this first of May.[1]

May 2nd, Sunday. Again a heavenly morning. Letter from Coleridge.

May 4th, Tuesday. William had slept pretty well and though he went to bed nervous, and jaded in the extreme, he rose refreshed. I wrote *The Leech Gatherer* for him, which he had begun the night before, and of which he wrote several stanzas in bed this morning. It was very hot ; we called at Mr. Simpson's door as we passed, but did not go in. We rested several times by the way, read, and repeated *The Leech Gatherer*. We were almost melted before we were at the top of the hill. We saw Coleridge on the Wytheburn side of the water ; he crossed the beck to us. Mr. Simpson was fishing there. William and I ate a luncheon, then went on towards the waterfall. It is a glorious wild solitude under that lofty purple crag. It stood upright by itself. Its own self, and its shadow below, one mass — all else was sunshine. We went on further. A bird at the top of the crags was flying round and round, and looked in thinness and transparency, shape and motion like a moth. We climbed the hill, but looked in vain for a shade, except at the foot of the great waterfall, and there we did not like to stay on account of the loose stones above our heads. We came down, and rested upon a moss-covered rock, rising out of the bed of the river. There we lay, ate our dinner, and stayed there till about 4 o'clock or later. William and C. repeated and read verses. I drank a little brandy and water, and was in Heaven. The stag's horn is very beautiful and fresh, springing upon the fells. Mountain ashes, green. We drank tea at a farm house. The woman had not a pleasant countenance, but was civil enough. She had a pretty boy, a year old, whom she suckled. We parted from Coleridge at Sara's crag, after having looked at the letters which C. carved in the morning. I kissed them all. William deepened the T with C.'s pen-knife. We sate afterwards on the wall, seeing the sun go down, and the reflections in the still water. C.

---

[1] This sentence is written large, vertically across the page.

looked well, and parted from us chearfully, hopping up upon the side stones. On the Rays we met a woman with two little girls, one in her arms, the other, about four years old, walking by her side, a pretty little thing, but half-starved. She had on a pair of slippers that had belonged to some gentleman's child, down at the heels, but it was not easy to keep them on, but, poor thing! young as she was, she walked carefully with them; alas, too young for such cares and such travels. The mother, when we accosted her, told us that her husband had left her, and gone off with another woman, and how she "*pursued*" them. Then her fury kindled, and her eyes rolled about. She changed again to tears. She was a Cockermouth woman, thirty years of age — a child at Cockermouth when I was. I was moved, and gave her a shilling — I believe 6d. more than I ought to have given. We had the crescent moon with the " auld moon in her arms ".[1] We rested often, always upon the bridges. Reached home at about ten o'clock. The Lloyds had been here in our absence. We went soon to bed. I repeated verses to William while he was in bed; he was soothed, and I left him. " This is the spot" over and over again.

May 5th, Wednesday. A very fine morning, rather cooler than yesterday. We planted ¾ of the bower. I made bread. We sate in the orchard. The thrush sang all day, as he always sings. I wrote to the Hutchinsons, and to Coleridge — packed off *Thalaba*. William had kept off work till near bed-time, when we returned from our walk. Then he began again, and went to bed very nervous. We walked in the twilight, and walked till night came on. The moon had the old moon in her arms, but not so plain to be seen as the night before. When we went to bed it was a boat without the circle. I read *The Lover's Complaint* to Wm. in bed, and left him composed.

May 6th, Thursday. A sweet morning. We have put the finishing stroke to our bower, and here we are sitting in the orchard. It is one o'clock. We are sitting upon a seat under the wall, which I found my brother building up, when I came to him with his apple. He had intended that it should have

---

[1] From the *Ballad of Sir Patrick Spens*, quoted as heading to Coleridge's *Dejection*.

been done before I came. It is a nice, cool, shady spot. The small birds are singing, lambs bleating, cuckow calling, the thrush sings by fits, Thomas Ashburner's axe is going quietly (without passion) in the orchard, hens are cackling, flies humming, the women talking together at their doors, plumb and pear trees are in blossom — apple trees greenish — the opposite woods green, the crows are cawing. We have heard ravens. The ash trees are in blossom, birds flying all about us. The stitchwort is coming out, there is one budding lychnis, the primroses are passing their prime, celandine, violets, and wood sorrel for ever more, little geraniums and pansies on the wall. We walked in the evening to Tail End, to enquire about hurdles for the orchard shed and about Mr. Luff's flower. The flower dead ! no hurdles. I went on to look at the falling wood ; Wm. also, when he had been at Benson's, went with me. They have left a good many small oak trees but we dare not hope that they are all to remain. The ladies are come to Mr. Gell's cottage. We saw them as we went, and their light when we returned. When we came in we found a Magazine, and Review, and a letter from Coleridge with verses to Hartley, and Sara H. We read the review, etc. The moon was a perfect boat, a silver boat, when we were out in the evening. The birch tree is all over green in *small* leaf, more light and elegant than when it is full out. It bent to the breezes, as if for the love of its own delightful motions. Sloe-thorns and hawthorns in the hedges.

May 7th, Friday. William had slept uncommonly well, so, feeling himself strong, he fell to work at *The Leech Gatherer* [1] ; he wrote hard at it till dinner time, then he gave over, tired to death — he had finished the poem. I was making Derwent's frocks. After dinner we sate in the orchard. It was a thick, hazy, dull air. The thrush sang almost continually ; the little birds were more than usually busy with their voices. The sparrows are now full fledged. The nest is so full that they lie upon one another, they sit quietly in their nest with closed mouths. I walked to Rydale after tea, which we drank by the kitchen fire. The evening very dull—a terrible kind of threaten-

---

[1] *i.e. Resolution and Independence.*

ing brightness at sunset above Easedale. The sloe-thorn beautiful in the hedges, and in the wild spots higher up among the hawthorns. No letters. William met me. He had been digging in my absence, and cleaning the well. We walked up beyond Lewthwaites. A very dull sky ; coolish ; crescent moon now and then. I had a letter brought me from Mrs. Clarkson while we were walking in the orchard. I observed the sorrel leaves opening at about 9 o'clock. William went to bed tired with thinking about a poem.

May 8th, Saturday Morning. We sowed the scarlet beans in the orchard, and read *Henry V.* there. William lay on his back on the seat. I wept " For names, sounds, faiths, delights and duties lost " — taken from a poem upon Cowley's wish to retire to the Plantations. Read in the Review. I finished Derwent's frocks. After dinner William added a step to the orchard steps.

May 9th, Sunday Morning. The air considerably colder to-day, but the sun shone all day. William worked at *The Leech Gatherer* almost incessantly from morning till tea-time. I copied *The Leech Gatherer* and other poems for Coleridge. I was oppressed and sick at heart, for he wearied himself to death. After tea he wrote two stanzas in the manner of Thomson's *Castle of Indolence*, and was tired out. Bad news of Coleridge.

May 10th, Monday. A fine clear morning, but coldish. William is still at work, though it is past ten o'clock—he will be tired out, I am sure. My heart fails in me. He worked a little at odd things, but after dinner he gave over. An affecting letter from Mary H. We sate in the orchard before dinner. Old Joyce spent the day. I wrote to Mary H. Mrs. Jameson and Miss Simpson called just when William was going to bed at 8 o'clock. I wrote to Coleridge, sent off reviews and poems. Went to bed at 12 o'clock. William did not sleep till 3 o'clock.

May 11th, Tuesday. A cool air. William finished the stanzas about C. and himself. He did not go out to-day. Miss Simpson came in to tea, which was lucky enough, for it inter-rupted his labours. I walked with her to Rydale. The evening cool ; the moon only now and then to be seen ; the Lake purple as we went ; primroses still in abundance. William did not meet me. He completely finished his poems, I finished Derwent's frocks. We went to bed at 12 o'clock. Wm. pretty well — he looked very well — he complains that he gets cold in his chest.

May 12th, Wednesday. A sunshiny, but coldish morning. We walked into Easedale and returned by George Rawnson's and the lane. We brought home heckberry blossom, crab blossom, the anemone nemorosa, marsh marigold, speedwell, — that beautiful blue one, the colour of the blue-stone or glass used in jewellery — with its beautiful pearl-like chives. Anemones are in abundance, and still the dear dear primroses, violets in beds, pansies in abundance, and the little celandine. I pulled a bunch of the taller celandine. Butterflies of all colours. I often see some small ones of a pale purple lilac, or emperor's eye colour, something of the colour of that large geranium which grows by the lake side. Wm. observed the beauty of Geordy Green's [1] house. We see it from our Orchard. Wm. pulled ivy with beautiful berries — I put it over the chimney-piece. Sate in the orchard the hour before dinner, coldish. We have now dined. My head aches — William is sleeping in the window. In the evening we were sitting at the table, writing, when we were rouzed by Coleridge's voice below. He had walked ; looked palish, but was not much tired. We sate up till one o'clock, all together ; then William went to bed, and I sate with C. in the sitting-room (where he slept) till a ¼ past 2 o'clock. Wrote to M. H.

May 13th, Thursday. The day was very cold, with snow showers. Coleridge had intended going in the morning to Keswick, but the cold and showers hindered him. We went with him after tea as far as the plantations by the roadside descending to Wytheburn. He did not look very well when we parted from him. We sate an hour at Mrs. Simpson's.

May 14th, Friday. A very cold morning — hail and snow showers all day. We went to Brother's wood, intending to get plants, and to go along the shore of the lake to the foot. We did go a part of the way, but there was no pleasure in stepping

---

[1] *i.e.* Pavement End.

along that difficult sauntering road in this ungenial weather. We turned again, and walked backwards and forwards in Brother's wood. William teased himself with seeking an epithet for the cuckow. I sate a while upon my last summer seat, the mossy stone. William's, unemployed, beside me, and the space between, where Coleridge has so often lain. The oak trees are just putting forth yellow knots of leaves. The ashes with their flowers passing away, and leaves coming out. The blue hyacinth is not quite full blown ; gowans are coming out, marsh marigolds in full glory ; the little star plant, a star without a flower. We took home a great load of gowans, and planted them in the cold about the orchard. After dinner, I worked bread, then came and mended stockings beside William ; he fell asleep. After tea I walked to Rydale for letters. It was a strange night. The hills were covered over with a slight covering of hail or snow, just so as to give them a hoary winter look with the black rocks. The woods looked miserable, the coppices green as grass, which looked quite unnatural, and they seemed half shrivelled up, as if they shrank from the air. O, thought I ! what a beautiful thing God has made winter to be, by stripping the trees, and letting us see their shapes and forms. What a freedom does it seem to give to the storms ! There were several new flowers out, but I had no pleasure in looking at them. I walked as fast as I could back again with my letter from S. H. which I skimmed over at Tommy Fleming's. Met Wm. at the top of White Moss. We walked a little beyond Olliff's. Near 10 when we came in. Wm. and Molly had dug the ground and planted potatoes in my absence. We wrote to Coleridge ; sent off a letter to Annette, bread and frocks to the C.'s. Went to bed at ½-past 11. William very nervous. After he was in bed, haunted with altering *The Rainbow*.

May 15th, Saturday Morning. It is now ¼ past 10, and he is not up. Miss Simpson called when I was in bed. I have been in the garden. It looks fresh and neat in spite of the frost. Molly tells me they had thick ice on a jug at their door last night. A very cold and chearless morning. I sate mending stockings all the morning. I read in Shakespeare. William lay very late because he slept ill last night. It snowed this morning just like Christmas. We had a melancholy letter from Coleridge just at bed-time. It distressed me very much, and I resolved upon going to Keswick the next day.

[*The following is written on the blotting-paper opposite this date :*]

S. T. Coleridge.
Dorothy Wordsworth. William Wordsworth.
Mary Hutchinson. Sara Hutchinson.
William. Coleridge. Mary.
Dorothy. Sara.
16th May
1802.
John Wordsworth.

[May] 6th, Sunday. William was at work all the morning. I did not go to Keswick. A sunny, cold, frosty day. A snow-shower at night. We were a good while in the orchard in the morning.

May 17th, Monday. William was not well, he went with me to Wytheburn water. He left me in a post-chaise. Hail showers, snow, and cold attacked me. The people were graving peats under Nadel Fell. A lark and thrush singing near Coleridge's house. Bancrofts there. A letter from M. H.

May 18th, Tuesday. Terribly cold, Coleridge not well. Froude called, Wilkinsons called, I not well. C. and I walked in the evening in the garden. Warmer in the evening. Wrote to M. and S.

May 19th, Wednesday. A grey morning — not quite so cold. C. and I set off at ½-past 9 o'clock. Met William near the 6-mile stone. We sate down by the road-side, and then went to Wytheburn water. Longed to be at the island. Sate in the sun. Coleridge's bowels bad, mine also. We drank tea at John Stanley's. The evening cold and clear. A glorious light on Skiddaw. I was tired. Brought a cloak down from Mr. Simpson's. Packed up books for Coleridge, then got supper, and went to bed.

May 20th, Thursday. A frosty, clear morning. I lay in bed late. William got to work. I was somewhat tired. We sate in the orchard sheltered all the morning. In the evening there was a fine rain. We received a letter from Coleridge, telling us that he wished us not to go to Keswick.

May 21st, Friday. A very warm gentle morning, a little rain. William wrote two sonnets on Buonaparte, after I had read Milton's sonnets to him. In the evening he went with Mr. Simpson with Borwick's boat to gather ling in Bainriggs. I planted about the well, was much heated, and I think I caught cold.

May 22nd, Saturday. A very hot morning. A hot wind, as if coming from a sand desert. We met Coleridge. He was sitting under Sara's rock when we reached him. He turned with us. We sate a long time under the wall of a sheep-fold. Had some interesting melancholy talk about his private affairs. We drank tea at a farmhouse. The woman was very kind. There was a woman with 3 children travelling from Workington to Manchester. The woman served them liberally. Afterwards she said that she never suffered any to go away without a trifle " sec as we have ". The woman at whose house we drank tea the last time was rich and senseless — she said " she never served any but their own poor ". C. came home with us. We sate some time in the orchard. Then they came in to supper — mutton chops and potatoes. Letters from S. and M. H.

[May 23rd,] Sunday. I sate with C. in the orchard all the morning. I was ill in the afternoon, took laudanum. We walked in Bainriggs after tea. Saw the juniper — umbrella shaped. C. went to S. and M. Points,[1] joined us on White Moss.

May 24th, Monday. A very hot morning. We were ready to go off with Coleridge, but foolishly sauntered, and Miss Taylor and Miss Stanley called. William and Coleridge and I went afterwards to the top of the Rays.

I had sent off a letter to Mary by C. I wrote again, and to C. Then went to bed. William slept not till 5 o'clock.

[May] 25th, Tuesday. Very hot — I went to bed after dinner. We walked in the evening. Papers and short note from C. ; again no sleep for Wm.

---

[1] Mary Point and Sara Point ; the " two heath-clad rocks " referred to in the last of the *Poems on the Naming of Places.*

[*May*] 26*th, Wednesday*. I was very unwell — went to bed again after dinner. We walked a long time backwards and forwards between John's Grove and the lane upon the turf. A beautiful night, not cloudless. It has never been so since May day.

[*May*] 27*th, Thursday*. I was in bed all day — very ill. William wrote to Rd., Cr. and Cook. Wm. went after tea into the orchard. I slept in his bed — he slept downstairs.

[*May*] 28*th, Friday*. I was much better than yesterday, though poorly. William tired himself with hammering at a passage. After dinner he was better and I greatly better. We sate in the orchard. The sky cloudy, the air sweet and cool. The young bullfinches, in their party-coloured raiment, bustle about among the blossoms, and poize themselves like wire-dancers or tumblers, shaking the twigs and dashing off the blossoms. There is yet one primrose in the orchard. The stitchwort is fading. The wild columbines are coming into beauty, the vetches are in abundance, blossoming and seeding. That pretty little wavy-looking dial-like yellow flower, the speedwell, and some others, whose names I do not yet know. The wild columbines are coming into beauty—some of the gowans fading. In the garden we have lilies, and many other flowers. The scarlet beans are up in crowds. It is now between 8 and nine o'clock. It has rained sweetly for two hours and a half ; the air is very mild. The heckberry blossoms are dropping off fast, almost gone — barberries are in beauty — snowballs coming forward — May roses blossoming.

[*May*] 29*th, Saturday*. I was much better — I made bread and a wee rhubarb tart and batter pudding for William. We sate in the orchard after dinner. William finished his poem on going for Mary.[1] I wrote it out. I wrote to Mary H., having received a letter from her in the evening. A sweet day. We nailed up the honeysuckles, and hoed the scarlet beans.

May 30*th, Sunday*. I wrote to Mrs. Clarkson. It was a clear but cold day. The Simpsons called in the evening. I had been obliged to go to bed before tea, and was unwell all day.

---

1 *i.e. A Farewell.*

Gooseberries, a present from Peggy Hodgson. I wrote to my Aunt Cookson.

[*May*] 31*st*, *Monday*. I was much better. We sat out all day. Mary Jameson dined. I wrote out the poem on " Our Departure ",[1] which he seemed to have finished. In the evening Miss Simpson brought us a letter from M. H., and a complimentary and critical letter to W. from John Wilson of Glasgow,[2] post-paid. I went a little way with Miss S. My tooth broke today. They will soon be gone. Let that pass, I shall be beloved — I want no more.

[*June* 1*st*,] *Tuesday*. A very sweet day, but a sad want of rain. We went into the orchard before dinner, after I had written to M. H. Then on to Mr. Olliff's intakes. We found some torn birds nests. The columbine was growing upon the rocks ; here and there a solitary plant, sheltered and shaded by the tufts and bowers of trees. It is a graceful slender creature, a female seeking retirement, and growing freest and most graceful where it is most alone. I observed that the more shaded plants were always the tallest. A short note and gooseberries from Coleridge.

June 2*nd*, *Wednesday*. In the morning we observed that the scarlet beans were drooping in the leaves in great numbers, owing, we guess, to an insect. We sate awhile in the orchard — then we went to the old carpenter's about the hurdles. Yesterday an old man called, a grey-headed man, above 70 years of age. He said he had been a soldier, that his wife and children had died in Jamaica. He had a beggar's wallet over his shoulders ; a coat of shreds and patches, altogether of a drab colour ; he was tall, and though his body was bent, he had the look of one used to have been upright. I talked a while, and then gave him a piece of cold bacon and a penny. Said he, " You're a fine woman ! " I could not help smiling ; I suppose he meant, " You're a kind woman ". Afterwards a woman called, travelling to Glasgow. After dinner we went into Frank's field, crawled up the little glen, and planned a seat, then went to Mr. Olliff's Hollins and sate there — found a beautiful

---

[1] *i.e. A Farewell.*   [2] *v. E.L.* p. 292.

shell-like purple fungus in Frank's field. After tea we walked to Butterlip How, and backwards and forwards there. All the young oak tree leaves are dry as powder. A cold south wind, portending rain. I ought to have said that on Tuesday evening, namely June 1st, we walked upon the turf near John's Grove. It was a lovely night. The clouds of the western sky reflected a saffron light upon the upper end of the lake. All was still. We went to look at Rydale. There was an Alpine, fire-like red upon the tops of the mountains. This was gone when we came in view of the lake. But we saw the Lake in a new and most beautiful point of view, between two little rocks, and behind a small ridge that had concealed it from us. This White Moss, a place made for all kinds of beautiful works of art and nature, woods and valleys, fairy valleys and fairy tarns, miniature mountains, alps above alps. Little John Dawson came in from the woods with a stick over his shoulder.

June 3rd, 1802, *Thursday.* A very fine rain. I lay in bed till ten o'clock. William much better than yesterday. We walked into Easedale — sheltered in a cow-house — came home wet. The cuckow sang, and we watched the little birds as we sate at the door of the cow-house. The oak copses are brown, as in autumn, with the late frosts — scattered over with green trees, birches or hazels. The ashes are coming into full leaf, some of them injured. We came home quite wet. We have been reading the life and some of the writings of poor Logan [1] since dinner. "And everlasting longings for the lost." It is an affecting line. There are many affecting lines and passages in his poem. William is now sleeping, with the window open, lying on the window seat. The thrush is singing. There are, I do believe, a thousand buds on the honeysuckle tree, all small and far from blowing, save one that is retired behind the twigs close to the wall, and as snug as a bird's nest. John's rose tree is very beautiful, blended with the honeysuckle.

On Tuesday evening when we were among the rocks we saw

---

[1] John Logan (1747–88), Scottish poet, author of *The Braes of Yarrow*. The line which D. W. quotes is from his *Ode written on a Visit to the Country in Autumn*. Logan was the reputed author of the poem *To the Cuckoo*, now attributed to Michael Bruce.

in the woods what seemed to be a man resting or looking about him — he had a piece of wood near him. William was on before me when we returned and as I was going up to him I found that this supposed man was John Dawson. I spoke to him and I suppose he thought I asked him what my Brother had said to him before, for he replied : '' *William* asks me how my head is ''. Poor fellow — he says it is worse and worse, and he walks as if he were afraid of putting his body in motion.

Yesterday morning William walked as far as the Swan with Aggy Fisher. She was going to attend upon Goan's [1] dying infant. She said, " There are many heavier crosses than the death of an infant " ; and went on, " There was a woman in this vale who buried 4 grown-up children in one year, and I have heard her say, when many years were gone by, that she had more pleasure in thinking of those 4 than of her living children, for as children get up and have families of their own, their duty to their parents ' *wears out and weakens* '. She could trip lightly by the graves of those who died when they were young with a light step, as she went to church on a Sunday."

We walked while dinner was getting ready up into Mr. King's Hollins. I was weak and made my way down alone, for Wm. took a difficult way. After dinner we walked upon the turf path — a showery afternoon. A very affecting letter came from M. H., while I was sitting in the window reading Milton's *Penseroso* to William. I answered this letter before I went to bed.

June 4th, Friday. It was a very sweet morning. There had been much rain in the night. Dined late. In the evening we walked on our favourite path.[2] Then we came in and sate in the orchard. The evening was dark and warm — a tranquil night. I left William in the orchard. I read *Mother Hubbard's Tale* before I went to bed.

---

[1] *i.e.* Goan Mackereth.

[2] The path is still traceable. Starting from the Wishing Gate road immediately under Dry Close it skirts the E. wall of John's Grove till the highest point of the latter is reached ; then it bears away to the left and skirts the hillside till it joins the road opposite White Moss Tarn. It commands beautiful views, and is at first fairly level, and would be sheltered in the days when John's Grove *was* a grove.—G. G. W.

[June] 5th, Saturday. A fine showery morning. I made both pies and bread ; but we first walked into Easedale, and sate under the oak trees, upon the mossy stones. There were one or two slight showers. The gowans were flourishing along the banks of the stream. The strawberry flower (Geum) hanging over the brook — all things soft and green. In the afternoon William sate in the orchard. I went there, was tired, and fell asleep. Mr. Simpson drank tea, Mrs. Smith called with her daughter. We began the letter to John Wilson.[1]

June 6th, Sunday. A showery morning. We were writing the letter to John Wilson when Ellen [2] came. Molly at Goan's child's funeral. After dinner I walked into John Fisher's intake with Ellen. She brought us letters from Coleridge, Mrs. Clarkson, and Sara Hutchinson. William went out in the evening and sate in the orchard, it was a showery day. In the evening there was one of the heaviest showers I ever remember.

June 7th, Monday. I wrote to Mary H. this morning, sent the C. Indolence poem. Copied the letter to John Wilson, and wrote to my brother Richard and Mrs. Coleridge. In the evening I walked with Ellen to Butterlip How and to George Mackareth's for the horse. It was a very sweet evening ; there was the cuckow and the little birds ; the copses still injured, but the trees in general looked most soft and beautiful in tufts. William was walking when we came in — he had slept miserably for 2 nights past, so we all went to bed soon. I went with Ellen in the morning to Rydale Falls. Letters from Annette, Mary H. and Cook.

June 8th, Tuesday. Ellen and I rode to Windermere. We had a fine sunny day, neither hot nor cold. I mounted the horse at the quarry. We had no difficulties or delays but at the gates. I was enchanted with some of the views. From the High Ray the view is very delightful, rich, and festive, water and wood, houses, groves, hedgerows, green fields, and mountains ; white houses, large and small. We passed 2 or 3 nice-looking statesmen's houses. Mr. Curwen's shrubberies

---

[1] *v.* May 31, *supra.*   [2] A servant of Mrs. Clarkson at Eusemere.

looked pitiful enough under the native trees. We put up our horses, ate our dinner by the water-side, and walked up to the Station. Then we went to the Island, walked round it, and crossed the lake with our horse in the ferry. The shrubs have been cut away in some parts of the island. I observed to the boatman that I did not think it improved. He replied : " We think it is, for one could hardly see the house before ". It seems to me to be, however, no better than it was. They have made no natural glades ; it is merely a lawn with a few miserable young trees, standing as if they were half-starved. There are no sheep, no cattle upon these lawns. It is neither one thing or another — neither *natural*, nor wholly cultivated and artificial, which it was before. And that great house ! Mercy upon us ! if it *could* be concealed, it *would* be well for all who are not pained to see the pleasantest of earthly spots deformed by man. But it *cannot* be covered. Even the tallest of our old oak trees would not reach to the top of it. When we went into the boat, there were two men standing at the landing-place. One seemed to be about 60, a man with a jolly red face ; he looked as if he might have lived many years in Mr. Curwen's house. He wore a blue jacket and trowsers, as the people who live close by Windermere, particularly at the places of chief resort, in affectation, I suppose. He looked significantly at our boatman just as we were rowing off, and said, " Thomas, mind you take off the directions off that cask. You know what I mean. It will serve as a blind for them, *you* know. It was a blind business, both for you, and the coachman, and me and all of us. Mind you take off the directions. A wink's as good as a nod with some folks " ; and then he turned round, looking at his companion with such an air of self-satisfaction, and deep insight into unknown things ! I could hardly help laughing outright at him. Laburnums blossom freely at the island, and in the shrubberies on the shore — they are blighted everywhere else. Roses of various sorts now out. The brooms were in full glory everywhere, " veins of gold " among the copses. The hawthorns in the valley fading away — beautiful upon the hills. We reached home at 3 o'clock. After tea William went out and walked and wrote that poem, " The sun has long been set ", etc.[1] He first went up to G. Mackareth's with the horse, afterwards he walked on our own path and wrote the lines ; he called me into the orchard, and there repeated them to me — he then stayed there till 11 o'clock.

June 9th, Wednesday. Wm. slept ill. A soaking all day rain. We should have gone to Mr. Simpson's to tea but we walked up after tea. Lloyds called. The hawthorns on the mountain sides like orchards in blossom. Brought rhubarb down. It rained hard. Ambleside fair. I wrote to Christr. and M. H.

June 10th, Thursday. I wrote to Mrs. Clarkson and Luff — went with Ellen to Rydale. Coleridge came in with a sack full of books, etc., and a branch of mountain ash. He had been attacked by a cow. He came over by Grisdale. A furious wind. Mr. Simpson drank tea. William very poorly — we went to bed latish — I slept in sitting room.

June 11th, Friday. A wet day. William had slept very ill. Wm. and C. walked out. I went to bed after dinner, not well. I was tired with making beds, cooking etc., Molly being very ill.

June 12th, Saturday. A rainy morning. C. set off before dinner. We went with him to the Rays, but it rained, so we went no further. Sheltered under a wall. He would be sadly wet, for a furious shower came on just when we parted. We got no dinner, but gooseberry pie to our tea. I baked both pies and bread, and walked with William, first on our own path, but it was too wet there, next over the rocks to the road, and backward and forward, and last of all up to Mr. King's. Miss Simpson and Robert had called. Letters from Sara and Annette.

June 13th, Sunday. A fine morning. Sunshiny and bright, but with rainy clouds. William had slept better but not well, he has been altering the poem to Mary this morning, he is now washing his feet. I wrote out poems for our journey and I wrote a letter to my Uncle Cookson. Mr. Simpson came when we were in the orchard in the morning, and brought us a beautiful drawing which he had done. In the evening we walked, first on our own path — there we walked a good while. It was a silent night. The stars were out by ones and twos,

---

[1] *Evening Voluntaries*, viii.

but no cuckow, no little birds, the air was not warm, and we have observed that since Tuesday, 8th, when William wrote, " The sun has long been set ", that we have had no birds singing after the evening is fairly set in. We walked to our new view of Rydale, but it put on a sullen face. There was an owl hooting in Bainriggs. Its first halloo was so like a human shout that I was surprized, when it made its second call tremulous and lengthened out, to find that the shout had come from an owl. The full moon (not quite full) was among a company of steady island clouds, and the sky bluer about it than the natural sky blue. William observed that the full moon, above a dark fir grove, is a fine image of the descent of a superior being. There was a shower which drove us into John's Grove before we had quitted our favourite path. We walked upon John's path before we went to view Rydale. We went to bed immediately upon our return home.

June 14th, Monday. I was very unwell — went to bed before I drank my tea — was sick and afterwards almost asleep when William brought me a letter from Mary, which he read to me sitting by the bed-side. Wm. wrote to Mary and Sara about *The Leech Gatherer*,[1] I wrote to both of them in one and to Annette, to Coleridge also. I was better after tea — I walked with Wm. when I had put up my parcel, on our own path. We were driven away by the horses that go on the commons ; then we went to look at Rydale, walked a little in the fir grove, went again to the top of the hill, and came home. A mild and sweet night. William stayed behind me. I threw him the cloak out of the window. The moon overcast. He sate a few minutes in the orchard, came in sleepy, and hurried to bed. I carried him his bread and butter.

[June] 15th, Tuesday. A sweet grey, mild morning. The birds sing soft and low. William has not slept all night. It wants only 10 minutes of 10, and he is in bed yet. After William rose we went and sate in the orchard till dinner time. We walked a long time in the evening upon our favourite path ; the owls hooted, the night hawk sang to itself incessantly, but

---

[1] *v. E.L.* pp. 305-7.

there were no little birds, no thrushes. I left William writing a few lines about the night-hawk [1] and other images of the evening, and went to seek for letters. None were come. We walked backwards and forwards a little, after I returned to William, and then up as far as Mr. King's. Came in. There was a basket of lettuces, a letter from M. H. about the delay of mine, and telling of one she had sent by the other post, one from Wade, and one from Sara to C. William did not read them. M. H. growing fat.

June 16th, Wednesday. We walked towards Rydale for letters — met Frank Batey with the expected one from Mary. We went up into Rydale woods and read it there. We sate near an old wall, which fenced a hazel grove, which Wm. said was exactly like the filbert grove at Middleham. It is a beautiful spot, a sloping or rather steep piece of ground, with hazels growing "tall and erect" in clumps at distances, almost seeming regular, as if they had been planted. We returned to dinner. I wrote to Mary after dinner, while William sate in the orchard. Old Mr. Simpson drank tea with us. When Mr. S. was gone I read my letter to William, speaking to Mary about having a cat. I spoke of the little birds keeping us company, and William told me that that very morning a bird had perched upon his leg. He had been lying very still, and had watched this little creature, it had come under the bench where he was sitting, and then flew up to his leg ; he thoughtlessly stirred himself to look further at it, and it flew on to the apple tree above him. It was a little young creature, that had just left its nest, equally unacquainted with man, and unaccustomed to struggle against storms and winds. While it was upon the apple tree the wind blew about the stiff boughs, and the bird seemed bemazed, and not strong enough to strive with it. The swallows come to the sitting-room window as if wishing to build, but I am afraid they will not have courage for it, but I believe they will build in my room window. They twitter, and make a bustle and a little chearful song, hanging against the panes of glass, with their soft white bellies close to the

---

[1] Probably a first draft of lines afterwards used for the opening of *The Waggoner*.

glass, and their forked fish-like tails. They swim round and round, and again they come. It was a sweet evening. We first walked to the top of the hill to look at Rydale, then to Butterlip How. I do not now see the brownness that was in the coppices. The lower hawthorn blossoms passed away. Those on the hills are a faint white. The wild guelder-rose is coming out, and the wild roses. I have seen no honey-suckles yet, except our own one nestling, and a tree of the yellow kind at Mrs. Townley's the day I went with Ellen to Windermere. Foxgloves are now frequent, the first I saw was that day with Ellen and the first ripe strawberries. William went to bed immediately.

[June] 17th, Thursday. William had slept well. I took castor oil and lay in bed till 12 o'clock. William injured himself with working a little. When I got up we sate in the orchard — a sweet mild day. Miss Hudson called — I went with her to the top of the hill. When I came home I found William at work attempting to alter a stanza in the poem on our going for Mary, which I convinced him did not need altering. We sate in the house after dinner. In the evening walked on our favourite path. A short letter from Coleridge. William added a little to the Ode he is writing.[1]

June 18th, Friday. When we were sitting after breakfast — William about to shave — Luff came in. It was a sweet morning — he had rode over the Fells. He brought news about Lord Lowther's intention to pay all debts, etc., and a letter from Mr. Clarkson. He saw our garden, was astonished at the scarlet beans, etc. etc. When he was gone, we wrote to Coleridge, M. H., and my brother Richard about the affair. William determined to go to Eusemere on Monday. In the afternoon we walked to Rydale with our letters — found no letters there. A sweet evening. I had a woful headache, and was ill in stomach from agitation of mind — went to bed at nine o'clock, but did not sleep till late.

[June] 19th, Saturday. The swallows were very busy under my window this morning. I slept pretty well, but William has got no sleep. It is after 11 and he is still in bed. A fine morning.

---

[1] Doubtless the *Ode, Intimations of Immortality.*—W. K.

Coleridge, when he was last here, told us that for many years, there being no Quaker meeting held at Keswick, a single old Quaker woman used to go regularly alone every Sunday to attend the meeting-house, and there used to sit and perform her worship, alone in that beautiful place among those fir trees, in that spacious vale, under the great mountain Skiddaw ! ! ! Poor old Willy [1] — we never pass by his grave close to the Churchyard gate without thinking of him and having his figure brought back to our minds. He formerly was an ostler at Hawkshead having spent a little estate. In his old age he was boarded or as they say *let* by the parish. A boy of the house that hired him was riding one morning pretty briskly beside John Fisher's — " Hullo ! has aught particular happened ? " said John to the boy — " Nay, naught at aw, nobbut auld Willy's dead." He was going to order the passing bell to be tolled. On Thursday morning Miss Hudson of Workington called. She said, " O ! I love flowers ! I sow flowers in the parks several miles from home, and my mother and I visit them, and watch them how they grow." This may show that botanists may be often deceived when they find rare flowers growing far from houses. This was a very ordinary young woman, such as in any town in the North of England one may find a score. I sate up a while after William — he then called me down to him. (I was writing to Mary H.) I read Churchill's *Rosciad*. Returned again to my writing, and did not go to bed till he called to me. The shutters were closed, but I heard the birds singing. There was our own thrush, shouting with an impatient shout — so it sounded to me. The morning was still, the twittering of the little birds was very gloomy. The owls had hooted a $\frac{1}{4}$ of an hour before, now the cocks were crowing. It was near daylight, I put out my candle, and went to bed. In a little time I thought I heard William snoring, so I composed myself to sleep. Charles Lloyd called. [?] at my sweet Brother.

June 20*th, Sunday.* He had slept better than I could have expected, but he was far from well all day ; we were in the

---

[1] Possibly " the poor Pensioner " of *The Excursion*, v, 880-90.—G. G. W.

orchard a great part of the morning. After tea we walked upon our own path for a long time. We talked sweetly together about the disposal of our riches. We lay upon the sloping turf. Earth and sky were so lovely that they melted our very hearts. The sky to the north was of a chastened yet rich yellow, fading into pale blue, and streaked and scattered over with steady islands of purple, melting away into shades of pink. It made my heart almost feel like a vision to me. We afterwards took our cloaks and sate in the orchard. Mr. and Miss Simpson called. We told them of our expected good fortune.[1] We were astonished and somewhat hurt to see how coldly Mr. Simpson received it — Miss S. seemed very glad. We went into the house when they left us, and Wm. went to bed. I sate up about an hour. He then called me to talk to him — he could not fall asleep. I wrote to Montagu.

[*June*] *21st, Monday.* William was obliged to be in bed late, he had slept so miserably. It was a very fine morning, but as we did not leave home till 12 o'clock it was very hot. I parted from my Beloved in the green lane above the Black-smith's, then went to dinner at Mr. Simpson's — we walked afterwards in the garden. Betty Towers and her son and daughter came to tea. The little lad is 4 years old, almost as little a thing as Hartley, and as sharp too, they say, but I saw nothing of this, being a stranger, except in his bonny eyes, which had such a sweet brightness in them when any thing was said to him that made him ashamed and draw his chin into his neck, while he sent his eyes upwards to look at you. His Mother is a delicate woman. She said she thought that both she and her husband were so tender in their health that they must be obliged to sell their land. Speaking of old Jim Jackson she said : " They might have looked up with the best in Grasmere, if they had but been careful " — " They began with a clear estate, and had never had but one child, he to be sure is a half-wit " — " How did they get through with their money ? " — " Why in eating and drinking. The wife would make tea 4 or 5 times in a day and sec' folks for sugar ! Then

---

[1] *v.* entry of June 18th *supra.*

she would have nea Teapot, but she would take the water out of a brass pan on the fire and pour it on to the tea in a quart pot. This all for herself, for she boiled the tea leaves always for her husband and their son."

I brought plants home, sunflowers, and planted them.

Aggy Fisher was talking with me on Monday morning, 21st of June, about her son. She went on — Old Mary Watson was at Goan's there when the child died. I had never seen her before since her son was drowned last summer, " we were all in trouble and trouble opens folks' hearts ". She began to tell about her daughter that's married to Leonard Holmes, how now that sickness is come upon him they are breaking down and failing in the world. Debts are coming in every day, and he can do nothing, and they fret and jar together. One day he came riding over to Grasmere — I wondered what was the matter, and I resolved to speak to him when he came back. He was as pale as a ghost, and he did not suffer the horse to gang quicker than a snail could crawl. He had come over in a trick of passion to auld Mary to tell her she might take her own again, her daughter and the bairns. Mary replied nobly (said Aggy) that she would not part man and wife, but that all should come together, and she would keep them while she had anything. Old Mary went to see them at Ambleside afterwards, and he begged her pardon. Aggy observed that they would never have known this sorrow, if it had pleased God to take him off suddenly.

[*June 22nd,*] *Tuesday Morning.* I had my breakfast in bed, being not quite well — I then walked to Rydale, I waited long for the post, lying in the field, and looking at the distant mountains, — looking and listening to the river. I met the post. Letters from Montagu and Richard. I hurried back, forwarded these to William, and wrote to Montagu. When I came home I wrote to my brother Christopher. I could settle to nothing. Molly washed and glazed the curtains. I read the *Midsummer Night's Dream*, and began *As You Like It*. Miss Simpson called — Tamar [1] brought me some berries. I

---

[1] Daughter of Robert Dockray, Underhow, baptized Dec. 27, 1759.— G. G. W.

resolved to go to William and for that purpose John Fisher promised to go over the fells with me. Miss Simpson ate pie, and then left me reading letters from Mary and Coleridge. The news came that a house was taken for Betsy. I wrote to Mary H. and put up a parcel for Coleridge. The L.B.[1] arrived. I went to bed at ½ past 11.

June 23rd, Wednesday. I slept till ½ past 3 o'clock — called Molly before 4, and had got myself dressed and breakfasted before 5, but it rained and I went to bed again. It is now 20 minutes past 10 — a sunshiny morning. I walked to the top of the hill and sate under a wall near John's Grove, facing the sun. I read a scene or two in *As You Like It*. I met Charles Lloyd, and old Mr. Lloyd was upstairs — Mrs. Ll. had been to meet me. I wrote a line to Wm. by the Lloyds. Coleridge and Leslie came just as I had lain down after dinner. C. brought me W.'s letter. He had got well to Eusemere. C. and I accompanied Leslie to the boat-house. It was a sullen, coldish evening, no sunshine ; but after we had parted from Leslie a light came out suddenly that repaid us for all. It fell only upon one hill, and the island, but it arrayed the grass and trees in gem-like brightness. I cooked C. his supper. We sate up till one o'clock.

June 24th, Thursday. I went with C. half-way up the Rays. It was a cool morning. I dined at Mr. Simpson's and helped Aggy Fleming to quilt a petticoat. Miss Simpson came with me after tea round by the White Bridge. I ground paint when I reached home, and was tired. Wm. came in just when Molly had left me. It was a mild rainy evening — he was cool and fresh and smelt sweetly — his clothes were wet. We sate together talking till the first dawning of day — a happy time. He was pale and not much tired. He thought I looked well too.

June 25th, Friday. Wm. had not fallen asleep till after 3 o'clock, but he slept tolerably. Miss Simpson came to colour the rooms. I began with whitewashing the ceiling. I worked with them (William was very busy) till dinner time, but after dinner I went to bed and fell asleep. When I rose I went just

---

[1] *i.e. Lyrical Ballads*, ed. 1802.

before tea into the garden. I looked up at my swallow's nest, and it was gone. It had fallen down. Poor little creatures, they could not themselves be more distressed than I was. I went upstairs to look at the ruins. They lay in a large heap upon the window ledge ; these swallows had been ten days employed in building this nest, and it seemed to be almost finished. I had watched them early in the morning, in the day many and many a time, and in the evenings when it was almost dark. I had seen them sitting together side by side in their unfinished nest, both morning and night. When they first came about the window they used to hang against the panes, with their white bellies and their forked tails, looking like fish ; but then they fluttered and sang their own little twittering song. As soon as the nest was broad enough, a sort of ledge for them, they sate both mornings and evenings, but they did not pass the night there. I watched them one morning, when William was at Eusemere, for more than an hour. Every now and then there was a feeling motion in their wings, a sort of tremulousness, and they sang a low song to one another.

[*June* 29*th*, *Tuesday*. . . .] [1] that they would not call here. I was going to tea. It is an uncertain day, sunshine, showers, and wind. It is now 8 o'clock ; I will go and see if my swallows are on their nest. Yes ! there they are, side by side, both looking down into the garden. I have been out on purpose to see their faces. I knew by looking at the window that they were there. Young George Mackareth is come down from London. Molly says : " I did not get him asked if he had got his la'al green purse yet ". When he went away he went round to see aw't neighbours and some gave him 6d., some a shilling, and I have heard his Mother say " 't la'al green purse was never out of his hand ". I wrote to M. H., my brother Christr. and Miss Griffith, then went to bed in the sitting room. C. and Wm. came in at about half-past eleven. They talked till after twelve.

June 30*th*, *Wednesday*. William slept ill, his head terribly bad. We walked part of the way up the Rays with Coleridge, a threatening windy coldish day. We did not go with C. far

---

[1] A page torn out of the MS. here. Among other things it must have told that the swallows had started rebuilding their nest.

up the Rays, but sate down a few minutes together before we parted. I was not very well — I was inclined to go to bed when we reached home, but Wm. persuaded me to have tea instead. We met an old man between the [?] shed and Lewthwaite's. He wore a rusty but untorn hat, an excellent blue coat, waistcoat, and breeches, and good mottled worsted stockings. His beard was very thick and grey, of a fortnight's growth we guessed, it was a regular beard, like grey *plush*. His bundle contained Sheffield ware. William said to him, after he had asked him what his business was, " You are a very old man ? " " Aye, I am 83." I joined in, " Have you any children ? " " Children ? Yes, plenty. I have children and grand-children, and great grand-children. I have a great grand-daughter, a fine lass, 13 years old." I then said, " What, they take care of you ? " He replied, half offended, " Thank God, I can take care of myself ". He said he had been a servant of the Marquis of Granby — " O he was a good man, he's in heaven — I hope he is ". He then told us how he shot himself at Bath, that he was with him in Germany, and travelled with him everywhere. " He was a famous boxer, sir." And then he told us a story of his fighting with his farmer. " He used always to call me hard and sharp." Then every now and then he broke out, " He was a good man ! When we were travelling he never asked at the public-houses, as it might be there " (pointing to the " Swan "), " what we were to pay, but he would put his hand into his pocket and give them what he liked ; and when he came out of the house he would say, Now, they would have charged me a shilling or tenpence. God help them, poor creatures ! ! " I asked him again about his children, how many he had. Says he, " I cannot tell you " (I suppose he confounded children and grand-children together) ; " I have one daughter that keeps a boarding-school at Skipton in Craven. She teaches flowering and marking. And another that keeps a boarding-school at Ingleton. I brought up my family under the Marquis." He was familiar with all parts of York-shire. He asked us where we lived. " At Grasmere." " The bonniest dale in all England ! " says the old man. I bought a pair of scissors of him, and we sate together by the road-side.

When we parted I tried to lift his bundle, and it was almost more than I could do. We got tea and I was somewhat better. After tea I wrote to Coleridge, and closed up my letter to M. H. We went soon to bed. A weight of children a poor man's blessing. I [?] myself.

July 1st, Thursday. A very rainy day. We did not go out at all, till evening. I laid down after dinner, but first we sate quietly together by the fire. In the evening we took my cloak and walked first to the top of White Moss, then round by the White Bridge, and up again beyond Mr. Olliff's — we had a nice walk, and afterwards sate by a nice snug fire, and William read Spenser, and I read *As you like it.* The saddle bags came from Keswick, with a letter from M. H. and from C., and Wilkinson's drawings, but no letter from Richard.

July 2nd, Friday. A very rainy morning. There was a gleam of fair weather, and we thought of walking into Easedale. Molly began to prepare the linen for putting out, but it rained worse than ever. In the evening we walked up to the view of Rydale, and afterwards towards Mr. King's. I left William, and wrote a short letter to M. H. and to Coleridge, and transcribed the alterations in *The Leech Gatherer.*

July 3rd, Saturday. I breakfasted in bed, being not very well. Aggy Ashburner helped Molly with the linen. I made veal and gooseberry pies. It was very cold. Thomas Ashburner went for coals for us. There was snow upon the mountain tops. Letters from M. H. and Annette — A.'s letter sent from G. Hill ¹ — written at Blois 23rd.

July 4th, Sunday. Cold and rain and very dark. I was sick and ill, had been made sleepless by letters. I lay in bed till 4 o'clock. When I rose, I was very far from well, but I grew better after tea. William walked out a little, I did not. We sate at the window together. It came on a terribly wet night. Wm. finished *The Leech Gatherer* today.

July 5th, Monday. A very sweet morning. William stayed some time in the orchard. I went to him there — it was a beautiful morning. I copied out *The L.-G.* for Coleridge, and

---

¹ *i.e.* Gallow Hill, the Hutchinsons' farm in Yorkshire.

for us. Wrote to Annette, — Mrs. Clarkson, M. H., and Coleridge. It came on a heavy rain, and we could not go to Dove Nest as we had intended, though we had sent Molly for the horse, and it was come. The roses in the garden are fretted and battered and quite spoiled, the honey suckle, though in its glory, is sadly teazed. The peas are beaten down. The scarlet beans want sticking. The garden is overrun with weeds.

July 6th, Tuesday. It was a very rainy day, but in the afternoon it cleared up a little and we set off towards Rydale to go for letters. The rain met us at the top of the White Moss, and it came on very heavily afterwards. It drove past Nab Scar in a substantial shape, as if going Grasmere-wards as fast [1] as it could go. We stopped at Willy Park's [2] and borrowed a plaid. I rested a little while till the rain seemed passing away, and then I went to meet William. I met him near Rydale with a letter from Christopher. We had a pleasant but very rainy walk home. A letter came from Mary in the morning, and in the evening one from Coleridge by Fletcher. The swallows have completed their beautiful nest. I baked bread and pies.

[July] 7th, Wednesday. A very fine day. William had slept ill, so he lay in bed till 11 o'clock. I wrote to John, ironed the linen, packed up. Lay in the orchard all the afternoon. In the morning Wm. nailed up the trees while I was ironing. We lay sweetly in the orchard. The well is beautiful. The orchard full of foxgloves. The honeysuckle beautiful — plenty of roses, but they are battered. Wrote to Molly Ritson [?] and Coleridge. Walked on the White Moss. Glow-worms. Well for them children are in bed when they shine.

[July] 8th, Thursday. A rainy morning. I paid Thomas Ashburner and Frank Baty. When I was coming home, a post-chaise passed with a little girl behind in a patched, ragged red cloak [?]. We sat in tranquillity together by the fire in the morning. In the afternoon, after we had talked a little, William fell asleep. I read the *Winter's Tale* ; then I went to bed, but did not sleep. The swallows stole in and out of their

---

[1] fast : *written* far.　　　　　　[2] Nab Cottage.

nest, and sate there, *whiles* quite still, *whiles* they sung low for two minutes or more at a time just like a muffled robin. William was looking at *The Pedlar* when I got up. He arranged it, and after tea I wrote it out — 280 lines. In the meantime the evening being fine he carried his coat to the tailor's, and went to George Mackareth's to engage the horse. He came in to me at about ½ past nine pressing me to go out ; he had got letters which we were to read out of doors — I was rather unwilling, fearing I could not see to read the letters, but I saw well enough. One was from M. H., a very tender affecting letter, another from Sara to C., from C. to us, and from my Br. Rd. The moon was behind. William hurried me out in hopes that I should see her. We walked first to the top of the hill to see Rydale. It was dark and dull, but our own vale was very solemn — the shape of Helm Crag was quite distinct, though black. We walked backwards and forwards on the White Moss path ; there was a sky-like white brightness on the lake. The Wyke cottage light at the foot of Silver How. Glow-worms out, but not so numerous as last night. O, beautiful place ! Dear Mary, William. The horse is come — Friday morning — so I must give over. William is eating his broth. I must prepare to go. The swallows, I must leave them, the well, the garden, the roses, all. Dear creatures ! ! they sang last night after I was in bed — seemed to be singing to one another, just before they settled to rest for the night. Well, I must go. Farewell.

On Friday morning, July 9th, William and I set forward to Keswick on our road to Gallow Hill. We had a pleasant ride, though the day was showery. It rained heavily when Nelly Mackareth took the horse from us, at the Blacksmith's. Coleridge met us at Sara's Rock. He had inquired about us before of Nelly Mackareth and we had been told by a handsome man, an inhabitant of Wytheburn, with whom he had been talking (and who seemed, by the bye, much pleased with his companion), that C. was waiting for us. We reached Keswick against tea-time. We called at Calvert's on the Saturday evening. On Sunday I was poorly and the day was wet, so we could not move from Keswick, but on Monday 12th July 1802

William teazed me out in hopes that
I should see ~~lazy~~. We walked up & to
the top of the hill to see Rydale. It
was dark & dull but our own vale
was very solemn. The shape of Silver
~~was~~ quite distinct, though
black. We walked backwards &
forwards on the white moss path.
There was a sky-like white brightness
~~on~~ the lake. The bright ~~looking~~
at the foot of Silver How bright
glowworms out but not so
many as last night — I have
~~put...~~ Dear Mary talks
the cow is come Friday by
morning so I must give over.
When is coming his Room I
must prepare to go — The
Swallows I must leave them
the bright. Dear creatures. They
sang last night after I was in
bed — seemed to be singing to one
another just before they settled

we went to Eusemere. Coleridge walked with us 6 or 7 miles. He was not well, and we had a melancholy parting after having sate together in silence by the road-side. We turned aside to explore the country near Hutton-John, and had a new and delightful walk. The valley, which is subject to the decaying mansion that stands at its head, seems to join its testimony to that of the house to the falling away of the family greatness. The hedges are in bad condition, the land wants draining, and is overrun with brackens, yet there is a something everywhere that tells of its former possessors. The trees are left scattered about as if intended to be like a park, and these are very interesting, standing as they do upon the sides of the steep hills that slope down to the bed of the river, a little stony-bedded stream that spreads out to a considerable breadth at the village of Dacre. A little above Dacre we came into the right road to Mr. Clarkson's, after having walked through woods and fields, never exactly knowing whether we were right or wrong. We learnt, however, that we had saved half-a-mile. We sate down by the river-side to rest, and saw some swallows flying about and about under the bridge, and two little schoolboys were loitering among the scars seeking after their nests. We reached Mr. Clarkson's at about eight o'clock after a sauntering walk, having lingered and loitered and sate down together that we might be alone. Mr. and Mrs. C. were just come from Luff's.

We spent Tuesday, the 13th of July, at Eusemere ; and on Wednesday morning, the 14th, we walked to Emont Bridge, and mounted the coach between Bird's Nest [1] and Hartshorn Tree. Mr. Clarkson's bitch followed us so far. A soldier and his young wife wanted to be taken up by that Coachman, but there was no room. We had a chearful ride though cold till we got on to Stainmoor, and then a heavy shower came on, but we buttoned ourselves up both together in the Guard's coat, and we liked the hills and the rain the better for bringing us so close to one another — I never rode more snugly. At last however it grew so very rainy that I was obliged to go into the coach at Bowes. Lough of Penrith was there and very impertinent — I

---

[1] An obsolete name for Brougham Hall, derived from the family of that name who owned it for about half a century from 1676 or earlier.—G. G. W.

was right glad to get out again to my own dear Brother at Greta Bridge ; the sun shone chearfully, and a glorious ride we had over Gaterly Moor. Every building was bathed in golden light. The trees were more bright than earthly trees, and we saw round us miles beyond miles — Darlington spire, etc. etc. We reached Leeming Lane [1] at about 9 o'clock : supped comfortably, and enjoyed our fire.

On Thursday morning, at a little before seven, being the 15th July, we got into a post-chaise and went to Thirsk [2] to breakfast. We were well treated, but when the landlady understood that we were going to *walk* off, and leave our luggage behind, she threw out some saucy words in our hearing. The day was very hot, and we rested often and long before we reached the foot of the Hambledon Hills, and while we were climbing them, still oftener. We had a sandwich in our pockets which we finished when we had climbed part of the hill, and we were almost overpowered with thirst, when I heard the trickling of a little stream of water. I was before William, and I stopped till he came up to me. We sate a long time by this water, and climbed the hill slowly. I was footsore, the sun shone hot, the little Scotch cattle panted and tossed fretfully about. The view was hazy, and we could see nothing from the top of the hill but an indistinct wide-spreading country, full of trees, but the buildings, towns, and houses were lost. We stopped to examine that curious stone, then walked along the flat common. It was now cooler, but I was still footsore and could not walk quick, so I left William sitting two or three times, and when he followed me he took a sheep for me, and then me for a sheep. I rested opposite the Sign of the Sportsman and was questioned by the Landlady. Arrived very hungry at Rivaux. Nothing to eat at the Millers, as we expected, but at an exquisitely neat farmhouse we got some boiled milk and bread ; this strengthened us, and I went down to look at the

---

[1] Leeming Lane, the local name for the section of the great trunk road between Boroughbridge and Piercebridge.—G. G. W.

[2] Thirsk, 13 m. from Leeming Lane. The inn was The Three Tuns, in the market-place, still the principal inn. The little stream of water on Sutton Bank is now given a spout and called Wordsworth's Well. The road climbs 600 feet in less than a mile, and the summit is 964 feet above the sea.—G. G. W.

ruins. Thrushes were singing, cattle feeding among green-grown hillocks about the ruins. These hillocks were scattered over with *grovelets* of wild roses and other shrubs, and covered with wild flowers. I could have stayed in this solemn quiet spot till evening, without a thought of moving, but William was waiting for me, so in a quarter of an hour I went away. We walked upon Mr. Duncombe's terrace and looked down upon the Abbey. It stands in a larger valley among a brotherhood of valleys, of different length and breadth, — all woody, and running up into the hills in all directions. We reached Helmsly just at dusk. We had a beautiful view of the castle from the top of the hill, slept at a very nice inn, and were well treated — bright bellows and floors as smooth as ice. On Friday morning, 16th July, we walked to Kirby. Met people coming to Helmsly fair. Were misdirected, and walked a mile out of our way — met a double horse at Kirby. A beautiful view above Pickering [1] — Sinnington village very beautiful. Met Mary and Sara seven miles from G. H. Sheltered from the rain ; beautiful glen, spoiled by the large house — sweet church and churchyard.[2] Arrived at Gallow Hill at 7 o'clock.

July 16th, Friday Evening. The weather bad, almost all the time. Sara, Tom, and I rode up Bedale. Wm., Mary, Sara, and I went to Scarborough, and we walked in the Abbey pasture, and to Wykeham ; and on Monday, the 26th, we went off with Mary in a post-chaise. We had an interesting ride over the Wolds, though it rained all the way. Single thorn bushes were scattered about on the turf, sheep-sheds here and there, and now and then a little hut. Swelling grounds, and sometimes a single tree or a clump of trees. Mary was very sick, and every time we stopped to open a gate she felt the motion in her whole body — indeed I was sick too, and perhaps the smooth gliding of the chaise over the turf made us worse. We passed through one or two little villages, embosomed in tall trees. After we had parted from Mary, there were gleams of

---

[1] The "beautiful view" is from Wrelton Park, 3 miles to the west.—G. G. W.
[2] The glen, church and churchyard are those of Brompton, where William was to be married and where the large house is no more beautiful than it was.—G. G. W.

sunshine, but with showers. We saw Beverley in a heavy rain, and yet were much pleased with the beauty of the town. Saw the Minster — a pretty, clean building, but injured very much with Grecian architecture. The country between Beverley and Hull very rich, but miserably flat — brick houses, windmills, houses again — dull and endless. Hull a frightful, dirty, *brick-housey*, tradesmanlike, rich, vulgar place ; yet the river, though the shores are so low that they can hardly be seen, looked beautiful with the evening lights upon it, and boats moving about. We walked a long time, and returned to our dull day-room but quiet evening one, quiet and our own, to supper.

July 27th, Tuesday. Market day. Streets dirty, very rainy, did not leave Hull till 4 o'clock, and left Barton at about six ; rained all the way almost. A beautiful village at the foot of a hill with trees. A gentleman's house converted into a lady's boarding-school. We had a woman in bad health in the coach, and took in a lady and her daughter — supped at Lincoln, duck and peas, and cream cheese — paid 2/-. We left Lincoln on Wednesday morning, 28th July, at six o'clock. It rained heavily, and we could see nothing but the antientry of some of the buildings as we passed along. The night before, however, we had seen enough to make us regret this. The minster stands at the edge of a hill overlooking an immense plain. The country very flat as we went along — the day mended. We went to see the outside of the Minster while the passengers were dining at Peterborough ; the West End very grand. The little girl, who was a great scholar and plainly her Mother's favourite, though she had a large family at home, had bought " The Farmer's Boy ". She said it was written by a man without education and was very wonderful.

On Thursday morning, 29th, we arrived in London. Wm. left me at the Inn. I went to bed, etc. etc. After various troubles and disasters, we left London on Saturday morning at ½-past 5 or 6, the 31st of July. (I have forgot which.) We mounted the Dover Coach at Charing Cross. It was a beautiful morning. The city, St. Paul's, with the river and a multitude of little boats, made a most beautiful sight as we crossed

Westminster Bridge. The houses were not overhung by their cloud of smoke, and they were spread out endlessly, yet the sun shone so brightly, with such a fierce light, that there was even something like the purity of one of nature's own grand spectacles.

We rode on chearfully, now with the Paris diligence before us, now behind. We walked up the steep hills, a beautiful prospect everywhere, till we even reached Dover. At first the rich, populous, wide-spreading, woody country about London, then the River Thames, ships sailing, chalk cliffs, trees, little villages. Afterwards Canterbury, situated on a plain, rich and woody, but the City and Cathedral disappointed me. Hop grounds on each side of the road some miles from Canterbury, then we came to a common, the race ground, an elevated plain, villages among trees in the bed of a valley at our right, and, rising above this valley, green hills scattered over with wood, neat gentlemen's houses. One white house, almost hid with green trees, which we longed for, and the parson's house, as neat a place as could be, which would just have suited Coleridge. No doubt we might have found one for Tom Hutchinson and Sara, and a good farm too. We halted at a half-way house — fruit carts under the shade of trees, seats for guests, a tempting place to the weary traveller. Still, as we went along, the country was beautiful, hilly, with cottages lurking under the hills, and their little plots of hop ground like vineyards. It was a bad hop year. A woman on the top of the coach said to me, " It is a sad thing for the poor people, for the hop-gathering is the women's harvest ; there is employment about the hops both for women and children ".

We saw the castle of Dover, and the sea beyond, 4 or 5 miles before we reached D. We looked at it through a long vale, the castle being upon an eminence, as it seemed, at the end of this vale, which opened to the sea. The country now became less fertile, but near Dover it seemed more rich again. Many buildings stand on the flat fields, sheltered with tall trees. There is one old chapel that might have been there just in the same state in which it now is when this vale was as retired, and as little known to travellers as our own Cumberland mountain wilds 30 years ago. There was also a very old building on the other side of the road, which had a strange effect among the many new ones that are springing up everywhere. It seemed odd that it could have kept itself pure in its ancientry among so many upstarts. It was near dark when we reached Dover. We were told that the packet was about to sail, so we went down to the custom-house in half-an-hour — had our luggage examined, etc. etc., and then we drank tea with the Honourable Mr. Knox and his tutor. We arrived at Calais at 4 o'clock on Sunday morning, the 1st of August.[1] We stayed in the vessel till ½-past 7, then William went for letters, at about ½-past 8 or 9 we found out Annette and C. chez Madame Avril dans la Rue de la Tête d'or. We lodged opposite two ladies,[2] in tolerably decent-sized rooms, but badly furnished and with large store of bad smells and dirt in the yard, and all about. The weather was very hot. We walked by the sea-shore almost every evening with Annette and Caroline, or Wm. and I alone. I had a bad cold, and could not bathe at first, but William did. It was a pretty sight to see, as we walked upon the sands when the tide was low, perhaps a hundred people bathing about a quarter of a mile distant from us, and we had delightful walks after the heat of the day was passed away — seeing far off in the west the coast of England like a cloud crested with Dover Castle, which was but like the summit of the cloud — the evening star and the glory of the sky.[3] The reflections in the water were more beautiful than the sky itself, purple waves brighter than precious stones, for ever melting away upon the sands. The fort, a wooden building, at the entrance of the harbour at Calais, when the evening twilight was coming on, and we could not see anything of the building but its shape, which was far more distinct than in perfect daylight, seemed to be reared upon pillars of ebony, between

---

[1] July 31.—D. W.
[2] Two ladies lived in the house opposite to us, and we, in our idle moods, often amused ourselves with observing their still more idle way of spending their time ; they seemed neither to have work nor books, but were mostly at the window. Our rooms were rather large but ill-furnished, etc. *as text. So separate MS. sheet, probably copied by D. W. to send to a friend.*
[3] Cf. the sonnet " Fair Star of evening, Splendour of the west ".

which pillars the sea was seen in the most beautiful colours that can be conceived. Nothing in romance was ever half so beautiful. Now came in view, as the evening star sank down, and the colours of the west faded away, the two lights of England, lighted up by Englishmen in our country, to warn vessels off rocks or sands. These we used to see from the pier, when we could see no other distant objects but the clouds, the sky, and the sea itself : All was dark behind. The town of Calais seemed deserted of the light of heaven, but there was always light and life and joy upon the sea. One night, though, I shall never forget — the day had been very hot, and William and I walked alone together upon the pier. The sea was gloomy, for there was a blackness over all the sky, except when it was overspread with lightning, which often revealed to us a distant vessel. Near us the waves roared and broke against the pier, and they were interfused with greenish fiery light. The more distant sea always black and gloomy. It was also beautiful, on the calm hot night, to see the little boats row out of harbour with wings of fire, and the sail boats with the fiery track which they cut as they went along, and which closed up after them with a hundred thousand sparkles, balls, shootings and streams of glow-worm light. Caroline was delighted.

On Sunday, the 29th of August, we left Calais at twelve o'clock in the morning, and landed at Dover at one on Monday the 30th. I was sick all the way. It was very pleasant to me, when we were in harbour at Dover, to breathe the fresh air, and to look up and see the stars among the ropes of the vessel. The next day was very hot. We both bathed, and sate upon the Dover Cliffs, and looked upon France with many a melancholy and tender thought. We could see the shores almost as plain as if it were but an English lake. We mounted the coach at ½ past 4, and arrived in London at 6, the 30th August. It was misty, and we could see nothing. We stayed in London till Wednesday the 22nd of September, and arrived at Gallow Hill on Friday.

[*Friday*], *September 24th.* Mary first met us in the avenue. She looked so fat and well that we were made very happy by the sight of her ; then came Sara, and last of all Joanna. Tom

O

was forking corn, standing upon the corn cart. We dressed ourselves immediately and got tea — the garden looked gay with asters and sweet peas. Jack and George came on Friday evening, 1st October. On Saturday, 2nd, we rode to Hackness, William, Jack, George, and Sara single — I behind Tom. On Sunday 3rd, Mary and Sara were busy packing.

On Monday, 4th October 1802, my brother William was married to Mary Hutchinson. I slept a good deal of the night, and rose fresh and well in the morning. At a little after 8 o'clock I saw them go down the avenue towards the church. William had parted from me upstairs. When they were absent my dear little Sara prepared the breakfast. I kept myself as quiet as I could, but when I saw the two men running up the walk, coming to tell us it was over, I could stand it no longer, and threw myself on the bed, where I lay in stillness, neither hearing or seeing anything till Sara came upstairs to me, and said, " They are coming ". This forced me from the bed where I lay, and I moved, I knew not how, straight forward, faster than my strength could carry me, till I met my beloved William, and fell upon his bosom. He and John Hutchinson led me to the house, and there I stayed to welcome my dear Mary. As soon as we had breakfasted, we departed. It rained when we set off. Poor Mary was much agitated, when she parted from her brothers and sisters, and her home. Nothing particular occurred till we reached Kirby. We had sunshine and showers, pleasant talk, love and chearfulness. We were obliged to stay two hours at K. while the horses were feeding. We wrote a few lines to Sara, and then walked out ; the sun shone, and we went to the churchyard after we had put a letter into the post-office for the *York Herald*.[1] We sauntered about, and read the grave-stones. There was one to the memory of five children, who had all died within five years, and the longest lived had only lived four years.[2] There was another

---

[1] A notice of the marriage appeared in the *York Herald* of Oct. 9 and the *York Courant* of Oct. 11. The latter runs : " On Monday last was married at Brompton Mr. Wordsworth of Grasmere to Miss Hutchinson of Gallow Hill near Scarboro'". Both papers are now incorporated in the *Yorkshire Herald*.— G. G. W.

[2] Kirby Moorside Churchyard. A tombstone on the left as you approach

stone erected to the memory of an unfortunate woman (as we supposed, by a stranger). The verses engraved upon it expressed that she had been neglected by her relations, and counselled the readers of those words to look within, and recollect their own frailties. We left Kirby at about half-past two. There is not much variety of prospect from K. to Helmsley, but the country is very pleasant, being rich and woody, and Helmsley itself stands very sweetly at the foot of the rising grounds of Duncombe Park, which is scattered over with tall woods ; and, lifting itself above the common buildings of the town, stands Helmsley Castle, now a ruin, formerly inhabited by the gay Duke of Buckingham. Every foot of the road was, of itself, interesting to us, for we had travelled along it on foot, Wm. and I, when we went to fetch our dear Mary, and had sate upon the turf by the roadside more than once. Before we reached Helmsley, our driver told us that he could not take us any further, so we stopped at the same inn where we had slept before.[1] My heart danced at the sight of its cleanly outside, bright yellow walls, casements overshadowed with jasmine, and its low, double gavel-ended front. We were not shown into the same parlour where Wm. and I were ; it was a small room with a drawing over the chimney piece which the woman told us had been bought at a sale. Mary and I warmed ourselves at the kitchen fire. We then walked into the garden, and looked over a gate, up to the old ruin which stands at the top of a mount, and round about it the moats are grown up into soft green cradles, hollows surrounded with green grassy hillocks, and these are overshadowed by old trees, chiefly ashes. I prevailed upon William to go up with me to the ruins. We left Mary sitting by the kitchen fire. The sun shone, it was warm and very pleasant. One part of the castle seems to

---

the south porch still bears the inscription : " In memory of John and Susanna Cullon's children—Elizabeth died 1795, aged 18 months, Mary d. 1796 aged 2 years, James d. 1796 aged 4 years, David d. 1797 aged 1 year, John d. 1798 aged 5 months, Thomas d. 1804 aged 7 weeks, Mary d. 1810 aged 9 months ". It will be seen that the Cullons were as unfortunate after D. W.'s visit to the churchyard as before it.—G. G. W.

[1] The inn at Helmsley, now called the Old Manor House, remains with its exterior just as it is described by D. W. except that the walls are nearly white. and that roses and clematis have replaced the jasmine.—G. G. W.

be inhabited. There was a man mowing nettles in the open space which had most likely once been the castle-court. There is one gateway exceedingly beautiful. Children were playing upon the sloping ground. We came home by the street. After about an hour's delay we set forward again, had an excellent driver, who opened the gates so dexterously that the horses never stopped. Mary was very much delighted with the view of the castle from the point where we had seen it before. I was pleased to see again the little path which we had walked upon, the gate I had climbed over, and the road down which we had seen the two little boys drag a log of wood, and a team of horses struggle under the weight of a great load of timber. We had felt compassion for the poor horses that were under the governance of oppressive and ill-judging drivers, and for the poor boys, who seemed of an age to have been able to have dragged the log of wood merely out of the love of their own activity, but from poverty and bad food they panted for weakness, and were obliged to fetch their father from the town to help them. Duncombe House looks well from the road — a large building, though I believe only two-thirds of the original design are completed. We rode down a very steep hill to Rivaux valley, with woods all round us. We stopped upon the bridge to look at the Abbey, and again when we had crossed it. Dear Mary had never seen a ruined abbey before except Whitby. We recognised the cottages, houses, and the little valleys as we went along. We walked up a long hill, the road carrying us up the cleft or valley with woody hills on each side of us. When we went to G. H. I had walked down the valley alone. William followed me.

It was not dark evening when we passed the little publick house, but before we had crossed the Hambledon Hill, and reached the point overlooking Yorkshire, it was quite dark.[1] We had not wanted, however, fair prospects before us, as we drove along the flat plain of the high hill. Far far off us, in the western sky, we saw shapes of castles, ruins among groves, a

---

[1] Cf. sonnet, " Dark and more dark the shades of evening fell ", composed, as Wordsworth tells us, " after a journey over the Hambleton Hills, on a day memorable to me—the day of my marriage "

great spreading wood, rocks, and single trees, a minster with its tower unusually distinct, minarets in another quarter, and a round Grecian Temple also ; the colours of the sky of a bright grey, and the forms of a sober grey, with a dome. As we descended the hill there was no distinct view, but of a great space ; only near us we saw the wild and (as the people say) bottomless tarn [1] in the hollow at the side of the hill. It seemed to be made visible to us only by its own light, for all the hill about us was dark. Before we reached Thirsk we saw a light before us, which we at first thought was the moon, then lime-kilns ; but when we drove into the market-place it proved a large bonfire, with lads dancing round it, which is a sight I dearly love. The inn was like an illuminated house — every room full. We asked the cause, and were told by the girl that it was " Mr. John Bell's birthday,[2] that he had heired his estate ! " The landlady was very civil. She did not recognise the despised foot-travellers. We rode nicely in the dark, and reached Leeming Lane at eleven o'clock. I am always sorry to get out of a chaise when it is night. The people of the house were going to bed and we were not very well treated, though we got a hot supper. We breakfasted next morning and set off at about ½-past 8 o'clock. It was a chearful, sunny morning. We soon turned out of Leeming Lane and passed a nice village [3] with a beautiful church. We had a few showers, but when we came to the green fields of Wensley, the sun shone upon them all, and the Ure in its many windings glittered as it flowed along under the green slopes of Middleham and Middleham Castle. Mary looked about for her friend Mr. Place, and thought she had him sure on the contrary side of the vale from that on which we afterwards found that he lived. We went to a new built house at Leyburn, the same village where William and I had dined with George Hutchinson on our road to Grasmere 2 years and ¾ ago, but not the same house. The landlady was very civil, giving us cake and wine, but the

---

[1] *i.e.* Gormire, which from the top of Sutton Bank resembles the crater of an extinct volcano.—G. G. W.

[2] John Bell, of Thirsk, was born Oct. 3, 1764. As his birthday fell in 1802 on a Sunday, the celebration took place on the 4th. Tradition of his lavish hospitality still lingers.—G. G. W.   [3] Bedale.—G. G. W.

horses being out we were detained at least two hours, and did not set off till 2 o'clock. We paid for 35 miles, *i.e.* to Sedbergh, but the landlady did not encourage us to hope to get beyond Hawes. A shower came on just after we left the inn — while the rain beat against the windows we ate our dinners, which M. and W. heartily enjoyed — I was not quite well. When we passed through the village of Wensley my heart was melted away with dear recollections — the bridge, the little water-spout, the steep hill, the church. They are among the most vivid of my own inner visions, for they were the first objects that I saw after we were left to ourselves,[1] and had turned our whole hearts to Grasmere as a home in which we were to rest. The vale looked most beautiful each way. To the left the bright silver stream inlaid the flat and very green meadows, winding like a serpent. To the right we did not see it so far, it was lost among trees and little hills. I could not help observing, as we went along, how much more varied the prospects of Wensley Dale are in the summer time than I could have thought possible in the winter. This seemed to be in great measure owing to the trees being in leaf, and forming groves and screens, and thence little openings upon recesses and concealed retreats, which in winter only made a part of the one great vale. The *beauty* of the summer time here as much excels that of the winter, as the variety, owing to the excessive greenness of the fields, and the trees in leaf half concealing, and, where they do not conceal, softening the hard bareness of the limey white roofs. One of our horses seemed to grow a little restive as we went through the first village, a long village on the side of a hill.[2] It grew worse and worse, and at last we durst not go on any longer. We walked a while, and then the post boy was obliged to take the horse out, and go back for another. We seated ourselves again snugly in the post-chaise. The wind struggled about us and rattled the window, and gave a gentle motion to the chaise, but we were warm and at our ease within. Our station was at the top of a hill, opposite Bolton Castle, the Ure flowing beneath. William

---

[1] *i.e.* in Dec. 1799 : *v. E.L.* p. 238.   [2] West Wilton.—G. G. W.

has since wrote a sonnet on this our imprisonment. " Hard was thy durance, Queen ! compared with ours." Poor Mary !

Wm. fell asleep, lying upon my breast, and I upon Mary. I lay motionless for a long time, but I was at last obliged to move. I became very sick and continued so for some time after the boy brought the horse to us. Mary had been a little sick, but it soon went off. We had a sweet ride till we came to a publick-house on the side of a hill, where we alighted and walked down to see the waterfalls.[1] The sun was not set, and the woods and fields were spread over with the yellow light of evening, which made their greenness a thousand times more green. There was too much water in the river for the beauty of the falls, and even the banks were less interesting than in winter. Nature had entirely got the better in her struggles against the giants who first cast the mould of these works ; for, indeed, it is a place that did not in winter remind one of God, but one could not help feeling as if there had been the agency of some " mortal instruments ", which Nature had been struggling against without making a perfect conquest. There was something so wild and new in this feeling, knowing, as we did in the inner man, that God alone had laid his hand upon it, that I could not help regretting the want of it ; besides, it is a pleasure to a real lover of Nature to give winter all the glory he can, for summer *will* make its own way, and speak its own praises. We saw the pathway which William and I took at the close of evening, the path leading to the rabbit warren where we lost ourselves.[2] The farm, with its holly hedges, was lost among the green hills and hedgerows in general, but we found it out, and were glad to look at it again. When William had left us to seek the waterfalls, Mary and I were frightened by a cow.

At our return to the inn, we found new horses and a new driver, and we went on nicely to Hawes, where we arrived before it was quite dark. Mary and I got tea and William had a partridge and mutton chops and tarts for his supper.

---

[1] *i.e.* those of Aysgarth. Cf. W.'s description in his letter to Coleridge, Dec. 24, 1799, referred to above, which D. W. probably had in her mind.— G. G. W. [2] In Dec. 1799, same letter (*E.L.* pp. 234-42).

Mary sate down with him. We also had a shilling's worth of negus, and Mary made me some broth, for all which supper we were only charged 2/-. I could not sit up long, I vomited and took the broth and then slept sweetly. We rose at six o'clock — a rainy morning. We had a good breakfast and then departed. There was a very pretty view about a mile from Hawes, where we crossed a bridge ; bare and very green fields with cattle, a glittering stream, cottages, a few ill-grown trees, and high hills. The sun shone now. Before we got upon the bare hills, there was a hunting lodge on our right, exactly like Greta Hill, with fir plantations about it. We were very fortunate in the day, gleams of sunshine, passing clouds, that travelled with their shadows below them. Mary was much pleased with Garsdale. It was a dear place to William and me. We noted well the publick-house (Garsdale Hall) where we had baited, and drunk our pint of ale, and afterwards the mountain which had been adorned by Jupiter in his glory when we were here before. It was mid-day when we reached Sedbergh, and *market* day. We were in the same room where we had spent the evening together in our road to Grasmere. We had a pleasant ride to Kendal, where we arrived at about 2 o'clock. The day favoured us. M. and I went to see the house where dear Sara had lived, then we went to seek Mr. Bonsfield's shop, but we found him not. He had sold all his goods the day before. We then went to the Pot-woman's and bought 2 jugs and a dish, and some paper at Pennington's. When we came to the Inn William was almost ready for us. The afternoon was not chearful but it did not rain till we came near Windermere. I am always glad to see Stavely ; it is a place I dearly love to think of — the first mountain village that I came to with Wm. when we first began our pilgrimage together. Here we drank a bason of milk at a publick house, and here I washed my feet in the brook, and put on a pair of silk stockings by Wm.'s advice. Nothing particular occurred till we reached Ings chapel. The door was open, and we went in. It is a neat little place, with a marble floor and marble communion table, with a painting over it of the last supper, and Moses and Aaron on each side. The woman told us that " they had painted them as near as they could by the dresses as they are described in the Bible ", and gay enough they are. The marble had been sent by Richard Bateman [1] from Leghorn. The woman told us that a man had been at her house a few days before, who told her he had helped to bring it down the Red Sea, and she had believed him gladly ! It rained very hard when we reached Windermere. We sate in the rain at Wilcock's to change horses and arrived at Grasmere at about 6 o'clock on Wednesday evening, the 6th of October 1802. Molly was overjoyed to see us, for my part I cannot describe what I felt, and our dear Mary's feelings would I dare say not be easy to speak of. We went by candle light into the garden, and were astonished at the growth of the brooms, Portugal laurels, etc. etc. etc. The next day, Thursday, we unpacked the boxes. On Friday, 8th, we baked bread and Mary and I walked, first upon the hill-side, and then in John's Grove, then in view of Rydale, the first walk that I had taken with my sister.

[October] 9th, Saturday. William and I walked to Mr. Simpson's.

[October] 10th, Sunday. Rain all day.

[October] 11th, Monday. A beautiful day. We walked to the Easedale hills to hunt waterfalls.[2] William and Mary left me sitting on a stone on the solitary mountains, and went to Easedale tarn. I grew chilly and followed them. This approach to the tarn is very beautiful. We expected to have found C. at home, but he did not come till after dinner. He was well, but did not look so.

October 12th, Tuesday. We walked with C. to Rydale.

[October] 13th, Wednesday. Set forwards with him towards Keswick, and he prevailed us to go on. We consented, Mrs. C. not being at home. The day was delightful. We drank tea at John Stanley's. Wrote to Annette.

[October] 14th, Thursday. We went in the evening to Calvert's. Moonlight. Stayed supper.

[October] 15th, Friday. Walked to Lord William Gordon's.

[October] 16th, Saturday. Came home, Mary and I. William

---

[1] For the story of Robert (*not* Richard, an error made by both W. and D. W.) Bateman, *v. Michael*, ll. 258-70.   [2] Cf. *Louisa*, l. 24.

returned to Coleridge before we reached Nadel Fell. Mary and I had a pleasant walk, the day was very bright ; the people busy getting in their corn, reached home at about five o'clock. I was not quite well, but better after tea. We made cakes etc.

[*October*] 17*th, Sunday*. We had thirteen of our neighbours to tea. William came in just as we began tea.

[*October*] 18*th, Monday*. I was not very well. I walked up in the morning to the Simpsons.

[*October*] 19*th, Tuesday*. The Simpsons drank tea and supped. William was much oppressed.

[*October*] 20*th, Wednesday*. We all walked on Butterlip How. It rained.

[*October*] 21*st, Thursday*. I walked with William to Rydale.

[*October*] 22*nd, Friday*.

[*October*] 23*rd, Saturday*. Mary was baking. I walked with Wm. to see Langdale, Rydale and the foot of Grasmere. We had a heavenly walk, but I came home in the toothache and have since that day been confined upstairs till now, namely, *Saturday*, 30th October, 1802.

October 30*th, Saturday*. William is gone to Keswick. Mary went with him to the top of the Rays. She is returned, and is now sitting near me by the fire. It is a breathless, grey day, that leaves the golden woods of autumn quiet in their own tranquillity, stately and beautiful in their decaying ; the lake is a perfect mirror.

William met Stoddart at the bridge at the foot of Legberthwaite dale. He returned with him and they surprized us by their arrival at four o'clock in the afternoon. Stoddart and W. dined. I went to bed, and after tea S. read Chaucer to us.

October 31*st, Sunday*.[1] John Monkhouse called. William and S. went to K[eswick]. Mary and I walked to the top of the hill and looked at Rydale. I was much affected when I stood upon the second bar of Sara's gate.[2] The lake was perfectly still, the sun shone on hill and vale, the distant birch trees looked like large golden flowers. Nothing else in colour

---

[1] D. W. heads this entry Saturday, Oct. 30, but it clearly records the events of the following day. [2] The Wishing Gate.

was distinct and separate, but all the beautiful colours seemed to be melted into one another, and joined together in one mass, so that there were no differences, though an endless variety, when one tried to find it out. The fields were of one sober yellow brown. After dinner we both lay on the floor — Mary slept. I could not for I was thinking of so many things. We sate nicely together after tea looking over old letters. Molly was gone up to Mr. Simpson's to see Mrs. S. who was very ill.

November 1st, Monday. I wrote to Miss Lamb. After dinner Mary walked to Mr. Simpson's. Letters from Cook, Wrangham, Mrs. C.

November 2nd, Tuesday. William returned from K. — he was not well. Baking day. Mr. B. S. came in at tea time. Molly sate up with Mrs. S. William was not well this evening.

[November] 3rd, Wednesday. Mr. Luff came in to tea.

[November] 4th, Thursday. I scalded my foot with coffee after having been in bed in the afternoon — I was near fainting and then bad in my bowels. Mary waited upon me till 2 o'clock, then we went to bed, and with applications of vinegar I was lulled to sleep about 4.

[November] 5th, Friday. I was laid up all day. I wrote to Montagu and Cook, and sent off letters to Miss Lamb and Coleridge.

[November] 6th, Saturday.

[November] 7th, Sunday. Fine weather. Letters from Coleridge that he was gone to London. Sara at Penrith. I wrote to Mrs. Clarkson. Wm. began to translate Ariosto.

[November] 8th, Monday. A beautiful day. William got to work again at Ariosto, and so continued all the morning, though the day was so delightful that it made my very heart linger to be out of doors, and see and feel the beauty of the autumn in freedom. The trees on the opposite side of the lake are of a yellow brown, but there are one or two trees opposite our windows (an ash tree, for instance) quite green, as in spring. The fields are of their winter colour, but the island is as green as ever it was. Mary has been baking today, she is now sitting

in the parlour. William is writing out his stanzas from Ariosto. We have a nice fire — the evening is quiet. Poor Coleridge! Sara is at Keswick, I hope. William has been ill in his stomach, but he is better tonight. I have read one canto of Ariosto today.

December 24th, Christmas Eve. William is now sitting by me, at ½ past 10 o'clock. I have been beside him ever since tea running the heel of a stocking, repeating some of his sonnets to him, listening to his own repeating, reading some of Milton's, and the *Allegro* and *Penseroso*. It is a quiet keen frost. Mary is in the parlour below attending to the baking of cakes, and Jenny Fletcher's pies. Sara is in bed in the toothache, and so we are [?]. My beloved William is turning over the leaves of Charlotte Smith's sonnets, but he keeps his hand to his poor chest, pushing aside his breastplate. Mary is well and I am well, and Molly is as blithe as last year at this time. Coleridge came this morning with Wedgwood. We all turned out of Wm.'s bedroom one by one, to meet him. He looked well. We had to tell him of the birth of his little girl, born yesterday morning at 6 o'clock. Wm. went with them to Wytheburn in the chaise, and M. and I met W. on the Rays. It was not an unpleasant morning to the feeling! far from it. The sun shone now and then, and there was no wind, but all things looked chearless and distinct; no meltings of sky into mountains, the mountains like stone work wrought up with huge hammers. Last Sunday was as mild a day as I ever remember. We all set off together to walk. I went to Rydale and Wm. returned with me. M. and S. went round the lakes. There were flowers of various kinds — the topmost bell of a foxglove, geraniums, daisies, a buttercup in the water (but this I saw two or three days before), small yellow flowers (I do not know their name) in the turf, a large bunch of strawberry blossoms. Wm. sate a while with me, then went to meet M. and S. Last Saturday I dined at Mr. Simpson's, also a beautiful mild day. Monday was a frosty day and it has been frost ever since. It is to-day Christmas Day, Saturday, 25th December 1802. I am thirty-one years of age. It is a dull, frosty day.

Again I have neglected to write my Journal — New Year's

Day is passed, Old Christmas day and I have recorded nothing. It is today *Tuesday*, January 11th. On Christmas day I dressed myself ready to go [to] Keswick in a returned chaise, but did not go. On Thursday, 30th December, I went to K. William rode before me to the foot of the hill nearest K. There we parted close to a little watercourse, which was then noisy with water, but on my return a dry channel. We ate some potted beef on horseback and sweet cake. We stopped our horse close to the hedge, opposite a tuft of primroses, three flowers in full blossom and a bud. They reared themselves up among the green moss. We debated long whether we should pluck [them], and at last left them to live out their day, which I was right glad of at my return the Sunday following ; for there they remained, uninjured either by cold or wet. I stayed at K. over New Year's Day, and returned on Sunday, the 2nd January. Wm. Mackareth fetched me — (M. and S. walked as far as John Stanley's) — Wm. was alarmed at my long delay, and came to within three miles of Keswick. He mounted before me. It had been a sweet mild day and was a pleasant evening. C. stayed with us till Tuesday, January 4th. Wm. and I walked up to George M.'s to endeavour to get the horse, then walked with him to Ambleside. We parted with him at the turning of the lane, he going on horseback to the top of Kirkstone. On Thursday 6th, C. returned, and on Friday, the 7th, he and Sara went to Keswick. W. accompanied them to the foot of Wytheburn. I to Mrs. Simpson's, and dined, and called on Aggy Fleming sick in bed. It was a gentle day, and when Wm. and I returned home just before sunset, it was a heavenly evening. A soft sky was among the hills, and a summer sunshine above, blending with this sky, for it was more like sky than clouds. The turf looked warm and soft.

Jan[uary] 8th, Saturday. Wm. and I walked to Rydale — no letters. Still as mild as spring — a beautiful moonlight evening and a quiet night, but before morning the wind rose, and it became dreadfully cold. We were not well, Mary and I.

[January] 9th, Sunday. Mary lay long in bed and did not

walk. Wm. and I walked in Brother's Wood. I was *astonished* with the beauty of the place for I had never been here since my return home — never since before I went away in June ! ! Wrote to Miss Lamb.

January 10th, 1803, Monday. I lay in bed to have a drench of sleep till one o'clock. Worked all day — petticoats — Mrs. C.'s wrists. Ran Wm.'s woollen stockings, for he put them on today for the first time. We walked to Rydale and brought letters from Sara, Annette and [?] — furiously cold.

January 11th, Tuesday. A very cold day. Wm. promised me he would rise as soon as I had carried him his breakfast, but he lay in bed till between 12 and 1. We talked of walking, but the blackness of the cold made us slow to put forward, and we did not walk at all. Mary read the Prologue to Chaucer's tales to me in the morning. William was working at his poem to C. Letter from Keswick and from Taylor on Wm.'s marriage. C. poorly, in bad spirits. Canaries.[1] Before tea I sate 2 hours in the parlour. Read part of *The Knight's Tale* with exquisite delight. Since tea Mary has been down stairs copying out Italian poems for Stuart. William has been working beside me, and here ends this imperfect summary. I will take a nice Calais Book,[2] and *will* for the future write regularly and, if I can, legibly ; so much for this my resolution on *Tuesday* night, January 11th, 1803. Now I am going to take tapioca for my supper, and Mary an egg, William some cold mutton — his poor chest is tired.

Jan[uary] 12th, Wednesday. Very cold, and cold all the week.

[January] 16th, Sunday. Intensely cold. Wm. had a fancy for some ginger bread. I put on Molly's cloak and my Spenser, and we walked towards Matthew Newton's. I went into the house. The blind man and his wife and sister were sitting by the fire, all dressed very clean in their Sunday clothes, the sister reading. They took their little stock of gingerbread out of the cupboard, and I bought 6 pennyworth. They were so grateful when I paid them for it that I could not find it in my heart to

---

[1] *i.e.* Coleridge thinks of a voyage to the Canaries.
[2] *i.e.* presumably, a note-book D. W. had bought when in Calais.

tell them we were going to make gingerbread ourselves. I had asked them if they had no thick — " No," answered Matthew, " there was none on Friday, but we'll *endeavour* to get some." The next day the woman came just when we were baking and we bought 2 pennyworth.

IV

Recollections of A TOUR MADE IN SCOTLAND

A.D. 1803

CONTENTS

PART I

PART II

CONTENTS

PART III

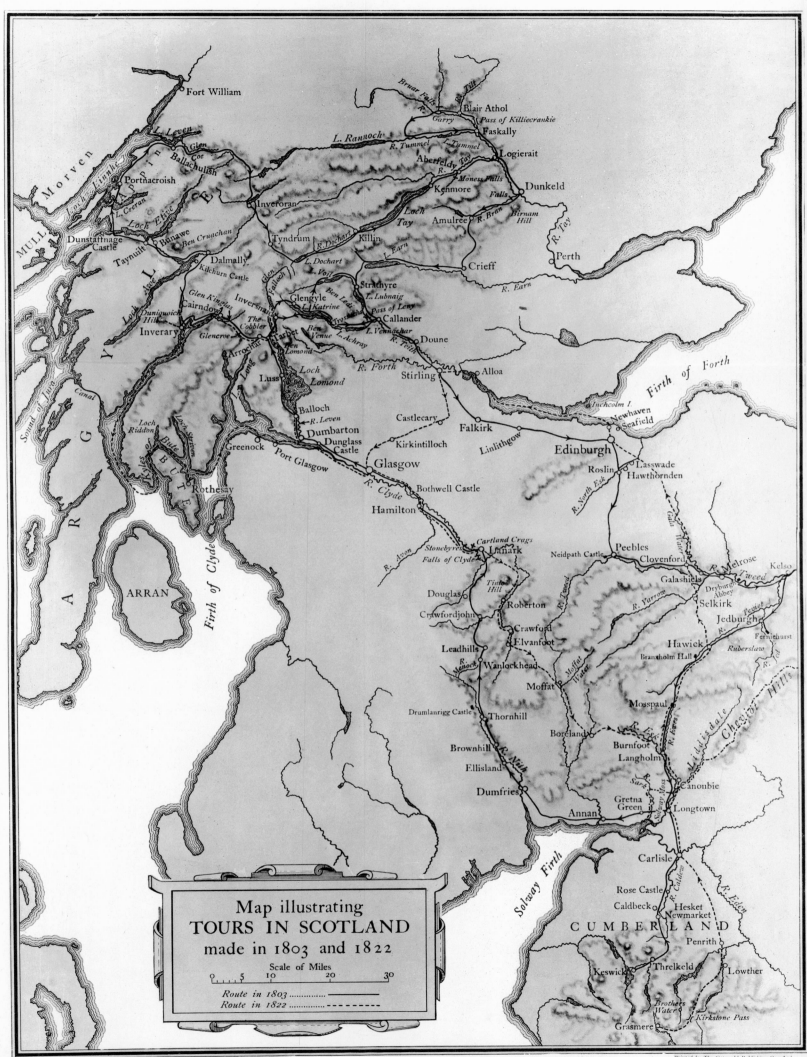

Map illustrating
TOURS IN SCOTLAND
made in 1803 and 1822

Scale of Miles

0 5 10 20 30

Route in 1803 ....
Route in 1822 ....

Based on the Ordnance Survey Map with the sanction of the Controller of H. M. Stationery Office

Printed by The Cotswold Publishing Co., Ltd.

RECOLLECTIONS OF A TOUR MADE IN SCOTLAND A.D. 1803

Part I

WILLIAM and I parted from Mary on Sunday afternoon, August 14th 1803 ; and Wm., Coleridge, and I left Keswick on Monday morning, the 15th, at twenty minutes after eleven o'clock. The day was very hot ; we walked up the hills, and along all the rough road, which made our walking half the day's journey. Travelled under the foot of Carrock, a mountain covered with stones on the lower part ; above, it is very rocky, but sheep pasture there ; we saw several where there seemed to be no grass to tempt them. Passed the foot of Grisdale and Mosedale, both pastoral vallies, narrow, and soon terminating in the mountains — green, with scattered trees and houses, and each a beautiful stream. At Grisdale our horse backed upon a steep bank where the road was not fenced, just above a pretty mill at the foot of the valley ; and we had a second threatening of a disaster in crossing a narrow bridge between the two dales ; but this was not the fault of either man or horse. Slept at Mr. Younghusband's publick-house, Hesket Newmarket. In the evening walked to Caldbeck Falls, a delicious spot in which to breathe out a summer's day — limestone rocks, hanging trees, pools, and waterbreaks — caves and caldrons which have been honoured with fairy names, and no doubt continue in the fancy of the neighbourhood to resound with fairy revels.

August 16th, Tuesday. Passed Rose Castle upon the Caldew, an ancient building of red stone with sloping gardens, an ivied gateway, velvet lawns, old garden walls, trim flower-borders with stately and luxuriant flowers. We walked up to the house and stood some minutes watching the swallows that flew about restlessly, and flung their shadows upon the sun-bright walls of the old building ; the shadows glanced and

195

twinkled, interchanged and crossed each other, expanded and shrunk up, appeared and disappeared every instant; as I observed to Wm. and Coleridge, seeming more like living things than the birds themselves. Dined at Carlisle; the town in a bustle with the assizes; so many strange faces known in former times and recognised, that it half seemed as if I ought to know them all, and, together with the noise, the fine ladies, etc., they put me into confusion. This day Hatfield [1] was condemned. I stood at the door of the gaoler's house, where he was; Wm. entered the house, and Coleridge saw him; I fell into conversation with a debtor, who told me in a dry way that he was "far over-learned", and another man observed to Wm. that we might learn from Hatfield's fate "not to meddle with pen and ink". We gave a shilling to my companion, whom we found out to be a friend of the family, a fellow-sailor with my brother John in Captain Wordsworth's ship. Walked upon the city walls, which are broken down in places and crumbling away, and most disgusting from filth. The city and neighbourhood of Carlisle disappointed me; the banks of the river quite flat, and, though the holms are rich, there is not much beauty in the vale from the want of trees — at least to the eye of a person coming from England, and (I scarcely know how), but to me the holms had not a *natural* look; there was something townish in their appearance, a dulness in their strong deep green. To Longtown — not very interesting, except from the long views over the flat country; the road rough, chiefly newly mended. Reached Longtown after sunset, a town of brick houses belonging chiefly to the Graham family. Being in the form of a cross and not long, it had been better called Crosstown. There are several shops, and it is not a very small place; but I could not meet with a silver thimble, and bought a halfpenny brass one. Slept at the Graham's Arms, a large inn. Here, as everywhere else, the people seemed utterly insensible of the enormity of Hatfield's

---

[1] A notorious forger who passed himself off as the Hon. A. A. Hope, M.P., and under that name franked letters, cheated the tradesmen of the district, and committed bigamy with Mary, "the Maid of Buttermere". (*v. Prelude* (1805), vii. 321.)

offences ; the ostler told William that he was quite a gentleman, paid every one genteelly, etc. etc. He and Mary had walked together to Gretna Green ; a heavy rain came on when they were there ; a returned chaise happened to pass, and the driver would have taken them up ; but Mr. Hope's carriage was to be sent for ! he did not choose to accept the chaise-driver's offer.

August 17th, Wednesday. Left Longtown after breakfast. About half a mile from the town a guide-post and two roads, to Edinburgh and Glasgow ; we took the left-hand road, to Glasgow. Here saw a specimen of the luxuriance of the heath-plant, as it grows in Scotland ; it was in the enclosed plantations (perhaps sheltered by them). These plantations appeared to be not well grown for their age ; the trees were stunted.[1] Afterwards the road, treeless, over a peat-moss common — the Solway Moss ; here and there an earth-built hut with its peat stack, a scanty growing willow hedge round the kail-garth, perhaps the cow pasturing near, — a little lass watching it, — the dreary waste cheared by the endless singing of larks.

We enter Scotland by crossing the river Sark ; on the Scotch side of the bridge the ground is unenclosed pasturage ; it was very green, and scattered over with that yellow flowered plant which we call grunsel ; the hills heave and swell prettily enough ; cattle feeding ; a few corn fields near the river. At the top of the hill opposite is Springfield, a village built by Sir William Maxwell — a dull uniformity in the houses, as is usual when all built at one time, or belonging to one individual, each just big enough for two people to live in, and in which a family, large or small as it may happen, is crammed. There the marriages are performed. Further on, though almost contiguous, is Gretna Green, upon a hill and among trees — this sounds well, but it is a dreary place ; the stone houses dirty and miserable, with broken windows. There is a pleasant view from the churchyard over Solway Firth to the Cumberland mountains. Dined at Annan. On our left as we travelled along appeared the Solway Firth and the mountains beyond,

---

[1] Growing irregularly, they reminded me of the Hartz forest near Goslar and I was pleased ; besides Wm. had spoken to me two years before of the pleasure he had received from the hether plant in that very spot.—C. C.

but the near country dreary. Those houses by the roadside which are built of stone are comfortless and dirty ; but we peeped into a clay *biggin* that was very *canny*, and I daresay will be as warm as a swallow's nest in winter. The town of Annan made me think of France and Germany ; many of the houses large and gloomy, the size of them outrunning the comforts. One thing which was like Germany pleased me : the shopkeepers express their calling by some device or painting ; bread-bakers have biscuits, loaves, cakes, painted on their window-shutters ; blacksmiths horses' shoes, iron tools, etc. etc. ; and so on through all trades.

Reached Dumfries at about nine o'clock — market-day ; met crowds of people on the road, and every one had a smile for us and our car. The inn was a large house, and tolerably comfortable ; Mr. Rogers and his sister, whom we hah seen at our own cottage at Grasmere a few days before, had arrived there that same afternoon on their way to the Highlands ; but we did not see them till the next morning, and only for about a quarter of an hour.

August 18th, Thursday. Went to the churchyard where Burns is buried, a bookseller accompanied us. He showed us the outside of Burns's house, where he had lived the last three years of his life, and where he died. It has a mean appearance, and is in a bye situation, whitewashed — dirty about the doors, as almost all Scotch houses are — flowering plants in the windows.

Went on to visit his grave. He lies at a corner of the churchyard, and his second son, Francis Wallace, beside him ; there is no stone to mark the spot ; but a hundred guineas have been collected, to be expended on some sort of monument. " There ", said the Bookseller, pointing to a pompous monument, " there lies Mr. Such-a-one " (I have forgotten his name), " a remarkably clever man ; he was an attorney, and hardly ever lost a cause he undertook. Burns made many a lampoon upon him, and there they rest, as you see." We looked at the grave with melancholy and painful reflections, repeating to each other his own verses :—

> *Is there a man whose judgment clear*
> *Can others teach the course to steer,*

> *Yet runs himself life's mad career*
>> *Wild as the wave ? —*
> *Here let him pause, and through a tear*
>> *Survey this grave.*

> *The poor Inhabitant below*
> *Was quick to learn, and wise to know,*
> *And keenly felt the friendly glow*
>> *And softer flame ;*
> *But thoughtless follies laid him low,*
>> *And stain'd his name.*

The churchyard is full of grave-stones and expensive monuments in all sorts of fantastic shapes — obelisk-wise, pillar-wise, etc. In speaking of Gretna Green, I forgot to mention that we visited the churchyard. The church is like a huge house ; indeed, so are all the churches, with a steeple, not a square tower or spire, — a sort of thing more like a glass-house chimney than a Church of England steeple ; grave-stones in abundance, few verses, yet there were some — no texts. Over the graves of married women the maiden name instead of that of the husband, spouse instead of wife, and the place of abode preceded by *in* instead of *of*.[1] When our guide had left us, we turned again to Burns's house. Mrs. Burns was gone to spend some time by the seashore with her children. We spoke to the servant-maid at the door, who invited us forward, and we sate down in the parlour. The walls were coloured with a blue wash ; on one side of the fire was a mahogany desk, opposite to the window a clock, and over the desk a print from the *Cotter's Saturday Night*, which Burns mentions in one of his letters having received as a present. The house was cleanly and neat in the inside, the stairs of stone, scoured white, the kitchen on the right side of the passage, the parlour on the left. In the room above the parlour the poet died, and his son after him in the same room. The servant told us she had lived five years with Mrs. Burns, who was now in great sorrow for the death of "Wallace". She said that Mrs. B.'s youngest son was at Christ's Hospital.

---

[1] As, for instance, Mary Hutchinson, spouse of W. W. *in* Grasmere, instead of *of*.—C. C.

We were glad to leave Dumfries, which is no agreeable place to them who do not love the bustle of a town that seems to be rising up to wealth. We could think of little else but poor Burns, and his moving about on that " unpoetic ground ". In our road to Brownhill, the next stage, we passed Ellisland at a little distance on our right, his farmhouse. We might there have had more pleasure in looking round, if we had been nearer to the spot ; but there is no thought surviving in connexion with Burns's daily life that is not heart-depressing. Travelled through the vale of Nith, here little like a vale, it is so broad, with irregular hills rising up on each side, in outline resembling the old-fashioned valances of a bed. There is a great deal of arable land — the corn ripe — trees here and there, plantations, clumps, coppices, and a newness in everything. So *much* of the gorse and broom rooted out that you wonder why it is not *all* gone, and yet there seems to be almost as much gorse and broom as corn ; and they grow one among another you know not how. Crossed the Nith ; the vale becomes narrow, and very pleasant ; corn fields, green hills, clay cottages ; the river's bed rocky, with woody banks. Left the Nith about a mile and a half, and reached Brownhill, a lonely inn, where we slept. The view from the windows was pleasing, though some travellers might have been disposed to quarrel with it for its general nakedness ; yet there was abundance of corn. It is an open country — open, yet all over hills. At a little distance were many cottages among trees, that looked very pretty. Brownhill is about seven or eight miles from Ellisland. I fancied to myself, while I was sitting in the parlour, that Burns might have caroused there, for most likely his rounds extended so far, and this thought gave a melancholy interest to the smoky walls. It was as pretty a room as a thoroughly dirty one could be, a square parlour painted green, but so covered over with smoke and dirt that it looked not unlike green seen through black gauze — there were three windows, looking three ways, a buffette ornamented with tea-cups, a superfine *largeish* looking-glass with gilt ornaments spreading far and wide, the glass spotted with dirt, some ordinary alehouse pictures, and above the chimney-piece a print in a much better style (as Wm. guessed, taken from a painting by Sir Joshua Reynolds) of some lady of quality, in the character of Euphrosyne. " Ay," said the servant-girl, seeing that we looked at it, " there's many travellers would give a deal for that, it's more admired than any in the house ". We could not but smile ; for the rest were such as may be found in the basket of any Italian image and picture hawker.

William and I walked out after dinner ; C. was not well, and slept upon the carriage cushions. We made our way to the cottages among the little hills and knots of wood, and then saw what a delightful country this part of Scotland might be made by planting forest trees. The ground all over heaves and swells like a sea ; but for miles there are neither trees nor hedgerows, only *mound* fences and tracts, or slips of corn, potatoes, clover — with hay between, and barren land ; but near the cottages many hills and hillocks covered with wood. We passed some fine trees, and paused under the shade of one close by an old mansion that seemed from its neglected state to be inhabited by farmers. (But I must say that many of the *gentleman's* houses which we have passed in Scotland have an air of neglect, and even of desolation.) It was a beech, in the full glory of complete and perfect growth, very tall, with one thick stem mounting to a considerable height, which was split into four *thighs*, as Coleridge afterwards called them, each in size a fine tree. Passed another mansion, now tenanted by a schoolmaster ; many boys playing upon the lawn. I cannot take leave of the country which we passed through to-day, without mentioning that we saw the Cumberland mountains within half a mile of Ellisland, Burns's house, the last view we had of them. Drayton has prettily described the connexion which this neighbourhood has with ours when he makes Skiddaw say —

Scurfell [1] from the sky,
That Anandale doth crown, with a most amorous eye,
Salutes me every day, or at my pride looks grim,
Oft threatening me with clouds, as I oft threatening him.

These lines recurred to Wm.'s memory, and we talked of

---

[1] Criffel.—J. C. S.

Burns, and of the prospect he must have had, perhaps from his own door, of Skiddaw and his companions, indulging ourselves in the fancy that we *might* have been personally known to each other, and he have looked upon those objects with more pleasure for our sakes. We talked of Coleridge's children and family, then at the foot of Skiddaw, and our own new-born John a few miles behind it ; while the grave of Burns's son, which we had just seen by the side of his father, and some stories heard at Dumfries respecting the dangers his surviving children were exposed to, filled us with melancholy concern, which had a kind of connexion with ourselves. In recollection of this, William long afterwards wrote the following Address to the sons of the ill-fated poet : —

Ye now are panting up life's hill,
'Tis twilight time of good and ill,
And more than common strength and skill
      Must ye display,
If ye would give the better will
      Its lawful sway.

Strong-bodied if ye be to bear
Intemperance with less harm, beware,
But if your Father's wit ye share,
      Then, then indeed,
Ye Sons of Burns, for watchful care
      There will be need.

For honest men delight will take
To shew you favour for his sake,
Will flatter you, and Fool and Rake
      Your steps pursue,
And of your Father's name will make
      A snare for you.

Let no mean hope your souls enslave,
Be independent, generous, brave ;
Your Father such example gave,
      And such revere,
But be admonished by his grave,
      And think and fear.

August 19th, Friday. Open country for a considerable way. Passed through the village of Thornhill, built by the Duke of Queensberry ; the brother-houses so small that they might have been built to stamp a character of insolent pride on his own huge mansion of Drumlanrigg, which is full in view on the opposite side of the Nith. This mansion is indeed very large ; but to us it appeared like a gathering together of little things — the roof is broken into a hundred pieces, cupolas, etc., in the shape of casters, conjuror's balls, cups, and the like. The situation would be noble if the woods had been left standing ; but they have been cut down not long ago, and the hills above and below the house are quite bare. About a mile and a half from Drumlanrigg is a turnpike gate at the top of a hill. We left our car with the man, and turned aside into a field where we looked down upon the Nith, which runs far below in a deep and rocky channel ; the banks woody. The view was pleasant down the river towards Thornhill, an open country — corn fields, pastures, and scattered trees. Returned to the turnpike house, a cold spot upon a common, black cattle feeding close to the door. Our road led us down the hill to the side of the Nith, and we travelled along its banks for some miles ; here were clay cottages perhaps every half or quarter of a mile, the bed of the stream rough with rocks ; banks irregular, now woody, now bare ; here a patch of broom, there of corn, then of pasturage ; and hills green or heathy, above. We were to have given our horse meal and water at a publick-house in one of the hamlets we passed through, but missed the house, for, as is common in Scotland, it was without a sign-board. Travelled on, still beside the Nith, till we came to a turnpike house, which stood rather high on the hill-side, and from the door we looked a long way up and down the river. The air coldish, the wind strong.

We asked the turnpike man to let us have some meal and water ; he had no meal, but luckily we had part of a feed of corn brought from Keswick, and he procured some hay at a neighbouring house. In the meantime I went into the house, where was an old man with a grey plaid over his shoulders, reading a newspaper. On the shelf lay a volume of the Scotch

Encyclopædia, a History of England, and some other books. The old man was a caller by the way. The man of the house came back, and we began to talk — he was very intelligent ; had travelled all over England, Scotland, and Ireland as a gentleman's servant, and now lived alone in that lonesome place. He said he was tired of his bargain, for he feared he should lose by it ; and he had indeed a troublesome office, for coal-carts without number were passing by, and the drivers seemed to do their utmost to cheat him. There is always something peculiar in the house of a man living alone. *This* was but half-furnished, yet nothing seemed wanting for *his* comfort, though a female who had travelled half as far would have needed fifty other things. He had no other meat or drink in the house but oat bread and cheese (the cheese was made with the addition of seeds) and some skimmed milk. He gave us of his bread and cheese, and milk (which proved to be sour).

We had yet ten or eleven miles to travel, and no food with us. Wm. lay under the wind in a corn field below the house, being not well enough to partake of the milk and bread. C. gave our host a pamphlet, *The Crisis of the Sugar Colonies* ; he was well acquainted with Burns's poems. There was a politeness and a manly freedom in this man's manners which pleased me very much. He told us that he had served a gentleman, a Captain in the army — he did not know *who* he was, for none of his relations had ever come to see him, but he used to receive many letters ; that he had lived near Dumfries till they would let him stay no longer, he made such havoc with the game — his whole delight from morning till night, and the long year through, was in field sports ; he would be on his feet the worst days in winter, and wade through snow up to the middle after his game. If he had company he was in tortures till they were gone ; he would then throw off his coat and put on an old jacket not worth half-a-crown ; he drank his bottle of wine every day, and two if he had better sport than usual. Ladies sometimes came to stay with his wife, and he often carried them out in an Irish jaunting-car, and if they vexed him he would choose the dirtiest roads possible, and spoil their clothes by jumping in and out of the car, and treading upon them. " But for all that " (and so he ended all) " he was a good fellow, and a clever fellow, and he liked him well." He would have ten or a dozen hares in the larder at once, he half maintained his family with game, and he himself was very fond of eating of the spoil — unusual with true heart-and-soul sportsmen.

The man gave us an account of his farm where he had lived, which was so cheap and pleasant that we thought we should have liked to have had it ourselves. Soon after leaving the turnpike house we turned up a hill to the right, the road for a little way very steep, bare hills, with sheep.

After ascending a little while we heard the murmur of a stream far below us, and saw it flowing downwards on our left, towards the Nith, and before us, between steep green hills, coming along a winding valley. The simplicity of the prospect impressed us very much. There was a single cottage by the brook side ; the dell was not heathy, but it was impossible not to think of Peter Bell's Highland Girl.

We now felt indeed that we were in Scotland ; there was a natural peculiarity in this place. In the scenes of the Nith it had not been the same as England, but yet not simple, naked Scotland. The road led us down the hill, and now there was no room in the vale but for the river and the road ; we had sometimes the stream to the right, sometimes to the left. The hills were pastoral, but we did not see many sheep ; green smooth turf on the left, no ferns. On the right the heath-plant grew in abundance, of the most exquisite colour ; it covered a whole hill-side, or it was in streams and patches. We travelled along the vale without appearing to ascend for some miles ; all the reaches were beautiful, in exquisite proportion, the hills seeming very high from being so near to us. It might have seemed a valley which nature had kept to herself for pensive thoughts and tender feelings, but that we were reminded at every turning of the road of something beyond by the coal-carts which were travelling towards us. Though these carts broke in upon the tranquillity of the glen, they added much to the picturesque effect of the different views, which indeed wanted nothing, though perfectly bare, houseless, and treeless.

After some time our road took us upwards towards the end of the valley. Now the steeps were heathy all around. Just as we began to climb the hill we saw three boys who came down the cleft of a brow on our left ; one carried a fishing-rod, and the hats of all were braided with honeysuckles ; they ran after one another as wanton as the wind. I cannot express what a character of *beauty* those few honeysuckles in the hats of the three boys gave to the place : what bower could they have come from ? We walked up the hill, met two well-dressed travellers, the woman barefoot. Our little lads before they had gone far were joined by some half-dozen of their companions, all without shoes and stockings. They told us they lived at Wanlockhead, the village above, pointing to the top of the hill ; they went to school and learned Latin (Virgil), and some of them Greek (Homer), but when Coleridge began to inquire further, off they ran, poor things ! I suppose afraid of being examined.

When, after a steep ascent, we had reached the top of the hill, we saw a village about half a mile before us on the side of another hill, which rose up above the spot where we were, after a descent, a sort of valley or hollow. Nothing grew upon this ground, or the hills above or below, but hether, yet round about the village (which consisted of a great number of huts, all alike, and all thatched, with a few larger slated houses among them, and a single modern-built one of a considerable size) were a hundred patches of cultivated ground, potatoes, oats, hay, and grass. We were struck with the sight of haycocks fastened down with aprons, sheets, pieces of sacking (as we supposed, to prevent the wind from blowing them away). We afterwards found that this practice was very general in Scotland. Every cottage seemed to have its little plot of ground, fenced by a ridge of earth ; this plot contained two or three different divisions, kail, potatoes, oats, hay ; the houses all standing in lines, or never far apart ; the cultivated ground was all together also, and made a very strange appearance with its many greens among the dark brown hills, neither tree nor shrub growing ; yet the grass and the potatoes looked greener than elsewhere, owing to the bareness of the neighbouring hills ; it was indeed a wild and singular spot (to use a woman's illustration) like a collection of patchwork, made of pieces as they might have chanced to have been cut by the mantua-maker, only just smoothed to fit each other, the different sorts of produce being in such a multitude of plots, and those so small and of such irregular shapes. Add to the strangeness of the village itself, that we had been climbing upwards, though gently, for many miles, and for the last mile and a half up a steep ascent, and did not know of any village till we saw the boys who had come out to play. The air was very cold, and one could not help thinking what it must be in winter, when those hills (now " red brown ") should have their three months' covering of snow.

The village, as we guessed, is inhabited by miners ; the mines belong to the Duke of Queensberry. The road to the village, down which the lads scampered away, was straight forward. I must mention that we met, just after we had parted from them, another little fellow, about six years old, carrying a bundle over his shoulder ; he seemed poor and half starved, and was scratching his fingers, which were covered with the itch. He was a miner's son, and lived at Wanlockhead ; did not go to school, but this was probably on account of his youth. I mention him because he seemed to be a proof that there was poverty and wretchedness among these people, though we saw no other symptom of it ; and afterwards we met scores of the inhabitants of this same village. Our road turned to the right, and we saw, at the distance of less than a mile, a tall upright building of grey stone, with several men standing upon the roof, as if they were looking out over battle-ments. It stood beyond the village, upon higher ground, as if presiding over it, — a kind of enchanter's castle, which it might have been, a place which Don Quixote would have gloried in. When we drew nearer we saw, coming out of the side of the building, a large machine or lever, in appearance like a great forge-hammer, as we supposed for raising water out of the mines. It heaved upwards once in half a minute with a slow motion, and seemed to rest to take breath at the bottom, its motion being accompanied with a sound between

Q

a groan and *jike*.[1] There would have been something in this object very striking in any place, as it was impossible not to invest the machine with some faculty of intellect ; it seemed to have made the first step from brute matter to life and purpose, showing its progress by great power. William made a remark to this effect, and Coleridge observed that it was like a giant with one idea. At all events, the object produced a striking effect in that place, where everything was in unison with it, particularly the building itself, which was turret-shaped, and with the figures upon it resembled much one of the fortresses in the wooden cuts of Bunyan's *Holy War*.

After ascending a considerable w y we began to descend again ; and now we met a team of horses dragging an immense tree to the lead mines (to repair or add to the building), and presently after we came to a cart, with another large tree, and one horse left in it, right in the middle of the highway. We were a little out of humour, thinking we must wait till the team came back. There were men and boys without number all staring at us ; after a little consultation they set their shoulders to the cart, and with a good heave all at once they moved it, and we passed along. These people were decently dressed, and their manners decent ; there was no hooting or impudent laughter. Leadhills, another mining village, was the place of our destination for the night ; and soon after we had passed the cart we came in sight of it. This village and the mines belong to Lord Hopetoun ; it has more stone houses than Wanlockhead, one large old mansion, and a considerable number of old trees — beeches, I believe. The trees told of the coldness of the climate ; they were more brown than green — far browner than the ripe grass of the little hay-garths. Here, as at Wanlockhead, were haycocks, hay-stacks, potato-beds, and kail-garths in every possible variety of shape, but (I suppose from the irregularity of the ground) it looked far less artificial — indeed, I should think that a painter might make several beautiful pictures in this village. It straggles down both sides of a mountain glen. As I have said, there is

---

[1] jike : a word used in the dialect of Cumberland for a creaking noise, *e.g.* the creaking of shoe leather.

a large mansion ; there is also a stone building that looks like a school, and the houses are single, or in clusters, or rows as it may chance.

We passed a decent-looking inn, the Hopetoun Arms ; but the house of Mrs. Otto, a widow, had been recommended to us with high encomiums. We did not then understand Scotch inns, and were not quite satisfied at first with our accommodations, but all things were smoothed over by degrees ; we had a fire lighted in our dirty parlour, tea came after a reasonable waiting ; and the fire with the gentle aid of twilight, burnished up the room into chearful comfort. C. was weary ; but W. and I walked out after tea. We talked with one of the miners, who informed us that the building which we had supposed to be a school was a library belonging to the village. He said they had got a book into it a few weeks ago, which had cost thirty pounds, and that they had all sorts of books. " What ! have you Shakespeare ? " " Yes, we have that ", and we found, on further inquiry, that they had a large library, of long standing, that Lord Hopetoun had subscribed liberally to it, and that gentlemen who came with him were in the habit of making larger or smaller donations. Each man who had the benefit of it paid a small sum monthly (I think about fourpence).

The man we talked with spoke much of the comfort and quiet in which they lived one among another ; he made use of a noticeable expression, saying that they were " very peaceable people considering they lived so much under-ground " ; — wages were about thirty pounds a year ; they had land for potatoes, warm houses, plenty of coals, and only six hours' work each day, so that they had leisure for reading if they chose ; he said the place was healthy, that the inhabitants lived to a great age ; and indeed we saw no appearance of ill-health in their countenances ; but it is not common for people working in lead mines to be healthy ; and I have since heard that it is *not* a healthy place. However this may be, they are unwilling to allow it ; for the landlady the next morning, when I said to her " You have a cold climate ", replied, " Ay, but it is *varra halesome* ". We inquired of the man respecting the large mansion ; he told us that it was built, as we might see, in the form of an H, and belonged to the Hopetouns, and they took their title from thence,[1] and that part of it was used as a chapel. We went close to it, and were a good deal amused with the building itself, standing forth in bold contradiction of the story which I daresay every man of Leadhills tells, and every man believes, that it is in the shape of an H ; it is but half an H, and one must be very accommodating to allow it even *so* much, for the legs are far too short. ☐ This is the shape of the building.

We visited the burying-ground, a plot of land not very small, crowded with graves, and upright grave-stones, over-looking the village and the dell. It was now the closing in of evening. Women and children were gathering in the linen for the night, which was bleaching by the burn-side. The graves overgrown with grass, such as, by industrious culture. had been raised up about the houses ; but there were bunches ot hether here and there, and with the blue-bells that grew among the grass the small plot of ground had a beautiful and wild appearance.

William left me, and I went to a shop to purchase some thread ; the woman had none that suited me ; but she would send a " *wee* lad " to the other shop. In the meantime I sat with the mother, and was much pleased with her manner and conversation. She had an excellent fire, and her cottage, though very small, looked comfortable and cleanly ; but re-member I saw it only by firelight. She confirmed what the man had told us of the quiet manner in which they lived ; and indeed her house and fireside seemed to need nothing to make it a chearful happy spot, but health and good humour. There was a bookishness, a certain formality in this woman's language, which was very remarkable. She had a dark com-plexion, dark eyes, and wore a *very white* cap, much over her face, which gave her the look of a French woman, and indeed afterwards the women on the roads frequently reminded us of French women, partly from the extremely white caps of the elder women, and still more perhaps from a certain gaiety and

---

[1] There is some mistake here. The Hopetoun title was not taken from any place in the Leadhills, much less from the house shaped like an H.—J. C. S.

party-coloured appearance in their dress in general. White bed-gowns are very common, and you rarely meet a young girl with either hat or cap ; they buckle up their hair often in a graceful manner.

I returned to the inn, and went into the kitchen to speak with the landlady ; she had made a hundred hesitations when I told her we wanted three beds. At last she confessed she *had* three beds, and showed me into a parlour which looked damp and cold, but she assured me in a tone that showed she was unwilling to be questioned further, that all *her* beds were well aired. I sat a while by the kitchen fire with the landlady, and began to talk to her ; but, much as I had heard in her praise (for the shopkeeper had told me she was a *varra discreet* woman) I cannot say that her manners pleased me much ; but her servant made amends, for she was as pleasant and chearful a lass as was ever seen ; and when we asked her to do anything, she answered, " Oh yes ", with a merry smile, and almost ran to get it for us. She was about sixteen years old : wore shoes and stockings, and had her hair tucked up with a comb. The servant at Brownhill was a coarse-looking wench, barefoot and bare-legged. I examined the kitchen round about ; it was crowded with furniture, drawers, cupboards, dish-covers, pictures, pans, and pots, arranged without order, except that the plates were on shelves, and the dish-covers hung in rows. These were very clean, but floors, passages, staircase, everything else dirty. There were two beds in recesses in the wall ; above one of them I noticed a shelf with some books :—it made me think of Chaucer's Clerke of Oxenforde :—

> *Liever had he at his bed's head*
> *Twenty books clothed in black and red.*

They were baking oat-bread, which they cut into quarters, and half-baked over the fire, and half-toasted before it. There was a suspiciousness about Mrs. Otto, almost like ill-nature ; she was very jealous of any inquiries that might appear to be made with the faintest idea of a comparison between Leadhills and any other place, except the advantage was evidently on the side of Leadhills. We had nice honey to breakfast. When ready to depart, we learned that we might have seen the library, which we had not thought of till it was too late, and we were very sorry to go away without seeing it.

Saturday, August 20th. Left Leadhills at nine o'clock, re-gretting much that we could not stay another day, that we might have made more minute inquiries respecting the manner of living of the miners, and been able to form an estimate, from our own observation, of the degree of knowledge, health, and comfort that there was among them. The air was keen and cold ; we might have supposed it to be three months later in the season and two hours earlier in the day. The landlady had not lighted us a fire ; so I was obliged to get myself toasted in the kitchen, and when we set off I put on both grey cloak and spencer.

Our road carried us down the valley, and we soon lost sight of Leadhills, for the valley made a turn almost immediately, and we saw two miles, perhaps, before us ; the glen sloped somewhat rapidly — heathy, bare, no hut or house. Passed by a shepherd, who was sitting upon the ground, reading, with the book on his knee, screened from the wind by his plaid, while a flock of sheep were feeding near him among the rushes and coarse grass (for, as we descended we came among lands where grass grew with the hether). Travelled through several reaches of the glen, which somewhat resembled the valley of Menock on the other side of Wanlockhead ; but it was not near so beautiful ; the forms of the mountains did not melt so exquisitely into each other, and there was a coldness, and, if I may so speak, a want of simplicity in the surface of the earth ; the hether was poor, not covering a whole hill-side ; not in luxuriant streams and beds interveined with rich verdure; but patchy and stunted, with here and there coarse grass and rushes. But we soon came in sight of a spot that impressed us very much. At the lower end of this new reach of the vale was a decayed tree, beside a decayed cottage, the vale spreading out into a level area which was one large field, without fence and without division, of a dull yellow colour ; the vale seemed to partake of the desolation of the cottage, and to participate in its decay ; and yet the spot was in its nature so dreary that one would rather have wondered how it ever came to be tenanted by man, than lament that it was left to waste and solitude. Yet the encircling hills were so exquisitely formed that it was impossible to conceive anything more lovely than this place would have been if the valley and hill-sides had been interspersed with trees, cottages, green fields, and hedgerows ; but all was desolate ; the one large field which filled up the area of the valley appeared, as I have said, in decay, and seemed to retain the memory of its connection with man in some way analogous to the ruined building ; for it was as much of a *field* as Mr. King's best pasture [1] scattered over with his fattest cattle.

We went on, looking before us, the place losing nothing of its hold upon our minds, when we discovered a woman sitting right in the middle of the field, alone, wrapped up in a grey cloak or plaid. She sat motionless all the time we looked at her, which might be nearly half an hour. We could not conceive why she sat there, for there were neither sheep nor cattle in the field ; her appearance was very melancholy. In the meantime our road carried us nearer to the cottage, though we were crossing over the hill to the left, leaving the valley below us, and we perceived that a part of the building was inhabited, and that what we had supposed to be *one* blasted tree was eight trees, four of which were entirely blasted, the others partly so, and round about the place was a little potato and cabbage garth, fenced with earth. No doubt, that woman had been an inhabitant of the cottage ; however this might be, there was so much obscurity and uncertainty about her, and her figure agreed so well with the desolation of the place, that we were indebted to the chance of her being there for some of the most interesting feelings that we had ever had from natural objects connected with man in dreary solitariness.

We had been advised to go along the *new* road, which would have carried us down the vale ; but we met some travellers who recommended us to climb the hill, and go by the village of Crawfordjohn as being much nearer. We had a long hill, and after having reached the top, steep and bad roads, so we

---

[1] *i.e.* at the Hollins, Grasmere.

continued to walk for a considerable way. The air was cold and clear — the sky blue; we walked chearfully along in the sunshine, each of us alone, only Wm. had the charge of the horse and car, so he sometimes took a ride, which did but poorly recompense him for the trouble of driving. I never travelled with more chearful spirits than this day; our road was along the side of a high moor. I can always walk over a moor with a light foot; I seem to be drawn more closely to nature in such places than anywhere else; or rather I feel more strongly the power of nature over me, and am better satisfied with myself for being able to find enjoyment in what unfortunately to many persons is either dismal or insipid. This moor, however, was more than commonly interesting; we could see a long way, and on every side of us were larger or smaller tracts of cultivated land. Some were extensive farms (yet in so large a waste they did but look small), with farm-houses, barns, etc., others (like little cottages) with enough to feed a cow, and supply the family with vegetables. In looking at these farms we had always one feeling. Why did the plough stop there? Why might not they as well have carried it twice as far? There were no hedgerows near the farms, and very few trees. As we were passing along, we saw an old man, the first we had seen in a Highland bonnet, walking with a staff at a very slow pace by the edge of one of the moorland corn-fields; he wore a grey plaid, and a dog was by his side. There was a scriptural solemnity in this man's figure, a sober simplicity which was most impressive. Scotland is the country above all others that I have seen, in which a man of imagination may carve out his own pleasures; there are so many *inhabited* solitudes, and the employments of the people are so immediately connected with the places where you find them, and their dresses so simple, so much alike, yet, from their being folding garments, admitting of an endless variety, and falling often so gracefully.

After some time we descended towards a broad vale, passed one farm-house, sheltered by fir trees, with a burn close to it; children playing, linen bleaching. The vale was open pastures and corn-fields unfenced, the land poor. The village of Crawfordjohn on the slope of a hill a long way before us to the

214

left — asked about our road of a man who was driving a cart ; he told us to go through the village, then along some fields, and we should come to a " herd's house by the burn side ". The highway was right through the vale, unfenced on either side ; the people of the village, who were making hay, all stared at us and our carriage. We inquired the road of a middle-aged man, dressed in a shabby black coat, at work in one of the hay fields ; he looked like the minister of the place, and when he spoke we felt assured that he was so, for he was not sparing of hard words, which, however, he used with great propriety, and he spoke like one who had been accustomed to dictate. Our car wanted mending in the wheel, and we asked him if there was a blacksmith in the village. " Yes," he replied, but when we showed him the wheel he told Wm. that he might mend it himself without a blacksmith, and he would put him in the way ; so he fetched hammer and nails and gave his directions, which Wm. obeyed, and repaired the damage entirely to his own satisfaction and the priest's, who did not offer to lend any assistance himself ; not as if he would not have been willing in case of need ; but as if it were more natural for him to dictate, and because he thought it more fit that Wm. should do it himself. He spoke much about the propriety of every man's lending all the assistance in his power to travellers, and with some ostentation or self-praise. Here I observed a honey-suckle and some flowers growing in a garden, the first I had seen in Scotland. It is a pretty chearful-looking village, but must be very cold in winter, standing on a hillside (and the vale itself is very high ground) unsheltered by trees.

Left the village behind us, and our road led through arable ground for a considerable way, on which were growing very good crops of corn and potatoes. Our friend accompanied us to show us the way, and C. and he had a scientific conversation concerning the uses and properties of lime and other manures. He seemed to be a well-informed man, somewhat pedantic in his manners ; but this might be only the difference between Scotch and English.[1]

---

[1] Probably the Rev. John Aird, minister of the parish, 1801-15.— J. C. S.

Soon after he had parted from us, we came upon a stony, rough road over a black moor ; and presently to the " herd's house by the burn side " ; we could hardly cross the burn dry-. shod, over which was the only road to the cottage. In England there would have been stepping-stones or a bridge ; but the Scotch need not be afraid of wetting their bare feet. The hut had its little kail-garth fenced with earth ; there was no other enclosure ; the common, heathy with coarse grass. Travelled along the common for some miles, before we joined the great road from Longtown to Glasgow — saw on the bare hill-sides at a distance, sometimes a solitary farm, now and then a plantation, and one very large wood, with an appearance of richer ground above ; but it was so very high we could not think it possible. Having descended considerably, the common was no longer of a peat-mossy brown heath colour, but grass with rushes was its chief produce ; there was sometimes a solitary hut (no enclosures except the kail-garth), and sheep pasturing in flocks, with shepherd-boys tending them. I remember one boy in particular ; he had no hat on, and only had a grey plaid wrapped round him : — it is nothing to describe, but on a bare moor, alone with his sheep, standing, as he did, in utter quietness and silence, there was something uncommonly impressive in his appearance, a solemnity which recalled to our minds the old man in the corn-field. We passed many people who were mowing, or raking the grass of the common ; it was little better than rushes ; but they did not mow straight forward, only here and there, where it was the best ; in such a place hay-cocks had an uncommon appearance to us.

After a long descent we came to some plantations which were not far from Douglas Mill. The country for some time had been growing into cultivation, and now it was a wide vale with large tracts of corn ; trees in clumps, no hedgerows, which always make a country look bare and unlovely. For my part, I was better pleased with the desert places we had left behind, though no doubt the inhabitants of this place think it " a varra bonny spot ", for the Scotch are always pleased with their own abode, be it what it may ; and afterwards at Edinburgh, when we were talking with a bookseller of our travels, he observed that it was " a fine country near Douglas Mill ". Douglas Mill is a single house, a large inn, being one of the regular stages between Longtown and Glasgow, and therefore a fair specimen of the best of the country inns of Scotland. As soon as our car stopped at the door we felt the difference ; at an English inn of this size, a waiter, or the master or mistress, would have been at the door immediately, but we remained some time before anybody came ; then a barefooted lass made her appearance, but she only looked at us and went away. The mistress, a remarkably handsome woman, showed us into a large parlour ; we ordered mutton-chops, and I finished my letter to Mary ; writing on the same window-ledge on which Wm. had written to me two years before.

After dinner, Wm. and I sat by a little mill-race in the garden. We had left Leadhills and Wanlockhead far above us, and now were come into a warmer climate ; but there was no richness in the face of the country. The shrubs looked cold and poor, and yet there were some very fine trees within a little distance of Douglas Mill, so that the reason, perhaps, why the few low shrubs and trees which were growing in the gardens seemed to be so unluxuriant, might be, that there being no hedgerows, the general appearance of the country was naked, and I could not help seeing the same coldness where, perhaps, it did not exist in itself to any great degree, for the corn crops are abundant, and I should think the soil is not bad. While we were sitting at the door, two of the landlady's children came out ; the elder, a boy about six years old, was running away from his little brother, in petticoats ; the ostler called out, " Sandy, tak' your wee brither wi' you " ; another voice from the window, " Sawny, dinna leave your wee brither " ; the mother then came, " Alexander, tak' your wee brother by the hand " ; Alexander obeyed, and the two went off in peace together. We were charged eightpence for hay at this inn, another symptom of our being in Scotland. Left Douglas Mill at about three o'clock ; travelled through an open corn country, the tracts of corn large and unenclosed. We often passed women or children who were watching a single cow while it fed upon the slips of grass between the corn. William asked a strong woman, about thirty years of age, who looked like the mistress of a family (I suppose moved by some sentiment of compassion for her being so employed) — if the cow would eat the corn if it were left to itself — she smiled at his simplicity. It is indeed a melancholy thing to see a full-grown woman thus waiting, as it were, body and soul devoted to the poor beast ; yet even this is better than working in a manufactory the day through.

We came to a moorish tract ; saw before us the hills of Loch Lomond, Ben Lomond and another, distinct each by itself. Not far from the roadside were some benches placed in rows in the middle of a large field, with a sort of covered shed like a sentry-box, but much more like those boxes which the Italian puppet-showmen in London use. We guessed that it was a pulpit or tent for preaching, and were told that a sect met there occasionally, who held that toleration was unscriptural, and would have all religions but their own exterminated. I have forgotten what name the man gave to this sect ; we could not learn that it differed in any other respect from the Church of Scotland. Travelled for some miles along the open country, which was all without hedgerows, sometimes arable, sometimes moorish, and often whole tracts covered with grunsel.[1] There was one field, which one might have believed had been sown with grunsel, it was so regularly covered with it — a large square field upon a slope, its boundary marked to our eyes only by the termination of the bright yellow ; contiguous to it were other fields of the same size and shape, one of clover, the other of potatoes, all equally regular crops. The oddness of this appearance, the grunsel being uncommonly luxuriant, and the field as yellow as gold, made Wm. laugh. C. was melancholy upon it, observing that there was land enough wasted to rear a healthy child.

We left behind us, considerably to the right, a single high mountain [2] (I have forgotten its name) ; we had had it long in view. Saw before us the river Clyde, its course at right angles to our road, which now made a turn, running parallel

---

[1] Ragweed.—J. C. S.   [2] Tinto.—J. C. S.

with the river ; the town of Lanerk in sight long before we
came to it. I was somewhat disappointed with the first view
of the Clyde ; the banks, though swelling and varied, had a
poverty in their appearance, chiefly from the want of wood
and hedgerows. Crossed the river and ascended towards
Lanerk, which stands upon a hill. When we were within about
a mile of the town, Wm. parted from C. and me, to go to the
celebrated waterfalls. C. did not attempt to drive the horse ;
but led him all the way. We inquired for the best inn, and
were told that the New Inn was the best ; but that they had
very " genteel apartments " at the Black Bull, and made less
charges, and the Black Bull was at the entrance of the town,
so we thought we would stop there, as the horse was obstinate
and weary. But when we came to the Black Bull we had no
wish to enter the apartments ; for it seemed the abode of dirt
and poverty, yet it was a large building. The town showed a
sort of French face, and would have done much more, had it
not been for the true British tinge of coal-smoke ; the doors
and windows dirty, the shops dull, the women too seemed to
be very dirty in their dress. The town itself is not ugly ; the
houses are of grey stone, the streets not very narrow, and the
market-place decent. The New Inn is a handsome old stone
building, formerly a gentleman's house. We were conducted
into a parlour, where people had been drinking ; the tables
were unwiped, chairs in disorder, the floor dirty, and the smell
of liquors was most offensive. We were tired, however, and
rejoiced in our tea.

The evening sun was now sending a glorious light through
the street, which ran from west to east ; the houses were of a
fire red, and the faces of the people as they walked westward
were almost like a blacksmith when he is at work by night. I
longed to be out, and meet with Wm., that we might see the
Falls before the day was gone. Poor Coleridge was unwell,
and could not go. I inquired my road, and a little girl told
me she would go with me to the porter's lodge, where I might
be admitted. I was grieved to hear that the Falls of the Clyde
were shut up in a gentleman's grounds, and to be viewed only
by means of lock and key. Much, however, as the pure feeling

with which one would desire to visit such places is disturbed by
useless, impertinent, or even unnecessary interference with
nature, yet when I was there the next morning I seemed to
feel it a less disagreeable thing than in smaller and more delicate
spots, if I may use the phrase. My guide, a sensible little girl,
answered my inquiries very prettily. She was eight years old,
read in the " Collection ", a book which all the Scotch children
whom I have questioned read in. I found it was a collection
of hymns ; she could repeat several of Dr. Watts's. We passed
through a great part of the town, then turned down a steep
hill, and came in view of a long range of cotton mills,[1] the
largest and loftiest I had ever seen ; climbed upwards again,
our road leading us along the top of the left bank of the river ;
both banks very steep and richly wooded. The girl left me at
the porter's lodge. Having asked after Wm., I was told that
no person had been there, or could enter but by the gate. The
night was coming on, therefore I did not venture to go in, as I
had no hope of meeting Wm. I had a delicious walk alone
through the wood ; the sound of the water was very solemn,
and even the cotton mills in the fading light of evening had
somewhat of the majesty and stillness of the natural objects.
It was nearly dark when I reached the inn. I found C. sitting
by a good fire, which always makes an inn room look comfortable. In a few minutes Wm. arrived ; he had heard of me at
the gate, and followed as quickly as he could, shouting after
me. He was pale and exceedingly tired. After he had left us
he had taken a wrong road, and while looking about to set
himself right had met with a barefooted boy, who said he would
go with him. The little fellow carried him by a wild path to
the upper of the Falls, the Boniton Linn, and coming down unexpectedly upon it, he was exceedingly affected by the solemn
grandeur of the place. This fall is not much admired or spoken
of by travellers ; you have never a full, breast view of it ; it
does not make a complete self-satisfying place, an abode of its

---

[1] New Lanark, Robert Owen's mills.—J. C. S. Robert Owen (1771–1858)
had bought the mills from his father-in-law, Dale, in 1800. It was here that
he conducted his famous experiments in education and in village community
life. For D. W.'s visit to him on his second Tour, in 1822, when his schemes
were already celebrated, v. Vol. II, pp. 381-9.

own, as a perfect waterfall seems to me to do ; but the river, down which you look through a long vista of steep and ruin-like rocks, the roaring of the waterfall, and the solemn evening lights, must have been most impressive. One of the rocks on the near bank, even in broad daylight, as we saw it the next morning, is exactly like the fractured arch of an abbey. With the lights and shadows of evening upon it, the resemblance must have been much more striking.

Wm.'s guide was a pretty boy, and he was exceedingly pleased with him. Just as they were quitting the waterfall, Wm.'s mind being full of the majesty of the scene, the little fellow pointed to the top of a rock, " There's a fine slae-bush there ". " Ay," said Wm., " but there are no slaes upon it ", which was true enough ; but I suppose the child remembered the slaes of another summer, though, as he said, he was but " half seven years old ", namely, six and a half. He conducted Wm. to the other fall, and as they were going along a narrow path, they came to a small cavern, where Wm. lost him, and looking about, saw his pretty figure in a sort of natural niche fitted for a statue, from which the boy jumped out laughing, delighted with the success of his trick. Wm. told us a great deal about him, while he sat by the fire, and of the pleasure of his walk, often repeating, " I wish you had been with me ". Having no change, he gave the boy sixpence, which was cer-tainly, if he had formed any expectations at all, far beyond them ; but he received it with the utmost indifference, without any remark of surprise or pleasure ; most likely he did not know how many halfpence he could get for it, and twopence would have pleased him more. My little girl was delighted with the sixpence I gave her, and said she would buy a book with it on Monday morning. What a difference between the manner of living and education of boys and of girls among the lower classes of people in towns ! she had never seen the Falls of the Clyde, nor had ever been further than the porter's lodge ; the boy, I daresay, knew every hiding-place in every accessible rock, as well as the fine " slae bushes " and the nut trees.

August 21st, Sunday. The morning was very hot, a morning

to tempt us to linger by the water-side. I wished to have had the day before us, expecting so much from what Wm. had seen ; but when we went there, I did not desire to stay longer than till the hour which we had prescribed to ourselves ; for it was a rule not to be broken in upon, that the person who conducted us to the Falls was to remain by our side till we chose to depart. We left our inn immediately after breakfast. The lanes were full of people going to church ; many of the middle-aged women wore long scarlet cardinals, and were without hats : they brought to my mind the women of Goslar as they used to go to church in their silver or gold caps, with their long cloaks, black or coloured.

The banks of the Clyde from Lanerk to the Falls rise immediately from the river ; they are lofty and steep, and covered with wood. The road to the Falls is along the top of one of the banks, and to the left you have a prospect of the open country — corn fields and scattered houses. To the right, over the river, the country spreads out, as it were, into a plain covered over with hills, no one hill much higher than another, but hills all over ; there were endless pastures overgrown with broom, and scattered trees, without hedges or fences of any kind, and no distinct footpaths. It was delightful to see the lasses in gay dresses running like cattle among the broom, making their way straight forward towards the river, here and there, as it might chance. They waded across the stream, and, when they had reached the top of the opposite bank, sate down by the road-side (about half a mile from the town) to put on their shoes and cotton stockings, which they brought tied up in pocket-handkerchiefs. The porter's lodge is about a mile from Lanerk, and the lady's house (for the whole belongs to a lady, whose name I have forgotten [1]) is upon a hill at a little distance. We walked, after we had entered the private grounds, perhaps two hundred yards along a gravel carriage-road, then came to a little side gate, which opened upon a narrow gravel path under trees, and in a minute and a half, or less, were directly opposite to the great waterfall. I was much affected

---

[1] Lady Mary Ross.—J. C. S. : *v.* Vol. ii, p. 383.

by the first view of it. The majesty and strength of the water (for I had never before seen so large a cataract), struck me with astonishment, which died away, giving place to more delightful feelings ; though there were some buildings that I could have wished had not been there, though at first unnoticed. The chief of them was a neat, white, lady-like house,[1] very near to the waterfall. Wm. and C., however, were in a better and perhaps wiser humour, and did not dislike the house ; indeed, it was a very nice-looking place, with a moderate-sized garden, leaving the green fields free and open. This house is on the side of the river opposite to the grand house and the pleasure-grounds. The waterfall (Cora Linn) is composed of two falls, with a sloping space (which *appears* to be about twenty yards) between, but is much more. The basin which receives the fall is enclosed by noble rocks, with trees (chiefly hazels, birch, and ash) growing out of their sides whenever there is any hold for them ; and a magnificent resting-place it is for such a river ; I think more grand than the Falls themselves.

After having stayed some time, we returned by the same footpath into the main carriage-road, and soon came upon what Wm. calls an ell-wide gravel walk, from which we had different views of the Linn. We sat upon a bench, placed for the sake of one of these views, whence we looked down upon the water-fall, and over the open country, and saw a ruined tower (called Wallace's Tower), which stands at a very little distance from the fall, and is an interesting object. A lady and gentleman, more expeditious tourists than we, came to the spot ; they left us at the seat, and we found them again at another station above the Falls. C., who is always good-natured enough to enter into conversation with anybody whom he meets in his way, began to talk with the gentleman, who observed that it was a " *majestic* waterfall ". Coleridge was delighted with the accuracy of the epithet, particularly as he had been settling in his own mind the precise meaning of the words grand, majestic, sublime, etc., and had discussed the subject with Wm. at some length the day before. " Yes, sir," says Coleridge, " it *is* a

---

[1] Corehouse.—J. C. S.

majestic waterfall." " Sublime and beautiful ", replied his friend. Poor C. could make no answer, and, not very desirous to continue the conversation, came to us and related the story, laughing heartily.

The distance from one Linn to the other may be half a mile or more, along the same ell-wide walk. We came to a pleasure-house, of which the little girl had the key ; she said it was called the Fog-house, because it was lined with *fog*, namely moss. On the outside it resembled some of the huts in the prints belonging to Captain Cook's Voyages, and within was like a hay-stack scooped out. It was circular, with a dome-like roof, a seat all round fixed to the wall, and a table in the middle, — seat, wall, roof, and table all covered with moss in the neatest manner possible. It was as snug as a bird's nest ; I wish we had such a one at the top of our orchard, only a great deal smaller. We afterwards found that huts of the same kind were common in the pleasure-grounds of Scotland ; but we never saw any that were so beautifully wrought as this. It had, however, little else to recommend it, the situation being chosen without judgment ; there was no prospect from it, nor was it a place of seclusion and retirement, for it stood close to the ell-wide gravel walk. We wished we could have shoved it about a hundred yards further on, when we arrived at a bench which was also close to the walk, for just below the bench, the walk elbowing out into a circle, there was a beautiful spring of clear water, which we could see rise up continually, at the bottom of a round stone basin full to the brim, the water gushing out at a little outlet and passing away under the walk. A reason was wanted for placing the hut where it is ; what a good one would this little spring have furnished for bringing it hither ! Along the whole of the path were openings at intervals for views of the river, but, as almost always happens in gentlemen's grounds, they were injudiciously managed ; you were prepared for a dead stand, by a parapet, a painted seat, or some other device.

We stayed some time at the Boniton Fall, which has one great advantage over the other falls, that it is at the termination of the pleasure-grounds, and we see no traces of the boundary-line ; yet, except under some accidental circumstances, such as a sunset like that of the preceding evening, it is greatly inferior to the Cora Linn. We returned to the inn to dinner. The landlord set the first dish upon the table, as is common in England, and we were well waited upon. This first dish was true Scottish — a boiled sheep's head, with the hair singed off ; C. and I ate heartily of it ; we had barley broth, in which the sheep's head had been boiled. A party of tourists whom we had met in the pleasure-grounds drove from the door while we were waiting for dinner ; I guess they were fresh from England, for they had stuffed the pockets of their carriage with bundles of hether, roots and all, just as if Scotland grew no hether but on the banks of the Clyde. They passed away with their treasure towards Loch Lomond. A party of boys, dressed all alike in blue, very neat, were standing at the chaise-door ; we con-jectured they were charity scholars ; but found on inquiry that they were apprentices to the cotton factory ; we were told that they were well instructed in reading and writing. We had seen in the morning a flock of girls dressed in grey coming out of the factory, probably apprentices also.

After dinner set off towards Hamilton, but on foot, for we had to turn aside to the Cartland Rocks, and our car was to meet us on the road. A guide attended us, who might almost in size, and certainly in activity, have been compared with Wm.'s companion who hid himself in the niche of the cavern. His method of walking and very quick step soon excited our attention ; I could hardly keep up with him ; he paddled by our side, just reaching to my shoulder, like a little dog, with his long snout pushed before him (for he had an enormous nose) and walked with his head foremost. I said to him, " How quick you walk ! " he replied, " *That* was *not* quick walking ", and when I asked him what he called so, he said " Five miles an hour ", and then related in how many hours he had lately walked from Lanerk to Edinburgh, done some errands, and returned to Lanerk (I have forgotten the particulars, but it was a very short time), and added that he had an old father who could walk at the rate of four miles an hour, for twenty-four miles, any day, and had never had an hour's sickness in his life. " Then ", said I, " he has not drunk much strong liquor ? "

" Yes, enough to drown him." From his eager manner of uttering this, I inferred that he himself was a drinker ; and the man who met us with the car told Wm. that he gained a great deal of money as an errand-goer, but spent it all in tippling. He had been a shoe-maker, but could not bear the confinement on account of a weakness in his chest.

The neighbourhood of Lanerk is exceedingly pleasant ; we came to a sort of district of glens or little valleys that cleave the hills, leaving a chearful, open country above them, with no superior hills, but an undulating surface. Our guide pointed to the situation of the Cartland Crags. We were to cross a narrow valley, and walk down on the other side, and then we should be at the spot ; but the little fellow made a sharp turn down a footpath to the left, saying, " We must have some conversation here ". He paddled on with his small pawing feet till we came right opposite to a gentleman's house on the other side of the valley, when he halted, repeating some words (I have forgotten what) which were taken up by the most distinct echo I ever heard — this is saying little : it was the most distinct echo that it is possible to conceive. It shouted the names of our fireside friends in the very tone in which Wm. and C. spoke ; but it seemed to make a joke of me, and I could not help laughing at my own voice, it was so shrill and pert, exactly as if some one had been mimicking it very successfully, with an intention of making me ridiculous. ·I wished Joanna had been there to laugh for the echo is an excellent laugher, and would have almost made her believe that it was a true story which Wm. has told of her and the mountains.[1] We turned back, crossed the valley, went through the orchard and plantations belonging to the gentleman's house. By the bye, we observed to our guide that the echo must bring many troublesome visitors to disturb the quiet of the owner of that house. " Oh no," said he, " he glories in much company." He was a native of that neighbourhood, had made a moderate fortune abroad, purchased an estate, built the house, and raised the plantations ; and further, had made a convenient walk through

---

[1] v. W.'s poem, To Joanna.

his woods to the Cartland Crags. The house was modest and neat, and though not adorned in the best taste, and though the plantations were of fir, we looked at it with great pleasure, there was such true liberality and kindheartedness in leaving his orchard path open, and his walks unobstructed by gates. I hope this goodness is not often abused by plunderers of the apple-trees, which were hung with tempting apples close to the path.

At the termination of the little valley, we descended through a wood along a very steep path to a muddy stream running over limestone rocks; turned up to the left along the bed of the stream, and soon we were closed in by rocks on each side. They were very lofty — of limestone, trees starting out of them, high and low, overhanging the stream or shooting up towards the sky. No place of the kind could be more beautiful if the stream had been clear, but it was of a muddy yellow colour; had it been a large river, one might have got the better of the unpleasantness of the muddy water in the grandeur of its roaring, the boiling up of the foam over the rocks, or the obscurity of its pools.

We had been told that the Cartland Crags were better worth going to see than the Falls of the Clyde. I did not think so; but I have seen rocky dells resembling this before, with clear water instead of that muddy stream, and never saw anything like the Falls of the Clyde. It would be a delicious spot to have near one's house; one would linger out many a day in the cool shade of the caverns, and the stream would soothe one by its murmuring; still, being an old friend, one would not love it the less for its homely face. Even we, as we passed along, could not help stopping for a long while to admire the beauty of the lazy foam, for ever in motion, and never moved away, in a still place of the water, covering the whole surface of it with streaks and lines and ever-varying circles. Wild marjoram grew upon the rocks in great perfection and beauty; our guide gave me a bunch, and said he should come hither to collect a store for tea for the winter, and that it was " varra halesome " : he drank none else. We walked perhaps half a mile along the bed of the river; but it might *seem* to be much further than it was, owing to the difficulty of the path, and the sharp and many turnings of the glen. Passed two of Wallace's Caves. There is scarce a noted glen in Scotland that has not a cave for Wallace or some other hero. Before we left the river the rocks became less lofty, turned into a wood through which was a convenient path upwards, met the owner of the house and the echo-ground, and thanked him for the pleasure which he had provided for us and other travellers by making such pretty pathways.

It was four o'clock when we reached the place where the car was waiting. We were anxious to be off, as we had fifteen miles to go ; but just as we were seating ourselves we found that the cushions were missing. Wm. was forced to go back to the town, a mile at least, and C. and I waited with the car. It rained, and we had some fear that the evening would be wet, but the rain soon ceased, though the sky continued gloomy — an unfortunate circumstance, for we had to travel through a beautiful country, and of that sort which is most set off by sunshine and pleasant weather.

Travelled through the Vale or *Trough* of the Clyde, as it is called, for ten or eleven miles, having the river on our right. We had fine views both up and down the river for the first three or four miles, our road being not close to it, but above its banks, along the open country, which was here occasionally intersected by hedgerows.

Left our car in the road, and turned down a field to the Fall of Stonebyres, another of the falls of the Clyde, which I had not heard spoken of ; therefore it gave me the more pleasure. We saw it from the top of the bank of the river at a little distance. It has not the imposing majesty of Cora Linn ; but it has the advantage of being left to itself, a grand solitude in the heart of a populous country. We had a prospect above and below it, of cultivated grounds, with hay-stacks, houses, hills ; but the river's banks were lonesome, steep, and woody, with rocks near the fall.

A little further on, came more into company with the river ; sometimes we were close to it, sometimes above it, but always at no great distance ; and now the vale became more interesting and amusing. It is very populous, with villages, hamlets, single cottages, or farmhouses embosomed in orchards, and scattered over with gentlemen's seats, some of them very ugly, tall and obtrusive, others neat and comfortable. We seemed now to have got into a country where poverty and riches were shaking hands together ; pears and apples, of which the crop was abundant, hung over the road, often growing in orchards unfenced ; or there might be bunches of broom along the road-side in an interrupted line, that looked like a hedge till we came to it and saw the gaps. Bordering on these fruitful orchards perhaps would be a patch, its chief produce being gorse or broom. There was nothing like a moor or common anywhere ; but small plots of uncultivated ground were left high and low, among the potatoes, corn, cabbages, which grew intermingled, now among trees, now bare. The Trough of the Clyde is, indeed, a singular and very interesting region ; it is somewhat like the upper part of the vale of Nith, but above the Nith is much less cultivated ground — without hedgerows or orchards, or anything that looks like a rich country. We met crowds of people coming from the kirk ; the lasses were gaily dressed, often in white gowns, coloured satin bonnets, and coloured silk handkerchiefs, and generally with their shoes and stockings in a bundle hung on their arm. Before we left the river the vale became much less interesting, resembling a poor English country, the fields being large, and unluxuriant hedges.

It had been dark long before we reached Hamilton, and Wm. had some difficulty in driving the tired horse through the town. At the inn they hesitated about being able to give us beds, the house being brim-full — lights at every window. We were rather alarmed for our accommodations during the rest of the tour, supposing the house to be filled with *tourists* ; but they were in general only regular travellers ; for out of the main road from town to town we saw scarcely a carriage, and the inns were empty. There was nothing remarkable in the treatment we met with at this inn, except the lazy impertinence of the waiter. It was a townish place, with a great larder set out ; the house throughout dirty.

August 22nd, Monday. Immediately after breakfast walked to the Duke of Hamilton's house to view the picture-gallery, chiefly the famous picture of Daniel in the Lions' Den, by Rubens. It is a large building, without grandeur, a heavy, lumpish mass, after the fashion of the Hopetoun H,[1] only five times the size, and with longer legs, which makes it gloomy. We entered the gate, passed the porter's lodge, where we saw nobody, and stopped at the front door, as William had done two years before with Sir William Rush's family. We were met by a little mean-looking man, shabbily dressed, out of livery, who, we found, was the porter. After scanning us over, he told us that we ought not to have come to that door ; we said we were sorry for the mistake, but as one of our party had been there two years before, and was admitted by the same entrance, we had supposed it was the regular way. After many hesitations, and having kept us five minutes waiting in the large hall, while he went to consult with the housekeeper, he informed us that we could not be admitted at that time, the housekeeper being unwell ; but that we might return in an hour : he then conducted us through long gloomy passages to an obscure door at the corner of the house. We asked if we might be permitted to walk in the park in the meantime ; and he told us that this would not be agreeable to the Duke's family. We returned to the inn discontented enough, but resolved not to waste an hour, if there were anything else in the neighbourhood worth seeing. The waiter told us there was a curious place called Baroncleugh, with gardens cut out in rocks, and we determined to go thither. We had to walk through the town (which may be about as large as Penrith), and perhaps a mile further, along a dusty turnpike road. The morning was hot, sunny, and windy, and we were half tired before we reached the place ; but were amply repaid for our trouble.

The general face of the country near Hamilton is much in the ordinary English style ; not very hilly, with hedgerows, corn fields, and stone houses. The Clyde is here an open river with low banks, and the country spreads out so wide that there is no appearance of a regular vale. Baroncleugh is in a beautiful deep glen through which runs the river Avon, a stream that

---

[1] The house belonging to the Earls of Hopetoun at Leadhills, not that which bears this name about twelve miles from Edinburgh.—J. C. S.

falls into the Clyde. The house stands very sweetly in complete retirement ; it has its gardens and terraces one above another, with flights of steps between, box-trees and yew-trees cut in fantastic shapes, flower-borders and summer-houses ; and, still below, apples and pears were hanging in abundance on the branches of large old trees, which grew intermingled with the natural wood, elms, beeches, etc., even to the water's edge. The whole place is in perfect harmony with the taste of our ancestors, and the yews and hollies are shaven as nicely, and the gravel walks and flower-borders kept in as exact order, as if the spirit of the first architect of the terraces still presided over them. The opposite bank of the river is left in its natural wildness, and nothing was to be seen higher up but the deep dell, its steep banks being covered with fine trees, a beautiful relief or contrast to the garden, which is one of the most elaborate old things ever seen, a little hanging garden of Babylon.

I was sorry to hear that the owner of this sweet place did not live there always. He had built a small thatched house to eke out the old one : it was a neat dwelling, with no false ornaments. We were exceedingly sorry to quit this spot, which is left to nature and past times, and should have liked to have pursued the glen further up ; we were told that there was a ruined castle ; and the walk itself must be very delightful ; but we wished to reach Glasgow in good time, and had to go again to Hamilton House. Returned to the town by a much shorter road, and were very angry with the waiter for not having directed us to it ; but he was too great a man to speak three words more than he could help.

We stopped at the proper door of the Duke's house, and seated ourselves humbly upon a bench, waiting the pleasure of the porter, who, after a little time, informed us that we could not be admitted, giving no reason whatever. When we got to the inn, we could just gather from the waiter that it was not usual to refuse admittance to strangers ; but *that was all* : he could not, or would not, help us, so we were obliged to give it up, which mortified us, for I had wished much to see the picture. Wm. vowed that he would write that very night to

Lord Archibald Hamilton, stating the whole matter, which he did from Glasgow.

I ought to have mentioned the park, though, as we were not allowed to walk there, we saw but little of it. It looked pleasant, as all parks with fine trees must be, but, as it seemed to be only a large, nearly level, plain, it could not be a particularly beautiful park, though it borders upon the Clyde, and the Avon runs, I believe, through it, after leaving the solitude of the glen of Baroncleugh.

Quitted Hamilton at about eleven o'clock. There is nothing interesting between Hamilton and Glasgow till we came to Bothwell Castle, a few miles from Hamilton. The country is cultivated, but not rich, the fields large, a perfect contrast to the huddling together of hills and trees, corn and pasture grounds, hay-stacks, cottages, orchards, broom and gorse (but chiefly broom), that had amused us so much the evening before in passing through the Trough of the Clyde. A native of Scotland would not probably be satisfied with the account I have given of the Trough of the Clyde, for it is one of the most celebrated scenes in Scotland. We certainly received less pleasure from it than we had expected ; but it was plain that this was chiefly owing to the unfavourable circumstances under which we saw it — a gloomy sky and a cold blighting wind. It is a very beautiful district, yet there, as in all the other scenes of Scotland celebrated for their fertility, we found something which gave us a notion of barrenness, of what was not altogether genial. The new fir and larch plantations, here as in almost every other part of Scotland, contributed not a little to this effect.

Crossed the Clyde not far from Hamilton, and had the river for some miles at a distance from us, on our left ; but after having gone, it might be, three miles, we came to a porter's lodge on the left side of the road, where we were to turn to Bothwell Castle, which is in Lord Douglas's grounds. The woman who keeps the gate brought us a book, in which we wrote down our names. Went about half a mile before we came to the pleasure-grounds. Came to a large range of stables, where we were to leave the car ; but there was no one to unyoke the horse, so Wm. was obliged to do it himself, a task which he performed very awkwardly, being then new to it. We saw the ruined castle embosomed in trees, passed the house, and soon found ourselves on the edge of a steep brow immediately above and overlooking the course of the river Clyde through a deep hollow between woods and green steeps. We had approached at right angles from the main road to the place over a flat, and had seen nothing before us but a nearly level country terminated by distant slopes, the Clyde hiding himself in his deep bed.

It was exceedingly delightful to come thus unexpectedly upon such a beautiful region. The Castle stands nobly, overlooking the Clyde. When we came up to it I was hurt to see that flower-borders had taken [the] place of the natural overgrowings of the ruin, the scattered stones and wild plants. It is a large and grand pile, of red freestone, harmonizing perfectly with the rocks of the river, from which, no doubt, it has been hewn. When I was a little accustomed to the unnaturalness of a modern garden, I could not help admiring the excessive beauty and luxuriance of some of the plants, particularly the purple-flowered clematis, and a broad-leaved creeping plant without flowers, which scrambled up the castle wall along with the ivy, and spread its vine-like branches so lavishly that it seemed to be in its natural situation, and one could not help thinking that, though not self-planted among the ruins of this country, it must somewhere have its natural abode in such places. If Bothwell Castle had not been close to the Douglas mansion we should have been disgusted with the possessor's miserable conception of *adorning* such a venerable ruin ; but it is so very near to the house that of necessity the pleasure-grounds must have extended beyond it, and perhaps the neatness of a shaven lawn and the complete desolation natural to a ruin might have made an unpleasing contrast ; and besides, being within the precincts of the pleasure-grounds, and so very near to the modern mansion of a noble family, it has forfeited in some degree its independent majesty, and becomes a tributary to the mansion ; its solitude being interrupted, it has no longer the same command over the mind in sending it back into past times, or excluding the ordinary feelings which we bear about us in daily life. We had then only to regret that the castle and house were so near to each other ; and it was impossible *not* to regret it ; for the ruin presides in state over the river, far from city or town, as if it might have had a peculiar privilege to preserve its memorials of past ages and maintain its own character for centuries to come.

We sat upon a bench under the high trees, and had beautiful views of the different reaches of the river above and below. On the opposite bank, which is finely wooded with elms and other trees, are the remains of an ancient priory, built upon a rock : and rock and ruin are so blended together that it is impossible to separate the one from the other. Nothing can be more beautiful than the little remnants of this holy place ; elm trees (for we were near enough to distinguish them by their branches) grow out of the walls, and overshadow a small but very elegant window. It can scarcely be conceived what a grace the castle and priory impart to each other ; and the river Clyde flows on smooth and unruffled below, seeming to my thoughts more in harmony with the sober and stately images of former times, than if it had roared over a rocky channel, forcing its sound upon the ear. It blended gently with the warbling of the smaller birds and chattering of the larger ones that had made their nests in the ruins. In this fortress the chief of the English nobility were confined after the battle of Bannockburn. If a man is to be a prisoner, he scarcely could have a more pleasant place to solace his captivity ; but I thought that for close confinement I should prefer the banks of a lake or the sea-side. The greatest charm of a brook or river is in the liberty to pursue it through its windings ; you can then take it in whatever mood you like ; silent or noisy, sportive or quiet. The beauties of a brook or river must be sought, and the pleasure is in going in search of them ; those of a lake or of the sea come to you of themselves. These rude warriors cared little perhaps about either ; and yet if one may judge from the writings of Chaucer and from the old romances, more interesting passions were connected with natural objects in the days of chivalry than now, though going in search of scenery, as it is called, had not then been thought of. I had heard nothing of Bothwell Castle, at least nothing that I remembered, therefore, perhaps, my pleasure was greater, compared with what I received elsewhere, than others might feel.

At our return to the stables we found an inferior groom, who helped Wm. to yoke the horse, and was very civil. We grew hungry before we had travelled many miles, and seeing a large publick-house (it was in a walled court some yards from the road) C. got off the car to inquire if we could dine there, and was told we could have nothing but eggs. It was a miserable place, very like a French house ; indeed we observed, in almost every part of Scotland, except Edinburgh, that we were reminded ten times of France and Germany for once of England.

Saw nothing remarkable after leaving Bothwell, except the first view of Glasgow, at some miles distance, terminated by the mountains of Loch Lomond. The suburbs of Glasgow extend very far, houses on each side of the highway, — all ugly ; and the inhabitants dirty. The roads are very wide ; and everything seems to tell of the neighbourhood of a large town. We were annoyed by carts and dirt, and the road was full of people, who all noticed our car in one way or other ; the children often sent a hooting after us.

Wearied completely, we at last reached the town, and were glad to walk, leading the car to the first decent inn, which was luckily not far from the end of the town. Wm., who gained most of his road-knowledge from ostlers, had been informed of this house by the ostler at Hamilton ; it proved quiet and tolerably cheap, a new building — the Saracen's Head. I shall never forget how glad I was to be landed in a little quiet backparlour, for my head was beating with the noise of carts which we had left, and the wearisomeness of the disagreeable objects near the highway ; but with my first pleasant sensations also came the feeling that we were not in an English inn — partly from its half-unfurnished appearance, which is common in Scotland, for in general the deal wainscots and doors are unpainted, and partly from the dirtiness of the floors. Having dined, Wm. and I walked to the post-office, and after much seeking found out a quiet timber-yard wherein to sit down and read our letter. We then walked a considerable time in the streets, which are perhaps as handsome as streets can be, which derive no particular effect from their situation in connexion with natural advantages, such as rivers, sea, or hills. The Trongate, an old street, is very picturesque — high houses, with an intermixture of gable fronts towards the street. The New Town is built of fine stone, in the best style of the very best London streets at the west end of the town, but, not being of brick, they are greatly superior. One thing must strike every stranger in his first walk through Glasgow — an appearance of business and bustle, but no coaches or gentlemen's carriages. During all the time we walked in the streets I only saw three carriages, and these were travelling chaises. I also could not but observe a want of cleanliness in the appearance of the lower orders of the people, and a dulness in the dress and outside of the whole mass, as they moved along. We returned to the inn before it was dark. I had a bad headache, and was tired, and we all went to bed soon.

August 23rd, Tuesday. A cold morning. Walked to the bleaching-ground,[1] a large field bordering on the Clyde, the banks of which are perfectly flat, and the general face of the country is nearly so in the neighbourhood of Glasgow. This field, the whole summer through, is covered with women of all ages, children, and young girls spreading out their linen, and watching it while it bleaches. The scene must be very chearful on a fine day, but it rained when we were there, and though there was linen spread out in all parts, and great numbers of women and girls were at work, yet there would have been many more on a fine day, and they would have appeared happy, instead of stupid and chearless. In the middle of the field is a wash-house, whither the inhabitants of this large town, rich and poor, send or carry their linen to be washed. There are two very large rooms, with each a cistern in the middle for hot water ; and all round the rooms are benches for the women to set their tubs upon. Both the rooms were crowded with washers ; there might be a hundred, or two, or even three ; for it is not easy to form an accurate notion of so great a

---

[1] Glasgow Green.—J. C. S.

number ; however, the rooms were large, and they were both full. It was amusing to see so many women, arms, head, and face all in motion, all busy in an ordinary household employment, in which we are accustomed to see, at the most, only three or four women employed in one place. The women were very civil. I learnt from them the regulations of the house ; but I have forgotten the particulars. The substance of them is, that *so* much is to be paid for each tub of water, *so* much for a tub, and the privilege of washing for a day, and, *so* much to the general overlookers of the linen, when it is left to be bleached. An old man and woman have this office, who were walking about, two melancholy figures.

The shops at Glasgow are large, and like London shops, and we passed by the largest coffee-room I ever saw. You look across the piazza of the Exchange, and see to the end of the coffee-room, where there is a circular window, the width of the room. Perhaps there might be thirty gentlemen sitting on the circular bench of the window, each reading a newspaper. They had the appearance of figures in a fantoccine, or men seen at the extremity of the opera-house, diminished into puppets.

I am sorry I did not see the High Church : both Wm. and I were tired, and it rained very hard after we had left the bleaching-ground ; besides, I am less eager to walk in a large town than anywhere else ; so we put it off, and I have since repented of my irresolution.

Dined, and left Glasgow at about three o'clock, in a heavy rain. We were obliged to ride through the streets to keep our feet dry, and, in spite of the rain, every person as we went along stayed his steps to look at us ; indeed, we had the pleasure of spreading smiles from one end of Glasgow to the other (for we travelled the whole length of the town). A set of schoolboys (perhaps there might be eight) with satchels over their shoulders, and, except one or two, without shoes and stockings, yet very well dressed in jackets and trousers, like gentlemen's children, followed us in great delight, admiring the car and longing to jump up. At last, though we were seated, they made several attempts to get on behind ; and they looked so pretty and wild, and at the same time so modest, that we wished to give them a ride, and there being a little hill near the end of the town, we got off, and four of them who still remained, the rest having dropped into their homes by the way, took our places ; and indeed I would have walked two miles willingly, to have had the pleasure of seeing them so happy. When they were to ride no longer, they scampered away, laughing and rejoicing. New houses are rising up in great numbers round Glasgow, citizen-like houses, and new plantations, chiefly of fir ; the fields are frequently enclosed by hedgerows, but there is no richness, nor any particular beauty for some miles.

The first object that interested us was a gentleman's house upon a green plain or holm, almost close to the Clyde, sheltered by tall trees, a quiet modest mansion, and, though white-washed, being an old building, and no other house near it, or in connexion with it, and standing upon the level field, which belonged to it, its own domain, the whole scene together brought to our minds an image of the retiredness and sober elegance of a nunnery ; but this might be owing to the greyness of the afternoon, and our having come immediately from Glasgow, and through a country which, till now, had either had a townish taint, or at best little of rural beauty. While we were looking at the house we overtook a foot-traveller, who, like many others, began to talk about our car. We alighted to walk up a hill, and, continuing the conversation, the man told us, with something like a national pride, that it belonged to a Scotch Lord (Lord Semple) ; he added, that a little further on we should see a much finer prospect, as fine a one as ever we had seen in our lives ; accordingly, when we came to the top of the hill, it opened upon us most magnificently. We saw the Clyde, now a stately sea-river, winding away mile after mile, spotted with boats and ships, each side of the river hilly, the right populous with single houses and villages — Dunglass Castle upon a promontory, the whole view terminated by the rock of Dumbarton, at five or six miles' distance, which stands by itself, without any hills near it, like a sea-rock.

We travelled for some time near the river, passing through clusters of houses which seemed to owe their existence rather to the wealth of the river than the land, for the banks were mostly bare, and the soil appeared poor, even near the water. The left side of the river was generally uninhabited and moorish, yet there are some beautiful spots : for instance, a nobleman's house,[1] where the fields and trees were rich, and, in combination with the river, looked very lovely. As we went along Wm. and I were reminded of the views upon the Thames in Kent, which, though greatly superior in richness and softness, are much inferior in grandeur. Not far from Dumbarton, we passed under some rocky, copse-covered hills, which were so like some of the hills near Grasmere that we could have half believed they were the same. Arrived at Dumbarton before it was dark, having pushed on briskly that we might have start of a traveller at the inn, who was following us as fast as he could in a gig. Every front room was full, and we were afraid we should not have been admitted. They put us into a little parlour, dirty, and smelling of liquors, the table uncleaned, and not a chair in its place ; we were glad, however, of our sorry accommodations.

While tea was preparing we lolled at our ease, and though the room-window overlooked the stable-yard, and at our entrance there appeared to be nothing but gloom and un-loveliness, yet while I lay stretched upon the carriage cushions on three chairs, I discovered a little side peep which was enough to set the mind at work. It was no more than a smoky vessel lying at anchor, with its bare masts, a clay hut and the shelving bank of the river, with a green pasture above. Perhaps you will think that there is not much in this, as I describe it : it is true ; but the effect produced by these simple objects, as they happened to be combined, together with the gloom of the evening, was exceedingly wild. Our room was parted by a slender partition from a large dining-room, in which were a number of officers and their wives, who, after the first hour, never ceased singing, dancing, laughing, or loud talking. The ladies sang some pretty songs, a great relief to us. We went early to bed ; but poor C. could not sleep for the noise at the street door ; he lay in the parlour below stairs. It is no uncommon thing

---

[1] No doubt Erskine House, the seat of Lord Blantyre.—J. C. S.

in the best inns of Scotland to have shutting-up beds in the sitting-rooms.

August 24th, Wednesday. As soon as breakfast was over, Wm. and I walked towards the Castle, a short mile from the town. We overtook two young men, who, on our asking the road, offered to conduct us, though it might seem it was not easy to miss our way, for the rock rises singly by itself from the plain on which the town stands. The rock of Dumbarton is very grand when you are close to it, but at a little distance, under an ordinary sky, and in open day, it is not grand, but curiously wild. The castle and fortifications add little effect to the general view of the rock, especially since the building of a modern house, which is white-washed, and consequently jars, wherever it is seen, with the natural character of the place. There is a path up to the house, but it being low water we could walk round the rock, which we resolved to do. On that side next the town green grass grows to a considerable height up the rock, but wherever the river borders upon it, it is naked stone. I never saw rock in nobler masses, or more deeply stained by time and weather, nor is this to be wondered at, for it is in the very eye of sea-storms and land-storms, of mountain winds and water winds. It is of all colours, but a rusty yellow predominates. As we walked along, we could not but look up continually, and the mass above being on every side so huge, it appeared more wonderful than when we saw the whole together.

We sat down on one of the large stones which lie scattered near the base of the rock, with sea-weed growing amongst them. Above our heads the rock was perpendicular for a considerable height, nay, as it seemed, to the very top, and on the brink of the precipice a few sheep (two of them rams with twisted horns) stood, as if on the look-out over the wide country. At the same time we saw a sentinel in his red coat, walking backwards and forwards between us and the sky, with his firelock over his shoulder. The sheep, I suppose owing to our being accustomed to see them in similar situations, appeared to retain their real size, while, on the contrary, the soldier seemed to be diminished by the distance till he almost looked like a puppet moved with wires for the pleasure of children, or an eight years' old drummer in his stiff, manly dress beside a company of grenadiers. I had never before, perhaps, thought of sheep and men in soldiers' dresses at the same time, and here they were brought together in a strange fantastic way. As will be easily conceived, the fearlessness and stillness of those quiet creatures, on the brow of the rock, pursuing their natural occupations, contrasted with the restless and apparently unmeaning motions of the dwarf soldier, added not a little to the general effect of this place, which is that of wild singularity, and the whole was aided by a blustering wind and a gloomy sky. C. joined us, and we went up to the top of the rock.

The road to a considerable height is through a narrow cleft, in which a flight of steps is hewn ; the steps nearly fill the cleft, and on each side the rocks form a high and irregular wall ; it is almost like a long sloping cavern, only that it is roofed by the sky. We came to the barracks ; soldiers' wives were hanging out linen upon the rails, while the wind beat about them furiously : there was nothing which it could set in motion but the garments of the women and the linen upon the rails ; the grass (for we had now come to green grass) was close and smooth, and not one pile an inch above another, and neither tree nor shrub — the standard pole stood erect without a flag. The rock has two summits, one much broader and higher than the other. When we were near to the top of the lower eminence we had the pleasure of finding a little garden of flowers and vegetables belonging to the soldiers. There are three distinct and very noble prospects — the first up the Clyde towards Glasgow — Dunglass Castle, seen on its promontory — boats, sloops, hills, and many buildings ; the second, down the river to the sea — Greenock and Port-Glasgow, and the distant mountains at the entrance of Loch Long ; and the third extensive and distant view is up the Leven (which here falls into the Clyde), to the mountains of Loch Lomond. The distant mountains in all these views were obscured by mists and dingy clouds, but if the grand outline of any one of the views can be seen, it is sufficient recompense for the trouble of climbing the rock of Dumbarton.

The soldier who was our guide told us that an old ruin which we came to at the top of the higher eminence had been a wind-mill — an inconvenient situation, though certainly a glorious place for wind ; perhaps if it really *had* been a wind-mill it was only for the use of the garrison. We looked over cannons on the battery-walls, and saw in an open field below the yeomanry cavalry exercising, while we could hear from the town (which was full of soldiers) " Dumbarton's drums beat bonny, O ! " Yet while we stood upon this eminence, rising up so far as it does — inland, and having the habitual old English feeling of our own security as islanders, we could not help looking upon the fortress, in spite of its cannon and soldiers, and the rumours of invasion, as set up against the hostilities of wind and weather rather than for any other warfare. On our return we were invited into the guard-room, about half-way down the rock, where we were shown a large rusty sword, which they called Wallace's Sword, and a trout boxed up in a well close by, where they said he had been confined for upwards of thirty years. For the pleasure of the soldiers, who were anxious that we should see him, we took some pains to spy him out in his black den, and at last succeeded. It was pleasing to observe how much interest the poor soldiers (though themselves probably new to the place) seemed to attach to this antiquated inhabitant of their garrison.

When we had reached the bottom of the rock along the same road by which we had ascended, we made our way over the rough stones left bare by the tide, round the bottom of the rock, to the point whence we had set off. This is a wild and melancholy walk on a blustering cloudy day — the naked bed of the river, scattered over with sea-weed ; grey swampy fields on the other shore ; sea-birds flying overhead — the high rock perpendicular and bare. We came to two very large fragments, which had fallen from the main rock ; C. thought that one of them was as large as Bowder-Stone, William and I did not ; but it is impossible to judge accurately ; we probably, without knowing it, compared them with the whole mass from which they had fallen, which, from its situation, we consider as one rock or stone, and there is no object of the kind for comparison with Bowder-Stone. When we leave the shore of the Clyde grass begins to show itself on the rock ; go a considerable way (still under the rock) along a flat field, and pass immediately below the white house, which wherever seen looks so ugly.

Left Dumbarton at about eleven o'clock. The sky was chearless and the air ungenial, which we regretted, as we were going to Loch Lomond, and wished to greet the first of the Scottish lakes with our chearfullest and best feelings. Crossed the Leven at the end of Dumbarton, and, when we looked behind, had a pleasing view of the town, bridge, and rock ; but when we took in a reach of the river at the distance of perhaps half a mile, the swampy ground (being so near a town, and not in its natural wildness, but seemingly half cultivated, with houses here and there) gave us an idea of extreme poverty of soil, or that the inhabitants were either indolent or miserable. We had to travel four miles on the banks of the " Water of Leven " before we should come to Loch Lomond. Having expected a grand river from so grand a lake, we were disappointed ; for it appeared to me not to be very much larger than the Emont, and is not near so beautiful ; but we must not forget that the day was cold and gloomy. Near Dumbarton it is like a river in a flat country, or under the influence of tides ; but a little higher up it resembles one of our rivers, flowing through a vale of no extreme beauty, though prettily wooded ; the hills on each side not very high, sloping backwards from the bed of the vale, which is neither very narrow nor very wide — the prospect terminated by Ben Lomond and other mountains. The vale is populous, but looks as if it were not inhabited by cultivators of the earth ; the houses are chiefly of stone ; often in rows by the river-side ; they stand pleasantly, but have a tradish look, as if they might have been off-sets from Glasgow. We saw many bleach-yards, but no other symptom of a manufactory, except something in the houses that was not rural, and a want of independent comforts. Perhaps if the river had been glittering in the sun, and the smoke of the cottages rising in distinct volumes towards the sky, as I have seen in the vale or basin below Pillsden in Dorsetshire, when every cottage, hidden from the eye, pointed out its lurking-place by an upright wreath of white smoke, the whole scene might have excited ideas of perfect chearfulness.

Here, as on the Nith, and much more than in the Trough of the Clyde, a great portion of the ground was uncultivated, but the hills being less wild, the river more stately, and the ground not heaved up so irregularly and tossed about, the imperfect cultivation was the more to be lamented, particularly as there were so many houses near the river. In a small enclosure by the wayside is a pillar erected to the memory of Dr. Smollett, who was born in a village at a little distance, which we could see at the same time, and where, I believe, some of the family still reside. There is a long Latin inscription, which C. translated for my benefit. The Latin is miserably bad [1] — as Wm. and C. said, such as poor Smollett, who was an excellent scholar, would have been ashamed of.

Before we came to Loch Lomond the vale widened, and became less populous. We climbed over a wall into a large field to have a better first view of the lake than from the road. This view is very much like that from Mr. Clarkson's windows : the mountain in front resembles Hallan ; indeed, is almost the same ; but Ben Lomond is not seen standing in such majestic company as Helvellyn, and the meadows are less beautiful than at Ulswater. The reach of the lake is very magnificent ; you see it (as Ulswater is seen beyond the promontory of Old Church) winding away behind a large woody island that looks like a promontory. The outlet of the lake (we had a distinct view of it in the field) is very insignificant. The bulk of the river is frittered away by small alder bushes, as I recollect,— I do not remember that it was reedy, but the ground had a swampy appearance ; and here the vale spreads out wide and shapeless, as if the river were born to no inheritance, had no sheltering cradle, no hills of its own. As we have seen, this does not continue long ; it flows through a distinct, though not a magnificent vale. But, having lost the pastoral

---

[1] The inscription on the pillar was written by Professor George Stuart of Edinburgh, John Ramsay of Ochtertyre and Dr. Samuel Johnson ; for Dr. Johnson's share in the work see Croker's Boswell, p. 392.—J. C. S.

character which it had in the youthful days of Smollett (if the description in his ode to his native stream be a faithful one) it is less interesting than it was then.

The road carried us sometimes close to the lake, sometimes at a considerable distance from it, over moorish grounds, or through half-cultivated enclosures ; we had the lake on our right, which is here so wide that the opposite hills, not being high, are cast into insignificance, and we could not distinguish any buildings near the water, if any there were. It is however always delightful to travel by a lake of clear waters, if you see nothing else but a very ordinary country ; but we had some beautiful distant views, one in particular, down the high road, through a vista of over-arching trees ; and the near shore was frequently very pleasing, with its gravel banks, bendings, and small bays. In one part it was bordered for a considerable way by irregular groupes of forest trees or single stragglers, which, although not large, seemed old ; their branches were stunted and knotty, as if they had been striving with storms, and had half yielded to them. Under these trees we had a variety of pleasing views across the lake, and the very rolling over the road and looking at its smooth and beautiful surface was itself a pleasure ; it was as smooth as a gravel walk, and of the bluish colour of some of the roads among the lakes of the North of England.

Passed no very remarkable place till we came to Sir James Colquhoun's house, which stands upon a large, flat, woody peninsula, looking towards Ben Lomond. There must be many beautiful walks among the copses of the peninsula, and delicious views over the water ; but the general surface of the country is poor, and looks as if it ought to be rich and well peopled, for it is not mountainous ; nor had we passed any hills which a Cumbrian would dignify with the name of mountains. There was many a little plain or gently-sloping hill covered with poor heath or broom without trees, where one should have liked to see a cottage in a bower of wood, with its patch of corn and potatoes, and a green field with a hedge to keep it warm. As we advanced we perceived less of the coldness of poverty, the hills not having so large a space between them and the lake.

The surface of the *hills*, being in its natural state, is always beautiful ; but where there is only a half cultivated and half peopled soil near the banks of a lake or river, the idea is forced upon one that they who *do* live there have not much of chearful enjoyment.

But soon we came to just such a place as we had wanted to see. The road was close to the water, and a hill, bare, rocky, or with scattered copses rose above it. A deep shade hung over the road, where some little boys were at play ; we expected a dwelling-house of some sort ; and when we came nearer, saw three or four thatched huts under the trees, and at the same moment felt that it was a paradise. We had before seen the lake only as one wide plain of water ; but here the portion of it which we saw was bounded by a high and steep, heathy and woody island opposite, which did not appear like an island, but the main shore, and framed out a little oblong lake apparently not so broad as Rydale-water, with one small island covered with trees, resembling some of the most beautiful of the holms of Windermere, and only a narrow river's breadth from the shore. This was a place where we should have liked to have lived, and the only one we had seen near Loch Lomond : —how delightful to have a little shed concealed under the branches of the fairy island ! the cottages and the island might have been made for the pleasure of each other. It was but like a natural garden, the distance was so small ; nay, one could not have forgiven any one living there, not compelled to daily labour, if he did not connect it with his dwelling by some feeling of domestic attachment, like what he has for the orchard where his children play. I thought, what a place for Wm. ! he might row himself over with twenty strokes of the oars, escaping from the business of the house, and as safe from intruders, with his boat anchored beside him, as if he had locked himself up in the strong tower of a castle. We were unwilling to leave this sweet spot ; but it was so simple, and therefore so rememberable, that it seemed almost as if we could have carried it away with us. It was nothing more than a small lake enclosed by trees at the ends and by the way-side, and opposite by the island, a steep bank on which the purple heath was seen under low oak coppice-wood, a group of houses over-shadowed by trees, and a bending road. There was one remarkable tree, an old larch with hairy branches, which sent out its main stem horizontally across the road, an object that seemed to have been singled out for injury where everything else was lovely and thriving, tortured into that shape by storms, which one might have thought could not have reached it in that sheltered place.

We were now entering into the Highlands. I believe Luss is the place where we were told that country begins ; but at these cottages I would have gladly believed that we were there, for it was like a new region. The huts were after the Highland fashion, and the boys who were playing wore the Highland dress and philabeg. On going into a new country I seem to myself to waken up, and afterwards it surprises me to remember how much alive I have been to the distinctions of dress, house-hold arrangements, etc. etc., and what a spirit these little things give to wild, barren, or ordinary places. The cottages are within about two miles of Luss. Came in view of several islands ; but the lake being so very wide, we could see little of their peculiar beauties, and they, being large, hardly looked like islands.

Passed another gentleman's house, which stands prettily in a bay,[1] and soon after reached Luss, where we intended to lodge. On seeing the outside of the inn we were glad that we were to have such pleasant quarters. It is a nice-looking white house, by the road-side ; but there was not much promise of hospitality when we stopped at the door : no person came out till we had shouted a considerable time. A barefooted lass showed me up-stairs, and again my hopes revived ; the house was clean for a Scotch inn, and the view very pleasant to the lake, over the top of the village — a cluster of thatched houses among trees, with a large chapel in the midst of them. Like most of the Scotch kirks which we had seen, this building resembles a big house ; but it is a much more pleasing building than they generally are, and has one of our rustic belfries, not

---

[1] Camstraddan House and bay.—J. C. S.

unlike that at Ambleside, with two bells hanging in the open air. We chose one of the back rooms to sit in, being more snug, and they looked upon a very sweet prospect — a stream tumbling down a cleft or glen on the hill-side, rocky coppice ground, a rural lane, such as we have from house to house at Grasmere, and a few out-houses. We had a poor dinner, and sour ale ; but as long as the people were civil we were contented.

C. was not well, so he did not stir out, but Wm. and I walked through the village to the shore of the lake. When I came close to the houses, I could not but regret a want of loveliness correspondent with the beauty of the situation and the appearance of the village at a little distance — not a single ornamented garden ; we saw potatoes and cabbages, but never a honeysuckle. Yet there were *wild* gardens, as beautiful as any that ever man cultivated, overgrowing the roofs of some of the cottages — flowers and creeping plants. How elegant were the wreaths of the bramble that had " built its own bower " upon the riggins in several parts of the village ; therefore we had chiefly to regret the want of gardens, as they are symptoms of leisure and comfort, or at least of no painful industry. Here we first saw houses without windows, the smoke coming out of the open window-places ; the chimneys were like stools with four legs, a hole being left in the roof for the smoke, and over that a slate placed upon four sticks — sometimes the whole leaned as if it were going to fall. The fields close to Luss lie flat to the lake, and a river, as large as our stream near the church at Grasmere, flows by the end of the village, being the same which comes down the glen behind the inn ; it is very much like our stream — beds of blue pebbles upon the shores.

We walked towards the head of the lake, and from a large pasture field near Luss, a gentle eminence, had a very interesting view back upon the village and the lake and islands beyond. We then perceived that Luss stood in the centre of a spacious bay, and that close to it lay another small one, within the larger, where the boats of the inhabitants were lying at anchor, a beautiful natural harbour. The islands, as we look down the water, are seen in great beauty. Inch-ta-vannach, the same that framed out the little peaceful lake which we had passed in the morning, towers above the rest. The lake is very wide here, and the opposite shores not being lofty the chief part of the permanent beauty of this view is among the islands, and on the near shore, including the low promontories of the bay of Luss, and the village ; and we saw it under its dullest aspect — the air cold, the sky gloomy, without a glimpse of sunshine. On a splendid evening, with the light of the sun diffused over the whole — islands, distant hills, and the broad expanse of the lake, with its creeks, bays, and little slips of water among the islands, it must be a glorious sight.

Up the lake there are no islands ; Ben Lomond terminates the view, without any other large mountains ; no clouds were upon it, therefore we saw the whole size and form of the mountain, yet it did not appear to me so large as Skiddaw does from Derwent-water. Continued our walk a considerable way towards the head of the lake, and went up a high hill, but saw no other reach of the water. The hills on the Luss side become much steeper, and the lake, having narrowed a little above Luss, was no longer a very wide lake where we lost sight of it.

Came to a bark hut by the shores, and sate for some time under the shelter of it. While we were here a poor woman with a little child by her side begged a penny of me, and asked where she could " find quarters in the village ". She was a travelling beggar, a native of Scotland, had often " heard of that water ", but was never there before. This woman's appearance, while the wind was rustling about us, and the waves breaking at our feet, was very melancholy : the waters looked wide, the hills many, and dark, and far off — no house but at Luss. I thought what a dreary waste must this lake be to such poor creatures, struggling with fatigue and poverty and unknown ways !

We ordered tea when we reached the inn, and desired the girl to light us a fire ; she replied, " I dinna ken whether she'll gie fire ", meaning her mistress. We told her we did not wish her mistress to *give* fire, we only desired her to let *her* make a fire and we would pay for it. The girl brought in the tea-things, but no fire, and when I asked if she was coming to light it, she said " her mistress was not varra willing to gie fire ". At last, however, on our insisting upon it, the fire was lighted : we got tea by candlelight, and spent a comfortable evening. I had seen the landlady before we went out, for, as had been usual in all the country inns, there was a demur respecting beds, notwithstanding the house was empty, and there were at·least half-a-dozen spare beds. Her countenance corresponded with the unkindness of denying us a fire on a cold night, for she was the most cruel and even hateful-looking woman I ever saw. She was overgrown with fat, and was sitting with her feet and legs in a tub of water for the dropsy (probably brought on by whisky-drinking). The sympathy which I felt and expressed for her, on seeing her in this wretched condition (for her legs were swoln as thick as mill-posts), seemed to produce no effect ; and I was obliged, after five minutes' conversation, to leave the affair of the beds undecided. C. had some talk with her daughter, a smart lass in a cotton gown, with a bandeau round her head, without shoes and stockings. She told C. with some pride that she had not spent all her time at Luss, but was then fresh from Glasgow.

It came on a very stormy night ; the wind rattled every window in the house, and it rained heavily. Wm. and C. had bad beds, in a two-bedded room in the garrets, though there were empty rooms on the first floor, and they were disturbed by a drunken man, who had come to the inn when we were gone to sleep.

August 25th, Thursday. We were glad when we awoke to see that it was a fine morning — the sky was bright blue, with quick-moving clouds, the hills chearful, lights and shadows vivid and distinct. The village looked exceedingly beautiful this morning from the garret windows — the stream glittering near it, while it flowed under trees through the level fields to the lake. After breakfast, Wm. and I went down to the waterside. The roads were as dry as if no drop of rain had fallen, which added to the pure chearfulness of the appearance of the village, and even of the distant prospect, an effect which I always seem to perceive from clearly bright roads (for they are always brightened by rain) after a storm ; but when we came among the houses I regretted even more than last night, because the contrast was greater, the slovenliness and dirt near the doors ; and could not but remember, with pain from the contrast, the cottages of Somersetshire, covered with roses and myrtle, and their small gardens of herbs and flowers. While lingering by the shore we began to talk with a man who offered to row us to Inch-ta-vannach ; but the sky began to darken ; and the wind being high, we doubted whether we should venture, therefore made no engagement ; he offered to sell me some thread, pointing to his cottage, and added that many English ladies carried thread away from Luss.

Presently after C. joined us, and we determined to go to the island. I was sorry that the man who had been talking with us was not our boatman ; Wm. by some chance had engaged another. We had two rowers and a strong boat ; so I felt myself bold, though there was a great chance of a high wind. The nearest point of Inch-ta-vannach is not perhaps more than a mile and a quarter from Luss ; we did not land there, but rowed round the end, and landed on that side which looks towards our favourite cottages, and their own island, which, wherever seen, is still their own. It rained a little when we landed, and I took my cloak, which afterwards served us to sit down upon in our road up the hill, when the day grew much finer, with gleams of sunshine. This island belongs to Sir James Colquhoun, who has made a convenient road that winds gently to the top of it.

We had not climbed far before we were stopped by a sudden burst of prospect, so singular and beautiful that it was like a flash of images from another world. We stood with our backs to the hill of the island, which we were ascending, and which shut out Ben Lomond entirely, and all the upper part of the lake, and we looked towards the foot of the lake, scattered over with islands without beginning and without end. The sun shone, and the distant hills were visible, some through sunny mists, others in gloom with patches of sunshine ; the lake was lost under the low and distant hills, and the islands lost in the lake, which was all in motion with travelling fields of light, or dark shadows under rainy clouds. There are many hills, but no commanding eminence at a distance to confine the prospect, so that the land seemed endless as the water.

What I had heard of Loch Lomond, or any other place in Great Britain, had given me no idea of anything like what we beheld : it was an outlandish scene — we might have believed ourselves in North America. The islands were of every possible variety of shape and surface — hilly and level, large and small, bare, rocky, pastoral, or covered with wood. Immediately under my eyes lay one large flat island, bare and green, so flat and low that it scarcely appeared to rise above the water, with straggling peat-stacks and a single hut upon one of its out-shooting promontories (for it was of a very irregular shape, though perfectly flat). Another, its next neighbour, and still nearer to us, was covered over with heath and coppice-wood, the surface undulating, with flat or sloping banks towards the water, and hollow places, cradle-like valleys, behind. These two islands, with Inch-ta-vannach, where we were standing, were intermingled with the water, I might say interbedded and interveined with it, in a manner that was exquisitely pleasing. There were bays innumerable, straits or passages like calm rivers, landlocked lakes, and, to the main water, stormy promontories. The solitary hut on the flat green island seemed unsheltered and desolate, and yet not wholly so, for it was but a broad river's breadth from the covert of the wood of the other island. Near to these is a miniature, an islet covered with trees, on which stands a small ruin that looks like the remains of a religious house ; it is overgrown with ivy, and were it not that the arch of a window or gateway may be distinctly seen, it would be difficult to believe that it was not a tuft of trees growing in the shape of a ruin, rather than a ruin overshadowed by trees. When we had walked a little further we saw below us, on the nearest large island, where some of the wood had been cut down, a hut, which we conjectured to be a bark hut. It appeared to be on the shore of a little forest lake, enclosed by Inch-ta-vannach (where we were), and the woody island on which the hut stands.

Beyond we had the same intricate view as before, and

could discover Dumbarton rock with its double head. There being a mist over it, it had a ghost-like appearance (as I observed to Wm. and C.) something like the Tor of Glastonbury from the Dorsetshire hills. Right before us, on the flat island mentioned before, were several small single trees or shrubs, growing at different distances from each other, close to the shore, but some optical delusion had detached them from the land on which they stood, and they had the appearance of so many little vessels sailing along the coast of it. I mention the circumstance, because, with the ghostly image of Dumbarton Castle, and the ambiguous ruin on the small island, it was much in the character of the scene, which was throughout magical and enchanting — a new world in its great permanent outline and composition, and changing at every moment in every part of it by the effect of sun and wind, and mist and shower and cloud, and the blending lights and deep shades which took the place of each other, traversing the lake in every direction. The whole was indeed a strange mixture of soothing and restless images, of images inviting to rest, and others hurrying the fancy away into an activity still more pleasing than repose ; yet, intricate and homeless, that is, without lasting abiding-place for the mind, as the prospect was, there was no perplexity ; we had still a guide to lead us forward.

Wherever we looked, it was a delightful feeling that there was something beyond. Meanwhile, the sense of quiet was never lost sight of ; the little peaceful lakes among the islands might make you forget that the great water, Loch Lomond, was so near ; and yet are more beautiful, because you know that it is so : they have their own bays and creeks sheltered within a shelter. When we had ascended to the top of the island we had a view up to Ben Lomond, over the long, broad water without spot or rock ; and, looking backwards, saw the islands below us as on a map. This view, as may be supposed, was not nearly so interesting as those we had seen before. We hunted out all the houses on the shore, which were very few : there was the village of Luss, the two gentlemen's houses, our favourite cottages, and here and there a hut ; but I do not recollect any comfortable-looking farm-houses, and on the opposite shore not a single dwelling. The whole scene was a combination of natural wildness, loveliness, beauty, and barrenness, or rather bareness, yet not comfortless or cold ; but the whole was beautiful. We were too far off the more distant shore to distinguish any particular spots which we might have regretted were not better cultivated, and near Luss there was no want of houses.

After we had left the island, having been so much taken with the beauty of the bark hut and the little lake by which it appeared to stand, we desired the boatman to row us through it, and we landed at the hut. Walked upon the island for some time, and found out sheltered places for cottages. There were several woodmen's huts, which, with some scattered fir-trees, and others in irregular knots, that made a delicious murmuring in the wind, added greatly to the romantic effect of the scene. They were built in the form of a cone from the ground, like savages' huts, the door being just large enough for a man to enter with stooping. Straw beds were raised on logs of wood, tools lying about, and a forked bough of a tree was generally suspended from the roof in the middle to hang a kettle upon. It was a place that might have been just visited by new settlers. I thought of Ruth and her dreams of romantic love :

> *And then he said how sweet it were,*
> *A fisher or a hunter there,*
> *A gardener in the shade,*
> *Still wandering with an easy mind,*
> *To build a household fire, and find*
> *A home in every glade.*[1]

We found the main lake very stormy when we had left the shelter of the islands, and there was again a threatening of rain, but it did not come on. I wanted much to go to the old ruin, but the boatmen were in a hurry to be at home. They told us it had been a stronghold built by a man who lived there alone, and was used to swim over and make depredations on the shore, — that nobody could ever lay hands on him, he was such a good swimmer, but at last they caught him in a net.

---

[1] *Ruth*, stanza xiii.

The men pointed out to us an island belonging to Sir James Colquhoun, on which were a great quantity of deer.

Arrived at the inn at about twelve o'clock, and prepared to depart immediately : we should have gone with great regret if the weather had been warmer and the inn more comfortable. When we were leaving the door, a party with smart carriage and servants drove up, and I observed that the people of the house were just as slow in their attendance upon them as on us, with our single horse and outlandish Hibernian vehicle.

When we had travelled about two miles the lake became considerably narrower, the hills rocky, covered with copses, or bare, rising more immediately from the bed of the water, and therefore we had not so often to regret the want of inhabitants. Passed by, or saw at a distance, sometimes a single cottage, or two or three together, but the whole space between Luss and Tarbet is a solitude to the eye. We were reminded of Ulswater, but missed the pleasant farms, and the mountains were not so interesting : we had not seen them in companies or brotherhoods rising one above another at a long distance. Ben Lomond stood alone, opposite to us, majestically overlooking the lake ; yet there was something in this mountain which disappointed me, — a want of massiveness and simplicity, perhaps from the top being broken into three distinct stages. The road carried us over a bold promontory by a steep and high ascent, and we had a long view of the lake pushing itself up in a narrow line through an avenue of mountains, terminated by the mountains at the head of the lake, of which Ben Lui, if I do not mistake, is the most considerable. The afternoon was showery and misty, therefore we did not see this prospect so distinctly as we could have wished, but there was a grand obscurity over it which might make the mountains appear more numerous.

I have said so much of this lake that I am tired myself, and I fear I must have tired my friends. We had a pleasant journey to Tarbet ; more than half of it on foot, for the road was hilly, and after we had climbed one small hill we were not desirous to get into the car again, seeing another before us, and our path was always delightful, near the lake, and frequently through woods. When we were within about half a mile of Tarbet, at a

T

sudden turning, looking to the left, we saw a very craggy-topped mountain amongst other smooth ones ; the rocks on the summit distinct in shape as if they were buildings raised up by man, or uncouth images of some strange creature. We called out with one voice, " That's what we wanted ! " alluding to the frame-like uniformity of the side-screens of the lake for the last five or six miles. As we conjectured, this singular mountain was the famous Cobbler, near Arrochar. Tarbet was before us in the recess of a deep, large bay, under the shelter of a hill. When we came up to the village we had to inquire for the inn, there being no signboard. It was a well-sized white house, the best in the place ; we were conducted up-stairs into a sitting-room that might make any good-humoured travellers happy — a square room, with windows on each side, looking, one way, towards the mountains, and across the lake to Ben Lomond, the other.

There was a pretty stone house before (*i.e.* towards the lake) some huts, scattered trees, two or three green fields with hedgerows, and a little brook making its way towards the lake ; the fields are almost flat, and screened on that side nearest the head of the lake by a hill, which, pushing itself out, forms the bay of Tarbet, and, towards the foot, by a gentle slope and trees. The lake is narrow, and Ben Lomond shuts up the prospect, rising directly from the water. We could have believed ourselves to be by the side of Ulswater, at Glenridden, or in some other of the inhabited retirements of that lake ; we were in a sheltered place among mountains ; it was not an open joyous bay, with a chearful populous village, like Luss ; but a pastoral and retired spot, with a few single dwellings. The people of the inn stared at us when we spoke, without giving us an answer immediately, which we were at first disposed to attribute to coarseness of manners, but found afterwards that they did not understand us at once, Erse being the language spoken in the family. Nothing but salt meat and eggs for dinner — no potatoes ; the house smelt strongly of herrings, which were hung to dry over the kitchen fire.

Walked in the evening towards the head of the lake ; the

road was steep over the hill, and when we had reached the top of it we had long views up and down the water. Passed a troop of women who were resting themselves by the roadside, as if returning from their day's labour. Amongst them was a man, who had walked with us a considerable way in the morning, and told us he was just come from America, where he had been for some years, — was going to his own home, and should return to America. He spoke of emigration as a glorious thing for them who had money ; poor fellow ! I do not think that he had brought much back with him, for he had worked his passage over : I much suspected that a bundle, which he carried upon a stick, tied in a pocket-handkerchief, contained his all. He was almost blind, he said, as were many of the crew. He intended crossing the lake at the ferry ; but it was stormy, and he thought he should not be able to get over that day. I could not help smiling when I saw him lying by the roadside with such a company about him, not like a wayfaring man, but seeming as much at home and at his ease as if he had just stepped out of his hut among them, and they had been neighbours all their lives. Passed one pretty house, a large thatched dwelling with outhouses, but the prospect above and below was solitary.

The sun had long been set before we returned to the inn. As travellers, we were glad to see the moon over the top of one of the hills, but it was a cloudy night, without any peculiar beauty or solemnity. After tea we made inquiries respecting the best way to go to Loch Ketterine ; the landlord could give but little information, and nobody seemed to know anything distinctly of the place, though it was but ten miles off. We applied to the maid-servant who waited on us : she was a fine-looking young woman, dressed in a white bed-gown, her hair fastened up by a comb, and without shoes and stockings. When we asked her about the Trossachs she could give us no information, but on our saying, " Do you know Loch Ketterine ? " she answered with a smile, " I *should* know that loch, for I was bred and born there ". After much difficulty we learned from her that the Trossachs were at the foot of the lake, and that by the way we were to go we should come upon them at the head, should have to travel ten miles to the foot [1] of the water, and that there was no inn by the way. The girl spoke English very distinctly ; but she had few words, and found it difficult to understand us. She did not much encourage us to go, because the roads were bad, and it was a long way, " and there was no putting-up for the like of us ". We determined, however, to venture, and throw ourselves upon the hospitality of some cottager or gentleman. We desired the landlady to roast us a couple of fowls to carry with us ; there are always plenty of fowls at the doors of a Scotch inn, and eggs are as regularly brought to table at breakfast as bread and butter.

---

[1] This distinction between the foot and head is not very clear. What is meant is this : They would have to travel the whole length of the lake, from the west to the east end of it, before they came to the Trossachs, the pass leading away from the east end of the lake.—J. C. S.

Part II

August 26th, Friday. We did not set off till between ten and eleven o'clock, much too late for a long day's journey. Our boatman lived at the pretty white house which we saw from the windows : we called at his door by the way, and, even when we were near the house, the outside looked comfortable ; but within I never saw anything so miserable from dirt, and dirt alone : it reminded one of the house of a decayed weaver in the suburbs of a large town, with a sickly wife and a large family ; but Wm. says it was far worse, that it was quite Hottentotish.

After long waiting, and many clumsy preparations, we got ourselves seated in the boat ; but we had not floated five yards before we perceived that if any of the party (and there was a little Highland woman who was going over the water with us, the boatman, his helper, and ourselves) should stir but a few inches, leaning to one side or the other, the boat would be full in an instant, and we at the bottom ; besides, it was very leaky, and the woman was employed to lade out the water continually. It appeared that this crazy vessel was not the man's own, and that *his* was lying in a bay at a little distance. He said he would take us to it as fast as possible, but I was so much frightened I would gladly have given up the whole day's journey ; indeed not one of us would have attempted to cross the lake in that boat for a thousand pounds. We reached the larger boat in safety after coasting a considerable way near the shore, but just as we were landing, Wm. dropped the bundle which contained our food into the water. The fowls were no worse, but some sugar, ground coffee, and pepper-cake seemed to be entirely spoiled. We gathered together as much of the coffee and sugar as we could and tied it up, and again trusted ourselves to the lake. The sun shone, and the air was calm (luckily it had been so while we were in the crazy boat) we had rocks and woods on each side of us, or

259

bare hills ; seldom a single cottage, and there was no rememberable place till we came opposite to a waterfall of no inconsiderable size, that appeared to drop directly into the lake ; close
to it was a hut, which we were told was the ferry-house. On the
other side of the lake was a pretty farm under the mountains,
beside a river, the cultivated grounds lying all together, and
sloping towards the lake from the mountain hollow down
which the river came. It is not easy to conceive how beautiful
these spots appeared after moving on so long between the
solitary steeps.

We went a considerable way further, and landed at Rob
Roy's Caves, which are in fact no caves, but some fine rocks
on the brink of the lake, in the crevices of which a man might
hide himself cunningly enough ; the water is very deep below
them, and the hills above steep and covered with wood. The
little Highland woman, who was in size about a match for our
guide at Lanerk, accompanied us hither. There was something
very gracious in the manners of this woman ; she could scarcely
speak five English words, yet she gave me, whenever I spoke
to her, as many intelligible smiles as I had needed English
words to answer me, and helped me over the rocks in the most
obliging manner. She had left the boat out of good-will to
us, or for her own amusement. She had never seen these caves
before ; but no doubt had heard of them, the tales of Rob
Roy's exploits being told familiarly round the *ingles* hereabouts, for this neighbourhood was his home. We landed at
Inversneyde, the ferry-house by the waterfall, and were not
sorry to part with our boatman, who was a coarse hard-
featured man, and, speaking of the French, uttered the basest
and most cowardly sentiments. His helper, a youth fresh from
the Isle of Skye, was innocent of this fault, and though but a
bad rower, was a far better companion ; he could not speak a
word of English, and sang a plaintive Gaelic air in a low tone
while he plied his oar.

The ferry-house stood on the bank a few yards above the
landing-place where the boat lies. It is a small hut under a
steep wood, and a few yards to the right (looking towards the
hut) is the waterfall. The fall is not very high, but the stream

is considerable, as we could see by the large black stones that were lying bare, but the rains, if they had reached this place, had had little effect upon the waterfall ; its noise was not so great as to form a contrast with the stillness of the bay into which it falls, where the boat, and house, and waterfall itself seemed all sheltered and protected. The Highland woman was to go with us the two first miles of our journey — she led us along a bye foot-path a shorter way up the hill from the ferry-house. There is a considerable settling in the hills that border Loch Lomond, at the passage by which we were to cross to Loch Ketterine ; Ben Lomond, terminating near the ferry-house, is on the same side of the water with it, and about three miles above Tarbet.

We had to climb right up the hill, which is very steep, and, when close under it, seemed to be high, but we soon reached the top, and when we were there had lost sight of the lake ; and now our road was over a moor, or rather through a wide moorland hollow. Having gone a little way, we saw before us, at the distance of about half a mile, a very large stone building, a singular structure, with a high wall round it, naked hill above, and neither field nor tree near ; but the moor was not over-grown with heath merely, but grey grass, such as cattle might pasture upon. We could not conjecture what this building was ; it appeared as if it had been built strong to defend it from storms ; but for what purpose ? Wm. called out to us that we should observe that place well, for it was exactly like one of the spittals of the Alps, built for the reception of travellers, and indeed I had thought it must be so before he spoke. This building, from its singular structure and appearance, made the place, which is itself in a country like Scotland nowise remarkable, take a character of unusual wildness and desolation — this when we first came in view of it ; and afterwards, when we had passed it and looked back, three pyramidal mountains on the opposite side of Loch Lomond terminated the view, which under certain accidents of weather must be very grand. Our Highland companion had not English enough to give us any information concerning this strange building ; we could only get from her that it was a " large house ", which was plain enough.

We walked about a mile and a half over the moor without seeing any other dwelling but one hut by the burn-side, with a peat-stack and a ten-yards-square enclosure for potatoes ; then we came to several clusters of houses, even hamlets they might be called, but where there is any land belonging to the Highland huts there are so many out-buildings near, which differ in no respect from the dwelling-houses except that they send out no smoke, that one house looks like two or three. Near these houses was a considerable quantity of cultivated ground, potatoes and corn, and the people were busy making hay in the hollow places of the open vale, and all along the sides of the becks. It was a pretty sight altogether — men and women, dogs, the little running streams, with linen bleaching near them, and chearful sunny hills and rocks on every side. We passed by one patch of potatoes that a florist might have been proud of ; no carnation-bed ever looked more gay than this square plot of ground on the waste common. The flowers were in very large bunches, and of an extraordinary size, and of every conceivable shade of colouring from snow-white to deep purple. It was pleasing in that place, where perhaps was never yet a flower cultivated by man for his own pleasure, to see these blossoms grow more gladly than elsewhere, making a summer garden near the mountain dwellings.

At one of the clusters of houses we parted with our companion, who had insisted on bearing my bundle while she stayed with us. I often tried to enter into conversation with her, and seeing a small tarn before us, was reminded of the pleasure of fishing and the manner of living there, and asked her what sort of food was eaten in that place, if they lived much upon fish, or had mutton from the hills ; she looked earnestly at me, and shaking her head, replied, " Oh yes ! eat fish — no papishes, eat everything ". The tarn had one small island covered with wood ; the stream that runs from it falls into Loch Ketterine, which, after we had gone a little beyond the tarn, we saw at some distance before us.

Pursued the road, a mountain horse-track, till we came to a corner of what seemed the head of the lake, and there sate down completely tired, and hopeless as to the rest of our journey. The road ended at the shore, and no houses were to be seen on the opposite side except a few widely parted huts, and on the near side was a trackless heath. The land at the head of the lake was but a continuation of the common we had come along, and was covered with hether, intersected by a few straggling foot-paths.

C. and I were faint with hunger, and could go no further till we had refreshed ourselves, so we ate up one of our fowls, and drank of the water of Loch Ketterine ; but Wm. could not be easy till he had examined the coast, so he left us, and made his way along the moor across the head of the lake. C. and I, as we sate, had what seemed to us but a dreary prospect — a waste of unknown ground which we guessed we must travel over before it was possible for us to find a shelter. We saw a long way down the lake ; it was all moor on the near side ; on the other the hills were steep from the water, and there were large coppice-woods, but no chearful green fields, and no road that we could see ; we knew, however, that there must be a road from house to house ; but the whole lake appeared a solitude — neither boats, islands, nor houses, no grandeur in the hills, nor any loveliness in the shores. When we first came in view of it we had said it was like a barren Ulswater — Ulswater dismantled of its grandeur, and cropped of its lesser beauties. When I had swallowed my dinner I hastened after Wm., and C. followed me. Walked through the hether with some labour for perhaps half a mile, and found Wm. sitting on the top of a small eminence, whence we saw the real head of the lake, which was pushed up into the vale a considerable way beyond the promontory where we now sate. The view up the lake was very pleasing, resembling Thirlemere below Armath ; there were rocky promontories and woody islands, and, what was most chearing to us, a neat white house on the opposite shore ; but we could see no boats, so, in order to get to it we should be obliged to go round the head of the lake, a long and weary way.

After C. came up to us, while we were debating whether we should turn back or go forward, we espied a man on horseback at a little distance, with a boy following him on foot, no doubt a welcome sight, and we hailed him. We should have been glad to have seen either man, woman, or child at this time, but there was something uncommon and interesting in this man's appearance, which would have fixed our attention wherever we had met him. He was a complete Highlander in dress, figure, and face, and a very fine-looking man, hardy and vigorous, though past his prime. While he stood waiting for us in his bonnet and plaid, which never look more graceful than on horseback, I forgot our errand, and only felt glad that we were in the Highlands. Wm. accosted him with, " Sir, do you speak English ? " He replied, " A little ". He spoke however, sufficiently well for our purpose, and very distinctly, as all the Highlanders do who learn English as a foreign language ; but in a long conversation they want words ; he informed us that he himself was going beyond the Trossachs, to Callander, that no boats were kept to let ; but there were two gentlemen's houses at this end of the lake, one of which we could not yet see, it being hidden from us by a part of the hill on which we stood. The other house was that which we saw opposite to us ; both the gentlemen kept boats, and probably might be able to spare one of their servants to go with us. After we had asked many questions, which the Highlander answered with patience and courtesy, he parted from us, going along a sort of horse-track, which a foot-passenger, if he once get into it, need not lose if he be careful.

When he was gone we again debated whether we should go back to Tarbet, or throw ourselves upon the mercy of one of the two gentlemen for a night's lodging. What we had seen of the main body of the lake made us little desire to see more of it ; the Highlander upon the naked heath, in his Highland dress, upon his careful-going horse, with the boy following him, was worth it all ; but after a little while we resolved to go on, ashamed to shrink from an adventure. Pursued the horse-track, and soon came in sight of the other gentleman's house, which stood on the opposite side of the vale, a little above the lake. It was a white house ; no trees near it except a new plantation of firs ; but the fields were green, sprinkled over with hay-cocks, and the brook which comes down the valley and falls into the lake ran through them. It was like a new-made farm in a mountain vale, and yet very pleasing after the depressing prospect which had been before us.

Our road was rough, and not easy to be kept. It was between five and six o'clock when we reached the brook side, where C. and I stopped, and Wm. went up towards the house, which was in a field, where about half a dozen people were at work. He addressed himself to one who appeared like the master, and all drew near him, staring at Wm. as nobody could have stared but out of sheer rudeness, except in such a lonely place. He told his tale, and inquired about boats ; there were no boats, and no lodging nearer than Callander, ten miles beyond the foot of the lake. A laugh was on every face when Wm. said we were come to see the Trossachs ; no doubt they thought we had better have stayed at our own homes. Wm. endeavoured to make it appear not so very foolish, by informing them that it was a place much celebrated in England, though perhaps little thought of by them, and that we only differed from many of our countrymen in having come the wrong way in consequence of an erroneous direction.

After a little time the gentleman said we should be accommodated with such beds as they had, and should be welcome to rest in their house if we pleased. Wm. came back for C. and me ; the men all stood at the door to receive us, and now their behaviour was perfectly courteous. We were conducted into the house by the same man who had directed us hither on the other side of the lake, and afterwards we learned that he was the father of our hostess. He showed us into a room upstairs, begged we would sit at our ease, walk out, or do just as we pleased. It was a large square deal wainscoted room, the wainscot black with age, yet had never been painted : it did not look like an English room, and yet I do not know in what it differed, except that in England it is not common to see so large and well-built a room so ill-furnished : there were two or three large tables, and a few old chairs of different sorts, as if they had been picked up one did not know how, at sales, or had belonged to different rooms of the house ever since it was built. We sate perhaps three-quarters of an hour, and I was about to carry down our wet coffee and sugar and ask leave to boil it, when the mistress of the house entered — a tall fine-looking woman, neatly dressed in a dark-coloured gown, with a white handkerchief tied round her head ; she spoke to us in a very pleasing manner, begging permission to make tea for us, an offer which we thankfully accepted. Encouraged by the sweetness of her manners, I went down-stairs to dry my feet by the kitchen fire ; she lent me a pair of stockings, and behaved to me with the utmost attention and kindness. She carried the tea-things into the room herself, leaving me to make tea, and set before us cheese and butter and barley cakes. These cakes are as thin as our oat-bread, but, instead of being crisp, are soft and leathery, yet we, being hungry, and the butter delicious, ate them with great pleasure, but when the same bread was set before us afterwards we did not like it.

After tea Wm. and I walked out ; we amused ourselves with watching the Highlanders at work : they went leisurely about everything, and whatever was to be done, all followed, old men, and young, and little children. We were driven into the house by a shower, which came on with the evening darkness, and the people leaving their work paused at the same time. I was pleased to see them a while after sitting round a blazing fire in the kitchen, father and son-in-law, master and man, and the mother with her little child on her knee. When I had been there before tea I had observed what a contrast there was between the mistress and her kitchen ; she did not differ in appearance from an English country lady ; but her kitchen, roof, walls, and floor of mud, was all black alike ; yet now, with the light of a bright fire upon so many happy countenances, the whole room made a pretty sight.

We heard the company laughing and talking long after we were in bed ; indeed I believe they never work till they are tired.[1] The children could not speak a word of English : they were very shy at first ; but after I had caressed the eldest, and given her a red leather purse, with which she was delighted, she took hold of my hand and hung about me, changing her

---

[1] She means that they stop work before they are tired.—W. K.

side-long looks for pretty smiles. Her mother lamented they were so far from school, they should be obliged to send the children down into the Lowlands to be taught reading and English. Callander, the nearest town, was twenty miles from them, and it was only a small place : they had their groceries from Glasgow. She said that at Callander was their nearest church, but they sometimes " got a preaching at the Garrison ". In explaining herself she informed us that the large building which had puzzled us in the morning had been built by Government, at the request of one of the Dukes of Montrose, for the defence of his domains against the attacks of Rob Roy. I will not answer for the truth of this ; perhaps it might have been built for this purpose, and as a check on the Highlands in general ; certain it is, however, that it was a garrison ; soldiers used to be constantly stationed there, and have only been withdrawn within the last thirteen or fourteen years. Mrs. Macfarlane attended me to my room ; she said she hoped I should be able to sleep upon blankets, and said they were " fresh from the fauld ".

August 27th, Saturday. Before I rose, Mrs. Macfarlane came into my room to see if I wanted anything, and told me she should send the servant up with a basin of whey, saying, " We make very good whey in this country " ; indeed, I thought it the best I had ever tasted ; but I cannot tell how this should be, for they only make skimmed-milk cheeses. I asked her for a little bread and milk for our breakfast, but she said it would be no trouble to make tea, as she must make it for the family ; so we all breakfasted together. The cheese was set out, as before, with plenty of butter and barley-cakes, and fresh baked oaten cakes, which, no doubt, were made for us : they had been kneaded with cream, and were excellent. All the party pressed us to eat, and were very jocose about the necessity of helping out their coarse bread with butter, and they themselves ate almost as much butter as bread. In talking of the French and the present times, their language was what most people would call Jacobinical. They spoke much of the oppressions endured by the Highlanders further up, of the absolute impossibility of their living in any comfort, and of the cruelty of laying so many restraints on emigration. Then they spoke with animation of the attachment of the clans to their lairds : " The laird of this place, Glengyle, where we live, could have commanded so many men who would have followed him to the death ; and now there are none left ". It appeared that Mr. Macfarlane, and his wife's brother, Mr. Macalpine, farmed the place, inclusive of the whole vale upwards to the mountains, and the mountains themselves, under the lady of Glengyle, the mother of the young laird, a minor. It was a sheep-farm.

Speaking of another neighbouring laird, they said he had gone, like the rest of them, to Edinburgh, left his lands and his own people, spending his money where it brought him not any esteem, so that he was of no value either at home or abroad. We mentioned Rob Roy, and the eyes of all glistened ; even the lady of the house, who was very diffident, and no great talker, exclaimed, " He was a good man, Rob Roy ! " He had been dead only about eighty years, had lived in the next farm, which belonged to him, and there his bones were laid.[1] He was a famous swordsman. Having an arm much longer than other men, he had a greater command with his sword. As a proof of the length of his arm, they told us that he could garter his tartan stockings below the knee without stooping, and added a dozen different stories of single combats, which he had fought, all in perfect good-humour, merely to prove his prowess. I daresay they had stories of this kind which would hardly have been exhausted in the long evenings of a whole December week, Rob Roy being as famous here as ever Robin Hood was in the Forest of Sherwood ; *he* also robbed from the rich, giving to the poor, and defending them from oppression. They tell of his confining the factor of the Duke of Montrose in one of the islands of Loch Ketterine, after having taken his money from him (the Duke's rents) in open

---

[1] There is a mistake here. His bones were laid about fifteen or twenty miles from thence, in Balquhidder kirkyard. But it was under the belief that his " grave is near the head of Loch Ketterine, in one of those pinfold-like burial grounds, of neglected and desolate appearance, which the traveller meets with in the Highlands of Scotland ", that W.'s well-known poem on *Rob Roy's Grave* was composed.—J. C. S.

day, while they were sitting at table. He was a formidable enemy of the Duke, but being a small laird against a greater, was overcome at last, and forced to resign all his lands on the Braes of Loch Lomond (including the caves which we visited), on account of the money he had taken from the Duke and could not repay.

When breakfast was ended the mistress desired the person whom we took to be her husband to " return thanks ". He said a short grace, and in a few minutes they all went off to their work. We saw them about the door following one another like a flock of sheep, with the children after, whatever job they were engaged in. Mrs. Macfarlane told me she would show me the burying-place of the lairds of Glengyle, and took me to a square enclosure like a pinfold, with a stone ball at every corner ; we had noticed it the evening before, and wondered what it could be. It was in the middle of a *planting*, as they call plantations, which was enclosed for the preservation of the trees, therefore we had to climb over a high wall : it was a dismal spot, containing four or five graves overgrown with long grass, nettles, and brambles. Against the wall was a marble monument to the memory of one of the lairds, of whom they spoke with veneration : some English verses were inscribed upon the marble, purporting that he had been the father of his clan, a brave and good man. When we returned to the house she said she would show me what curious feathers they had in their country, and brought out a bunch carefully wrapped up in paper. On my asking her what bird they came from, " Oh ! " she replied, " it is a great beast ". We conjectured it was an eagle, and from her description of its ways, and the manner of destroying it, we knew it was so. She begged me to accept of some of the feathers, telling me that some ladies wore them in their heads. I was much pleased with the gift, which I shall preserve in memory of her kindness and simplicity of manners, and the Highland solitude where she lived.

We took leave of the family with regret : they were handsome, healthy, and happy-looking people. It was ten o'clock when we departed. We had learned that there was a ferry-boat kept at three miles' distance, and if the man was at home he would row us down the lake to the Trossachs. Our walk was mostly through coppice-woods, along a horse-road, upon which narrow carts might travel. Passed that white house which had looked at us with such a friendly face when we were on the other side ; it stood on the slope of a hill, with green pastures below it, plots of corn and coppice-wood, and behind, a rocky steep covered with wood. It was a very pretty place, but the morning being cold and dull the opposite shore appeared dreary. Near to the white house we passed by another of those little pinfold squares, which we knew to be a burying-place ; it was in a sloping green field among woods, and within sound of the beating of the water against the shore, if there were but a gentle breeze to stir it : I thought if I lived in that house, and my ancestors and kindred were buried there, I should sit many an hour under the walls of this plot of earth, where all the household would be gathered together.

We found the ferryman at work in the field above his hut, and he was at liberty to go with us, but, being wet and hungry, we begged that he would let us sit by his fire till we had re-freshed ourselves. This was the first genuine Highland hut we had been in. We entered by the cow-house, the house-door being within, at right angles to the outer door. The woman was distressed that she had a bad fire, but she heaped up some dry peats and hether, and, blowing it with her breath, in a short time raised a blaze that scorched us into comfortable feelings. A small part of the smoke found its way out of the hole of the chimney, the rest through the open window-places, one of which was within the recess of the fireplace, and made a frame to a little picture of the restless lake and the opposite shore, seen when the outer door was open. The woman of the house was very kind : whenever we asked her for anything it seemed a fresh pleasure to her that she had it for us ; she always answered with a sort of softening down of the Scotch exclama-tion, " Hoot ! " " Ho ! yes, ye'll get that ", and hied to her cupboard in the spence. We were amused with the phrase " Ye'll get that " in the Highlands, which appeared to us as if it came from a perpetual feeling of the difficulty with which most things are procured. We *got* oatmeal, butter, bread and milk, made some porridge, and then departed. It was rainy and cold, with a strong wind.

C. was afraid of the cold in the boat, so he determined to walk down the lake, pursuing the same road we had come along. There was nothing very interesting for the first three or four miles on either side of the water : to the right, uncultivated heath or poor coppice-wood, and to the left, a scattering of meadow ground, patches of corn, coppice-woods, and here and there a cottage. The wind fell, and it began to rain heavily. On this Wm. wrapped himself in the boatman's plaid, and lay at the bottom of the boat till we came to a place where I could not help rousing him. We were rowing down that side of the lake which had hitherto been little else than a moorish ridge. After turning a rocky point we came to a bay closed in by rocks and steep woods, chiefly of full-grown birch. The lake was elsewhere ruffled, but at the entrance of this bay the breezes sunk, and it was calm : a small island was near, and the opposite shore, covered with wood, looked soft through the misty rain. Wm., rubbing his eyes, for he had been asleep, called out that he hoped I had not let him pass by anything that was so beautiful as this ; and I was glad to tell him that it was but the beginning of a new land. After we had left this bay we saw before us a long reach of woods and rocks and rocky points, that promised other bays more beautiful than what we had passed. The ferryman was a good-natured fellow, and rowed very industriously, following the ins and outs of the shore ; he was delighted with the pleasure we expressed, continually repeating how pleasant it would have been on a fine day. I believe he was attached to the lake by some sentiment of pride, as his own domain (his being almost the only boat upon it), which made him (seeing we were willing gazers) take far more pains than an ordinary boatman ; he would often say, after he had compassed the turning of a point, " This is a bonny part ", and he always chose the bonniest, with greater skill than our prospect-hunters and " picturesque travellers " ; places screened from the winds — that was the first point ; the rest followed of course,— richer growing trees, rocks and banks, and curves which the eye delights in.

The second bay we came to differed from the rest ; the hills retired a short space from the lake, leaving a few level fields between, on which was a cottage embosomed in trees : the bay was defended by rocks at each end, and the hills behind made a shelter for the cottage, the only dwelling, I believe, except one, on this side of Loch Ketterine. We now came to steeps that rose directly from the lake, and passed by a place called in the Gaelic the Den of the Ghosts,[1] which reminded us of Lodore ; it is a rock, or mass of rock, with a stream of large black stones like the naked or dried-up bed of a torrent down the side of it ; birch-trees start out of the rock in every direction, and cover the hill above, further than we could see. The water of the lake below was very deep, black, and calm. Our delight increased as we advanced, till we came in view of the termination of the lake, seeing where the river issues out of it through a narrow chasm between the hills.

Here I ought to rest, as we rested, and attempt to give utterance to our pleasure : but indeed I can impart but little of what we felt. We were still on the same side of the water, and, being immediately under the hill, within a considerable bending of the shore, we were enclosed by hills all round, as if we had been upon a smaller lake of which the whole was visible. It was an entire solitude ; and all that we beheld was the perfection of loveliness and beauty ; we had been through many solitary places since we came into Scotland, but this place differed as much from any we had seen before, as if there had been nothing in common between them ; no thought of dreariness or desolation found entrance here ; yet nothing was to be seen but water, wood, rocks, and hether, and bare mountains above. We saw the mountains by glimpses as the clouds passed by them, and were not disposed to regret, with our boatman, that it was not a fine day, for the near objects were not concealed from us, but softened by being seen through the mists. The lake is not very wide here, but appeared to be much narrower than it really is, owing to the many pro-

---

[1] Goblins' Cave.—J. C. S.

montories, which are pushed so far into it that they are much more like islands than promontories. We had a longing desire to row to the outlet and look up into the narrow passage through which the river went ; but the point where we were to land was on the other side, so we bent our course right across, and just as we came in sight of two huts, which have been built by Lady Perth as a shelter for those who visit the Trossachs, C. hailed us with a shout of triumph from the door of one of them, exulting in the glory of Scotland. The huts stand at a small distance from each other, on a high and perpendicular rock, that rises from the bed of the lake. A road, which has a very wild appearance, has been cut through the rock ; yet even here, among these bold precipices, the feeling of excessive beautifulness overcomes every other. While we were upon the lake, on every side of us were bays within bays, often more like tiny lakes or pools than bays, and these not in long succession only, but all round, some almost on the broad breast of the water, the promontories shot out so far.

After we had landed we walked along the road to the uppermost of the huts, where C. was standing. From the door of this hut we saw Benvenue opposite to us — a high mountain, but clouds concealed its top ; its side, rising directly from the lake, is covered with birch-trees to a great height, and seamed with innumerable channels of torrents ; but now there was no water in them, nothing to break in upon the stillness and repose of the scene ; nor do I recollect hearing the sound of water from any side, the wind being fallen and the lake perfectly still ; the place was all eye, and completely satisfied the sense and the heart. Above and below us, to the right and to the left, were rocks, knolls, and hills, which, wherever anything could grow (and that was *every*where between the rocks) were covered with trees and hether ; the trees did not in any place grow so thick as an ordinary wood ; yet I think there was never a bare space of twenty yards : it was more like a natural forest where the trees grow in groups or singly, not hiding the surface of the ground, which, instead of being green and mossy, was of the richest purple. The hether was indeed the most luxuriant I ever saw ; it was so tall that a child of ten years old struggling through it would often have been buried head and shoulders, and the exquisite beauty of the colour, near or at a distance, seen under the trees, is not to be conceived. But if I were to go on describing for evermore, I should give but a faint, and very often a false, idea of the different objects and the various combinations of them in this most intricate and delicious place ; besides, I tired myself out with describing at Loch Lomond, so I will hasten to the end of my tale. This reminds me of a sentence in a little pamphlet written by the minister of Callander, descriptive of the environs of that place. After having taken up at least six closely-printed pages with the Trossachs, he concludes thus, " In a word, the Trossachs beggar all description ",— a conclusion in which everybody who has been there will agree with him. I believe the word Trossachs signifies many hills : it is a name given to all the eminences at the foot of Loch Ketterine, and about half a mile beyond.

We left the hut, retracing the few yards of road which we had climbed ; our boat lay at anchor under the rock in the last of all the compartments of the lake, a small oblong pool, almost shut up within itself, as several others had appeared to be, by jutting points of rock. It was the termination of a long out-shooting of the water, pushed up between the steeps of the main shore (where the huts stand) and a broad promontory which, with its hillocks and points and lesser promontories, occupies the centre of the foot of the lake. A person sailing through the lake up the middle of it, would just as naturally suppose that the outlet was here as on the other side ; and so it might have been, with the most trifling change in the disposition of the ground, for at the end of this slip of water the lake is confined only by a gentle rising of a few yards towards an opening between the hills, a narrow pass or valley through which the river might have flowed. The road is carried through this valley, which only differs from the lower part of the vale of the lake in being excessively narrow, and without water ; it is enclosed by mountains, rocky mounds, hills and hillocks scattered over with birch-trees, and covered with Dutch myrtle and hether, even surpassing what we had seen before. Our mother Eve had no fairer, though a more diversified garden, to tend, than we found within this little close valley. It rained all the time, but the mists and calm air made us ample amends for a wetting.

At the opening of the pass we climbed up a low eminence, and had an unexpected prospect suddenly before us — another lake, small compared with Loch Ketterine, though perhaps four miles long, but the misty air concealed the end of it. The transition from the solitary wildness of Loch Ketterine and the narrow valley or pass to this scene was very delightful : it was a gentle place, with lovely open bays, one small island, corn fields, woods, and a groupe of cottages. This vale seemed to have been made to be tributary to the comforts of man, Loch Ketterine for the lonely delight of Nature, and kind spirits delighting in beauty. The sky was grey and heavy,— floating mists on the hill-sides, which softened the objects, and where we lost sight of the lake it appeared so near to the sky that they almost touched one another, giving a visionary beauty to the prospect. While we overlooked this quiet scene we could hear the stream rumbling among the rocks between the lakes, but the mists concealed any glimpse of it which we might have had. This small lake is called Loch Achray.

We returned, of course, by the same road. Our guide repeated over and over again his lamentations that the day was so bad, though we had often told him (not indeed with much hope that he would believe us) that we were glad of it. As we walked along he pulled a leafy twig from a birch-tree, and, after smelling it, gave it to me, saying, how " sweet and hale-some " it was, and that it was pleasant and very halesome on a fine summer's morning to sail under the banks where the birks are growing. This reminded me of the old Scotch songs, in which you continually hear of the " pu'ing the birks ". Common as birches are in the north of England, I believe their sweet smell is a thing unnoticed among the peasants. We returned again to the huts to take a farewell look. We had shared our food with the ferryman and a traveller whom we had met here, who was going up the lake, and wished to lodge at the ferry-house, so we offered him a place in the boat. C.

275

chose to walk. We took the same side of the lake as before, and had much delight in visiting the bays over again ; but the evening began to darken, and it rained so heavily before we had gone two miles that we were completely wet. It was dark when we landed, and on entering the house I was sick with cold.

The good woman had provided, according to her promise, a better fire than we had found in the morning ; and indeed when I sate down in the chimney-corner of her smoky biggin' I thought I had never been more comfortable in my life. C. had been there long enough to have a pan of coffee boiling for us, and having put our clothes in the way of drying, we all sate down, thankful for a shelter. We could not prevail upon the man of the house to draw near the fire, though he was cold and wet, or to suffer his wife to get him dry clothes till she had served us, which she did, though most willingly, not very expeditiously. A Cumberland man of the same rank would not have had such a notion of what was fit and right in his own house, or if he had, one would have accused him of servility ; but in the Highlander it only seemed like politeness (however erroneous and painful to us) naturally growing out of the dependence of the inferiors of the clan upon their laird ; he did not, however, refuse to let his wife bring out the whisky-bottle at our request : " she keeps a dram ", as the phrase is ; indeed, I believe there is scarcely a lonely house by the wayside in Scotland where travellers may not be accommodated with a dram. We asked for sugar, butter, barley-bread, and milk, and with a smile and a stare more of kindness than wonder, she replied, " Ye'll get that ", bringing each article separately. We caroused our cups of coffee, laughing like children at the strange atmosphere in which we were : the smoke came in gusts, and spread along the walls and above our heads in the chimney, where the hens were roosting like light clouds in the sky ; we laughed and laughed again, in spite of the smarting of our eyes, yet had a quieter pleasure in observing the beauty of the beams and rafters gleaming between the clouds of smoke. They had been crusted over and varnished by many winters, till, where the firelight fell upon them, they were as glossy as black rocks on a sunny day cased in ice. When we had eaten our supper we sate about half an hour, and I think I had never felt so deeply the blessing of a hospitable welcome and a warm fire. The man of the house repeated from time to time that we should often tell of this night when we got to our homes, and interposed praises of this, his own lake, which he had more than once, when we were returning in the boat, ventured to say was " bonnier than Loch Lomond ".

Our companion from the Trossachs, who it appeared was an Edinburgh drawing-master going during the vacation on a pedestrian tour to Johnny Groat's house, was to sleep in the barn with Wm. and Coleridge, where the man said he had plenty of dry hay. I do not believe that the hay of the Highlands is often very dry, but this year it had a better chance than usual : wet or dry, however, the next morning they said they had slept comfortably. When I went to bed, the mistress, desiring me to " go *ben* ", attended me with a candle, and assured me that the bed was dry, though not " sic as I had been used to ". It was of chaff ; there were two others in the room, a cupboard and two chests, on one of which stood the milk in wooden vessels covered over ; I should have thought that milk so kept could not have been sweet, but the cheese and butter were good. The walls of the whole house were of stone unplaistered. It consisted of three apartments, — the cow-house at one end, the kitchen or house in the middle, and the spence at the other end. The rooms were divided, not up to the riggin, but only to the beginning of the roof, so that there was a free passage for light and smoke from one end of the house to the other.

I went to bed some time before the family. The door was shut between us, and they had a bright fire, which I could not see ; but the light it sent up among the varnished rafters and beams, which crossed each other in almost as intricate and fantastic a manner as I have seen the under-boughs of a large beech-tree withered by the depth of the shade above, produced the most beautiful effect that can be conceived. It was like what I should suppose an underground cave or temple to be, with a dripping or moist roof, and the moonlight entering in upon it by some means or other, and yet the colours were more like the colours of melted gems. I lay looking up till the light of the fire faded away, and the man and his wife and child had crept into their bed at the other end of the room. I did not sleep much, but passed a comfortable night, for my bed, though hard, was warm and clean : the unusualness of my situation prevented me from sleeping. I could hear the waves beat against the shore of the lake ; a little *syke* close to the door made a much louder noise ; and when I sate up in my bed I could see the lake through an open window-place at the bed's head. Add to this, it rained all night. I was less occupied by remembrance of the Trossachs, beautiful as they were, than the vision of the Highland hut, which I could not get out of my head. I thought of the Fairyland of Spenser, and what I had read in romance at other times, and then, what a feast would it be for a London pantomime-maker, could he but transplant it to Drury Lane, with all its beautiful colours !

August 28th, Sunday. We were desirous to have crossed the mountains above Glengyle to Glenfalloch, at the head of Loch Lomond, but it rained so heavily that it was impossible, so the ferryman engaged to row us to the point where C. and I had rested, while Wm. was going on our doubtful adventure. The hostess provided us with tea and sugar for our breakfast ; the water was boiled in an iron pan, and dealt out to us in a jug, a proof that she does not often drink tea, though she said she had always tea and sugar in the house. She and the rest of the family breakfasted on curds and whey, as taken out of the pot in which she was making cheese ; she insisted upon my taking some also ; and her husband joined in with the old story, that it was " varra halesome ". I thought it exceedingly good, and said to myself that they lived nicely with their cow : she was meat, drink, and company. Before breakfast the housewife was milking behind the chimney, and I thought I had seldom heard a sweeter fire-side sound ; in an evening, sitting over a sleepy, low-burnt fire, it would lull one like the purring of a cat.

When we departed, the good woman shook me cordially by the hand, saying she hoped that if ever we came into

Scotland again, we would come and see her. The lake was calm, but it rained so heavily that we could see little. Landed at about ten o'clock, almost wet to the skin, and, with no prospect but of streaming rains, faced the mountain-road to Loch Lomond. We recognised the same objects passed before, — the tarn, the potato-bed, and the cottages with their *burnies*, which were no longer, as one might say, household streams, but made us only think of the mountains and rocks they came from. Indeed, it is not easy to imagine how different everything appeared ; the mountains with mists and torrents alive and always changing : but the low grounds where the inhabitants had been at work the day before were melancholy, with here and there a few haycocks and hay scattered about.

Wet as we were, Wm. and I turned out of our path to the Garrison house. A few rooms of it seemed to be inhabited by some wretchedly poor families, and it had all the desolation of a large decayed mansion in the suburbs of a town, abandoned of its proper inhabitants, and become the abode of paupers. In spite of its outside bravery, it was but a poor protection against " the sword of winter, keen and cold ". We looked at the building through the arch of a broken gateway of the courtyard, in the middle of which it stands. Upon that stormy day it appeared *more* than desolate ; there was something about it even frightful.

When beginning to descend the hill towards Loch Lomond, we overtook two girls, who told us we could not cross the ferry till evening, for the boat was gone with a number of people to church. One of the girls was exceedingly beautiful ; and the figures of both of them, in grey plaids falling to their feet, their faces only being uncovered, excited our attention before we spoke to them ; but they answered us so sweetly that we were quite delighted, at the same time that they stared at us with an innocent look of wonder. I think I never heard the English language sound more sweetly than from the mouth of the elder of these girls, while she stood at the gate answering our inquiries, her face flushed with the rain ; her pronunciation was clear and distinct : without difficulty, yet slow, like that of a foreign speech. They told us we might sit in the ferry-house till the return of the boat, went in with us, and made a good fire as fast as possible to dry our wet clothes. We learnt that the taller was the sister of the ferryman, and had been left in charge with the house for the day, that the other was his wife's sister, and was come with her mother on a visit, — an old woman, who sate in a corner beside the cradle, nursing her little grand-child. We were glad to be housed, with our feet upon a warm hearth-stone ; and our attendants were so active and good-humoured that it was pleasant to have to desire them to do anything. The younger was a delicate and unhealthy-looking girl ; but there was an uncommon meekness in her countenance, with an air of premature intelligence, which is often seen in sickly young persons. The other made me think of Peter Bell's Highland Girl :

> *As light and beauteous as a squirrel,*
> *As beauteous and as wild !* [1]

She moved with unusual activity, which was chastened very delicately by a certain hesitation in her looks when she spoke, being able to understand us but imperfectly. They were both exceedingly desirous to get me what I wanted to make me comfortable. I was to have a gown and petticoat of the mistress's ; so they turned out her whole wardrobe upon the parlour floor, talking Erse to one another, and laughing all the time. It was long before they could decide which of the gowns I was to have ; they chosé at last, no doubt thinking that it was the best, a light-coloured sprigged cotton, with long sleeves, and they both laughed while I was putting it on, with the blue lindsey petticoat, and one or the other, or both together, helped me to dress, repeating at least half a dozen times, " You never had on the like of that before ". They held a consultation of several minutes over a pair of coarse woollen stockings, gabbling Erse as fast as their tongues could move, and looked as if uncertain what to do : at last, with great diffidence, they offered them to me, adding, as before, that I had never worn " the like of them ". When we entered the house we had been not a little glad to see a fowl stewing in

---

[1] *Peter Bell*, part iii. stanza 31.

barley-broth ; and now when the wettest of our clothes were stripped off, began again to recollect that we were hungry, and asked if we could have dinner. " Oh yes, ye may get that ", the elder replied, pointing to the pan on the fire.

Conceive what a busy house it was — all our wet clothes to be dried, dinner prepared and set out for us four strangers, and a second cooking for the family ; add to this, two rough *callans*, as they called them, about eight years old, were playing beside us ; the poor baby was fretful all the while ; the old woman sang doleful Erse songs, rocking it in its cradle the more violently the more it cried ; then there were a dozen cookings of porridge, and it could never be fed without the assistance of all three. The hut was after the Highland fashion, but without anything beautiful except its situation ; the floor was rough, and wet with the rain that came in at the door, so that the lasses' bare feet were as wet as if they had been walking through street puddles, in passing from one room to another ; the windows were open, as at the other hut ; but the kitchen had a bed in it, and was much smaller, and the shape of the house was like that of a common English cottage, without its comfort ; yet there was no appearance of poverty — indeed, quite the contrary. The peep out of the open door-place across the lake made some amends for the want of the long roof and elegant rafters of our boatman's cottage, and all the while the waterfall, which we could not see, was roaring at the end of the hut, which seemed to serve as a sounding-board for its noise, so that it was not unlike sitting in a house where a mill is going. The dashing of the waves against the shore could not be distinguished ; yet in spite of my know-ledge of this I could not help fancying that the tumult and storm came from the lake, and went out several times to see if it was possible to row over in safety.

After long waiting we grew impatient for our dinner ; at last the pan was taken off, and carried into the other room ; but we had to wait at least another half hour before the cere-money of dishing up was completed ; yet with all this bustle and difficulty, the manner in which they (and particularly the elder of the girls) performed everything, was perfectly graceful.

We ate a hearty dinner, and had time to get our clothes quite dry before the arrival of the boat. The girls could not say at what time it would be at home ; on our asking them if the church was far off they replied, " Not very far " ; and when we asked *how* far, they said, " Perhaps about four or five miles ". I believe a Church of England congregation would hold themselves excused for non-attendance three parts of the year, having but half as far to go ; but in the lonely parts of Scotland they make little of a journey of nine or ten miles to a preaching. They have not perhaps an opportunity of going more than once in a quarter of a year, and, setting piety aside, have other motives to attend : they hear the news, public and private, and see their friends and neighbours ; for though the people who meet at these times may be gathered together from a circle of twenty miles' diameter, a sort of neighbourly connexion must be so brought about. There is something exceedingly pleasing to my imagination in this gathering together of the inhabitants of these secluded districts — for instance, the borderers of these two large lakes meeting at the deserted garrison which I have described. The manner of their travelling is on foot, on horseback, and in boats across the waters, — young and old, rich and poor, all in their best dress.

If it were not for these Sabbath-day meetings one summer month would be like another summer month, one winter month like another — detached from the goings-on of the world, and solitary throughout ; from the time of earliest childhood they will be like landing-places in the memory of a person who has passed his life in these thinly peopled regions ; they must generally leave distinct impressions, differing from each other so much as they do in circumstances, in time and place, etc., — some in the open fields, upon hills, in houses, under large rocks, in storms, and in fine weather.

But I have forgotten the fireside of our hut. After long waiting, the girls, who had been on the look-out, informed us that the boat was coming. I went to the water-side, and saw a cluster of people on the opposite shore ; but being yet at a distance, they looked more like soldiers surrounding a carriage than a groupe of men and women ; red and green were the distinguishable colours. We hastened to get ourselves ready as soon as we saw the party approach, but had longer to wait than we expected, the lake being wider than it appears to be. As they drew near we could distinguish men in tartan plaids, women in scarlet cloaks, and green umbrellas by the half-dozen. The landing was as pretty a sight as ever I saw. The bay, which had been so quiet two days before, was all in motion with small waves, while the swoln waterfall roared in our ears. The boat came steadily up, being pressed almost to the water's edge by the weight of its cargo ; perhaps twenty people landed, one after another. It did not rain much, but the women held up their umbrellas ; they were dressed in all the colours of the rainbow, and, with their scarlet cardinals, the tartan plaids of the men, and Scotch bonnets, made a gay appearance. There was a joyous bustle surrounding the boat, which even imparted something of the same character to the waterfall in its tumult, and the restless grey waves ; the young men laughed and shouted, the lasses laughed, and the elder folks seemed to be in a bustle to be away. I remember well with what haste the mistress of the house where we were ran up to seek after her child, and seeing us, how anxiously and kindly she inquired how we had fared, if we had had a good fire, had been well waited upon, etc. etc. All this in three minutes — for the boatman had another party to bring from the other side and hurried us off.

The hospitality we had met with at the two cottages and Mr. Macfarlane's gave us very favourable impressions on this our first entrance into the Highlands, and at this day the innocent merriment of the girls, with their kindness to us, and the beautiful figure and face of the elder, come to my mind whenever I think of the ferry-house and waterfall of Loch Lomond, and I never think of the two girls but the whole image of that romantic spot is before me, a living image, as it will be to my dying day. The following poem was written by Wm. not long after our return from Scotland :—

Sweet Highland Girl, a very shower
Of beauty is thy earthly dower !

283

Twice seven consenting years have shed
Their utmost bounty on thy head,
And these grey rocks, this household lawn,
These trees, a veil just half withdrawn,
This fall of water that doth make
A murmur near the silent Lake ;
This little Bay, a quiet road
That holds in shelter thy abode ;
In truth together ye do seem
Like something fashion'd in a dream ;
Such forms as from their covert peep
When earthly cares are laid asleep,
Yet dream and vision as thou art
I bless thee with a human heart :
God shield thee to thy latest years !
I neither know thee nor thy peers,
And yet my eyes are fill'd with tears.

With earnest feeling I shall pray
For thee when I am far away :
For never saw I mien or face
In which more plainly I could trace
Benignity and home-bred sense
Ripening in perfect innocence ;
Here, scattered like a random seed,
Remote from men, thou dost not need
Th' embarrass'd look of shy distress
And maidenly shamefacedness ;
Thou wear'st upon thy forehead clear
The freedom of a mountaineer.
A face with gladness overspread !
Sweet looks by human-kindness bred !
And seemliness complete that sways
Thy courtesies about thee plays ;
With no restraint but such as springs
From quick and eager visitings
Of thoughts that lie beyond the reach
Of thy few words of English speech :

A bondage sweetly brook'd, a strife
That gives thy gestures grace and life !
So have I not unmoved in mind
Seen birds of tempest-loving kind,
Thus beating up against the wind.

What hand but would a garland cull
For thee who art so beautiful ?
O happy pleasure ! here to dwell
Beside thee in some heathy dell,
Adopt your homely ways and dress,
A Shepherd, thou a Shepherdess !
But I could frame a wish for thee
More like a grave reality :
Thou art to me but as a wave
Of the wild sea : and I would have
Some claim upon thee if I could,
Though but of common neighbourhood.
What joy to hear thee and to see !
Thy elder brother I would be,
Thy father, anything to thee.

Now thanks to Heaven that of its grace
Hath led me to this lonely place !
Joy have I had, and going hence
I bear away my recompence.
In spots like these it is we prize
Our memory, feel that she hath eyes,
Then why should I be loth to stir ?
I feel this place is made for her ;
To give new pleasure like the past
Continued long as life shall last.
Nor am I loth, though pleased at heart,
Sweet Highland Girl, from thee to part ;
For I, methinks, till I grow old
As fair before me shall behold
As I do now, the Cabin small,
The Lake, the Bay, the Waterfall,
And thee, the Spirit of them all.

285

We were rowed over speedily by the assistance of two youths, who went backwards and forwards for their own amusement, helping at the oars, and pulled as if they had strength and spirits to spare for a year to come. We noticed that they had uncommonly fine teeth, and that they and the boatman were very handsome people. Another merry crew took our place in the boat.

We had three miles to walk to Tarbet. It rained, but not heavily; the mountains were not concealed from us by the mists, but appeared larger and more grand; twilight was coming on, and the obscurity under which we saw the objects, with the sounding of the torrents, kept our minds alive and wakeful; all was solitary and huge — sky, water, and mountains mingled together. While we were walking forward, the road leading us over the top of a brow, we stopped suddenly at the sound of a half-articulate Gaelic hooting from the field close to us; it came from a little boy, whom we could see on the hill between us and the lake, wrapped up in a grey plaid; he was probably calling home the cattle for the night. His appearance was in the highest degree moving to the imagination : mists were on the hillsides, darkness shutting in upon the huge avenue of mountains, torrents roaring, no house in sight to which the child might belong; his dress, cry, and appearance all different from anything we had been accustomed to. It was a text, as Wm. has since observed to me, containing in itself the whole history of the Highlander's life — his melancholy, his simplicity, his poverty, his superstition, and above all, that visionariness which results from a communion with the unworldliness of nature.

When we reached Tarbet the people of the house were anxious to know how we had fared, particularly the girl who had waited upon us. Our praises of Loch Ketterine made her exceedingly happy, and she ventured to say (of which we had heard not a word before) that it was " bonnier to *her* fancy than Loch Lomond ". The landlord, who was not at home when we had set off, told us that if he had known of our going he would have recommended us to Mr. Macfarlane's or the other farmhouse, adding that they were hospitable people in that vale. C. and I got tea, and Wm. and the drawing-master chose supper ; they asked to have a broiled fowl, a dish very common in Scotland, to which the mistress replied, " Would not a ' boiled ' one do as well ? " They consented, supposing that it would be more easily cooked ; but when the fowl made its appearance, to their great disappointment it proved a cold one that had been stewed in the broth at dinner.

August 29th, Monday. It rained heavily this morning, and, having heard so much of the long rains since we came into Scotland, as well as before, we had no hope that it would be over in less than three weeks at the least ; so poor C. being very unwell, determined to send his clothes to Edinburgh and make the best of his way thither, being afraid to face much wet weather in an open carriage. Wm. and I were unwilling to be confined at Tarbet, so we resolved to go to Arrochar, a mile and a half on the road to Inverary, where there is an inn celebrated as a place of good accommodation for travellers. C. and I set off on foot, and Wm. was to follow with the car, but a heavy shower coming on, C. left me to shelter in a hut and wait for Wm., while he went on before. This hut was un-plaistered, and without windows, crowded with beds, uncomfortable, and not in the simplicity of the ferryman's house. A number of good clothes were hanging against the walls, and a green silk umbrella was set up in a corner. I should have been surprised to see an umbrella in such a place before we came into the Highlands ; but umbrellas are not so common anywhere as there, a plain proof of the wetness of the climate ; even five minutes after this a girl passed us without shoes and stockings, whose gown and petticoat were not worth half a crown, holding an umbrella over her bare head.

We turned at a guide-post, " To the New Inn ", and, after descending a little, and winding round the bottom of a hill, saw, at a small distance, a white house half hidden by tall trees upon a lawn that slopes down to the side of Loch Long, a sea-loch, which is here very narrow. Right before us, across the lake, was the Cobbler, which *appeared* to rise directly from the water ; but, in fact, it overtopped another hill, being a considerable way behind. The inn looked so much like a gentleman's house that we could hardly believe it *was* an inn. We drove down the broad gravel walk, and, making a sweep, stopped at the front door, were shown into a large parlour with a fire, and my first thought was, How comfortable we should be ! but C., who had arrived before us, checked my pleasure : the waiter had shown himself disposed to look coolly upon us, and there had been a hint that we could not have beds ; a party was expected, who had engaged all the beds. We conjectured this might be but a pretence, and ordered dinner in the hope that matters would clear up a little, and we thought they could not have the heart to turn us out in so heavy a rain if it were possible to lodge us. We had a nice dinner, yet would have gladly changed our roasted lamb and pickles, and the gentleman-waiter with his napkin in his pocket, for the more homely fare of the smoky hut at Loch Ketterine, and the good woman's busy attentions, with the certainty of a hospitable shelter at night. After dinner I spoke to the landlord himself, but he was not to be moved : he could not even provide one bed for me, so nothing was to be done but either to return to Tarbet with C., or that Wm. and I should push on the next stage, to Cairndow. We had an interesting close view from the windows of the room where we sate, looking across the lake, which did not differ in appearance, as we saw it here, from a fresh-water lake. The sloping lawn on which the house stood was prettily scattered over with trees ; but we had seen the place to great advantage at our first approach, owing to the mists upon the mountains, which had made them seem exceedingly high, while the strange figures on the Cobbler appeared and disappeared, like living things ; but, as the day cleared we were disappointed in what was more like the permanent effect of the scene : the mountains were not so lofty as we had supposed, and the low grounds not so fertile ; yet still it is a very interesting, I may say *beautiful* place.

The rain ceased entirely, so we resolved to go on to Cairndow, and had the satisfaction of seeing that our landlord had not told us an untruth concerning the expected company ; for just before our departure we saw, on the opposite side of the vale, a coach with four horses, another carriage, and two or three men on horseback, a striking procession, as it moved along between the bare mountain and the lake. Twenty years ago, perhaps, such a sight had not been seen here except when the Duke of Argyle, or some other Highland chieftain, might chance to be going with his family to London or Edinburgh. They had to cross a bridge at the head of the lake (which we could not see), so, after disappearing about ten minutes, they drove up to the door — three old ladies, two waiting-women, and store of men-servants ; the old ladies were as gaily dressed as bullfinches in spring-time. We heard the next day that they were the renowned Miss Waughs of Carlisle, and that they enjoyed themselves over a game of cards in the evening.

Left Arrochar at about four o'clock in the afternoon. C. accompanied us a little way ; we portioned out the contents of our purse before our parting ; and, after we had lost sight of him, drove heavily along. Crossed the bridge, and looked to the right, up the vale, which is soon terminated by moun-tains : it was of a yellow green, with but few trees and few houses ; sea-gulls were flying above it. Our road (the same along which the carriages had come) was directly under the mountains on our right hand, and the lake was close to us on our left, the waves breaking among stones overgrown with yellow sea-weed ; fishermen's boats, and other larger vessels than are seen on fresh-water lakes were lying at anchor near the opposite shore ; sea-birds flying overhead ; the noise of torrents mingled with the beating of the waves, and misty mountains enclosed the vale ; a melancholy but not a dreary scene. Often have I, in looking over a map of Scotland, followed the intricate windings of one of these sea-lochs, till, pleasing myself with my own imaginations, I have felt a longing, almost painful, to travel among them by land or by water.

This was the first sea-loch we had seen. We came prepared for a new and great delight, and the first impression which Wm. and I received, as we drove rapidly through the rain down the lawn of Arrochar, the objects dancing before us, was even more delightful than we had expected ; but, as I have said, when we looked through the window, as the mists disappeared and the objects were seen more distinctly, there was less of sheltered valley-comfort than we had fancied to ourselves, and the mountains were not so grand ; and now that we were near to the shore of the lake, and could see that it was not of fresh water, the wreck, the broken sea-shells, and scattered sea-weed gave somewhat of a dull and uncleanly look to the whole lake, and yet the water was clear, and might have appeared as beautiful as that of Loch Lomond, if with the same pure pebbly shore. Perhaps, had we been in a more chearful mood of mind we might have seen everything with a different eye ; the stillness of the mountains, the motion of the waves, the streaming torrents, the sea-birds, the fishing-boats were all melancholy ; yet still, occupied as my mind was with other things, I thought of the long windings through which the waters of the sea had come to this inland retreat, visiting the inner solitudes of the mountains, and I could have wished to have mused out a summer's day on the shores of the lake. From the foot of these mountains whither might not a little barque carry one away ? Though so far inland, it is but a slip of the great ocean : seamen, fishermen, and shepherds here find a natural home. We did not travel far down the lake, but, turning to the right through an opening of the mountains, entered a glen called Glen Croe.

Our thoughts were full of Coleridge, and when we were enclosed in the narrow dale, with a length of winding road before us, a road that seemed to have insinuated itself into the very heart of the mountains (the brook, the road, bare hills, floating mists, scattered stones, rocks, and herds of black cattle being all that we could see) I shivered at the thought of his being sickly and alone, travelling from place to place. The Cobbler, on our right, was pre-eminent above the other hills ; the singular rocks on its summit, seen so near, were like ruins — castles or watch-towers. After we had passed one reach of the glen, another opened out, long, narrow, deep, and house-less, with herds of cattle and large stones ; but the third reach was softer and more *beautiful*, as if the mountains had there made a warmer shelter, and there were a more gentle climate ; the rocks by the river-side had dwindled away, the mountains were smooth and green, and towards the end, where the glen sloped upwards, it was a cradle-like hollow, and at that point where the slope became a hill, at the very bottom of the curve of the cradle, stood one cottage, with a few fields and beds of potatoes. There was also another house near the roadside, which appeared to be a herdsman's hut. The dwelling in the middle of the vale was a very pleasing object ; I said within myself, how quietly might a family live in this pensive solitude, cultivating and loving their own fields ; but the herdsman's hut, being the only one in the vale, had a melancholy face ; not being attached to any particular plot of land, one could not help considering it as just kept alive and above ground by some dreary connexion with the long barren tract we had travelled through.

The afternoon had been exceedingly pleasant after we had left the vale of Arrochar ; the sky was often threatening, but the rain blew off, and the evening was uncommonly fine. The sun had set a short time before we had dismounted from the car to walk up the steep hill at the end of the glen ; clouds were moving all over the sky, some of a brilliant yellow hue, which shed a light like bright moonlight upon the mountains. We could not have seen the head of the valley under more favourable circumstances ; the passing away of a storm is always a time of life and chearfulness, especially in a mountainous country ; but that afternoon and evening the sky was in an extraordinary degree vivid and beautiful. We often stopped in ascending the hill to look down the long reach of the glen. The road, following the course of the river as far as we could see, the farm and cottage, hills smooth towards the base and rocky higher up, were the sole objects before us. This part of Glen Croe reminded us of some of the dales of the north of England — Grisdale above Ulswater, for instance ; but the length of it, and the broad highway, which is always to be seen at a great distance, a sort of centre of the vale, a point of reference, gives to the whole of the glen, and each division of it, a very different character.

At the top of the hill we came to a seat with the well-known inscription, " Rest and be thankful ". On the same stone it was recorded that the road had been made by Col. Wade's

regiment. The seat is placed so as to command a full view of
the valley, and the long, long road, which, with the fact recorded, and the exhortation, makes it an affecting resting-place.
We called to mind with pleasure a seat under the braes of
Loch Lomond on which I had rested, where the traveller is
informed by an inscription upon a stone that the road was
made by Col. Lascelles's regiment. There, the spot had not
been chosen *merely* as a resting-place, for there was no steep
ascent in the highway, but it might be for the sake of a spring
of water and a beautiful rock, or, more probably, because at
that point the labour had been more than usually toilsome in
hewing through the rock. Soon after we had climbed the hill
we began to descend into another glen, called Glen Kinglas.
We now saw the western sky, which had hitherto been hidden
from us by the hill — a glorious mass of clouds uprising from a
sea of distant mountains, stretched out in length before us,
towards the west, and close by us was a small lake or tarn.
From the reflection of the crimson clouds the water appeared
of a deep red, like melted rubies, yet with a mixture of a grey
or blackish hue : the gorgeous light of the sky, with the singular
colour of the lake, made the scene exceedingly romantic ; yet
it was more melancholy than chearful. With all the power
of light from the clouds, there was an overcasting of the gloom
of evening, a twilight upon the hills.

We descended rapidly into the glen, which resembles the
lower part of Glen Croe, though it seemed to be inferior in
beauty ; but before we had passed through one reach it was
quite dark, and I only know that the steeps were high, and
that we had the company of a foaming stream ; and many a
vagrant torrent crossed us, dashing down the hills. The road
was bad, and, uncertain how we should fare, we were eager
and somewhat uneasy to get forward ; but when we were out
of the close glen, and near to Cairndow (as a traveller had told
us), the moon showed her clear face in the sky, revealing a
spacious vale, with a broad loch and sloping corn fields ; the
hills not very high. This chearful sight put us into spirits,
and we thought it was at least no dismal place to sit up all
night in, if they had no beds, and they could not refuse us a

shelter. We were, however, well received, and sate down in a neat parlour with a good fire.

August 30th, Tuesday. Breakfasted before our departure, and ate a herring, fresh from the water, at our landlord's earnest recommendation — much superior to the herrings we get in the north of England.[1] Though we rose at seven, could not set off before nine o'clock ; the servants were in bed ; the kettle did not boil — indeed, we were completely out of patience ; but it had always been so, and we resolved to go off in future without breakfast. Cairndow is a single house by the side of the loch, I believe resorted to by gentlemen in the fishing season : it is a pleasant place for such a purpose ; but the vale did not look so beautiful as by moonlight — it had a sort of sea-coldness without mountain grandeur. There is a ferry for foot-passengers from Cairndow to the other side of the water, and the road along which all carriages go is carried round the head of the lake, perhaps a distance of three miles.

After we had passed the landing-place of the ferry opposite to Cairndow we saw the lake spread out to a great width, more like an arm of the sea or a great river than one of our lakes ; it reminded us of the Severn at the Chepstow passage ; but the shores were less rich and the hills higher. The sun shone, which made the morning chearful, though there was a cold wind ; our road never carried us far from the lake, and with the beating of the waves, the sparkling sunshiny water, boats, the opposite hills, and, on the side on which we travelled, the chance cottages, the coppice woods, and common business of the fields, the ride could not but be amusing. But what most excited our attention was, at one particular place, a cluster of fishing-boats at anchor in a still corner of the lake, a small bay or harbour by the wayside ; they were overshadowed by fishermen's nets hung out to dry, which formed a dark awning that covered them like a tent, overhanging the water on each side, and falling in the most exquisitely graceful folds. There was a monastic pensiveness, a funereal gloom in the appearance of this little company of vessels, which was the more interesting

---

[1] I should rather think so !—J. C. S.

from the general liveliness and glancing motions of the water, they being perfectly still and silent in their sheltered nook.

When we had travelled about seven miles from Cairndow, winding round the bottom of a hill, we came in view of a great basin or elbow of the lake. Completely out of sight of the long track of water we had coasted, we seemed now to be on the edge of a very large, almost circular, lake, the town of Inverary before us, a line of white buildings on a low promontory right opposite, and close to the water's edge ; the whole landscape a showy scene, and bursting upon us at once. A traveller who was riding by our side called out, " Can that be the Castle ? " Recollecting the prints which we had seen, we knew it could not ; but the mistake is a natural one at that distance : it is so little like an ordinary town, from the mixture of regularity and irregularity in the buildings. With the expanse of water and pleasant mountains, the scattered boats and sloops, and those gathered together, it had a truly festive appearance. A few steps more brought us in view of the Castle, a stately turreted mansion, but with a modern air, standing on a lawn, retired from the water, and screened behind by woods covering the sides of high hills to the top, and still beyond, by bare mountains. Our road wound round the semicircular shore, crossing two bridges of lordly architecture. The town looked pretty when we drew near to it in connexion with its situation, different from any place I had ever seen, yet exceedingly like what I imaged to myself from representations in raree-shows, or pictures of foreign places (Venice, for example) painted on the scene of a play-house, which one is apt to fancy are as cleanly and gay as they look through the magnifying-glass of the raree-show or in the candle-light dazzle of a theatre. At the door of the inn, though certainly the buildings had not that delightful outside which they appeared to have at a distance, yet they looked very pleasant. The range bordering on the water consisted of little else than the inn, being a large house, with very large stables, the county gaol, the opening into the main street into the town, and an arched gateway, the entrance into the Duke of Argyle's private domain.

We were decently well received at the inn, but it was over-rich in waiters and large rooms to be exactly to our taste, though quite in harmony with the neighbourhood. Before dinner we went into the Duke's pleasure-grounds, which are extensive, and of course command a variety of lively and interesting views. Walked through avenues of tall beech-trees, and observed some that we thought even the tallest we had ever seen ; but they were all scantily covered with leaves, and the leaves exceedingly small — indeed, some of them, in the most exposed situations, were almost bare, as if it had been winter. Travellers who wish to view the inside of the Castle send in their names, and the Duke appoints the time of their going ; but we did not think that what we should see would repay us for the trouble, there being no pictures, and the house (which I believe has not been built above half a century) is fitted up in the modern style ; if there had been any reliques of the ancient costume of the castle of a Highland chieftain, we should have been sorry to have passed it.

Sate after dinner by the fireside till near sunset, for it was very cold, though the sun shone all day. At the beginning of this our second walk we passed through the town, which is but a doleful example of Scotch filth. The houses are plaistered or rough-cast, and washed yellow — well built, well sized, and sash-windowed, bespeaking a connexion with the Duke, such a dependence as may be expected in a small town so near to his mansion ; and indeed he seems to have done his utmost to make them comfortable, according to our English notions of comfort : they are fit for the houses of people living decently upon a decent trade ; but the windows and door-steads were as dirty as in a dirty by-street of a large town, making a most unpleasant contrast with the comely face of the buildings towards the water, and the ducal grandeur and natural festivity of the scene. Smoke and blackness are the wild growth of a Highland hut : the mud floors cannot be washed, the door-steads are trampled by cattle, and if the inhabitants be not very cleanly it gives one little pain ; but dirty people living in two-storied stone houses, with *dirty* sash windows, are a melancholy spectacle anywhere, giving the notion either of vice or the extreme of wretchedness.

Returning through the town, we went towards the Castle, and entered the Duke's grounds by a porter's lodge, following the carriage-road through the park, which is prettily scattered over with trees, and slopes gently towards the lake. A great number of lime-trees were growing singly, not beautiful in their shape, but I mention them for the resemblance to one of the same kind we had seen in the morning, which formed a shade as impenetrable as the roof of any house. The branches did not spread far, nor any one branch much further than another ; on the outside it was like a green bush shorn with shears, but when we sate upon a bench under it, looking upwards, in the middle of the tree we could not perceive any green at all ; it was like a hundred thousand magpies' nests clustered and matted together, the twigs and boughs being so intertwined that neither the light of the mid-day sun nor showers of hail or rain could pierce through them. The lime-trees on the lawn resembled this tree both in shape and in the manner of inter-twisting their twigs, but they were much smaller, and not an impenetrable shade.

The views from the Castle are delightful. Opposite is the lake, girt with mountains, or rather smooth high hills ; to the left appears a very steep rocky hill, called Duniquoich Hill, on the top of which is a building like a watch-tower ; it rises boldly and almost perpendicular from the plain, at a little distance from the river Arey, that runs through the grounds. To the right is the town, overtopped by a sort of spire or pinnacle of the church, a thing unusual in Scotland, except in the large towns, and which would often give an elegant appearance to the villages, which, from the uniformity of the huts, and the frequent want of tall trees, they seldom exhibit.

In looking at an extensive prospect, or travelling through a large vale (the Trough of the Clyde for instance), I could not help thinking that in England there would have been some-where a tower or spire to warn us of a village lurking under the covert of a wood or bank, or to point out some particular spot on the distant hills which we might look at with kindly feelings. I well remember how we used to love the little nest of trees out of which Ganton spire rose on the distant Wolds opposite to the windows at Gallow Hill. The spire of Inverary is not of so beautiful a shape as those of the English churches, and, not being one of a class of buildings which is understood at once, seen near or at a distance, is a less interesting object ; but it suits well with the outlandish trimness of the buildings bordering on the water ; indeed, there is no one thing of the many gathered together in the extensive circuit of the basin or vale of Inverary, that is not in harmony with the effect of the whole place. The Castle is built of a beautiful hewn stone, in colour resembling our blue slates. The author-tourists have quarrelled with the architecture of it, but we did not find much that we were disposed to blame. A castle in a deep glen, over-looking a roaring stream, and defended by precipitous rocks, is, no doubt, an object far more interesting ; but, dropping all ideas of danger or insecurity, the natural retinue in our minds of an ancient Highland chieftain, — take a Duke of Argyle at the end of the eighteenth century, let him have his house in Grosvenor Square, his London liveries, and daughters glittering at St. James's, and I think you will be satisfied with his present mansion in the Highlands, which seems to suit with the present times and its situation, and that is indeed a noble one for a modern Duke of the mountainous district of Argyleshire, with its bare valleys, its rocky coasts, and sea lochs.

There is in the natural endowments of Inverary something akin to every feature of the general character of the county ; yet even the very mountains and the lake itself have a kind of princely festivity in their appearance ; I do not know how to communicate the feeling, but it seemed as if it were no insult to the hills to look on them as the shield and enclosure of the ducal domain, to which the water might delight in bearing its tribute. The hills near the lake are smooth, so smooth that they might have been shaven or swept ; the shores, too, had somewhat of the same effect, being bare, and having no rough-ness, no woody points ; yet the whole circuit being very large, and the hills so extensive, the scene was not the less chearful and festive, rejoicing in the light of heaven. Behind the Castle the hills are planted to a great height, and the pleasure-grounds extend far up the valley of Arey. We continued our walk a short way along the river, and were sorry to see it stripped of its natural ornaments, after the fashion of Mr. Brown,[1] and left to tell its tale (for it would not be silent like the river at Blenheim) to naked fields and the planted trees on the hills. We were disgusted with the stables, out-houses, or farm-houses in different parts of the grounds behind the Castle : they were broad, out-spreading, fantastic, and unintelligible buildings.

Sate in the park till the moonlight was perceived more than the light of day. We then walked near the town by the water-side. I observed that the children who were playing did not speak Erse, but a much worse English than is spoken by those Highlanders whose common language is the Erse. I went into the town to purchase tea and sugar to carry with us on our journey. We were tired when we returned to the inn, and went to bed directly after tea. My room was at the very top of the house — one flight of steps after another ! — but when I drew back the curtains of my window I was repaid for the trouble of panting up-stairs by one of the most splendid moonlight prospects that can be conceived : the whole circuit of the hills, the Castle, the two bridges, the tower on Duniquoich Hill, and the lake with many boats — fit scene for summer midnight festivities ! I should have liked to have seen a bevy of Scottish ladies sailing, with music, in a gay barge. William, to whom I have read this, tells me that I have used the very words of Browne of Ottery, Coleridge's fellow-townsman : —

> *As I have seen when on the breast of Thames*
> *A heavenly bevy of sweet English dames,*
> *In some calm evening of delightful May,*
> *With music give a farewell to the day,*
> *Or as they would (with an admired tone)*
> *Greet night's ascension to her ebon throne.*

BROWNE's Britannia's Pastorals.

August 31st, Wednesday. We had a long day's journey before us, without a regular baiting-place on the road, so we

---

[1] John Brown, D.D. (1715-66), author of the popular *Estimate of the Manners and Principles of the Times* (1757). He wrote also a *Letter to a Friend,* dilating on the beauties of Keswick. *v.* W. W.'s *Guide to the Lakes,* ed. 1906, pp. 50, 68, 183.

breakfasted at Inverary, and did not set off till nine o'clock, having, as usual, to complain of the laziness of the servants. Our road was up the valley behind the Castle, the same we had gone along the evening before. Further up, though the plantations on the hills are noble, the valley was cold and naked, wanting hedgerows and comfortable houses. We travelled several miles under the plantations, the vale all along seeming to belong almost exclusively to the Castle. It might have been better distinguished and adorned, as we thought, by neater farm-houses and cottages than are common in Scotland, and snugger fields with warm hedgerows, at the same time testifying as boldly its adherence to the chief.

At that point of the valley where the pleasure-grounds appear to end, we left our horse at a cottage door, and turned a few steps out of the road to see a waterfall, which roared so loud that we could not have gone by without looking about for it, even if we had not known that there was one near Inverary. The waterfall is not remarkable for anything but the good taste with which it has been left to itself, though there is a pleasure-road from the Castle to it. As we went further up the valley the woods died away, and it became an ordinary Scotch glen, the poor pasturage of the hills creeping down into the valley, where it was little better for the shelter, I mean little greener than on the hill-sides ; but a man must be of a churlish nature if, with a mind free to look about, he should not find such a glen a pleasing place to travel through, though seeing little but the busy brook, with here and there a bush or tree, and cattle pasturing near the thinly-scattered dwellings. But we came to one spot which I cannot forget, a single green field at the junction of another brook with the Arey, a peninsula surrounded with a close row of trees, which overhung the streams, and under their branches we could just see a neat white house that stood in the middle of the field enclosed by the trees. Before us was nothing but bare hills, and the road through the bare glen. A person who has not travelled in Scotland can scarcely imagine the pleasure we have had from a stone house, though fresh from the workmen's hands, square and sharp ; there is generally such an appearance of equality in poverty through

the long glens of Scotland, giving the notion of savage ignorance
— no house better than another, and barns and houses all
alike. This house had, however, other recommendations of its
own ; even in the fertile parts of Somersetshire it would have
been a delicious spot ; here, " 'Mid mountain wild set like a
little nest ", it was a resting-place for the fancy, and to this
day I often think of it, the cottage and its green covert, as an
image of romance, a place of which I have the same sort of
knowledge as of some of the retirements, the little vallies,
described so livelily by Spenser in his *Fairy Queen*.

We travelled on, the glen now becoming entirely bare.
Passed a miserable hut on a naked hill-side, not far from the
road, where we were told by a man who came out of it that.
we might refresh ourselves with a dram of whisky. Went over
the hill, and saw nothing remarkable till we came in view of
Loch Awe, a large lake far below us, among high mountains —
one very large mountain right opposite, which we afterwards
found was called Cruachan. The day was pleasant — sunny
gleams and a fresh breeze ; the lake (we looked across it) as
bright as silver, which made the islands, three or four in number,
appear very green. We descended gladly, invited by the prospect
before us, travelling downwards, along the side of the hill, above
a deep glen, woody towards the lower part near the brook ; the
hills on all sides were high and bare, and not very stony : it
made us think of the descent from Newlands into Buttermere,
though on a wider scale, and much inferior in simple majesty.

After walking down the hill a long way we came to a bridge,
under which the water dashed through a dark channel of rocks
among trees, the lake being at a considerable distance below,
with cultivated lands between. Close upon the bridge was a
small hamlet,[1] a few houses near together, and huddled up in
trees — a very sweet spot, the only retired village we had yet
seen which was characterized by *beautiful* wildness with
sheltering warmth. We had been told at Inverary that we
should come to a place where we might give our horse a feed of
corn, and found on inquiry that there was a little publick-

---

[1] Cladich.—J. C. S.

house here, or rather a hut " where they kept a dram ". It was a cottage, like all the rest, without a sign-board. The woman of the house helped to take the horse out of harness, and, being hungry, we asked her if she could make us some porridge, to which she replied that " we should get that ", and I followed her into the house, and sate over her hearth while she was making it ; as to fire, there was little sign of it, save the smoke, for a long time, she having no fuel but green wood, and no bellows but her breath. My eyes smarted exceedingly, but the woman seemed so kind and chearful that I was willing to endure it for the sake of warming my feet in the ashes and talking to her. The fire was in the middle of the room, a crook being suspended from a cross-beam, and a hole left at the top for the smoke to find its way out by : it was a rude Highland hut, unadulterated by Lowland fashions, but it had not the elegant shape of the ferry-house at Loch Ketterine, and the fire, being in the middle of the room, could not be such a snug place to draw to on a winter's night.

We had a long afternoon before us, with only eight miles to travel to Dalmally, and, having been told that a ferry-boat was kept at one of the islands, we resolved to call for it, and row to the island, so we went to the top of an eminence, and the man who was with us set some children to work to gather sticks and withered leaves to make a smoky fire, a signal for the boatman, whose hut is on a flat green island, like a sheep pasture, without trees, and of a considerable size : the man told us it was a rabbit-warren. There were other small islands, on one of which was a ruined house, fortification, or small castle : we could not learn anything of its history, only a girl told us that formerly gentlemen lived in such places. Immediately from the water's edge rose the mountain Cruachan on the opposite side of the lake ; it is woody near the water and craggy above, with deep hollows on the surface. We thought it the grandest mountain we had seen, and on saying to the man who was with us that it was a fine mountain, " Yes," he replied, " it is an excellent mountain ", adding that it was higher than Ben Lomond, and then told us some wild stories of the enormous profits it brought to Lord Breadalbane, its lawful owner. The shape of Loch Awe is very remarkable, its outlet being at one side, and only about eight miles from the head, and the whole lake twenty-four miles in length. We looked with longing after that branch of it opposite to us out of which the water issues : it seemed almost like a river gliding under steep precipices. What we saw of the larger branch, or what might be called the body of the lake, was less promising, the banks being merely gentle slopes, with not very high mountains behind, and the ground moorish and cold.

The children, after having collected fuel for our fire, began to play on the green hill where we stood, as heedless as if we had been trees or stones, and amused us exceedingly with their activity : they wrestled, rolled down the hill, pushing one another over and over again, laughing, screaming, and chattering Erse : they were all without shoes and stockings, which, making them fearless of hurting or being hurt, gave a freedom to the action of their limbs which I never saw in English children : they stood upon one another, body, breast, or face, or any other part ; sometimes one was uppermost, sometimes another, and sometimes they rolled all together, so that we could not know to which body this leg or that arm belonged. We waited, watching them, till we were assured that the boatman had noticed our signal. By the bye, if we had received proper directions at Loch Lomond, on our journey to Loch Ketterine, we should have made our way down the lake till we had come opposite to the ferryman's house, where there is a hut, and the people who live there are accustomed to call him by the same signal as here. Luckily for us we were not so well instructed, for we should have missed the pleasure of receiving the kindness of Mr. and Mrs. Macfarlane and their family.

A young woman who wanted to go to the island accompanied us to the water-side ; the walk was pleasant, through fields with hedgerows, the greenest fields we had seen in Scotland ; but we were obliged to return without going to the island. The poor man had taken his boat to another place, and the waters were swoln so that we could not go close to the shore, and show ourselves to him, nor could we make him hear by shouting. On our return to the publick-house we asked the woman what we should pay her, and were not a little surprised when she answered, " Three shillings ". Our horse had had a sixpenny feed of miserable corn, not worth threepence ; the rest of the charge was for skimmed milk, oat-bread, porridge, and blue milk cheese : we told her it was far too much ; and, giving her half-a-crown, departed. I was sorry she had made this unreasonable demand, because we had liked the woman, and we had before been so well treated in the Highland cottages ; but, on thinking more about it, I satisfied myself that it was no scheme to impose upon us, for she was contented with the half-crown, and would, I daresay, have been so with two shillings, if we had offered it her at first. Not being accustomed to fix a price upon porridge and milk, to such as we, at least, when we asked her she did not know what to say ; but, seeing that we were travelling for pleasure, no doubt she concluded we were rich, and that what was a small gain to *her* could be no great loss to us.

When we had gone a little way we saw before us a young man with a bundle over his shoulder, hung on a stick, bearing a great boy on his back : seeing that they were travellers, we offered to take the boy on the car, to which the man replied that he should be more than thankful, and set him up beside me. They had walked from Glasgow, and that morning from Inverary ; the boy was only six years old, " But ", said his father, " he is a stout walker ", and a fine fellow he was, smartly dressed in tight clean clothes and a nice round hat : he was going to stay with his grandmother at Dalmally. I found him good company ; though I could not draw a single word out of him, it was a pleasure to see his happiness gleaming through the shy glances of his healthy countenance. Passed a pretty chapel by the lake-side, and an island with a farm-house upon it, and corn and pasture fields ; but, as we went along, we had frequent reason to regret the want of English hedgerows and English culture ; for the ground was often swampy or moorish near the lake where comfortable dwellings among green fields might have been. When we came near to the end of the lake we had a steep hill to climb, so Wm. and I walked ; and we had such confidence in our horse that we were not afraid to leave the car to his guidance with the child in it ; we were soon, however, alarmed at seeing him trot up the hill a long way before us ; the child, having raised himself up upon the seat, was beating him as hard as he could with a little stick which he carried in his hand ; and when he saw our eyes were on him he sate down, I believe very sorry to resign his office : the horse slackened his pace, and no accident happened.

When we had ascended half-way up the hill, directed by the man, I took a nearer footpath, and at the top came in view of a most impressive scene, a ruined castle on an island almost in the middle of the last compartment of the lake, backed by a mountain cove, down which came a roaring stream. The castle occupied every foot of the island that was visible to us, appearing to rise out of the water ; mists rested upon the mountain side, with spots of sunshine between ; there was a mild desolation in the low grounds, a solemn grandeur in the mountains, and the castle was wild, yet stately, not dismantled of its turrets, nor the walls broken down, though completely in ruin. After having stood some minutes I joined Wm. on the high road, and both wishing to stay longer near this place, we requested the man to drive his little boy on to Dalmally, about two miles further, and leave the car at the inn. He told us that the ruin was called Kilchurn Castle, that it belonged to Lord Breadalbane, and had been built by one of the ladies of that family for her defence during her Lord's absence at the Crusades, for which purpose she levied a tax of seven years' rent upon her tenants ; [1] he said that from that side of the lake it did not appear, in very dry weather, to stand upon an island ; but that it was possible to go over to it without being wet-shod. We were very lucky in seeing it after a great flood ; for its enchanting effect was chiefly owing to its situation in the lake, a decayed palace rising out of the plain of waters ! I have called it a palace, for such feeling it gave to me, though having been built as a place of defence, a castle or fortress. We turned again and re-ascended the hill, and sate a long time in the middle of it looking on the castle and the huge

---

[1] Not very probable.—D. W.

mountain cove opposite, and William, addressing himself to the ruin, poured out these verses : [1]—

> *Child of loud-throated War ! the mountain stream*
> *Roars in thy hearing ; but thy hour of rest*
> *Is come, and thou art silent in thy age.*

We walked up the hill again, and, looking down the vale, had a fine view of the lake and islands, resembling the views down Windermere, though much less rich. Our walk to Dalmally was pleasant : the vale makes a turn to the right, beyond the head of the lake, and the village of Dalmally (which is, in fact, only a few huts, the manse or minister's house, the chapel, and the inn) stands near the river, which flows into the head of the lake. The whole vale is very pleasing, the lower part of the hill-sides being sprinkled with thatched cottages, cultivated ground in small patches near them, which evidently belonged to the cottages.

We were overtaken by a gentleman who rode on a beautiful white pony (like Lilly) and was followed by his servant, a Highland boy, on another pony, a little creature, not much bigger than a large mastiff, on which were slung a pair of crutches and a tartan plaid. The gentleman entered into conversation with us, and on our telling him that we were going to Glen Coe, he advised us, instead of proceeding directly to Tyndrum, the next stage, to go round by the outlet of Loch Awe to Loch Etive, and thence to Glen Coe. We were glad to change our plan, for we wanted much to see more of Loch Awe, and he told us that the whole of the way by Loch Etive was pleasant, and the road to Tyndrum as dreary as possible ; indeed, we could see it at that time several miles before us upon the side of a bleak mountain ; and he said that there was nothing but moors and mountains all the way. We reached the inn a little before sunset, ordered supper, and I walked out. Crossed a bridge to look more nearly at the parsonage-house and the chapel, which stand upon a bank close to the river, a pretty stream overhung in some parts by trees. The vale is very pleasing ; but, like all the other Scotch vales we had yet

---

[1] *Address to Kilchurn Castle, upon Loch Awe.*

seen, it told of its kinship with the mountains and of poverty or some neglect on the part of man.

September 1st, Thursday. We had been attended at supper by a civil boy, whom we engaged to rouze us at six o'clock, and to provide us each a basin of milk and bread, and have the car ready ; all which he did punctually, and we were off in good time. The morning was not unpleasant, though rather cold, and we had some fear of rain. Crossed the bridge, and passed by the manse and chapel, our road carrying us back again in the direction we had come ; but on the opposite side of the river. Passed close to many of the houses we had seen on the hill-side, which the lame gentleman had told us belonged to Lord Breadalbane, and were attached to little farms, or *crofts*, as he called them. Lord B. had lately laid out a part of his estates in this way as an experiment, in the hope of preventing discontent and emigration. We were sorry we had not an opportunity of seeing into these cottages, and of learning how far the people were happy or otherwise. The dwellings certainly did not look so comfortable when we were near to them as from a distance ; but this might be chiefly owing to what the inhabitants did not feel as an evil — the dirt about the doors. We saw, however (a sight always painful to me), two or three women, each creeping after her single cow, while it was feeding on the slips of grass between the corn-grounds. Went round the head of the lake, and onwards close to the lake-side. Kilchurn Castle was always interesting, though not so grand as seen from the other side, with its own mountain cove and roaring stream. It combined with the vale of Dalmally and the distant hills — a beautiful scene, yet overspread with a gentle desolation. As we went further down we lost sight of the vale of Dalmally. The castle, which we often stopped to look back upon, was very beautiful seen in combination with the opposite shore of the lake — perhaps a little bay, a tuft of trees, or a slope of the hill. Travelled under the foot of the mountain Cruachan, along an excellent road, having the lake close to us on our left, woods overhead, and frequent torrents tumbling down the hills. The distant views across the lake were not peculiarly interesting after we were out of sight of

Kilchurn Castle, the lake being wide, and the opposite shore not rich, and those mountains which we could see were not high.

Came opposite to the village where we had dined the day before, and, losing sight of the body of the lake, pursued the narrow channel or pass,[1] which is, I believe, three miles long, out of which issues the river that flows into Loch Etive. We were now enclosed between steep hills, on the opposite side entirely bare, on *our* side bare or woody ; the branch of the lake generally filling the whole area of the vale. It was a pleasing, solitary scene ; the long reach of naked precipices on the other side rose directly out of the water, exceedingly steep, not rugged or rocky, but with scanty sheep pasturage and large beds of small stones, purple, dove-coloured, or red, such as are called Screes in Cumberland and Westmoreland. These beds, or rather streams of stones, appeared as smooth as the turf itself, nay, I might say, as soft as the feathers of birds, which they resembled in colour. There was no building on either side of the water ; in many parts only just room for the road, and on the other shore no footing, as it might seem, for any creature larger than the mountain sheep, and they, in treading amongst the shelving stones, must often send them down into the lake below.

After we had wound for some time through the valley, having met neither foot-traveller, horse, nor cart, we started at the sight of a single vessel, just as it turned round the point of a hill, coming into the reach of the valley where we were. She floated steadily through the middle of the water, with one large sail spread out, full swoln by the breeze, that blew her right towards us. I cannot express what romantic images this vessel brought along with her — how much more beautiful the mountains appeared, the lake how much more graceful. There was one man on board, who sate at the helm, and he, having no companion, made the boat look more silent than if we could not have seen him. I had almost said the *ship*, for on that narrow water it appeared as large as the ships which I have

---

[1] The Pass of Awe.—J. C. S.

watched sailing out of a harbour of the sea. A little further on we passed a stone hut by the lake-side, near which were many charcoal sacks, and we conjectured that the vessel had been depositing charcoal brought from other parts of Loch Awe to be carried to the iron-works at Loch Etive. A little further on we came to the end of the lake, but *where* exactly it ended was not easy to determine, for the river was as broad as the lake, and we could only say when it became positively a river by the rushing of the water. It is, indeed, a grand stream, the quantity of water being very large, frequently forming rapids, and always flowing very quickly ; but its greatness is short-lived, for, after a course of three miles, it is lost in the great waters of Loch Etive, a sea loch.

Crossed a bridge, and climbing a hill towards Taynuilt, our baiting-place, we saw a hollow to the right below us, through which the river continued its course between rocks and steep banks of wood. Wm. turned aside to look into the dell, but I was too much tired. We had left it, two or three hundred yards behind, an open river, the hills, enclosing the branch of the lake, having settled down into irregular slopes. We were glad when we reached Taynuilt, a village of huts, with a chapel and one stone house, which was the inn. It had begun to rain, and I was almost benumbed with the cold, besides having a bad headach ; so it rejoiced me to see kind looks on the landlady's face, and that she was willing to put herself in a bustle for our comfort ; we had a good fire presently, and breakfast was set out — eggs, preserved gooseberries, excellent cream, cheese, and butter, but no wheat bread, and the oaten cakes were so hard I could not chew them. We wished to go upon Loch Etive ; so, having desired the landlady to prepare a fowl for supper, and engaged beds, which she promised us *willingly* (a proof that we were not in the great road), we determined to find our way to the lake and endeavour to procure a boat. It rained heavily, but we went on, hoping the sky would clear.

Walked through unenclosed fields, a sort of half-desolate country ; but when we came to the mouth of the river which issues out of Loch Awe, and which we had to cross by a ferry, looking up that river we saw that the vale down which it flowed was richly wooded and beautiful.

We were now among familiar fireside names. We could see the town of Bunawe, a place of which the old woman with whom Wm. lodged ten years at Hawkshead used to tell tales half as long as an ancient romance. It is a small village or port on the same side of Loch Etive on which we stood, and at a little distance is a house built by a Mr. Knott of Coniston Water-head, a partner in the iron-foundry at Bunawe, in the service of whose family the old woman had spent her youth. It was an ugly yellow-daubed building, staring this way and that, but William looked at it with pleasure for poor Ann Tyson's sake.[1] We hailed the ferry-boat, and a little boy came to fetch us ; he rowed up against the stream with all his might for a considerable way, and then yielding to it, the boat was shot towards the shore almost like an arrow from a bow. It was pleasing to observe the dexterity with which the lad managed his oars, glorying in the *appearance* of danger (for he observed us watching him), and afterwards, while he conveyed us over, his pride redoubled ; for my part, I was completely dizzy with the swiftness of the motion.

We could not have a boat from the ferry, but were told that if we would walk to a house half a mile up the river, we had a chance of getting one. I went a part of the way with Wm., and then sate down under the umbrella near some houses. A woman came out to talk with me, and pressed me to take shelter in her house, which I refused, afraid of missing Wm. She eyed me with extreme curiosity, asking fifty questions respecting the object of our journey. She told me that it rained most parts of the year there, and that there was no chance of fine weather that day ; and I believe when Wm. came to tell me that we could have a boat, she thought I was half crazed. We went down to the shore of the lake, and, after having sate some time under a wall, the boatman came to us, and we went upon the water. At first it did not rain heavily, and the air was not cold, and before we had gone

---

[1] The village dame with whom he lived when a school-boy at Hawkshead.

far we rejoiced that we had not been faint-hearted. The loch is of a considerable width, but the mountains are so very high that, whether we were close under them or looked from one shore to the other, they maintained their dignity. I speak of the higher part of the loch, above the town of Bunawe and the large river, for downwards they are but hills, and the water spreads out wide towards undetermined shores. On our right was the mountain Cruachan, rising directly from the lake, and on the opposite side another mountain, called Ben Durinish, craggy, and exceedingly steep, with wild wood growing among the rocks and stones.

We crossed the water, which was very rough in the middle, but calmer near the shores, and some of the rocky basins and little creeks among the rocks were as still as a mirror, and they were so beautiful with the reflection of the orange-coloured seaweed growing on the stones or rocks, that a child, with a child's delight in gay colours, might have danced with joy at the sight of them. It never ceased raining, and the tops of the mountains were concealed by mists, but as long as we could see across the water we were contented ; for though little could be seen of the true shapes and permanent appearances of the mountains, we saw enough to give us the most exquisite delight : the powerful lake which filled the large vale, roaring torrents, clouds floating on the mountain sides, sheep that pastured there, sea-birds and land birds. We sailed a considerable way without coming to any houses or cultivated fields. There was no horse-road on either side of the loch, but a person on foot, as the boatman told us, might make his way at the foot of Ben Durinish, namely on that side of the loch on which we were ; there was, however, not the least track to be seen, and it must be very difficult and laborious.

We happened to say that we were going to Glen Coe, which would be the journey of a long day and a half, when one of the men, pointing to the head of the loch, replied that if we were there we should be but an hour's walk from Glen Coe. Though it continued raining, and there was no hope that the rain would cease, we could not help wishing to go by that way : it was an adventure ; we were not afraid of trusting ourselves to the hospitality of the Highlanders, and we wanted to give our horse a day's rest, his back having been galled by the saddle. The owner of the boat, who understood English much better than the other man, his helper, said he would make inquiries about the road at a farm-house a little further on. He was very ready to talk with us, and was rather an interesting companion ; he spoke after a slow and solemn manner, in book and sermon language and phrases :—

A stately speech,
Such as grave livers do in Scotland use.[1]

When we came to the farm-house of which the man had spoken, Wm. and he landed to make the necessary inquiries. It was a thatched house at the foot of the high mountain Ben Durinish — a few patches or little beds of corn belonging to it ; but the spot was pastoral, the green grass growing to the walls of the house. The dwelling-house was distinguished from the outer buildings (which were numerous, making it look like two or three houses, as is common in Scotland) by a chimney and one small window with sash-panes ; on one side was a little woody glen, with a precipitous stream that fell into the bay, which was perfectly still, and bordered with the rich orange-colour reflected from the sea-weed. Cruachan, on the other side of the lake, was exceedingly grand, and appeared of an enormous height, spreading out two large arms that made a cove down which fell many streams swoln by the rain, and in the hollow of the cove were some huts which looked like a village. The top of the mountain was concealed from us by clouds, and the mists floated high and low upon the sides of it.

Wm. came back to the boat highly pleased with the chearful hospitality and kindness of the woman of the house, who would scarcely permit him and his guide to go away without taking some refreshment. She was the only person at home, so they could not obtain the desired information ; but Wm. had been well repaid for the trouble of landing ; indeed, rainy as it was, I regretted that I had not landed also, for I should have wished to bear away in my memory a perfect image of

---

[1] *Resolution and Independence,* stanza xiv.

this place,— the view from the doors, as well as the simple Highland comforts and contrivances which were near it. I think I never saw a retirement that would have so completely satisfied me, if I had wanted to be altogether shut out from the world, and at the same time among the grandest of the works of God ; but it must be remembered that mountains are often so much dignified by clouds, mists, and other accidents of weather, that one could not know them again in the full sunshine of a summer's noon. But, whatever the mountains may be in their own shapes, the farm-house with its pastoral grounds and corn fields won from the mountain, its warm outhouses in irregular stages one above another on the side of the hill, the rocks, the stream, and sheltering bay, must at all times be interesting objects. The household boat lay at anchor, chained to a rock, which, like the whole border of the lake, was edged with sea-weed, and some fishing-nets were hung upon poles,— affecting images, which led our thoughts out to the wide ocean, yet made these solitudes of the mountains bear the impression of greater safety and more deep seclusion.

The rain became so heavy that we should certainly have turned back if we had not felt more than usual courage from the pleasure we had enjoyed, which raised hope where none was. There were some houses a little higher up, and we determined to go thither and make further inquiries. We could now hardly see to the other side of the lake, yet continued to go on, and presently heard some people pushing through a thicket close to us, on which the boatman called out, " There's one that can tell us something about the road to Glen Coe, for he was born there ". We looked up and saw a ragged, lame fellow, followed by some others, with a fishing-rod over his shoulder ; and he was making such good speed through the boughs that one might have half believed he was the better for his lame leg. He was the head of a company of tinkers, who, as the men told us, travel with their fishing-rods as duly as their hammers. On being hailed by us the whole company stopped ; and their lame leader and our boatmen shouted to each other in Erse — a savage cry to our ears, in that lonely and romantic place. We could not learn from the tinker all we wished to know, therefore when we came near to the houses Wm. landed again with the owner of the boat. The rain was now so heavy that we could see nothing at all — not even the houses whither Wm. was going.

We had given up all thought of proceeding further at that time, but were desirous to know how far that road to Glen Coe was practicable for us. They met with an intelligent man, who was at work with others in a hay field, though it rained so heavily ; he gave them the information they desired, and said that there was an acquaintance of his between that place and Glen Coe, who, he had no doubt, would gladly accommodate us with lodging and anything else we might need. When Wm. returned to the boat we shaped our course back again down the water, leaving the head of Loch Etive not only unvisited, but unseen — to our great regret. The rain was very heavy ; the wind had risen, and both wind and tide were against us, so that it was hard labour for the boatmen to push us on. They kept as close to the shore as they could, to be under the wind ; but at the doubling of many of the rocky points the tide was so strong that it was difficult to get on at all, and I was sometimes afraid that we should be dashed against the rocks, though I believe, indeed, there was not much danger.

Came down the same side of the lake under Ben Durinish, and landed at a ferry-house opposite to Bunawe, where we gave the men a glass of whisky ; but our chief motive for landing was to look about the place, which had a most wild aspect at that time. It was a low promontory, pushed far into the water, narrowing the lake exceedingly ; in the obscurity occasioned by the mist and rain it appeared to be an island ; it was stained and weatherbeaten, a rocky place, seeming to bear no produce but such as might be cherished by cold and storms, lichens or the incrustations of sea rocks. We rowed right across the water to the mouth of the river of Loch Awe, our boat following the ferry-boat which was conveying the tinker crew to the other side, whither they were going to lodge, as the men told us, in some kiln, which they considered as their right and privilege, a lodging always to be found where there was any arable land ; for every farm has its kiln to dry the corn in : another proof of the wetness of the climate. The kilns are built of stone, covered in, and probably as good a shelter as the huts in which these Highland vagrants were born. They gather sticks or hether for their fire, and, as they are obstinate beggars (for the men said they would not be denied), they probably have plenty of food with little other trouble than that of wandering in search of it, for their smutty faces and tinker equipage serve chiefly for a passport to a free and careless life. It rained very heavily, and the wind blew when we crossed the lake, and their boat and ours went tilting over the high waves. They made a romantic appearance ; three women were of the party ; two men rowed them over ; the lame fellow sate at one end of the boat, and his companion at the other, each with an enormous fishing-rod, which looked very graceful, something like masts to the boat. When we had landed at the other side we saw them, after having begged at the ferry-house, strike merrily through the fields, no doubt betaking themselves to their shelter for the night.

We were completely wet when we reached the inn ; the landlady wanted to make a fire for me up-stairs, but I went into her own parlour to undress, and her daughter; a pretty little girl, who could speak a few words of English, waited on me ; I rewarded her with one of the penny books bought at Dumfries for Johnny, with which she was greatly delighted. We had an excellent supper — fresh salmon, a fowl, goose-berries and cream, and potatoes ; good beds ; and the next morning boiled milk and bread, and were only charged seven shillings and sixpence for the whole — horse, liquor, supper, and the two breakfasts. We thought they had made a mis-take, and told them so — for it was only just half as much as we had paid the day before at Dalmally, the case being that Dalmally is in the main road of the tourists. The landlady insisted on my bringing away a little cup instead of our tin can, which she told me had been taken from the car by some children : we set no little value on this cup as a memorial of the good woman's honesty and kindness, and hoped to have brought it home.

September 2nd, Friday. Departed at about seven o'clock this morning, having to travel eight miles down Loch Etive, and then to cross a ferry. Our road was at first at a considerable distance from the lake, and out of sight of it, among undulating hills covered with coppice woods, resembling the country between Coniston and Windermere, but it afterwards carried us close to the water's edge ; and in this part of our ride we were disappointed. We knew that the high mountains were all at the head of the lake, therefore had not expected the same awful grandeur which we beheld the day before, and perceived by glimpses ; but the gentleman whom we met with at Dalmally had told us that there were many fine situations for gentlemen's seats on this part of the lake, which had made us expect greater loveliness near the shores, and better cultivation. It is true there are pleasant bays, with grounds prettily sloping to the water, and coppice woods, where houses would stand in shelter and sun, looking on the lake ; but much is yet wanting,—waste lands to be ploughed, peat-mosses drained, hedgerows reared ; and the woods demand a grant of longer life than is now their privilege.

But after we had journeyed about six miles a beautiful scene opened upon us. The morning had been gloomy, and at this time the sun shone out, scattering the clouds. We looked right down the lake, that was covered with streams of dazzling sunshine, which revealed the indentings of the dark shores. On a bold promontory, on the same side of the loch where we were, stood an old castle, an irregular tall building, not without majesty ; and beyond, with leagues of water between, our eyes settled upon the island of Mull, a high mountain, green in the sunshine, and overcast with clouds,— an object as inviting to the fancy as the evening sky in the west, and though of a terrestrial green, almost as visionary. We saw that it was an island of the sea, but were unacquainted with its name ; it was of a gem-like colour, and as soft as the sky. The shores of Loch Etive, in their moorish, rocky wildness, their earthly bareness, as they lay in length before us, produced a contrast which, with the pure sea, the brilliant sunshine, the long distance, contributed to the aërial and romantic power with which the mountain island was invested.

Soon after, we came to the ferry. The boat being on the other shore, we had to wait a considerable time, though the water was not wide, and our call was heard immediately. The boatmen moved with surly tardiness, as if glad to make us know that they were our masters. At this point the lake was narrowed to the breadth of not a very wide river by a round ear or promontory on the side on which we were, and a low ridge of peat-mossy ground on the other. It was a dreary place, shut out from the beautiful prospect of the Isle of Mull, and Dunstaffnage Castle (so the fortress was called). Four or five men came over with the boat ; the horse was unyoked, and being harshly driven over rough stones, which were as slippery as ice with slimy seaweed, he was in terror before he reached the boat, and they completed the work by beating and pushing him by main force over the ridge of the boat, for there was no open end, or plank, or any other convenience for shipping either horse or carriage. I was very uneasy when we were launched on the water. A blackguard-looking fellow, blind of one eye (which I could not but think had been put out in some strife or other), held him by force like a horse-breaker, while the poor creature fretted, and stamped with his feet against the bare boards, frightening himself more and more with every stroke ; and when we were in the middle of the water I would have given a thousand pounds to have been sure that we should reach the other side in safety. The tide was rushing violently in, making a strong eddy with the stream of the loch, so that the motion of the boat and the noise and foam of the waves terrified him still more, and we thought it would be impossible to keep him in the boat, and when we were just far enough from the shore to have been all drowned he became furious, and, plunging desperately, his hind-legs were in the water, then, recovering himself, he beat with such force against the boat-side that we were afraid he should send his feet through. All the while the men were swearing terrible oaths, and cursing the poor beast, redoubling their curses when we reached the landing-place, and whipping him ashore in brutal triumph.

We had only room for half a heartful of joy when we set foot on dry land, for another ferry was to be crossed five miles further. We had intended breakfasting at this house if it had been a decent place ; but after this affair we were glad to pay the men off and depart, though I was not well and needed refreshment.[1] The people made us more easy by assuring us that we might easily swim the horse over the next ferry. The first mile or two of our road was over a peat-moss ; we then came near to the sea-shore, and had beautiful views backward towards the Island of Mull and Dunstaffnage Castle, and forward where the sea ran up between the hills. In this part, on the opposite side of the small bay or elbow of the sea, was a gentleman's house on a hillside,[2] and a building on the hilltop which we took for a lighthouse, but were told that it belonged to the mansion, and was only lighted up on rejoicing days — the laird's birthday, for instance.

Before we had left the peat-moss to travel close to the sea-shore we delighted ourselves with looking on a range of green hills, in shape like those bordering immediately upon the sea, abrupt but not high ; they were, in fact, a continuation of the same ; but retiring backwards, and rising from the black peat-moss. These hills were of a delicate green, uncommon in Scotland ; a foaming rivulet ran down one part, and near it lay two herdsmen full in the sun, with their dogs, among a troop of black cattle which were feeding near, and sprinkled over the whole range of hills, a pastoral scene, to our eyes the more beautiful from knowing what a delightful prospect it must overlook. We now came under the steeps by the sea-side, which were bold rocks, mouldering scars, or fresh with green grass. Under the brow of one of these rocks was a burying-ground, with many upright grave-stones and hay-cocks between, and fenced round by a wall neatly sodded. Near it were one or two houses with out-houses, under a group of trees ; but no chapel. The neatness of the burying-ground would in itself have been noticeable in any part of Scotland where we have been ; but it was more interesting from its

---

[1] Though I was faint in my stomach and had a violent headache.—C. C.
[2] Lochnell House.—J. C. S.

situation than for its own sake, within the sound of the gentlest waves of the sea, and near so many quiet and beautiful objects. There was a range of hills opposite, which we were here first told were the hills of Morven, so much sung of by Ossian. We consulted with some men respecting the ferry, who advised us by all means to send our horse round the loch, and go ourselves over in the boat : they were very civil, and seemed to be intelligent men, yet all disagreed about the length of the loch, though we were not two miles from it : one said it was only six miles long, another ten or fifteen, and afterwards a man whom we met told us it was twenty.

We lost sight of the sea for some time, crossing a half-cultivated space, then reached Loch Creran, a large irregular sea loch, with low sloping banks, coppice woods, and uncultivated grounds, with a scattering of corn fields ; as it appeared to us, very thinly inhabited, mountains at a distance. We found only women at home at the ferry-house. I was faint and cold, and went to sit by the fire, but, though very much needing refreshment, I had not heart to eat anything there, the house was so dirty, and there were so many wretchedly dirty women and children ; yet perhaps I might have got over the dirt (though I believe there are few ladies who would not have been turned sick by it) if there had not been a most disgusting combination of laziness and coarseness in the countenances and manners of the women, though two of them were very handsome. It was a small hut, and four women were living in it : one, the mother of the children and mistress of the house ; the others I supposed to be lodgers, or perhaps servants ; but there was no work amongst them. They had just taken from the fire a great pan full of potatoes, which they mixed up with milk, all helping themselves out of the same vessel, and the little children put in their dirty hands to dig out of the mess at their pleasure. I thought to myself, How light the labour of such a house as this ! Little sweeping, no washing of floors, and as to scouring the table, I believe it was a thing never thought of.

After a long time the ferryman came home ; but we had to wait yet another hour for the tide. In the meanwhile our horse took fright in consequence of his terror at the last ferry, ran away with the car, and dashed out umbrellas, greatcoats, etc. ; but luckily he was stopped before any serious mischief was done. We had determined, whatever it cost, not to trust ourselves with him again in the boat ; but sending him round the lake seemed almost out of the question, there being no road, and probably much difficulty in going round with a horse ; so after some deliberation with the ferryman it was agreed that he should swim over. The usual place of ferrying was very broad, but he was led to the point of a peninsula at a little distance. It being an unusual affair (indeed, the people of the house said that he was the first horse that had ever swum over), we had several men on board, and the mistress of the house offered herself as an assistant : we supposed for the sake of a share in eighteen-pennyworth of whisky which her husband called for without ceremony, and of which she and the young lasses, who had helped to push the boat into the water, partook as freely as the men. At first I feared for the horse : he was frightened, and strove to push himself under the boat ; but I was soon tolerably easy, for he went on regularly and well, and after from six to ten minutes' swimming landed in safety on the other side. Poor creature ! he stretched out his nostrils and stared wildly while the man was trotting him about to warm him, and when he put him into the car he was afraid of the sound of the wheels.

For some time our road was up a glen, the banks chiefly covered with coppice woods, an unpeopled, but, though without grandeur, not a dreary tract. Came to a moor and descended into a broad vale, which opened to Loch Linnhe, an arm of the sea, the prospect being shut in by high mountains, on which the sun was shining among mists and resting clouds. A village and chapel stood on the opposite hill ; the hills sloped prettily down to the bed of the vale, a large level area, the grounds in general cultivated, but not rich. We went perhaps half a mile down the vale, when our road struck right across it towards the village on the hill-side. We overtook a tall, well-looking man, seemingly about thirty years of age, driving a cart, of whom we inquired concerning the road, and the distance to

Z

Portnacroish, our baiting-place. We made further inquiries respecting our future journey, which he answered in an intelligent manner, being perfectly acquainted with the geography of Scotland. He told us that the village which we saw before us and the whole tract of country was called Appin. Wm. said that it was a pretty wild place, to which the man replied, " Sir, it is a very bonny place if you did but see it on a fine day", mistaking Wm.'s praise for a half-censure ; I must say, however, that we hardly ever saw a thoroughly pleasing place in Scotland, which had not something of wildness in its aspect of one sort or other. It came from many causes here : the sea, or sea-loch, of which we only saw as it were a glimpse crossing the vale at the foot of it, the high mountains on the opposite shore, the unenclosed hills on each side of the vale, with black cattle feeding on them, the simplicity of the scattered huts, the half-sheltered, half-exposed situation of the village, the imperfect culture of the fields, the distance from any city or large town, and the very names of Morven and Appin, particularly at such a time, when old Ossian's old friends, sunbeams and mists, as like ghosts as any in the mid-afternoon could be, were keeping company with them. William did all he could to efface the unpleasant impression he had made on the Highlander, and not without success, for he was kind and communicative when we walked up the hill towards the village. He had been a great traveller, in Ireland and elsewhere ; but I believe that he had visited no place so beautiful to his eyes as his native home, the strath of Appin under the heathy hills.

We arrived at Portnacroish soon after parting from this man. It is a small village — a few huts and an indifferent inn by the side of the loch. Ordered a fowl for dinner, had a fire lighted, and went a few steps from the door up the road, and turning aside into a field stood at the top of a low eminence, from which, looking down the loch to the sea through a long vista of hills and mountains, we beheld one of the most delightful prospects that, even when we dream of fairer worlds than this, it is possible for us to conceive in our hearts. A covering of clouds rested on the long range of the hills of Morven, mists floated very near to the water on their sides, and were slowly shifting about : yet the sky was clear, and the sea, from the reflection of the sky, of an ethereal or sapphire blue, which was intermingled in many places, and mostly by gentle gradations, with beds of bright dazzling sunshine ; green islands lay on the calm water, islands far greener, for so it seemed, than the grass of other places ; and from their excessive beauty, their unearthly softness, and the great distance of many of them, they made us think of the islands of the Blessed in the *Vision of Mirza* — a resemblance more striking from the long tract of mist which rested on the top of the steeps of Morven. The view was endless, and though not so wide, had something of the intricacy of the islands and water of Loch Lomond as we saw them from Inch-ta-vannach ; and yet how different ! At Loch Lomond we could never forget that it was an inland lake of fresh water, nor here that it was the sea itself, though among multitudes of hills. Immediately below us, on an island a few yards from the shore, stood an old keep or fortress ; [1] the vale of Appin opened to the waterside, with cultivated fields and cottages. If there were trees near the shore they contributed little to the delightful effect of the scene : it was the immeasurable water, the lofty mist-covered steeps of Morven to the right, the emerald islands without a bush or tree, the celestial colour and brightness of the calm sea, and the innumerable creeks and bays, the communion of land and water as far as the eye could travel. My description must needs be languid ; for the sight itself was too fair to be remembered. We sate a long time upon the hill, and pursued our journey at about four o'clock. Had an indifferent dinner, but the cheese was so excellent that Wm. wished to buy the remainder ; but the woman would not consent to sell it, and forced us to accept a large portion of it.

We had to travel up the loch, leaving behind us the beautiful scene which we had viewed with such delight before dinner. Often, while we were climbing the hill, did we stop to look back, and when we had gone twenty or thirty yards beyond the point where we had the last view of it, we left the car to

---

[1] Castle Stalker.—J. C. S.

the care of some children who were coming from school, and went to take another farewell, always in the hope of bearing away a more substantial remembrance. Travelled for some miles along a road which was so smooth it was more like a gravel walk in a gentleman's grounds than a public highway. Probably the country is indebted for this excellent road to Lord Tweeddale,[1] now a prisoner in France. His house stands upon an eminence within a mile of Portnacroish, commanding the same prospect which I have spoken of, except that it must lose something in not having the old fortress at the foot of it — indeed, it is not to be seen at all from the house or grounds.

We travelled under steep hills, stony or smooth, with coppice-woods and patches of cultivated land, and houses here and there ; and at every hundred yards, I may almost venture to say, a streamlet, narrow as a ribband, came tumbling down, and, crossing our road, fell into the lake below. On the opposite shore, the hills (namely, the continuation of the hills of Morven) were stern and severe, rising like upright walls from the water's edge, and in colour more resembling rocks than hills, as they appeared to us. We did not see any house, or any place where it was likely a house could stand, for many miles ; but as the loch was broad we could not perhaps distinguish the objects thoroughly. A little after sunset our road led us from the vale of the loch. We came to a small river, a bridge, a mill, and some cottages at the foot of a hill, and close to the loch.

Did not cross the bridge, but went up the brook, having it on our left, and soon found ourselves in a retired valley, scattered over with many grey huts, and surrounded on every side by green hills. The hay grounds in the middle of the vale were unenclosed, which was enough to keep alive the Scottish wildness, here blended with exceeding beauty ; for there were trees growing irregularly or in clumps all through the valley, rocks or stones here and there, which, with the people at work, hay-cocks sprinkled over the fields, made the vale look full and populous. It was a sweet time of the evening : the moon was up ; but there was yet so much of day that her light was

---

[1] George, seventh Marquis of Tweeddale, being in France in 1803, was detained by Bonaparte, and died at Verdun, Aug. 9, 1804.—J. C. S.

not perceived. Our road was through open fields ; the people suspended their work as we passed along, and leaning on their pitchforks or rakes, with their arms at their sides, or hanging down, some in one way, some in another, and no two alike, they formed most beautiful groups, the outlines of their figures being much more distinct than by day, and all that might have been harsh or unlovely softened down. The dogs were, as usual, attendant on their masters, and, watching after us, they barked aloud ; yet even their barking hardly disturbed the quiet of the place.

I cannot say how long this vale was ; it made the larger half of a circle, or a curve deeper than that of half a circle, before it opened again upon the loch. It was less thoroughly cultivated and woody after the last turning — the hills steep and lofty. We met a very tall stout man, a fine figure, in a Highland bonnet, with a little girl, driving home their cow : he accosted us, saying that we were late travellers, and that we had yet four miles to go before we should reach Ballachulish, a long way, uncertain as we were respecting our accommodations. He told us that the vale was called the Strath of Duror, and when we said it was a pretty place, he answered, indeed it was, and that they lived very comfortably there, for they had a good master, Lord Tweeddale, whose imprisonment he lamented, speaking earnestly of his excellent qualities. At the end of the vale we came close upon a large bay of the loch, formed by a rocky hill, a continuation of the ridge of high hills on the left side of the strath, making a very grand promontory, under which was a hamlet, a cluster of huts, at the water's edge, with their little fleet of fishing-boats at anchor, and behind, among the rocks, a hundred slips of corn, slips and patches, often no bigger than a garden such as a child, eight years old, would make for sport : it might have been the work of a small colony from China. There was something touching to the heart in this appearance of scrupulous industry, and excessive labour of the soil, in a country where hills and mountains, and even vallies, are left to the care of nature and the pleasure of the cattle that feed among them. It was, indeed, a very interesting place, the more so being in perfect contrast with the few houses at the entrance of the strath — a sea hamlet, without trees, under a naked stony mountain, yet perfectly sheltered, standing in the middle of a large bay which half the winds that travel over the lake can never visit. The other, a little bowery spot, with its river, bridge, and mill, might have been a hundred miles from the sea-side.

The moon was now shining, and though it reminded us how far the evening was advanced, we stopped for many minutes before we could resolve to go on ; we saw nothing stirring, neither men, women, nor cattle ; but the linen was still bleaching by the stony rivulet, which ran near the houses in water-breaks and tiny cataracts. For the first half mile after we had left this scene there was nothing remarkable ; and afterwards we could only see the hills, the sky, the moon, and moonlight water. When we came within, it might be, half a mile of Ballachulish, the place where we were to lodge, the loch narrowed very much, the hills still continuing high. I speak inaccurately, for it split into two divisions, the one along which we went being called Loch Leven.

The road grew very bad, and we had an anxious journey till we saw a light before us, which with great joy we assured ourselves was from the inn ; but what was our distress when, on going a few steps further, we came to a bridge half broken down, with bushes laid across to prevent travellers from going over. After some perplexity we determined that *I* should walk on to the house before us (for we could see that the bridge was safe for foot-passengers) and ask for assistance. By great good luck, at this very moment four or five men came along the road towards us and offered to help Wm. in driving the car through the water, which was not very deep at that time, though, only a few days before, the damage had been done to the bridge by a flood.

I walked on to the inn, ordered tea, and was conducted into a lodging-room. I desired to have a fire, and was answered with the old scruple about " *giving* fire ", with, at the same time, an excuse " that it was so late " ; the girl, however, would ask the landlady, who was lying-in ; the fire was brought immediately, and from that time the girl was very civil. I was not, however, quite at ease, for Wm. stayed long, and I was going to leave my fire to seek after him, when I heard him at the door with the horse and car. The horse had taken fright with the roughness of the river-bed and the rattling of the wheels (the second fright in consequence of the ferry) and the men had been obliged to unyoke him and drag the car through, a troublesome affair for Wm. ; but he talked less of the trouble and alarm than of the pleasure he had felt in having met with such true goodwill and ready kindness in the Highlanders. They drank their glass of whisky at the door, wishing Wm. twenty good wishes, and asking him twice as many questions, if he was married, if he had an estate, where he lived, etc. etc. This inn is the ferry-house on the main road up into the Highlands by Fort-William, and here Coleridge, though unknown to us, had slept three nights before.

September 3rd, Saturday. When we have arrived at an unknown place by moonlight, it is never a moment of indifference when I greet it again with the morning light, especially if the objects have appeared beautiful, or in any other way impressive or interesting. I have kept back, unwilling to go to the window, that I might not lose the picture taken to my pillow at night. So it was at Ballachulish : and instantly I felt that the passing away of my own fancies was a loss. The place had appeared exceedingly wild by moonlight ; I had mistaken corn-fields for naked rocks, and the lake had appeared narrower and the hills more steep and lofty than they really were.

We rose at six o'clock, and took a basin of milk before we set forward on our journey to Glen Coe. It was a delightful morning, the road excellent, and we were in good spirits, happy that we had no more ferries to cross, and pleased with the thought that we were going among the grand mountains which we saw before us at the head of the loch. We travelled close to the water's edge, and were rolling along a smooth road, when the horse suddenly backed, frightened by the upright shafts of a roller rising from behind the wall of a field adjoining the road. Wm. pulled, whipped, and struggled in vain ; we both leapt upon the ground, and the horse dragged the car after him, he going backwards down the bank of the loch, and it was turned over, half in the water, the horse lying on his back, struggling in the harness, a frightful sight ! I gave up everything ; thought that the horse would be lamed, and the car broken to pieces. Luckily a man came up in the same moment, and assisted Wm. in extricating the horse, and, after an hour's delay, with the help of strings and pocket-handkerchiefs, we mended the harness and set forward again, Wm. leading the poor animal all the way, for the regular beating of the waves frightened him, and any little gushing stream that crossed the road would have sent him off. The village where the blacksmith lived was before us, a few huts under the mountains, and, as it seemed, at the head of the loch ; but it runs further up to the left, being narrowed by a hill above the village, near which, at the edge of the water, was a slate quarry, and many large boats with masts, on the water below, high mountains shutting in the prospect, which stood in single, distinguishable shapes, yet clustered together, simple and bold in their forms, and their surfaces of all characters and all colours ; some that looked as if scarified by fire, others green ; and there was one that might have been blasted by an eternal frost, its summit and sides for a considerable way down being as white as hoar-frost at eight o'clock on a winter's morning. No clouds were on the hills ; the sun shone bright, but the wind blew fresh and cold.

When we reached the blacksmith's shop, I left Wm. to help to take care of the horse, and went into the house. The mistress (with a child in her arms and two or three running about) received me very kindly, making many apologies for the dirty house, which she partly attributed to its being Saturday ; but I could plainly see that it was dirt of all days. I sate in the midst of it with great delight, for the woman's benevolent, happy countenance almost converted her slovenly and lazy way of leaving all things to take care of themselves into a comfort and a blessing.

It was not a Highland hut, but a slated house built by the master of the quarry for the accommodation of his blacksmith, the shell of an English cottage, as if left unfinished by the workmen, without plaister, and with floor of mud. Two beds, with not over-clean bedclothes, were in the room. Luckily for me, there was a good fire and a boiling kettle. The woman was very sorry she had no butter ; none was to be had in the village : she gave me oaten and barley bread. We talked over the fire ; I answered her hundred questions, and in my turn put some to her. She asked me, as usual, if I was married, how many brothers I had, etc. etc. I told her that Wm. was married, and had a fine boy ; to which she replied, " And the man's a decent man too ". Her next-door neighbour came in with a baby on her arm, to request that I would accept of some fish, which I broiled in the ashes. She joined in our conversation, but with more shyness than her neighbour, being a very young woman. She happened to say that she was a stranger in that place, and had been bred and born a long way off. On my asking her where, she replied, " At Leadhills " ; and when I told her that I had been there, a joy lighted up her countenance which I shall never forget, and when she heard that it was only a fortnight before, her eyes filled with tears. I was exceedingly affected with the simplicity of her manners ; her tongue was now let loose ; and she would have talked for ever of Leadhills, of her mother, of the quietness of the people in general, and the goodness of Mrs. Otto, who, she told me, was a " varra discreet woman ". She was sure we should be " well put up at Mrs. Otto's ", and praised her house and furniture ; indeed, it seemed she thought all earthly comforts were gathered together under the bleak heights that surround the villages of Wanlockhead and Leadhills : and afterwards, when I said it was a wild country thereabouts, she even seemed surprized, and said it was not half so wild as where she lived now. One circumstance which she mentioned of Mrs. Otto I must record, both in proof of her *discretion*, and the sobriety of the people at Leadhills, namely, that no liquor was ever drunk in her house after a certain hour of the night (I have forgotten what hour ; but it was an early one, I am sure not later than ten).

The blacksmith, who had come in to his breakfast, was impatient to finish our job, that he might go out into the hayfield, for, it being a fine day, every plot of hay-ground was scattered over with hay-makers. On my saying that I guessed much of their hay must be spoiled, he told me no, for that they had high winds, which dried it quickly, — the people understood the climate, " were clever at the work, and got it in with a *blink* ". He hastily swallowed his breakfast, dry bread and a basin of weak tea without sugar, and held his baby on his knee till he had done.

The women and I were again left to the fireside, and there were no limits to their joy in me, for they discovered another bond of connexion. I lived in the same part of England from which Mr. Rose, the superintendent of the slate-quarries, and his wife, had come. " Oh ! " said Mrs. Stuart (so her neighbour called her, they not giving each other their Christian names, as is common in Cumberland and Westmoreland), ".Oh ! " said she, " what would not I give to see anybody that came from within four or five miles of Leadhills ! " They both exclaimed that I must see Mrs. Rose ; she would make much of me — *she* would have given me tea and bread and butter and a good breakfast. I learned from the two women, Mrs. Stuart and Mrs. Duncan (so the other was called), that Stuart had come from Leadhills for the sake of better wages, to take the place of Duncan, who had resigned his office of blacksmith to the quarries (as far as I could learn) in a pet, intending to go to America, that his wife was averse to go, and that the scheme, for this cause and through other difficulties, had been given up. He appeared to be a good-tempered man, and made us a most reasonable charge for mending the car. His wife told me that they must give up the house in a short time to the other blacksmith ; she did not know whither they should go, but her husband, being a good workman, could find employment anywhere. She hurried me out to introduce me to Mrs. Rose, who was at work in the hay-field ; she was exceedingly glad to see one of her country-women, and entreated that I would go up to her house. It was a substantial plain house, that would have held half-a-dozen of the common huts ; she conducted me into a sitting-room up-stairs, and set before me red and white wine, with the remnant of a loaf of wheaten bread (which she took out of a cupboard in the sitting-room) and some delicious butter. She was a healthy and chearful-looking woman, dressed like one of our country lasses, and had certainly had no better education than Aggy Ashburner,[1] but she was as a chief in this secluded place, a Madam of the village, and seemed to be treated with the utmost respect.

In our way to and from the house we met several people who interchanged friendly greetings with her, but always as with one greatly superior. She attended me back to the black-smith's, and would not leave me till she had seen us set forward again on our journey. Mrs. Duncan and Mrs. Stuart shook me cordially, nay, affectionately, by the hand. I tried to prevail upon the former, who had been my hostess, to accept of some money, but in vain ; she would not take a farthing, and though I told her it was only to buy something for her little daughter, even seemed grieved that I should think it possible. I forgot to mention that while the blacksmith was repairing the car, we walked to the slate-quarry, where we saw again some of the kind creatures who had helped us in our difficulties the night before. The hovel under which they split their slates stood upon an outjutting rock, a part of the quarry rising immediately out of the water, and commanded a fine prospect down the loch below Ballachulish, and upwards towards the grand mountains, and the other horn of the vale where the lake was concealed. The blacksmith drove our car about a mile of the road ; we then hired a man and horse to take me and the car to the top of Glen Coe, being afraid that if the horse backed or took fright we might be thrown down some precipice.

But before we departed we could not resist our inclination to climb up the hill which I have mentioned as appearing to terminate the loch. The mountains, though inferior to those of Glen Coe on the other side are very majestic ; and the solitude in which we knew the unseen lake was bedded at their feet was enough to excite our longings. We climbed steep after steep, far higher than they appeared to us, and I was going to give up the accomplishment of our aim, when a glorious sight on the mountain before us made me forget my fatigue. A slight shower had come on, its skirts falling upon us,

---

[1] *v. Grasmere Journal*, and Appendix, p. 433.

and half the opposite side of the mountain was wrapped up in rainbow light, covered as by a veil with one dilated rainbow : so it continued for some minutes ; and the shower and rainy clouds passed away as suddenly as they had come, and the sun shone again upon the tops of all the hills. In the meantime we reached the wished-for point, and saw to the head of the loch. Perhaps it might not be so beautiful as we had imaged it in our thoughts, but it was beautiful enough not to disappoint us, — a narrow deep valley, a perfect solitude, without house or hut. One of the hills was thinly sprinkled with Scotch firs, which appeared to be the survivors of a large forest : they were the first natural wild Scotch firs we had seen. Though thinned of their numbers, and left, comparatively, to a helpless struggle with the elements, we were much struck with the gloom, and even grandeur, of the trees.

Hastened back again to join the car, but were tempted to go a little out of our way to look at a nice white house belonging to the laird of Glen Coe, which stood sweetly in a green field under the hill near some tall trees and coppice woods. At this house the horrible massacre of Glen Coe began, which we did not know when we were there ; but the house must have been rebuilt since that time. We had a delightful walk through fields, among copses, and by a river-side : we could have fancied ourselves in some part of the north of England unseen before, it was so much like it, and yet so different. I must not forget one place on the opposite side of the water, where we longed to live — a snug white house on the mountain-side, surrounded by its own green fields and woods, the high mountain above, the loch below, and inaccessible but by means of boats. A beautiful spot indeed it was ; but in the retired parts of Scotland a comfortable white house is itself such a pleasant sight, that I believe, without our knowing how or why, it makes us look with a more loving eye on the fields and trees than for their own sakes they deserve.

At about one o'clock we set off, Wm. on our own horse, and I with my Highland driver. He was perfectly acquainted with the country, being a sort of carrier or carrier-merchant or shopkeeper, going frequently to Glasgow with his horse and cart to fetch and carry goods and merchandise. He knew the name of every hill, almost every rock ; and I made good use of his knowledge ; but partly from laziness, and still more because it was inconvenient, I took no notes, and now I am little better for what he told me. He spoke English tolerably ; but seldom understood what was said to him without a " What's your wull ? " We turned up to the right, and were at the foot of the glen (the laird's house cannot be said to be *in* the glen). The afternoon was delightful, — the sun shone, the mountain-tops were clear, the lake glittered in the great vale behind us, and the stream of Glen Coe flowed down to it glittering among alder-trees. The meadows of the glen were of the freshest green ; one new-built stone house in the first reach, some huts, hillocks covered with wood, alder-trees scattered all over. Looking backward, we were reminded of Patterdale and the head of Ulswater, but forward the greatness of the mountains overcame every other idea.

The impression was, as we advanced up to the head of this first reach, as if the glen were nothing, its loneliness and retire-ment, as if it made up no part of my feeling : the mountains were all in all. That which fronted us (I have forgotten its name) was exceedingly lofty, the surface stony, nay, the whole mountain was one mass of stone, wrinkled and puckered up together. At the second and last reach (for it is not a winding vale) it makes a quick turning almost at right angles to the first ; and now we are in the depths of the mountains ; no trees in the glen, only green pasturage for sheep, and here and there a plot of hay-ground, and something that tells of former cultivation. I observed this to the guide, who said that formerly the glen had had many inhabitants, and that there, as elsewhere in the Highlands, there had been a great deal of corn where now the lands were left waste, and nothing fed upon them but cattle. I cannot attempt to describe the mountains. I can only say that I thought those on our right (for the other side was only a continued high ridge or craggy barrier, broken along the top into petty spiral forms) were the grandest I had ever seen. It seldom happens that mountains in a very clear air look exceedingly high, but these, though we could see the whole of them to their very summits, appeared to me more majestic in their own nakedness than our imaginations could have conceived them to be, had they been half hidden by clouds, yet showing some of their highest pinnacles. They were such forms as Milton might be supposed to have had in his mind when he applied to Satan that sublime expression —

His stature reached the sky.

The first division of the glen, as I have said, was scattered over with rocks, trees, and woody hillocks, and cottages were to be seen here and there. The second division is bare and stony, huge mountains on all sides, with a slender pasturage in the bottom of the valley ; and towards the head of it is a small lake or tarn, and near the tarn a single inhabited dwelling, and some unfenced hay-ground, a simple impressive scene ! Our road frequently crossed large streams of stones, left by the mountain-torrents, losing all appearance of a road. After we had passed the tarn the glen became less interesting, or rather the mountains, from the manner in which they are looked at ; but again, a little higher up, they resume their grandeur. The river is, for a short space, hidden between steep rocks ; we left the road, and, going to the top of one of the rocks, saw it foaming over stones, or lodged in dark black dens ; birch-trees grew on the inaccessible banks, and a few old Scotch firs towered above them. At the entrance of the glen the mountains had been all without trees, but here the birches clomb very far up the side of one of them opposite to us, half concealing a rivulet which came tumbling down as white as snow from the very top of the mountain. Leaving the rock, we ascended a hill which terminated the glen. We often stopped to look behind at the majestic company of mountains we had left. Before us was no single paramount eminence, but a mountain waste, mountain beyond mountain, and a barren hollow or basin into which we were descending.

We parted from our companion at the door of a whisky hovel, a building which, when it came out of the workmen's hands with its unglassed windows, would, in that forlorn region, have been little better than a howling place for the winds, and was now half unroofed. On seeing a smoke, I exclaimed, " Is it possible any people can live there ? " when at least half a dozen, men, women, and children, came to the door. They were about to rebuild the hut, and I suppose that they, or some other poor creatures, would dwell there through the winter, dealing out whisky to the starved travellers. The sun was now setting, the air very cold, the sky clear ; I could have fancied that it was winter-time, with hard frost. Our guide pointed out King's House to us, our resting-place for the night. We could just distinguish the house at the bottom of the moorish hollow or basin (I call it so, for it was nearly as broad as long) lying before us, with three miles of naked road winding through it, every foot of which we could see. The road was perfectly white, making a dreary contrast with the ground, which was of a dull earthy brown. Long as the line of road appeared before us, we could scarcely believe it to be three miles — I suppose owing to its being unbroken by any one object, and the moor naked as the road itself ; but we found it the longest three miles we had yet travelled, for the surface was so stony we had to walk most of the way.

The house looked respectable at a distance, a large square building, cased in blue slates to defend it from storms ; but when we came close to it the outside forewarned us of the poverty and misery within. Scarce a blade of grass could be seen growing upon the open ground ; the heath-plant itself found no nourishment there, appearing as if it had but sprung up to be blighted. There was no enclosure for a cow, no appropriated ground but a small plot like a church-yard, in which were a few starveling dwarfish potatoes, which had, no doubt, been raised by means of the dung left by travellers' horses ; they had not come to blossoming, and whether they would either yield fruit or blossom I know not. The first thing we saw on entering the door was two sheep hung up, as if just killed from the barren moor, their bones hardly sheathed in flesh. After we had waited a few minutes, looking about for a guide to lead us into some corner of the house, a woman, seemingly about forty years old, came to us in a great bustle, screaming in Erse, with the most horrible guinea-hen or peacock voice I ever heard, first to one person, then another. She could hardly spare time to show us up-stairs, for crowds of men were in the house — drovers, carriers, horsemen, travellers, all of whom she had to provide with supper, and she was, as she told us, the only woman there.

Never did I see such a miserable, such a wretched place, — long rooms with ranges of beds, no other furniture except benches, or perhaps one or two crazy chairs, the floors far dirtier than an ordinary house *could* be if it were never washed, — as dirty as a house after a sale on a rainy day, and the rooms being large, and the walls naked, they looked as if more than half the goods had been sold out. We sate shivering in one of the large rooms for three-quarters of an hour before the woman could find time to speak to us again ; she then promised a fire in another room, after two travellers, who were going a stage further, had finished their whisky, and said we should have supper as soon as possible. She had no eggs, no milk, no potatoes, no loaf-bread, or we should have preferred tea. With length of time the fire was kindled, and, after another hour's waiting, supper came, a shoulder of mutton so hard that it was impossible to chew the little flesh that might be scraped off the bones, and some sorry soup made of barley and water (for it had no other taste).

After supper, the woman, having first asked if we slept on blankets, brought in two pair of sheets, which she begged that I would air by the fire, for they would be dirtied below-stairs. I was very willing, but behold ! the sheets were so wet, that it would have been at least a two-hours' job before a far better fire than could be mustered at King's House, — for (that nothing might be wanting to make it a place of complete starvation) the peats were not dry, and if they had not been helped out by decayed wood dug out of the earth along with them, we should have had no fire at all. The woman was civil, in her fierce, wild way. She and the house, upon that desolate and extensive Wild, and everything we saw, made us think of one of those places of rendezvous which we read of in novels — Ferdinand Count Fathom, or Gil Blas, where there is one woman to receive the booty, and prepare the supper at night. She told us that she was only a servant, but that she had now lived there five years, and that, when but a " young lassie ", she had lived there also. We asked her if she had always served the same master, " Nay, nay, many masters, for they were always changing ". I verily believe that the woman was attached to the place like a cat to the empty house when the family who brought her up are gone to live elsewhere. The sheets were so long in drying that it was very late before we went to bed. We talked over our day's adventures by the fireside, and often looked out of the window towards a huge pyramidal mountain [1] at the entrance of Glen Coe. All between, the dreary waste was clear, almost, as sky, the moon shining full upon it. A rivulet ran amongst stones near the house, and sparkled with light ; I could have fancied that there was nothing else, in that extensive circuit over which we looked, that had the power of motion.

In comparing the impressions we had received at Glen Coe, we found that though the expectations of both had been far surpassed by the grandeur of the mountains, we had upon the whole both been disappointed, and from the same cause : we had been prepared for images of terror, had expected a deep, den-like valley with overhanging rocks, such as Wm. has described in these lines (speaking of the Alps) —

> *Brook and road*
> *Were fellow-travellers in this gloomy Pass,*
> *And with them did we journey several hours*
> *At a slow step. The immeasurable height*
> *Of woods decaying, never to be decayed !*
> *The stationary blasts of waterfalls ;*
> *And everywhere along the hollow rent*
> *Winds thwarting winds, bewilder'd and forlorn ;*
> *The torrents shooting from the clear blue sky,*
> *The rocks that mutter'd close upon our ears,*
> *Black drizzling crags that spake by the way-side*
> *As if a voice were in them ; the sick sight*
> *And giddy prospect of the raving stream ;*

---

[1] Buchail, the Shepherd of Etive.—J. C. S.

The unfetter'd clouds, and region of the heavens,
Tumult and peace, the darkness and the light,
Were all like workings of one mind, the features
Of the same face, blossoms upon one tree,
Characters of the great Apocalypse,
The Types and Symbols of Eternity,
Of first, and last, and midst, and without end.[1]

The place had nothing of this character, the glen being open to the eye of day, the mountains retiring in independent majesty. Even in the upper part of it, where the stream rushed through the rocky chasm, it was but a deep trench in the vale, not the vale itself, and could only be seen when we were close to it.

September 4th, Sunday. We had desired to be called at six o'clock, and rose at the first summons. Our beds had proved better than we expected, and we had not slept ill ; but poor Coleridge had passed a wretched night here four days before. This we did not know ; but since, when he told us of it, the notion of what he must have suffered, with the noise of drunken people about his ears all night, himself sick and tired, has made our discomfort cling to my memory, and given these recollections a twofold interest. I asked if it was possible to have a couple of eggs boiled before our departure ; the woman hesitated ; she thought I might, and sent a boy into the out-houses to look about, who brought in one egg after long searching. Early as we had risen it was not very early when we set off, for everything at King's House was in unison — equally uncomfortable. As the woman had told us the night before, " They had no hay and that was a loss ". There were neither stalls nor bedding in the stable, so that Wm. was obliged to watch the horse while it was feeding, for there were several others in the stable, all standing like wild beasts, ready to devour each other's portion of corn : this, with the slowness of the servant and other hindrances, took up much time, and we were completely starved, for the morning was very cold, as I believe all the mornings in that desolate place are.

---

[1] *The Simplon Pass*, " Poems of Imagination ", vii.

When we had gone about a quarter of a mile I recollected that I had left the little cup given me by the kind landlady at Taynuilt, which I had intended that John should hereafter drink out of, in memory of our wanderings. I would have turned back for it, but Wm. pushed me on, unwilling that we should lose so much time, though indeed he was as sorry to part with it as myself.

Our road was over a hill called the Black Mountain. For the first mile, or perhaps more, after we left King's House, we ascended on foot ; then came upon a new road, one of the finest that was ever trod ; and, as we went downwards almost all the way afterwards, we travelled very quickly. The motion was pleasant, the different reaches and windings of the road were amusing ; the sun shone, the mountain-tops were clear and chearful ; and we in good spirits, in a bustle of enjoyment, though there never was a more desolate region ; mountains behind, before, and on every side ; I do not remember to have seen either patch of grass, flower, or flowering hether within three or four miles of King's House. The low ground was not rocky, but black, and full of white frost-bleached stones, the prospect only varied by pools, seen everywhere both near and at a distance, as far as the ground stretched out below us : these were interesting spots, round which the mind assembled living objects, as they shone as bright as mirrors in the forlorn waste. We passed neither tree nor shrub for miles (I include the whole space from Glen Coe), yet we saw perpetually traces of a long decayed forest, pieces of black mouldering wood.

Through such a country as this we had travelled perhaps seven and a half miles this morning, when, after descending a hill, we turned to the right, and saw an unexpected sight in the moorland hollow into which we were entering, a small lake bounded on the opposite side by a grove of Scotch firs, two or three cottages at the head of it, and a lot of cultivated ground with scattered hay-cocks. The road along which we were going, after having made a curve considerably above the tarn, was seen winding through the trees on the other wide, a beautiful object, and, luckily for us, a drove of cattle happened to be passing there at the very time, a stream coursing the road, with off-stragglers to the borders of the lake, and under the trees on the sloping ground.

In conning over our many wanderings I shall never forget the gentle pleasure with which we greeted the lake of Inveroran and its few grey cottages : we suffered our horse to slacken his pace, having now no need of the comfort of quick motion, though we were glad to think that one of those cottages might be the publick-house where we were to breakfast. A forest (now, as it appeared, dwindled into the small grove bordering the lake) had, not many years ago, spread to that side of the vale where we were ; large stumps of trees which had been cut down were yet remaining undecayed, and there were some single trees left alive, as if by their battered black boughs to tell us of the storms that visit the valley which looked now so sober and peaceful. When we arrived at the huts, one of them proved to be the inn, a thatched house without a sign-board. We were kindly received, had a fire lighted in the parlour, and were in such good humour that we seemed to have a thousand comforts about us ; but we had need of a little patience in addition to this good humour before breakfast was brought, and at last it proved a disappointment : the butter not eatable, the barley-cakes fusty, the oat-bread so hard I could not chew it, and there were only four eggs in the house, which they had boiled as hard as stones.

Before we had finished breakfast two foot-travellers came in, and seated themselves at our table ; one of them was returning, after a long absence, to Fort-William, his native home ; he had come from Egypt, and, many years ago, had been on a recruiting party at Penrith, and knew many people there. He seemed to think his own country but a dismal land.

There being no bell in the parlour, I had occasion to go several times and ask for what we wanted in the kitchen, and I would willingly have given twenty pounds to have been able to take a lively picture of it. About seven or eight travellers (probably drovers), with as many dogs, were sitting in a complete circle round a large peat-fire in the middle of the floor, each with a mess of porridge, in a wooden vessel, upon his knee ; a pot, suspended from one of the black beams, was boiling on the fire ; two or three women pursuing their household business on the outside of the circle, children playing on the floor. There was nothing uncomfortable in this confusion : happy, busy, or vacant faces, all looked pleasant ; and even the smoky air (being a sort of natural indoor atmosphere of Scotland) served only to give a softening, I may say harmony, to the whole.

We departed immediately after breakfast ; our road leading us, as I have said, near the lake-side and through the grove of firs, which extended backward much further than we had imagined. After we had left it we came again among bare moorish wastes, as before, under the mountains, so that Inveroran still lives in our recollection as a favoured place, a flower in the desert.

Descended upon the whole, I believe, very considerably, in our way to Tyndrum ; but it was a road of long ups and downs, over hills and through hollows of uncultivated ground ; a chance farm perhaps once in three miles, a glittering rivulet bordered with greener grass than grew on the broad waste, or a broken fringe of alders or birches, partly concealing and partly pointing out its course.

Arrived at Tyndrum at about two o'clock. It is a cold spot. Though, as I should suppose, situated lower than Inveroran, and though we saw it in the hottest time of the afternoon sun, it had a far colder aspect from the want of trees. We were here informed that Coleridge, who, we supposed, was gone to Edinburgh, had dined at this very house a few days before, in his road to Fort-William. By the help of the cook, who was called in, the landlady made out the very day : it was the day after we parted from him ; as she expressed it, the day after the " great *speet* ", namely, the great rain. We had a moorfowl and mutton-chops for dinner, well cooked, and a reasonable charge. The house was clean for a Scotch inn, and the people about the doors were well dressed. In one of the parlours we saw a company of nine or ten, with the landlady, seated round a plentiful table, a sight which made us think of the fatted calf in the alehouse pictures of the Prodigal Son. There seemed to be a whole harvest of meats and drinks, and there was something of festivity and picture-like gaiety even in the fresh-coloured dresses of the people and their Sunday faces. The white table-cloth, glasses, English dishes, etc., were all in contrast with what we had seen at Inveroran : the places were but about nine miles asunder, both among hills ; the rank of the people little different, and each house appeared to be a house of plenty. We were I think better pleased with our treatment at this inn than any of the lonely houses on the road, except Taynuilt ; but Coleridge had not fared so well, and was dissatisfied, as he has since told us, and the two travellers who breakfasted with us at Inveroran had given a bad account of the house.

Left Tyndrum at about five o'clock, a gladsome afternoon ; the road excellent, and we bowled downwards through a pleasant vale, though not populous, or well cultivated, or woody, but enlivened by a river that glittered as it flowed. On the side of a sunny hill a knot of men and women were gathered together at a preaching. We passed by many droves of cattle and Shetland ponies, which accident stamped a character upon places, else unrememberable, not an *individual* character, but the soul, the spirit, and solitary simplicity of many a Highland region.

We had about eleven miles to travel before we came to our lodging, and had gone five or six, almost always descending, and still in the same vale, when we saw a small lake before us after the vale had made a bending to the left. It was about sunset when we came up to the lake ; the afternoon breezes had died away, and the water was in perfect stillness. One grove-like island, with a ruin that stood upon it overshadowed by the trees, was reflected on the water. This building, which, on that beautiful evening, seemed to be wrapped up in religious quiet, we were informed had been raised for defence by some Highland chieftain. All traces of strength, or war, or danger are passed away, and in the mood in which we were we could only look upon it as a place of retirement and peace. The lake is called Loch Dochart. We passed by two others of inferior beauty, and continued to travel along the side of the same river, the Dochart, through an irregular, undetermined vale ; — poor soil and much waste land.

At that time of the evening when, by looking steadily, we could discover a few pale stars in the sky, we saw upon an eminence (the bound of our horizon, though very near to us, and facing the bright yellow clouds of the west) a groupe of figures that made us feel how much we wanted in not being painters. Two herdsmen, with a dog beside them, were sitting on the hill, overlooking a herd of cattle scattered over a large meadow by the river-side. Their forms, looked at through a fading light, and backed by the bright west, were exceedingly distinct, a beautiful picture in the quiet of a Sabbath evening, exciting thoughts and images of almost patriarchal simplicity and grace. We were much pleased with the situation of our inn, where we arrived between eight and nine o'clock. The river was at the distance of a broad field from the door ; we could see it from the upper windows and hear its murmuring ; the moon shone, enlivening the large corn fields with chearful light. We had a bad supper, and the next morning they made us an unreasonable charge ; and the servant was uncivil, because, forsooth ! we had no wine.

N.B. The travellers in the morning had spoken highly of this inn.[1]

September 5th, Monday. After drinking a basin of milk we set off again at a little after six o'clock — a fine morning — eight miles to Killin — the river Dochart always on our left. The face of the country not very interesting, though not unpleasing, reminding us of some of the vales of the north of England, though meagre, nipped-up, or shrivelled compared with them. There were rocks, and rocky knolls, as about Grasmere and Wytheburn, and copses, but of a starveling growth ; the cultivated ground poor. Within a mile or two of Killin the land was better cultivated, and, looking down the vale, we had a view of Loch Tay, into which the Dochart falls. Close to the town, the river took up a roaring voice, beating its way over a rocky descent among large black stones — islands in the middle turning the stream this way and that —

---

[1] Suie. — J. C. S. *Quære*, Luib. — W. K.

the whole course of the river very wide. We crossed it by means of three bridges, which make one continued bridge of a great length. On an island below the bridge is a gateway with tall pillars, leading to an old burying-ground belonging to some noble family.[1] It has a singular appearance, and the place is altogether uncommon and romantic — a remnant of ancient grandeur : extreme natural wildness — the sound of roaring water, and withal, the ordinary half-village, half-town bustle of an every-day place.

The inn at Killin is one of the largest on the Scotch road : it stands pleasantly, near the chapel, at some distance from the river Dochart, and out of reach of its tumultuous noise ; and another broad, stately, and silent stream, which you cannot look at without remembering its boisterous neighbour, flows close under the windows of the inn, and beside the churchyard, in which are many graves. That river falls into the lake at the distance of nearly a mile from the mouth of the Dochart. It is bordered with tall trees and corn fields, bearing plentiful crops, the richest we had seen in Scotland.

After breakfast we walked onwards, expecting that the stream would lead us into some considerable vale ; but it soon became little better than a common rivulet, and the glen appeared to be short ; indeed, we wondered how the river had grown so great all at once. Our horse had not been able to eat his corn, and we waited a long time in the hope that he would be better. At eleven o'clock, however, we determined to set off, and give him all the ease possible by walking up the hills, and not pushing beyond a slow walk. We had fourteen miles to travel to Kenmore, by the side of Loch Tay. Crossed the same bridge again, and went down the south side of the lake. We had a delightful view of the village of Killin, among rich green fields, corn and wood, and up towards the two horns of the vale of Tay, the valley of the Dochart, and the other valley with its full-grown river, the prospect terminated by mountains. We travelled through lanes, woods, or open fields, never close to the lake, but always near it, for many miles, the

---

[1] The burial-place of Macnab of Macnab. — J. C. S.

road being carried along the side of a hill, which rose in an almost regularly receding steep from the lake. The opposite shore did not much differ from that down which we went, but it seemed more thinly inhabited, and not so well cultivated. The sun shone, the cottages were pleasant, and the goings-on of the harvest (for all the inhabitants were at work in the corn fields) made the way chearful. But there is an uniformity in the lake which (comparing it with other lakes) made it appear tiresome. It has no windings : I should even imagine, although it is so many miles long, that, from some points not very high on the hills, it may be seen from one end to the other ; there are few bays, no lurking-places where the water hides itself in the land, no outjutting points or promontories, no islands ; and there are no commanding mountains or precipices. I think that this lake would be the most pleasing in spring-time, or in summer before the corn begins to change colour, the long tracts of hills on each side of the vale having at this season a kind of patchy appearance, for the corn fields in general were very small, mere plots, and of every possible shade of bright yellow. When we came in view of the foot of the lake we perceived that it ended, as it had begun, in pride and loveliness. The village of Kenmore, with its neat church and cleanly houses, stands on a gentle eminence at the end of the water. The view, though not near so beautiful as that of Killin, is exceedingly pleasing. Left our car, and turned out of the road at about the distance of a mile from the town, and after having climbed perhaps a quarter of a mile, we were conducted into a locked-up plantation, and guessed by the sound that we were near the cascade, but could not see it. Our guide opened a door, and we entered a dungeon-like passage, and, after walking some yards in total darkness, found ourselves in a quaint apartment stuck over with moss, hung about with stuffed foxes and other wild animals, and ornamented with a library of wooden books covered with old leather backs, the mock furniture of a hermit's cell. At the end of the room, through a large bow-window, we saw the waterfall, and at the same time, looking down to the left, the village of Kenmore and a part of the lake — a very beautiful prospect.

Between Parts II and III of the " Recollections " D. W. has written ·

April 11th, 1805.   I am setting about a task which, how-ever free and happy the state of my mind, I could not have performed well at this distance of time ; but now, I do not know that I shall be able to go on with it at all.   I will strive, however, to do the best I can, setting before myself a different object from that hitherto aimed at, which was, to omit no incident, however trifling, and to describe the country so minutely that you should, where the objects were the most interesting, feel as if you had been with us.   I shall now only attempt to give you an idea of those scenes which pleased us most, dropping the incidents of the ordinary days, of which many have slipped from my memory, and others which remain it would be difficult, and often painful to me, to endeavour to draw out and disentangle from other thoughts.   I the less regret my inability to do more, because, in describing a great part of what we saw from the time we left Kenmore, my work would be little more than a repetition of what I have said before, or, where it was not so, a longer time was necessary to enable us to bear away what was most interesting than we could afford to give.

Part III

September 5th, Monday. We arrived at Kenmore after sunset.
September 6th, Tuesday. Walked before breakfast in Lord
Breadalbane's grounds, which border upon the river Tay. The
higher elevations command fine views of the lake ; and the
walks are led along the river's banks, and shaded with tall
trees : but it seemed to us that a bad taste had been at work,
the banks being regularly shaven and cut as if by rule and
line. One or two of such walks I should well have liked to
see ; but they are all equally trim, and I could not but regret
that the fine trees had not been left to grow out of a turf that
cattle were permitted to feed upon. There was one avenue
which would well have graced the ruins of an abbey, or some
stately castle. It was of a very great length, perfectly straight,
the trees meeting at the top in a cathedral arch, lessening in
perspective ; — the boughs the roofs, the stems the pillars : I
never saw so beautiful an avenue. We were told that some
improver of pleasure-grounds had advised Lord B. to cut down
the trees, and lay the whole open to the lawn, for the avenue
is very near his house. His own better taste, or that of some
other person, I suppose, had saved them from the axe. Many
workmen were employed in building a large mansion, something like that of Inverary, close to the old house, which was
yet standing ; the situation, as we thought, very bad, considering that Lord Breadalbane had the command of all the
ground at the foot of the lake, including hills both high and
low. It is in a hollow, without prospect either of the lake or
river, or anything else, seeing nothing, and adorning nothing.
After breakfast, left Kenmore, and travelled through the vale
of Tay, I believe fifteen or sixteen miles ; but in the course
of this we turned out of our way to the Falls of Moness, a
stream tributary to the Tay, which passes through a narrow
glen with very steep banks. A path like a woodman's track
has been carried through the glen, which, though the private

345

property of a gentleman, has not been taken out of the hands of Nature, but merely rendered accessible by this path, which ends at the waterfalls. They tumble from a great height, and are indeed very beautiful falls, and we could have sate with pleasure the whole morning beside the cool basin in which the waters rest, surrounded by high rocks and overhanging trees. In one of the most retired parts of the dell, we met a young man coming slowly along the path, intent upon a book which he was reading : he did not seem to be of the rank of a gentleman, though above that of a peasant.

Passed through the village of Aberfeldy, at the foot of the glen of Moness. The birks of Aberfeldy are spoken of in some of the Scotch songs, which no doubt grew in the stream of Moness ; but near the *village* we did not see any trees that were remarkable, except a row of laburnums, growing as a common field hedge ; their leaves were of a golden colour, and as lively as the yellow blossoms could have been in the spring. Afterwards we saw many laburnums in the woods, which we were told had been *planted* ; though I remember that Withering [1] speaks of the laburnum as one of the British plants, and growing in Scotland. The twigs and branches being stiff, were not so graceful as those of our garden laburnums, but I do not think I ever before saw any that were of so brilliant colour in their autumnal decay. In our way to and from Moness we crossed the Tay by a bridge of ambitious and ugly architecture. Many of the bridges in Scotland are so, having eye-holes between the arches, not in the battlements but at the outspreading of the pillar of the arch, which destroys its simplicity, and takes from the appearance of strength and security, without adding anything of lightness. We returned, by the same road, to the village of Weem, where we had left our car. The vale of Tay was very wide, having been so from within a short distance of Kenmore : the reaches of the river are long ; and the ground is more regularly cultivated than in

---

[1] William Withering (1741–99), eminent physician and botanist. In 1776 he published his famous book, *A Botanical Arrangement of all the Vegetables naturally growing in Great Britain, according to the System of the celebrated Linnaeus.*

any vale we had yet seen; chiefly corn, and very large tracts. Afterwards the vale becomes narrow and less cultivated, the reaches shorter — on the whole resembling the vale of Nith, but we thought it inferior in beauty.

One among the cottages in this narrow and wilder part of the vale fixed our attention almost as much as a Chinese or a Turk would do passing through the vale of Grasmere. It was a *cottage*, I believe, little differing in size and shape from all the rest ; but it was like a visitor, a stranger come into the Highlands, or a model set up of what may be seen in other countries. The walls were neatly plaistered or rough-cast, the windows of clean bright glass, and the door was painted. Before it was a flower-garden, fenced with a curiously-clipped hedge, and against the wall was placed the sign of a spinning-wheel. We could not pass this humble dwelling, so distinguished by an appearance of comfort and neatness, without some conjectures respecting the character and manner of life of the person inhabiting it : leisure he must have had ; and we pleased ourselves with thinking that some self-taught mind might there have been nourished by knowledge gathered from books, and the simple duties and pleasures of rural life.

At Logierait, the village where we dined, the vale widens again, and the Tummel joins the Tay and loses its name ; but the Tay falls into the channel of the Tummel, continuing its course in the same direction, almost at right angles to the former course of the Tay. We were sorry to find that we had to cross the Tummel by a *ferry*, and resolved not to venture in the same boat with the horse. Dined at a little publick-house, kept by a young widow, very talkative and laboriously civil. She took me out to the back-door, and said she would show me a place which had once been very grand, and, opening a door in a high wall, I entered a ruinous courtyard, in which was a large old mansion, the walls entire and very strong, but the roof broken in. The woman said it had been a palace of one of the kings of Scotland. It was a striking and even an affecting object, coming upon it, as I did, unawares ; a royal residence shut up and hidden, while yet in its strength, by mean cottages ; there was no appearance of violence, but decay

347

from desertion, and I should think that it may remain many years without undergoing further visible change. The woman and her daughter accompanied us to the ferry and crossed the water with us ; the woman said, but with not much appearance of honest heart-feeling, that she could not be easy to let us go without being there to know how we sped ; so I invited the little girl to accompany her, that she might have a ride in the car. The men were cautious, and the horse got over with less alarm than we could have expected. Our way was now up the vale, along the banks of the Tummel, an impetuous river ; the mountains higher than near the Tay, and the vale more wild, and the different reaches more interesting.

When we approached near to Fascally, near the junction of the Garry with the Tummel, the twilight was far advanced, and our horse not being perfectly recovered, we were fearful of taking him on to Blair-Athol, five miles further ; besides, the Pass of Killicrankie was within half a mile, and we were unwilling to go through a place so celebrated in the dark ; therefore, being joined by a traveller, we inquired if there was any publick-house near ; he said there was ; and that though the accommodations were not good, we might do well enough for one night, the host and his wife being very honest people. It proved to be rather better than a common cottage of the country ; we seated ourselves by the fire, Wm. called for a glass of whisky, and asked if they could give us beds. The woman positively refused to lodge us, though we had every reason to believe that she had, at least, one bed for me ; we entreated again and again in behalf of the poor horse, but all in vain ; she urged, though in an uncivil way, that she had been sitting up the whole of one or two nights before on account of a fair, and that now she wanted to go to bed and sleep ; so we were obliged to remount our car in the dark, and with a tired horse we moved on, and went through the Pass of Killi-crankie, hearing only the roaring of the river, and seeing a black chasm with jagged-topped black hills towering above. Afterwards the moon rose, and we should not have had an unpleasant ride if our horse had been in better plight, and we had not been annoyed (as we were almost at every twenty yards) by people coming from a fair held that day near Blair ; no pleasant prognostic of what might be our accommodation at the inn, where we arrived between ten and eleven o'clock, and found the house in an uproar ; but we were civilly treated, and were glad, after eating a morsel of cold beef, to retire to rest, and I fell asleep in spite of the noisy drunkards below stairs, who had outstayed the fair.

September 7th, Wednesday. Rose early, and went before breakfast to the Duke of Athol's gardens and pleasure-grounds, where we completely tired ourselves with a three-hours' walk. Having been directed to see *all* the waterfalls, we submitted ourselves to the gardener, who dragged us from place to place, calling our attention to, it might be, half-a-dozen (I cannot say how many) dripping streams ; very pretty in themselves, if we had had the pleasure of discovering them ; but they were generally robbed of their grace by the obtrusive ornaments which were first seen. The whole neighbourhood, a great country, seems to belong to the Duke of Athol. In his domain are hills and mountains, glens and spacious plains, rivers and innumerable torrents ; but near Blair are no old woods, and the plantations, except those at a little distance from the house, appear inconsiderable, being lost to the eye in so extensive a circuit.

The castle stands on low ground, not far from the Garry, commanding a prospect all round of distant mountains, a bare and cold scene, and, from the irregularity and width of it, not so grand as one should expect, knowing the great height of some of the mountains. Within the Duke's park are three glens, the glen of the river Tilt and two others, which, if they had been planted more judiciously, would have been very sweet retirements ; but they are choked up, the whole hollow of the glens (I do not speak of the Tilt, for that is rich in natural wood) being closely planted with trees, and those chiefly firs ; but many of the old fir-trees are, as single trees, very fine. On each side of the glen is an ell-wide gravel walk, which the gardener told us was swept once a week. It is conducted at the top of the banks, on each side, at nearly equal height, and equal distance from the stream ; they lead you up one of these paths, and down the other (very wearisome, as you will believe) mile after mile ! We went into the garden, where there was plenty of fruit — gooseberries, hanging as thick as possible upon the trees, ready to drop off ; I thought the gardener might have invited us to refresh ourselves with some of his fruit after our long fatigue. One part of the garden was decorated with statues, *images*, as poor Mr. Gill used to call those at Racedown, dressed in gay painted clothes ; and in a retired corner of the grounds, under some tall trees, appeared the figure of a favourite old gamekeeper of one of the former Dukes, in the attitude of pointing his gun at the game — " reported to be a striking likeness ", said the gardener. Looking at some of the tall larches, with long hairy twigs, very beautiful trees, he told us that they were among the first which had ever been planted in Scotland, that a Duke of Athol had brought a single larch from London in a pot, in his coach, from which had sprung the whole family that had overspread Scotland. This, probably, might not be accurate, for others might afterwards have come, or seed from other trees. He told us many anecdotes of the present Duke, which I wish I could perfectly remember. He is an indefatigable sportsman, hunts the wild deer on foot, attended by twelve Highlanders in the Highland dress, which he himself formerly used to wear ; he will go out at four o'clock in the morning, and not return till night. His fine family, " Athol's honest men, and Athol's bonny lasses ", to whom Burns, in his bumpers, drank health and long life, are dwindled away : of nine, I believe only four are left : the mother of them is dead in a consumption, and the Duke married again. We rested upon the hether seat which Burns was so loth to quit that moonlight evening when he first went to Blair Castle, and had a pleasure in thinking that he had been under the same shelter, and viewed the little waterfall opposite with some of the happy and pure feelings of his better mind. The castle has been modernized, which has spoiled its appearance. It is a large irregular pile, not handsome, but I think may have been picturesque, and even noble, before it was docked of its battlements and whitewashed.

The most interesting object we saw at Blair was the chapel, shaded by trees, in which the body of the impetuous Dundee lies buried. This quiet spot is seen from the windows of the inn, whence you look, at the same time, upon a high wall and a part of the town — a contrast which, I know not why, made the chapel and its grove appear more peaceful, as if kept so for some sacred purpose. We had a very nice breakfast, which we sauntered over after our weary walk.

Being come to the most northerly point of our destined course, we took out the map, loth to turn our backs upon the Highlands, and, looking about for something which we might yet see, we fixed our eyes upon two or three spots not far distant, and sent for the landlord to consult with him. One of them was Loch Rannoch, a fresh-water lake, which he told us was bordered by a natural pine forest, that its banks were populous, and that the place being very remote, we might there see much of the simplicity of the Highlander's life. The landlord said that we must take a guide for the first nine or ten miles ; but afterwards the road was plain before us, and very good, so at about ten o'clock we departed, having engaged a man to go with us. The Falls of Bruar, which we wished to visit for the sake of Burns, are about three miles from Blair, and our road was in the same direction for two miles.

After having gone for some time under a bare hill, we were told to leave the car at some cottages, and pass through a little gate near a brook which crossed the road. We walked upwards at least three quarters of a mile in the hot sun, with the stream on our right, both sides of which to a considerable height were planted with firs and larches intermingled — children of poor Burns's song ; for his sake we wished that they had been the natural trees of Scotland, birches, ashes, mountain-ashes, etc. ; however, sixty or seventy years hence they will be no unworthy monument to his memory. At present, nothing can be uglier than the whole chasm of the hillside with its formal walks. I do not mean to condemn them, for, for aught I know, they are as well managed as they could be ; but it is not easy to see the use of a pleasure-path leading to nothing, up a steep and naked hill in the midst of an unlovely tract of country, though by the side of a tumbling stream of clear water. It does not surely deserve the name of a pleasure-path. It is three miles from the Duke of Athol's house, and I do not believe that one person living within five miles of the place would wish to go twice to it. The falls are high, the rocks and stones fretted and gnawed by the water. I do not wonder at the pleasure which Burns received from this stream ; I believe we should have been much pleased if we had come upon it as he did. At the bottom of the hill we took up our car, and, turning back, joined the man who was to be our guide. Crossed the Garry, and went along a moor without any road but straggling cart-tracks. Soon began to ascend a high hill, and the ground grew so rough (road there was none) that we were obliged to walk most of the way — ascended to a considerable height, and commanded an extensive prospect bounded by lofty mountains, and having crossed the top of the fell we parted with our guide, being in sight of the vale into which we were to descend, and to pursue upwards till we should come to Loch Rannoch, a lake, as described to us, bedded in a forest of Scotch pines.

When left to ourselves we sate down on the hillside, and looked with delight into the deep vale below, which was exceedingly green, not regularly fenced or cultivated, but the level area scattered over with bushes and trees, and through that level ground glided a glassy river, not in serpentine windings, but in direct turnings backwards and forwards, and then flowed into the head of the Lake of Tummel ; but I will copy a rough sketch which I made while we sate upon the hill, which, imperfect as it is, will give a better idea of the course of the river (which I must add is more curious than beautiful) than my description. The ground must be often overflowed in winter, for the water seemed to touch the very edge of its banks. At this time the scene was soft and chearful, such as invited us downwards, and made us proud of our adventure. Coming near to a cluster of huts, we turned thither (a few steps out of our way) to inquire about the road ; these huts were on the hill, placed side by side, in a figure between a square and a circle, as if for the sake of mutual shelter, like haystacks in a farmyard — no trees near them. We called at one of the doors, and three hale, stout men came out, who could speak very little English, and stared at us with an almost savage look of wonder. One of them took much pains to set us forward, and went a considerable way down the hill till we came in sight of the cart road, which we were to follow ; but we had not gone far before we were disheartened ; it was with the greatest difficulty Wm. could lead the horse and car over the rough stones, and to sit in it was impossible ; the road grew worse and worse, therefore we resolved to turn back, having no reason to expect anything better, for we had been told that after we should leave the untracked ground all would be fair before us. We knew ourselves where we stood to be about eight miles distant from the point where the river Tummel, after having left the lake, joins the Garry at Fascally near the Pass of Killicrankie, therefore we resolved to make our way thither, and endeavour to procure a lodging at the same publick-house where it had been refused to us the night before. The road was likely to be very bad ; but, knowing the distance, we thought it more prudent than to venture farther with nothing before us but uncertainty. We were forced to unyoke the horse, and turn the car ourselves, owing to the steep banks on either side of the road, and after much trouble we got him in again, and set our faces down the vale towards Loch Tummel, Wm. leading the car and I walking by his side.

For the first two or three miles we looked down upon the lake, our road being along the side of the hill directly above it. On the opposite side another range of hills rose up in the same manner, — farm-houses thinly scattered among the copses near the water, and cultivated ground in patches. The lake does not wind, nor are the shores much varied by bays, — the mountains not commanding ; but the whole a pleasing scene. Our road took us out of sight of the water, and we were obliged to procure a guide across a high moor, where it was impossible that the horse should drag us at all, the ground being exceedingly rough and untracked : of course fatiguing for foot-travellers, and on *foot* we *must travel*. After some time, the river Tummel again served us for a guide, when it had left the lake. It was no longer a gentle stream, a mirror to the sky, but we could hear it roaring at a considerable distance between steep banks of rock and wood. We had to cross the Garry by a bridge, a little above the junction of the two rivers ; and were now not far from the publick-house, to our great joy, for we were very weary with our laborious walk. I do not think that I had walked less than sixteen miles, and Wm. much more, to which add the fatigue of leading the horse, and the rough roads, and you will not wonder that we longed for rest. We stopped at the door of the house, and Wm. entered as before, and again the woman refused to lodge us, in a most inhuman manner, giving no other reason than that she would not do it. We pleaded for the poor horse, entreated, soothed, and flattered, but all in vain, though the night was cloudy and dark. We begged to sit by the fire till morning, and to this she would not consent ; indeed, if it had not been for the sake of the horse, I would rather have lain in a barn than on the best of feather-beds in the house of such a cruel woman.

We were now, after our long day's journey, five miles from the inn at Blair, whither we, at first, thought of returning ; but finally resolved to go to a publick-house which we had seen in a village we passed through, about a mile above the ferry over the Tummel, having come from that point to Blair, for the sake of the Pass of Killicrankie and Blair itself, and had now the same road to measure back again. We were obliged to leave the Pass of Killicrankie unseen ; but this disturbed us little at a time when we had seven miles to travel in the dark, with a poor beast almost sinking with fatigue, for he had not baited once all day. We went on spiritless, and at a dreary pace — passed by one house which we were half inclined to go up to and ask for a night's lodging ; and soon after, being greeted by a gentle voice from a poor woman, whom, till she spoke, though we were close to her, we had not seen, we stopped, and asked if she could tell us where we might stay all night, and put up our horse. She mentioned the publick-house left behind, and we told our tale, and asked her if she had no house to which she could take us. " Yes, to be sure she had a house, but it was only a small cottage " ; and she had no place for the horse, and how we could lodge in *her* house

354

she could not tell ; but we should be welcome to whatever she had, so we turned the car, and she walked by the side of it, talking to us in a tone of human kindness which made us friends at once.

I remember thinking to myself, as I have often done in a stage-coach, though never with half the reason to prejudge favourably, What sort of countenance and figure shall we see in this woman when we come into the light ? And indeed it was an interesting moment when, after we had entered her house, she blew the embers on the hearth, and lighted a candle to assist us in taking the luggage out of the car. Her husband presently arrived, and he and Wm. took the horse to the publick-house. The poor woman hung the kettle over the fire. We had tea and sugar of our own, and she set before us barley cakes, and milk which she had just brought in ; I recollect she said she " had been west to fetch it ". The Highlanders always direct you by east and west, north and south — very confusing to strangers. She told us that it was her business to " keep the gate " for Mr. Butler, who lived at Fascally, just below, — that is, to receive messages, take in letters, etc. Her cottage stood by the side of the road leading to his house, within the gate, having, as we saw in the morning, a dressed-up porter's lodge outside ; but within was nothing but the naked walls, unplaistered, and floors of mud, as in the common huts. She said that they lived rent-free in return for their services ; but spoke of her place and Mr. Butler with little respect, hinting that he was very proud ; and indeed her appearance, and subdued manners, and that soft voice which had prepossessed us so much in her favour, seemed to belong to an injured and oppressed being. We talked a great deal with her, and gathered some interesting facts from her conversation, which I wish I had written down while they were fresh in my memory. They had only one child, yet seemed to be very poor, not discontented but languid, and willing to suffer rather than rouze to any effort. Though it was plain she despised and hated her master, and had no wish to conceal it, she hardly appeared to think it worth while to speak ill of him. We were obliged to sit up very late while our kind hostess was preparing our beds. William lay upon the floor on some hay, without sheets ; my bed was of chaff ; I had plenty of covering, and a pair of very nice strong clean sheets, — she said with some pride that she *had* good linen. I believe the sheets had been of her own spinning, perhaps when she was first married, or before, and she probably will keep them to the end of her life of poverty.

September 8th, Thursday. Before breakfast we walked to the Pass of Killicrankie. A very fine scene ; the river Garry forcing its way down a deep chasm between rocks, at the foot of high rugged hills covered with wood, to a great height. The Pass did not, however, impress us with awe, or a sensation of difficulty or danger, according to our expectations ; but, the road being at a considerable height on the side of the hill, we at first only looked into the dell or chasm. It is much grander seen from below, near the river's bed. Everybody knows that this Pass is famous in military history. When we were travelling in Scotland an invasion was hourly looked for, and one could not but think with some regret of the times when from the now depopulated Highlands forty or fifty thousand men might have been poured down for the defence of the country, under such leaders as the Marquis of Montrose or the brave man who had so distinguished himself upon the ground where we were standing. I will transcribe a sonnet suggested to Wm. by this place.

SONNET

Written October 1803

Six thousand Veterans practised in War's game,
Tried men, at Killicrankie were array'd
Against an equal host that wore the Plaid,
Shepherds and herdsmen. Like a whirlwind came
The Highlanders ; the slaughter spread like flame,
And Garry, thundering down his mountain road,
Was stopp'd, and could not breathe beneath the load
Of the dead bodies. 'Twas a day of shame
For them whom precept and the pedantry
Of cold mechanic battle do enslave.

Oh ! for a single hour of that Dundee
Who on that day the word of onset gave :
Like conquest might the men of England see,
And her Foes find a like inglorious grave.

We turned back again, and going down the hill below the Pass, crossed the same bridge we had come over the night before, and walked through Lady Perth's grounds by the side of the Garry till we came to the Tummel, and then walked up to the cascade of the Tummel. The fall is inconsiderable, scarcely more than an ordinary *wear* ; but it makes a loud roaring over large stones, and the whole scene is grand — hills, mountains, woods, and rocks. Fascally is a very pretty place, all but the house. Stoddart's print gives no notion of it. The house stands upon a small plain at the junction of the two rivers, a close deep spot, surrounded by high hills and woods. After we had breakfasted Wm. fetched the car, and, while we were conveying the luggage to the outside of the gate, where it stood, Mr. Butler, *mal apropos*, came very near to the door, called the woman out, and railed at her in the most abusive manner for *harbouring* people in that way. She soon slipped from him, and came back to us : I wished that Wm. should go and speak to her master, for I was afraid that he might turn the poor woman away ; but she would not suffer it, for she did not care whether they stayed or not. In the meantime, Mr. Butler continued scolding her husband ; indeed, he appeared to be not only proud, but very ignorant, insolent, and low-bred. The woman told us that she had sometimes lodged poor travellers who were passing along the road, and permitted others to cook their victuals in her house, for which Mr. B. had reprimanded her before ; but, as she said, she did not value her place, and it was no matter. In sounding forth the dispraise of Mr. Butler, I ought not to omit mentioning that the poor woman had great delight in talking of the excellent qualities of his mother, with whom she had been a servant, and lived many years. After having interchanged good wishes we parted with our charitable hostess, who, telling us her name, entreated us, if ever we came that way again, to inquire for her.

357

We travelled down the Tummel till it is lost in the Tay, and then, in the same direction, continued our course along the vale of Tay, which is very wide for a considerable way, but gradually narrows, and the river, always a fine stream, assumes more dignity and importance. Two or three miles before we reached Dunkeld, we observed whole hill-sides (the property of the Duke of Athol) planted with fir-trees till they are lost among the rocks near the tops of the hills. In forty or fifty years these plantations will be very fine, being carried from hill to hill, and not bounded by a visible artificial fence.

Reached Dunkeld at about three o'clock. It is a pretty, small town, with a respectable and rather large ruined abbey, which is greatly injured by being made the nest of a modern Scotch kirk, with sash windows, — very incongruous with the noble antique tower, — a practice which we afterwards found is not uncommon in Scotland. Sent for the Duke's gardener after dinner, and walked with him into the pleasure-grounds, intending to go to the Falls of the Bran, a mountain stream which here joins the Tay. After walking some time on a shaven turf under the shade of old trees, by the side of the Tay, we left the pleasure-grounds, and crossing the river by a ferry, went up a lane on the hill opposite till we came to a locked gate by the road-side, through which we entered into another part of the Duke's pleasure-grounds bordering on the Bran, the glen being for a considerable way (for aught I know, two miles) thridded by gravel walks. The walks are quaintly intersected, here and there by a baby garden of fine flowers among the rocks and stones. The waterfall (which we came to see) warned us by a loud roaring that we must expect it ; we were first, however, conducted into a small apartment, where the gardener desired us to look at a painting of the figure of Ossian, which, while he was telling us the story of the young artist who performed the work, disappeared, parting in the middle, flying asunder as if by the touch of magic, and lo ! we are at the entrance of a splendid room, which was almost dizzy and alive with waterfalls, that tumbled in all directions — the great cascade, which was opposite to the window that faced us, being reflected in innumerable mirrors upon the ceiling and against the walls. We both laughed heartily, which, no doubt, the gardener considered as high commendation ; for he was very eloquent in pointing out the beauties of the place.

We left the Bran, and pursued our walk through the plantations, where we readily forgave the Duke his little devices for their sakes. They are already no insignificant woods, where the trees happen to be oaks, birches, and others natural to the soil ; and under their shade the walks are delightful. From one hill, through different openings under the trees, we looked up the vale of Tay to a great distance, a magnificent prospect at that time of the evening ; woody and rich — corn, green fields, and cattle, the winding Tay, and distant mountains. Looked down the river to the town of Dunkeld, which lies low, under irregular hills, covered with wood to their rocky summits, and bounded by higher mountains, which are bare. The hill of Birnam, no longer Birnam *wood*, was pointed out to us. After a very long walk we parted from our guide when it was almost dark, and he promised to call on us in the morning to conduct us to the gardens.

September 9th, Friday. According to appointment, the gardener came with his keys in his hand, and we attended him whithersoever he chose to lead, in spite of past experience at Blair. We had, however, no reason to repent, for we were repaid for the trouble of going through the large gardens by the apples and pears of which he gave us liberally, and the walks through the woods on that part of the grounds opposite to where we had been the night before were very delightful. The Duke's house is neither large nor grand, being just an ordinary gentleman's house, upon a green lawn, and whitewashed, I believe. The old abbey faces the house on the [east] side, and appears to stand upon the same green lawn, which, though close to the town, is entirely excluded from it by high walls and trees.

We had been undetermined respecting our future course when we came to Dunkeld, whether to go on directly to Perth and Edinburgh, or to make a circuit and revisit the Trossachs. We decided upon the latter plan, and accordingly after breakfast set forward towards Crieff, where we intended to sleep, and the next night at Callander. The first part of our road, after having crossed the ferry, was up the glen of the Bran.

Looking backwards, we saw Dunkeld very pretty under the hills, and surrounded by rich cultivated ground, but we had not a good distant view of the abbey.

Left our car, and went about a hundred yards from the road to see the Rumbling Brig, which, though well worth our going out of the way even much further, disappointed us, as places in general do which we hear much spoken of as savage, tremendous, etc., — and no wonder, for they are usually described by people to whom rocks are novelties. The gardener had told us that we should pass through the most populous glen in Scotland, the glen of Amulree. It is not populous in the usual way, with scattered dwellings ; but many clusters of houses, hamlets such as we had passed near the Tummel, which had a singular appearance, being like small encampments, were generally without trees, and in high situations — every house the same as its neighbour, whether for men or cattle. There was nothing else remarkable in the glen. We halted at a lonely inn at the foot of a steep barren moor, which we had to cross ; then, after descending considerably, came to the Narrow Glen, which we had approached with no little curiosity, not having been able to procure any distinct description of it.

At Dunkeld, when we were hesitating what road to take, we wished to know whether that glen would be worth visiting, and accordingly put several questions to the waiter, and, among other epithets used in the course of interrogation, we stumbled upon the word *grand*, to which he replied, " No, I do not think there are any gentlemen's seats in it ". However, we drew enough from this describer and the gardener to determine us finally to go to Callander, the Narrow Glen being in the way.

Entered the glen at a small hamlet at some distance from the head, and turning aside a few steps, ascended a hillock which commanded a view to the top of it — a very sweet scene, a green valley, not very narrow, with a few scattered trees and huts, almost invisible in a misty gleam of afternoon light. At this hamlet we crossed a bridge, and the road led us down the glen, which had become exceedingly narrow, and so continued to the end : the hills on both sides heathy and rocky, very steep, but continuous ; the rocks not single or overhanging,

not scooped into caverns or sounding with torrents : there are
no trees, no houses, no traces of cultivation, not one out-
standing object. It is truly a solitude, the road even making
it appear still more so : the bottom of the valley is mostly
smooth and level, the brook not noisy : everything is simple
and undisturbed, and while we passed through it the whole
place was shady, cool, clear, and solemn. At the end of the
long valley we ascended a hill to a great height, and reached the
top, when the sun, on the point of setting, shed a soft yellow
light upon every eminence. The prospect was very extensive ;
over hollows and plains, no towns, and few houses visible ;— a
prospect, extensive as it was, in harmony with the secluded
dell, and fixing its own peculiar character of removedness from
the world, and the secure possession of the quiet of nature more
deeply in our minds. The following poem was written by
William on hearing of a tradition relating to it, which we did
not know when we were there :—

> In this still place remote from men
> Sleeps Ossian, in the Narrow Glen,
> In this still place where murmurs on
> But one meek streamlet, only one.
> He sung of battles and the breath
> Of stormy war, and violent death,
> And should, methinks, when all was pass'd,
> Have rightfully been laid at last
> Where rocks were rudely heap'd, and rent
> As by a spirit turbulent ;
> Where sights were rough, and sounds were wild,
> And everything unreconciled,
> In some complaining, dim retreat
> Where fear and melancholy meet ;
> But this is calm ; there cannot be
> A more entire tranquillity.
>
> Does then the bard sleep here indeed ?
> Or is it but a groundless creed ?
> What matters it ? I blame them not
> Whose fancy in this lonely spot

Was moved, and in this way express'd
Their notion of its perfect rest.
A convent, even a hermit's cell
Would break the silence of this Dell ;
It is not quiet, is not ease,
But something deeper far than these ;
The separation that is here
Is of the grave ; and of austere
And happy feelings of the dead :
And therefore was it rightly said
That Ossian, last of all his race,
Lies buried in this lonely place.

Having descended into a broad cultivated vale, we saw nothing remarkable. Observed a gentleman's house,[1] which stood pleasantly among trees. It was dark some time before we reached Crieff, a small town, though larger than Dunkeld.

September 10*th, Saturday.* Rose early, and departed without breakfast. We were to pass through one of the most celebrated vales of Scotland, Strath Erne. We found it a wide, long, and irregular vale, with many gentlemen's seats under the hills, woods, copses, frequent cottages, plantations, and much cultivation, yet with an intermixture of barren ground ; indeed, except at Killin and Dunkeld, there was always something which seemed to take from the composure and simplicity of the cultivated scenes. There is a struggle to overcome the natural barrenness, and the end not attained, an appearance of something doing or imperfectly done, a passing with labour from one state of society into another. When you look from an eminence on the fields of Grasmere Vale, the heart is satisfied with a simple undisturbed pleasure, and, no less, on one of the green or heathy dells of Scotland, where there is no appearance of change to be, or having been, but such as the seasons make. Strath Erne is so extensive a vale that, had it been in England, there must have been much inequality, as in Wensley Dale ; but at Wensley there is a unity, a softness, a melting together, which in the large vales of Scotland I never perceived. The

---

[1] Monzie probably. — J. C. S.

difference at Strath Erne may come partly from the irregularity, the undefined outline, of the hills which enclose it ; but it is caused still more by the broken surface, I mean broken as to colour and produce, the want of hedgerows, and also the great number of new fir plantations. After some miles it becomes much narrower as we approach nearer the mountains at the foot of the lake of the same name, Loch Erne.

Breakfasted at a small publick-house, a wretchedly dirty cottage, but the people were civil, and though we had nothing but barley cakes we made a good breakfast, for there were plenty of eggs. Walked up a high hill to view the seat of Mr. Dundas, now Lord Melville — a spot where, if he have gathered much wisdom from his late disgrace [1] or his long intercourse with the world, he may spend his days as quietly as he need desire. It is a secluded valley, not rich, but with plenty of wood : there are many pretty paths through the woods, and moss huts in different parts. After leaving the cottage where we breakfasted the country was very pleasing, yet still with a want of richness ; but this was less perceived, being huddled up in charcoal woods, and the vale narrow. Loch Erne opens out in a very pleasing manner, seen from a hill along which the road is carried through a wood of low trees ; but it does not improve afterwards, lying directly from east to west without any perceivable bendings : and the shores are not much broken or varied, not populous, and the mountains not sufficiently commanding to make up for the deficiencies. Dined at the head of the lake. I scarcely know its length, but should think not less than four or five miles, and it is wide in proportion. The inn is in a small village — a decent house.

Walked about half a mile along the road to Tyndrum, which is through a bare glen,[2] and over a mountain pass. It rained when we pursued our journey again, and continued to rain for several hours. The road which we were to take was up another glen, down which came a stream that fell into the lake

---

[1] Henry Dundas (1742–1811), first Viscount Melville, impeached before the House of Commons in April, 1805 (the month in which D. W. wrote this part of her narrative) for misappropriation of large sums of money when holding office as Treasurer of the Navy.   [2] Glen Ogle. — J. C. S.

on the opposite side at the head of it, so, after having crossed the main vale, a little above the lake, we entered into the smaller glen. The road delightfully smooth and dry — one gentleman's house very pleasant among large coppice woods. After going perhaps three miles up this valley, we turned to the left into another, which seemed to be much more beautiful. It was a level valley, not (like that which we had passed) a wide sloping cleft between the hills, but having a quiet, slow-paced stream, which flowed through level green grounds tufted with trees intermingled with cottages ; the tops of the hills were hidden by mists, and the objects in the valley seen through misty rain, which made them look exceedingly soft, and indeed partly concealed them, and we always fill up what we are left to guess at with something as beautiful as what we see. This valley seemed to have less of the appearance of barrenness or imperfect cultivation than any of the same character we had passed through ; indeed, we could not discern any traces of it. It is called Strath Eyer. *Strath* is generally applied to a broad vale ; but this, though open, is not broad.

We next came to a lake, called Loch Lubnaig, a name which signifies " winding ". In shape it somewhat resembles Ulswater, but is much narrower and shorter, being only four miles in length. The character of this lake is simple and grand. On the side opposite to where we were is a range of steep craggy mountains, one of which (like Place Fell), encroaching upon the bed of the lake, forces it to make a considerable bending. I have forgotten the name of this precipice : it is a very remarkable one, being almost perpendicular, and very rugged. We, on the other side, travelled under steep and rocky hills which were often covered with low woods to a considerable height ; there were one or two farm-houses, and a few cottages. A neat white dwelling [1] on the side of the hill over against the bold steep of which I have spoken, had been the residence of the famous traveller Bruce, who, all his travels ended, had arranged the history of them in that solitude (as deep as any Abyssinian one) among the mountains of his native country, where he

---

[1] Ardhullary. — J. C. S.

passed several years. Whether he died there or not we did not learn ; but the manner of his death was remarkable and affecting, — from a fall down-stairs in his own house, after so many dangers through which fortitude and courage had never failed to sustain him. The house stands sweetly, surrounded by coppice-woods and green fields. On the other side, I believe, were no houses till we came near to the outlet, where a few low huts looked very beautiful, with their dark brown roofs, near a stream which hurried down the mountain, and after its turbulent course travelled a short way over a level green, and was lost in the lake. Within a few miles of Callander we come into a grand region ; the mountains to a considerable height were covered with wood, enclosing us in a narrow passage ; the stream on our right, generally concealed by wood, made a loud roaring ; at one place, in particular, it fell down the rocks in a succession of cascades. The scene is much celebrated in Scotland, and is called the Pass of Leny. It was nearly dark when we reached Callander. We were wet and cold, and glad of a good fire. The inn was comfortable ; we drank tea ; and after tea the waiter presented us with a pamphlet descriptive of the neighbourhood of Callander, which we brought away with us, and I am very sorry I lost it.

September 11th, Sunday. Immediately after breakfast, the morning being fine, we set off with chearful spirits towards the Trossachs, intending to take up our lodging at the house of our old friend the ferryman. A boy accompanied us to convey the horse and car back to Callander from the head of Loch Achray. The country near Callander is very pleasing ; but, as almost everywhere else, imperfectly cultivated. We went up a broad vale, through which runs the stream from Loch Ketterine, and came to Loch Vennachar, a larger lake than Loch Achray, the small one which had given us such unexpected delight when we left the Pass of the Trossachs. Loch Vennachar is much larger, but greatly inferior in beauty to the image which we had conceived of its neighbour, and so the reality proved to us when we came up to that little lake, and saw it before us in its true shape in the chearful sunshine. The Trossachs, overtopped by Benledi and other high mountains, enclose the lake at the head ; and those houses which we had seen before, with their corn fields sloping towards the water, stood very prettily under low woods. The fields did not appear so rich as when we had seen them through the veil of mist ; but yet, as in framing our expectations we had allowed for a much greater difference, so we were even a second time surprized with pleasure at the same spot.

Went as far as these houses of which I have spoken, in the car, and then walked on, intending to pursue the road up the side of Loch Ketterine along which Coleridge had come ; but we had resolved to spend some hours in the neighbourhood of the Trossachs, and accordingly coasted the head of Loch Achray, and pursued the brook between the two lakes as far as there was any track. Here we found, to our surprize, for we had expected nothing but heath and rocks like the rest of the neighbourhood of the Trossachs, a secluded farm, a plot of verdant ground with a single cottage and its company of out-houses. We turned back, and went to the very point from which we had first looked upon Loch Achray when we were here with Coleridge. It was no longer a visionary scene : the sun shone into every crevice of the hills, and the mountain-tops were clear. After some time we went into the pass from the Trossachs, and were delighted to behold the forms of objects fully revealed, and even surpassing in loveliness and variety what we had conceived. The mountains, I think, appeared not so high ; but on the whole we had not the smallest disappointment ; the hether was fading, though still beautiful.

Sate for half-an-hour in Lady Perth's shed, and scrambled over the rocks and through the thickets at the head of the lake. I went till I could make my way no further, and left Wm. to go to the top of the hill, whence he had a distinct view, as on a map, of the intricacies of the lake and the course of the river. Returned to the huts, and, after having taken a second dinner of the food we had brought from Callander, set our faces towards the head of Loch Ketterine. I can add nothing to my former description of the Trossachs, except that we departed with our old delightful remembrances endeared, and many new ones. The path or road (for it was neither the one nor the other, but something between both) is the pleasantest I have ever travelled in my life for the same length of way ; now with marks of sledges or wheels, or none at all, bare or green, as it might happen ; now a little descent, now a level ; sometimes a shady lane, at others an open track through green pastures ; — then again it would lead us into thick coppice-woods, which often entirely shut out the lake, and again admitted it by glimpses. We have never had a more delightful walk than this evening. Ben Lomond and the three pointed-topped mountains of Loch Lomond, which we had seen from the Garrison, were very majestic under the clear sky, the lake perfectly calm, the air sweet and mild. I felt that it was much more interesting to visit a place where we have been before than it can possibly be the first time, except under peculiar circumstances. The sun had been set for some time, when, being within a quarter of a mile of the ferryman's hut, our path having led us close to the shore of the calm lake, we met two neatly dressed women, without hats, who had probably been taking their Sunday evening's walk. One of them said to us in a friendly, soft tone of voice, " What ! you are stepping westward ? " I cannot describe how affecting this simple expression was in that remote place, with the western sky in front, *yet* glowing with the departed sun. Wm. wrote the following poem long after, in remembrance of his feelings and mine :—

> " *What ! you are stepping westward ?* " *Yea,*
> *'Twould be a wildish destiny*
> *If we, who thus together roam*
> *In a strange land, and far from home,*
> *Were in this place the guests of chance :*
> *Yet who would stop, or fear to advance*
> *Though home or shelter he had none,*
> *With such a sky to lead him on ?*
>
> *The dewy ground was dark and cold,*
> *Behind all gloomy to behold,*
> *And stepping westward seem'd to be*
> *A kind of heavenly destiny ;*

I liked the greeting, 'twas a sound
Of something without place or bound ;
And seem'd to give me spiritual right
To travel through that region bright.

The voice was soft ; and she who spake
Was walking by her native Lake ;
The salutation was to me
The very sound of courtesy ;
Its power was felt, and while my eye
Was fix'd upon the glowing sky,
The echo of the voice enwrought
A human sweetness with the thought
Of travelling through the world that lay
Before me in my endless way.

We went up to the door of our boatman's hut as to a home, and scarcely less confident of a cordial welcome than if we had been approaching our own cottage at Grasmere. It had been a very pleasing thought, while we were walking by the side of the beautiful lake, that (few hours as we had been there) there was a home for us in one of its quiet dwellings. Accordingly, so we found it ; the good woman, who had been at a preaching by the lake-side, was in her holiday dress at the door, and seemed to be rejoiced at the sight of us. She led us into the hut, in haste to supply our wants ; we took once more a refreshing meal by her fireside, and, though not so merry as the last time, we were not less happy, bating our regrets that Coleridge was not in his old place. I slept in the same bed as before, and listened to the household stream, which now only made a very low murmuring.

September 12th, Monday. Rejoiced in the morning to see the sun shining upon the hills when I first looked out through the open window-place at my bed's head. We rose early, and after breakfast, our old companion (who was to be our guide for the day) rowed us over the water to the same point where Coleridge and I had sate down and eaten our dinner, while Wm. had gone to survey the unknown coast. We intended to cross Loch Lomond, follow the lake to Glenfalloch, above the head of it, and then come over the mountains to Glengyle, and so down the glen, and passing Mr. Macfarlane's house, back again to the ferry-house, where we should sleep. So, a third time we went through the mountain hollow, now familiar ground. The inhabitants had not yet got in all their hay, and were at work in the fields ; our guide often stopped to talk with them, and no doubt was called upon to answer many inquiries respecting us two strangers.

At the ferry-house of Inversneyde we had not the happy sight of the Highland girl and her companion, but the good woman received us cordially, gave me milk, and talked of Coleridge, who, the morning after we parted from him, had been at her house to fetch his watch, which he had forgotten two days before. He has since told me that he questioned her respecting the miserable condition of her hut, which, as you may remember, admitted the rain at the door, and retained it in the hollows of the mud floor : he told her how easy it would be to remove these inconveniences, and to contrive something, at least, to prevent the wind from entering at the window-places, if not a glass window for light and warmth by day. She replied that this was very true, but if they made any improvements the Laird would conclude that they were growing rich, and would raise their rent.

The ferryman happened to be just ready at the moment to go over the lake with a poor man, his wife and child ; the little girl, about three years old, cried all the way, terrified by the water. When we parted from this family, they going down the lake, and we up it, I could not but think of the difference in our condition to that poor woman, who, with her husband, had been driven from her home by want of work, and was now going a long journey to seek it elsewhere : every step was painful toil, for she had either her child to bear or a heavy burthen. *I* walked as she did, but pleasure was my object, and if toil came along with it, even *that* was pleasure, — pleasure, at least, it would be in the remembrance.

We were, I believe, nine miles from Glenfalloch when we left the boat. To us, with minds at ease, the walk was delightful ; it could not be otherwise, for we passed by a continual

369

succession of rocks, woods, and mountains ; but the houses were few, and the ground cultivated only in small portions near the water, consequently there was not that sort of variety which leaves distinct separate remembrances, but one impression of solitude and greatness. While the Highlander and I were plodding on together side by side, interspersing long silences with now and then a question or a remark, looking down to the lake he espied two small rocky islands, and pointing to them, said to me, " It will be *gay* [1] *and dangerous* sailing there in stormy weather when the water is high ". In giving my assent I could not help smiling, but I afterwards found that a like combination of words is not uncommon in Scotland, for, at Edinburgh, Wm. being afraid of rain, asked the ostler what he thought, who, looking up to the sky, pronounced it to be "*gay and dull* ", and therefore rain might be expected. The most remarkable object we saw was a huge single stone, I believe three or four times the size of Bowder Stone. The top of it, which on one side was sloping like the roof of a house, was covered with hether. Wm. climbed up the rock, which would have been no easy task but to a mountaineer, and we constructed a rope of pocket-handkerchiefs, garters, plaids, coats, etc., and measured its height. It was *so* many times the length of Wm.'s walking-stick, but, unfortunately, having lost the stick, we have lost the measure. The ferryman told us that a preaching was held there once in three months by a certain minister (I think of Arrochar) who engages, as a part of his office, to perform the service. The interesting feelings we had connected with the Highland Sabbath and Highland worship returned here with double force. The rock, though on one side a high perpendicular wall, in no place overhung so as to form a shelter, in no place could it be more than a screen from the elements. Why then had it been selected for such a purpose ? Was it merely from being a central situation and a conspicuous object ? Or did there belong to it some inheritance of superstition from old times ? It is impossible to look at the stone without asking, How came it hither ? Had then that

---

[1] *i.e. gey and*, Scottish for colloquial English *pretty, fairly.*

obscurity and unaccountableness, that mystery of power which is about it, any influence over the first persons who resorted hither for worship ? Or have they now on those who continue to frequent it ? The lake is in front of the perpendicular wall, and behind, at some distance, and totally detached from it, is the continuation of the ridge of mountains which forms the vale of Loch Lomond — a magnificent temple, of which this spot is a noble Sanctum Sanctorum.

We arrived at Glenfalloch at about one or two o'clock. It is no village ; there being only scattered huts in the glen, which may be four miles long, according to my remembrance : the middle of it is very green, and level, and tufted with trees. Higher up, where the glen parts into two very narrow ones, is the house of the Laird ; I daresay a pretty place. The view from the door of the publick-house is exceedingly beautiful ; the river flows smoothly into the lake, and the fields were at that time as green as possible. Looking backward, Ben Lomond very majestically shuts in the view. The top of the mountain, as seen here, being of a pyramidal form, it is much grander than with the broken outline, and stage above stage, as seen from the neighbourhood of Luss. We found nobody at home at the inn, but the ferryman shouted, wishing to have a glass of whisky, and a young woman came from the hay-field, dressed in a white bed-gown, without hat or cap. There was no whisky in the house, so he begged a little whey to drink with the fragments of our cold meat brought from Callander. After a short rest in a cool parlour we set forward again, having to cross the river and climb up a steep mountain on the opposite side of the valley. I observed that the people were busy bringing in the hay before it was dry into a sort of *fauld* or yard, where they intended to leave it, ready to be gathered into the house with the first threatening of rain, and if not completely dry brought out again. Our guide bore me in his arms over the stream, and we soon came to the foot of the mountain. The most easy rising, for a short way at first, was near a naked rivulet which made a fine cascade in one place. Afterwards, the ascent was very laborious, being frequently almost perpendicular.

It is one of those moments which I shall not easily forget, when at that point from which a step or two would have carried us out of sight of the green fields of Glenfalloch, being at a great height on the mountain, we sate down, and heard, as if from the heart of the earth, the sound of torrents ascending out of the long hollow glen. To the eye all was motionless, a perfect stillness. The noise of waters did not appear to come this way or that, from any particular quarter : it was every-where, almost, one might say, as if *exhaled* through the whole surface of the green earth. Glenfalloch, Coleridge has since told me, signifies the Hidden Vale ; but Wm. says, if we were to name it from our recollections of that time, we should call it the Vale of Awful Sound. We continued to climb higher and higher ; but the hill was no longer steep, and afterwards we pursued our way along the top of it with many small ups and downs. The walk was very laborious after the climbing was over, being often exceedingly stony, or through swampy moss, rushes, or rough hether. As we proceeded, continuing our way at the top of the mountain, encircled by higher mountains at a great distance, we were passing, without notice, a heap of scattered stones round which was a belt of green grass — green, and as it seemed rich, where all else was either poor hether and coarse grass, or unprofitable rushes and spongy moss. The Highlander made a pause, saying, " This place is much changed since I was here twenty years ago ". He told us that the heap of stones had been a hut where a family was then living, who had their winter habitation in the valley, and brought their goats thither in the summer to feed on the mountains, and that they were used to gather them together at night and morning to be milked close to the door, which was the reason why the grass was yet so green near the stones. It was affecting in that solitude to meet with this memorial of manners passed away ; we looked about for some other traces of humanity, but nothing else could we find in that place. We ourselves afterwards espied another of those ruins, much more extensive, the remains, as the man told us, of several dwellings. We were astonished at the sagacity with which our Highlander dis-covered the track where often no track was visible *to us*, and scarcely even when he pointed it out. It reminded us of what we read of the Hottentots and other savages ; he went on as confidently as if it had been a turnpike road — the more sur-prizing, as when he was there before it must have been a plain track, for he told us that fishermen from Arrochar carried herrings regularly over the mountains by that way to Loch Ketterine when the glens were much more populous than now.

Descended into Glengyle, above Loch Ketterine, and passed through Mr. Macfarlane's grounds, that is, through the whole of the glen, where there was now no house left but his. We stopped at his door to inquire after the family, though with little hope of finding them at home, having seen a large company at work in a hay field, whom we conjectured to be his whole household — as it proved, except a servant-maid, who answered our inquiries. We had sent the ferryman forward from the head of the glen to bring the boat round from the place where he left it to the other side of the lake. Passed the same farm-house we had such good reason to remember, and went up to the burying-ground that stood so sweetly near the water-side. The ferryman had told us that Rob Roy's grave was there, so we could not pass on without going up to the spot. There were several tomb-stones, but the inscriptions were either worn-out or unintelligible to us, and the place choked up with nettles and brambles. You will remember the description I have given of the spot. I have nothing here to add, except the following poem which it suggested to Wm. :—

> *A famous Man is Robin Hood,*
> *The English Ballad-singer's joy,*
> *And Scotland boasts of one as good,*
>   *She has her own Rob Roy !*
>
> *Then clear the weeds from off his grave,*
> *And let us chaunt a passing stave*
>   *In honour of that Outlaw brave.*
>
> *Heaven gave Rob Roy a daring heart*
> *And wondrous length and strength of arm,*
> *Nor craved he more to quell his foes,*
>   *Or keep his friends from harm.*

Yet Robin was as wise as brave,
As wise in thought as bold in deed,
For in the principles of things
    He sought his moral creed.

Said generous Rob, " What need of books ?
Burn all the statutes and their shelves :
They stir us up against our kind,
    And worse, against ourselves.

" We have a passion ; make a law,
Too false to guide us or control :
And for the law itself we fight
    In bitterness of soul.

" And puzzled, blinded thus, we lose
Distinctions that are plain and few :
These find I graven on my heart :
    That tells me what to do.

" The Creatures see of flood and field,
And those that travel on the wind !
With them no strife can last ; they live
    In peace, and peace of mind.

" For why ?   Because the good old rule
Suffices them, the simple plan
That they should take who have the power,
    And they should keep who can.

" A lesson which is quickly learn'd,
A signal this which all can see !
Thus nothing here provokes the strong
    To tyrannous cruelty.

" And freakishness of mind is check'd ;
He tamed who foolishly aspires,
While to the measure of their might
    All fashion their desires.

" *All kinds and creatures stand and fall*
By strength of prowess or of wit,
'Tis God's appointment who must sway,
    And who is to submit.

" *Since then," said Robin, " right is plain,*
And longest life is but a day ;
To have my ends, maintain my rights,
    I'll take the shortest way."

And thus among these rocks he lived
Through summer's heat and winter's snow ;
The Eagle, he was lord above,
    And Rob was lord below.

So was it — would at least have been
But through untowardness of fate ;
For polity was then too strong :
    He came an age too late.

Or shall we say an age too soon ?
For were the bold man living now,
How might he flourish in his pride
    With buds on every bough ?

Then Rents and Land-marks, Rights of chace,
Sheriffs and Factors, Lairds and Thanes,
Would all have seem'd but paltry things
    Not worth a moment's pains.

Rob Roy had never linger'd here,
To these few meagre vales confined,
But thought how wide the world, the times
    How fairly to his mind.

And to his Sword he would have said,
" *Do thou my sovereign will enact*
From land to land through half the earth ;
    Judge thou of law and fact.

" 'Tis fit that we should do our part :
Becoming that mankind should learn
That we are not to be surpass'd
    In fatherly concern.

" Of old things all are over old,
Of good things none are good enough ;
I'll shew that I can help to frame
    A world of other stuff.

" I, too, will have my Kings that take
From me the sign of life and death,
Kingdoms shall shift about like clouds
    Obedient to my breath."

And if the word had been fulfill'd
As might have been, then, thought of joy !
France would have had her present Boast,
    And we our brave Rob Roy.

Oh ! say not so, compare them not ;
I would not wrong thee, Champion brave !
Would wrong thee nowhere ; least of all
    Here, standing by thy Grave.

For thou, although with some wild thoughts,
Wild Chieftain of a savage Clan,
Hadst this to boast of — thou didst love
    The Liberty of Man.

And had it been thy lot to live
With us who now behold the light,
Thou wouldst have nobly stirr'd thyself,
    And battled for the right.

For Robin was the poor man's stay ;
The poor man's heart, the poor man's hand,
And all the oppress'd who wanted strength
    Had Robin's to command.

Bear witness many a pensive sigh
Of thoughtful Herdsman when he strays
Alone upon Loch Veol's heights,
*   And by Loch Lomond's Braes.*

And far and near, through vale and hill,
Are faces that attest the same ;
Kindling with instantaneous joy
*   At sound of Rob Roy's name.*

Soon after we saw our boat coming over the calm water. It was late in the evening, and I was stiff and weary, as well I might, after such a long and toilsome walk, so it was no poor gratification to sit down and be conscious of advancing in our journey without further labour. The stars were beginning to appear, but the brightness of the west was not yet gone ; — the lake perfectly still, and when we first went into the boat we rowed almost close to the shore under steep crags hung with birches : it was like a new-discovered country of which we had not dreamed, for in walking down the lake, owing to the road in that part being carried at a considerable height on the hill-side, the rocks and the indentings of the shore had been hidden from us. At this time, those rocks and their images in the calm water composed one mass, the surfaces of both equally distinct, except where the water trembled with the motion of our boat. Having rowed a while under the bold steeps, we launched out further when the shores were no longer abrupt. We hardly spoke to each other as we moved along receding from the west, which diffused a solemn animation over the lake. The sky was cloudless : and everything seemed at rest except our solitary boat, and the mountain-streams, — seldom heard, and but faintly. I think I have rarely experienced a more elevated pleasure than during our short voyage of this night. The good woman had long been looking out for us, and had prepared everything for our refreshment ; and as soon as we had finished supper, or rather tea, we went to bed. Wm., I doubt not, rested well, and, for my part, I slept as soundly on my chaff bed as ever I have done in childhood after the long

377

day's playing of a summer's holiday.

September 13th, Tuesday. Again a fine morning. I strolled into the green field in which the house stands while the woman was preparing breakfast, and at my return found one of her neighbours sitting by the fire, a feeble paralytic old woman. After having inquired concerning our journey the day before, she said, " I have travelled far in my time ", and told me she had married an English soldier who had been stationed at the Garrison ; they had had many children, who were all dead or in foreign countries ; and she had returned to her native place, where now she had lived several years, and was more comfortable than she could ever have expected to be, being very kindly dealt with by all her neighbours. Pointing to the ferryman and his wife, she said they were accustomed to give her a day of their labour in digging peats, in common with others, and in that manner she was provided with fuel, and, by like voluntary contributions, with other necessaries. While this infirm old woman was relating her story in a tremulous voice, I could not but think of the changes of things, and the days of her youth, when the shrill fife, sounding from the walls of the Garrison, made a merry noise through the echoing hills. I asked myself, if she were to be carried again to the deserted spot after her course of life, no doubt a troublesome one, would the silence appear to her the silence of desolation or of peace ?

After breakfast we took a final leave of our hostess, and, attended by her husband, again set forward on foot. My limbs were a little stiff, but the morning being uncommonly fine I did not fear to aim at the accomplishment of a plan we had laid of returning to Callander by a considerable circuit. We were to go over the mountains from Loch Ketterine, a little below the ferry-house on the same side of the water, descending to Loch Voil, a lake from which issues the stream that flows through Strath Eyer into Loch Lubnaig. Our road, as is generally the case in passing from one vale into another, was through a settling between the hills, not far from a small stream. We had to climb considerably, the mountain being much higher than it appears to be, owing to its retreating in what looks like a gradual slope from the lake, though we found it steep enough in the climbing. Our guide had been born near Loch Voil, and he told us that at the head of the lake, if we would look about for it, we should see the burying-place of a part of his family, the MacGregors, a clan who had long possessed that district, a circumstance which he related with no unworthy pride of ancestry. We shook hands with him at parting, not without a hope of again entering his hut in company with others whom we loved.

Continued to walk for some time along the top of the hill, having the high mountains of Loch Voil before us, and Ben Lomond and the steeps of Loch Ketterine behind. Came to several deserted mountain huts or shiels, and rested for some time beside one of them, upon a hillock of its green plot of monumental herbage. Wm. here threw off a stanza for the beginning of an ode upon the affecting subject of those relics of human society found in that grand and solitary region. The spot of ground where we sate was even beautiful, the grass being uncommonly verdant, and of a remarkably soft and silky texture. After this we rested no more till we came to the foot of the mountain, where there was a cottage, at the door of which a woman invited me to drink some whey : this I did, while Wm. went to inquire respecting the road at a new stone house a few steps further. He was told to cross the brook, and proceed to the other side of the vale, and that no further directions were necessary, for we should find ourselves at the head of the lake, and on a plain road which would lead us downward. We waded the river and crossed the vale — perhaps half a mile or more. The mountains all round are very high ; the vale pastoral and unenclosed, not many dwellings, and but few trees ; the mountains in general smooth near the bottom. They are in large unbroken masses, combining with the vale to give an impression of bold simplicity. Near the head of the lake, at some distance from us, we discovered the burial-place of the MacGregors, and did not view it without some interest, with its ornamental balls on the four corners of the wall, which, I dare say, have been often looked at with elevation of heart by our honest friend of Loch Ketterine. The lake is

379

divided right across by a narrow slip of flat land, making a
small lake at the head of the large one. The whole may be
about five miles long.

As we descended, the scene became more fertile, our way
being pleasantly varied ; through coppices or open fields, and
passing farm-houses, though always with an intermixture of
uncultivated ground. It was harvest-time, and the fields were
quietly (might I be allowed to say pensively ?) enlivened by
small companies of reapers. It is not uncommon in the more
lonely parts of the Highlands to see a *single* person so employed. The following poem was suggested to Wm. by a
beautiful sentence in Thomas Wilkinson's *Tour in Scotland* : —

> *Behold her single in the field,*
> *Yon solitary Highland Lass,*
> *Reaping and singing by herself —*
> *Stop here, or gently pass.*
> *Alone she cuts and binds the grain,*
> *And sings a melancholy strain.*
> *Oh ! listen, for the Vale profound*
> *Is overflowing with the sound.*
>
> *No nightingale did ever chaunt*
> *So sweetly to reposing bands*
> *Of travellers in some shady haunt*
> *Among Arabian Sands ;*
> *No sweeter voice was ever heard*
> *In spring-time from the cuckoo-bird*
> *Breaking the silence of the seas*
> *Among the farthest Hebrides.*
>
> *Will no one tell me what she sings ?*
> *Perhaps the plaintive numbers flow*
> *For old unhappy far-off things,*
> *And battles long ago ; —*
> *Or is it some more humble lay —*
> *Familiar matter of to-day —*
> *Some natural sorrow, loss or pain*
> *That has been, and may be again ?*

Whate'er the theme, the Maiden sung
As if her song could have no ending ;
I saw her singing at her work,
And o'er the sickle bending ;
I listen'd till I had my fill,
And as I mounted up the hill
The music in my heart I bore
Long after it was heard no more.

Towards the foot of the lake, on the opposite side (which was more barren than that on which we travelled), was a bare road up a steep hill, which leads to Glen Finlas, formerly a royal forest. It is a wild and rocky glen, as we had been told by a person who directed our notice to its outlet at Loch Achray. The stream which passes through it falls into that lake near the head. At the end of Loch Voil the vale is wide and populous — large pastures with many cattle, tracts of corn. We walked downwards a little way, and then crossed over to the same road along which we had travelled from Loch Erne to Callander, being once again at the entrance of Strath Eyer. It might be about four or five o'clock in the afternoon ; we were ten miles from Callander, exceedingly tired, and wished heartily for the poor horse and car. Walked up Strath Eyer, and saw in clear air and sunshine what had been concealed from us when we travelled before in the mist and rain. We found it less woody and rich than it had appeared to be, but, with all deductions, a very sweet valley.

Not far from Loch Lubnaig, though not in view of it, is a long village, with two or three publick-houses, and being in despair of reaching Callander that night without over-fatigue we resolved to stop at the most respectable-looking house, and, should it not prove wretched indeed, to lodge there if there were beds for us : at any rate it was necessary to take some refreshment. The woman of the house spoke with gentleness and civility, and had a good countenance, which reconciled me to stay (though I had been averse to the scheme, dreading the dirt usual in Scotch publick-houses by the way-side). She said she had beds for us, and clean sheets, and we desired her to prepare them immediately. It was a two-storied house, light built, though in other respects no better than the huts, and (as all the slated cottages are) much more uncomfortable in appearance, except that there was a chimney in the kitchen. At such places it is fit that travellers should make up their minds to wait at least an hour longer than the time necessary to prepare whatever meal they may have ordered, which we, I may truly say, did with most temperate philosophy. I went to talk with the mistress, who was baking barley cakes, which she wrought out with her hands as thin as the oaten bread we make in Cumberland. I asked her why she did not use a rolling-pin, and if it would not be much more convenient, to which she returned me no distinct answer, and seemed to give little attention to the question : she did not know, or that was what they were used to, or something of the sort. It was a tedious process, and I thought could scarcely have been managed if the cakes had been as large as ours ; but they are considerably smaller, which is a great loss of time in the baking.[1]

This woman, whose common language was the Gaelic, talked with me a very good English, asking many questions, yet without the least appearance of an obtrusive or impertinent curiosity ; and indeed I must say that I never, in those women with whom I conversed, observed anything on which I could put such a construction. They seemed to have a faith ready for all ; and as a child when you are telling him stories, asks for " more, more ", so they appeared to delight in being amused without effort of their own minds. Among other questions she asked me the old one over again, if I was married ; and when I told her that I was not, she appeared surprised, and, as if recollecting herself, said to me, with a pious seriousness and perfect simplicity, " To be sure, there is a great promise for virgins in Heaven " ; and then she began to tell how long she had been married, that she had had a large family and much sickness and sorrow, having lost several of her children. We had clean sheets and decent beds.

September 14th, Wednesday. Rose early, and departed before

---

[1] This practice prevailed in Cumberland and Westmorland seventy or eighty years ago.—D. W.

breakfast. The morning was dry, but cold. Travelled as before, along the shores of Loch Lubnaig, and along the pass of the roaring stream of Leny, and reached Callander at a little past eight o'clock. After breakfast set off towards Stirling, intending to sleep there ; the distance eighteen miles. We were now entering upon a populous and more cultivated country, having left the mountains behind, therefore I shall have little to tell ; for what is most interesting in such a country is not to be seen in passing through it as we did. Half way between Callander and Stirling is the village of Doune, and a little further on we crossed a bridge over a pleasant river (the Teith). Above the river stands a ruined castle of considerable size, upon a woody bank. We wished to have had time to go up to the ruin. Long before we reached the town of Stirling, saw the Castle, single, on its stately and commanding eminence. The rock or hill rises from a level plain ; the print in Stoddart's book does indeed give a good notion of its form. The surrounding plain appears to be of a rich soil, well cultivated. The crops of ripe corn were abundant. We found the town quite full ; not a vacant room in the inn, it being the time of the assizes : there was no lodging for us, and hardly even the possibility of getting anything to eat in a bye-nook of the house. Walked up to the Castle. The prospect from it is very extensive, and must be exceedingly grand on a fine evening or morning, with the light of the setting or rising sun on the distant mountains, but we saw it at an unfavourable time of day, the mid-afternoon, and were not favoured by light and shade. The Forth makes most intricate and curious turnings, so that it is difficult to trace them, even when you are overlooking the whole. It flows through a perfect level, and in one place cuts its way in the form of a large figure of eight. Stirling is the largest town we had seen in Scotland, except Glasgow. It is an old irregular place ; the streets towards the Castle on one side very steep. On the other, the hill or rock rises from the fields. The architecture of a part of the Castle is very fine, and the whole building in good repair : some parts, indeed, are modern. At Stirling we bought Burns's Poems in one volume, for two shillings. Went on to Falkirk, ten or eleven miles.

Dd

I do not recollect anything remarkable after we were out of sight of Stirling Castle, except the Carron Ironworks, seen at a distance ; — the sky above them was red with a fiery light. In passing through a turnpike gate we were greeted by a Highland drover, who, with many others, was coming from a fair at Falkirk, the road being covered all along with horsemen and cattle. He spoke as if we had been well known to him, asking us how we had fared on our journey. We were at a loss to conceive why he should interest himself about us, till he said he had passed us on the Black Mountain, near King's House. It was pleasant to observe the effect of solitary places in making men friends, and to see so much kindness, which had been produced in such a chance encounter, retained in a crowd. No beds in the inns at Falkirk — every room taken up by the people come to the fair. Lodged in a private house, a neat clean place — kind treatment from the old man and his daughter.

September 15*th*, *Thursday*. Breakfasted at Linlithgow, a small town. The house is yet shown from which the Regent Murray was shot. The remains of a royal palace, where Queen Mary was born, are of considerable extent ; the banks of gardens and fish-ponds may yet be distinctly traced, though the whole surface is transformed into smooth pasturage where cattle graze. The castle stands upon a gentle eminence, the prospect not particularly pleasing, though not otherwise ; it is bare and wide. The shell of a small ancient church is standing, into which are crammed modern pews, galleries, and pulpit, — very ugly, and discordant with the exterior. Nothing very interesting till we came to Edinburgh. Dined by the way at a small town or village upon a hill, the back part of the houses on one side overlooking an extensive prospect over flat corn fields. I mention this for the sake of a pleasant hour we passed sitting on the bank, where we read some of Burns's poems in the volume which we had bought at Stirling.

Arrived at Edinburgh a little before sunset. As we approached, the Castle rock resembling that of Stirling — in the same manner appearing to rise from a plain of cultivated ground, the Firth of Forth being on the other side, and not visible.

Drove to the White Hart in the Grassmarket,[1] an inn which had been mentioned to us, and which we conjectured would better suit us than one in a more fashionable part of the town. It was not noisy, and tolerably cheap. Drank tea, and walked up to the Castle, which luckily was very near. Much of the daylight was gone ; so that except it had been a clear evening, which it was not, we could not have seen the distant prospect.

September 16th, Friday. The sky the evening before, as you may remember the ostler told us, had been *gay and dull*, and this morning it was downright dismal : very dark, and promising nothing but a wet day, and before breakfast was over the rain began, though not heavily. We set out upon our walk, and went through many streets to Holyrood House, and thence to the hill called Arthur's Seat, a high hill, very rocky at the top, and below covered with smooth turf, on which sheep were feeding. We climbed up till we came to St. Anthony's Well and *Chapel*, as it is called, but it is more like a hermitage than a chapel, — a small ruin, which from its situation is exceedingly interesting, though in itself not remarkable. We sate down on a stone not far from the chapel, overlooking a pastoral hollow as wild and solitary as any in the heart of the Highland mountains : there, instead of the roaring of torrents, we listened to the noises of the city, which were blended in one loud indistinct buzz, a regular sound in the air, which in certain moods of feeling, and at certain times, might have a more tranquillizing effect upon the mind than those which we are accustomed to hear in such places. The Castle rock looked exceedingly large through the misty air : a cloud of black smoke overhung the city, which combined with the rain and mist to conceal the shapes of the houses, an obscurity which added much to the grandeur of the sound that proceeded from it. It was impossible to think of anything that was little or mean, the goings-on of trade, the strife of men, or every-day city business ; the impression was one, and it was visionary, like the conceptions of our childhood of Bagdad or Balsora when we have been reading the Arabian Nights' Entertain-

---

[1] Grassmarket—J. C. S. : Haymarket—D. W.

ments. Though the rain was very heavy we remained upon the hill for some time, then returned by the same road by which we had come, through green flat fields, formerly the pleasure-grounds of Holyrood House, on the edge of which stands the old roofless chapel of venerable architecture. It is a pity that it should be suffered to fall down, for the walls appear to be yet entire. Very near to the chapel is Holyrood House, which we could not but lament has nothing ancient in its appearance, being sash-windowed and not an irregular pile. It is very like a building for some national establishment, a hospital for soldiers or sailors. You have a description of it in Stoddart's Tour, therefore I need not tell you what we saw there.

When we found ourselves once again in the streets of the city, we lamented over the heavy rain, and indeed before leaving the hill, much as we were indebted to the accident of the rain for the peculiar grandeur and affecting wildness of those objects we saw, we could not but regret that the Firth of Forth was entirely hidden from us, and all distant objects ; and we strained our eyes till they ached, vainly trying to pierce through the thick mist. We walked industriously through the streets, street after street, and, in spite of wet and dirt, were exceedingly delighted. The old town, with its irregular houses, stage above stage, seen as we saw it, in the obscurity of a rainy day, hardly resembles the work of men, it is more like a piling up of rocks ; and I cannot attempt to describe what we saw so imperfectly, but must say that, high as my expectations had been raised, the city of Edinburgh far surpassed all expectation. Gladly would we have stayed another day ; but could not afford more time, and our notions of the weather of Scotland were so dismal, notwithstanding we ourselves had been so much favoured, that we had no hope of its mending. So at about six o'clock in the evening we departed, intending to sleep at an inn in the village of Roslin, about five miles from Edinburgh. The rain continued till we were almost at Roslin ; but then it was quite dark, so we did not see the Castle that night.

September 17th, Saturday. The morning very fine. We rose early and walked through the glen of Roslin, past Hawthornden, and considerably further, to the house of Mr. Walter Scott at Lasswade.[1] Roslin Castle stands upon a woody bank above a stream (the North Esk), too large, I think, to be called a brook, yet an inconsiderable river. We looked down upon the ruin from higher ground. Near it stands the Chapel, a most elegant building, a ruin, though the walls and roof are entire. I never passed through a more delicious dell than the glen of Roslin, though the water of the stream is dingy and muddy. The banks are rocky on each side, and hung with pine wood. About a mile from the Castle, on the contrary side of the water, upon the edge of a very steep bank, stands Hawthornden, the house of Drummond the poet, whither Ben Jonson came on foot from London to visit his friend. We did hear to whom the house at present belongs, and some other particulars, but I have a very indistinct recollection of what was told us, except that many old trees had been lately cut down. After Hawthornden the glen widens, ceases to be rocky, and spreads out into a rich vale, scattered over with gentlemen's seats.

Arrived at Lasswade before Mr. and Mrs. Scott had risen, and waited some time in a large sitting-room. Breakfasted with them, and stayed till two o'clock, and Mr. Scott accompanied us back almost to Roslin, having given us directions respecting our future journey, and promised to meet us at Melrose[2] two days after.

We ordered dinner on our return to the inn, and went to view the inside of the Chapel of Roslin, which is kept locked up, and so preserved from the injuries it might otherwise receive from idle boys ; but as nothing is done to keep it together, it must in the end fall. The architecture within is exquisitely beautiful. The stone both of the roof and walls is sculptured with leaves and flowers, so delicately wrought that I could have admired them for hours, and the whole of their groundwork is stained by time with the softest colours ; some of those leaves and flowers were tinged perfectly green, and at one part the effect was most exquisite : three or four leaves of a

---

[1] Lisswaede—D. W.   [2] Melross—D. W.

small fern, resembling that which we call adder's tongue, grew round a cluster of them at the top of a pillar, and the natural product and the artificial were so intermingled that at first it was not easy to distinguish the living plant from the other, they being of an equally determined green, though the fern was of a deeper shade. We set forward again after dinner. The afternoon was pleasant. Travelled through large tracts of ripe corn, interspersed with larger tracts of moorland — the houses at a considerable distance from each other, no longer thatched huts, but farm-houses resembling those of the farming counties in England, having many corn-stacks close to them. Dark when we reached Peebles ; found a comfortable old-fashioned publick-house, had a neat parlour, and drank tea.

September 18th, Sunday. The town of Peebles is on the banks of the Tweed. After breakfast walked up the river to Neidpath Castle, about a mile and a half from the town. The castle stands upon a green hill, overlooking the Tweed, a strong square-towered edifice, neglected and desolate, though not in ruin, the garden overgrown with grass, and the high walls that fenced it broken down. The Tweed winds between green steeps, upon which, and close to the river-side, large flocks of sheep pasturing ; higher still are the grey mountains ; but I need not describe the scene, for Wm. has done it better than I could do in a sonnet which he wrote the same day ; the five last lines, at least, of his poem will impart to you more of the *feeling* of the place than it would be possible for me to do : —

> *Degenerate Douglas ! thou unworthy Lord*
> *Whom mere despite of heart could so far please,*
> *And love of havoc (for with such disease*
> *Fame taxes him) that he could send forth word*
> *To level with the dust a noble horde,*
> *A brotherhood of venerable trees,*
> *Leaving an ancient Dome and Towers like these*
> *Beggar'd and outraged ! Many hearts deplored*
> *The fate of those old trees ; and oft with pain*
> *The Traveller at this day will stop and gaze*
> *On wrongs which Nature scarcely seems to heed ;*

A TOUR MADE IN SCOTLAND (A.D. 1803)

For shelter'd places, bosoms, nooks, and bays,
And the pure mountains, and the gentle Tweed,
And the green silent pastures yet remain.

I was spared any regret for the fallen woods when we were there, not then knowing the history of them. The soft low mountains, the castle, and the decayed pleasure-grounds, the scattered trees which have been left in different parts, and the road carried in a very beautiful line along the side of the hill, with the Tweed murmuring through the unfenced green pastures spotted with sheep, together composed an harmonious scene, and I wished for nothing that was not there. When we were with Mr. Scott he spoke of chearful days he had spent in that castle not many years ago, when it was inhabited by Professor Ferguson and his family, whom the Duke of Queensberry, its churlish owner, forced to quit it. We discovered a very fine echo within a few yards of the building.

The town of Peebles looks very pretty from the road in returning : it is an old town, built of grey stone, the same as the castle. Well-dressed people were going to church. Sent the car before, and walked ourselves, and while going along the main street Wm. was called aside in a mysterious manner by a person who gravely examined him — whether he was an Irishman or a foreigner, or what he was ; I suppose our car was the occasion of suspicion at a time when every one was talking of the threatened invasion. We had a day's journey before us along the banks of the Tweed, a name which has been sweet to my ears almost as far back as I can remember any-thing. After the first mile or two our road was seldom far from the river, which flowed in gentleness, though perhaps never silent ; the hills on either side high and sometimes stony, but excellent pasturage for sheep. In some parts the vale was wholly of this pastoral character, in others we saw extensive tracts of corn ground, even spreading along whole hill-sides, and without visible fences, which is dreary in a flat country ; but there is no dreariness on the banks of the Tweed ; the hills, whether smooth or stony, uncultivated or covered with ripe corn, had the same pensive softness. Near the corn tracts were large farm-houses, with many corn-stacks ; the stacks and house and out-houses together, I recollect, in one or two places upon the hills, at a little distance, seemed almost as large as a small village or hamlet. It was a clear autumnal day, without wind, and, being Sunday, the business of the harvest was suspended, and all that we saw, and felt, and heard, combined to excite one sensation of pensive and still pleasure.

Passed by several old halls yet inhabited, and others in ruin ; but I have hardly a sufficiently distinct recollection of any of them to be able to describe them, and I now at this distance of time regret that I did not take notes. In one very sweet part of the vale a gate crossed the road, which was opened by an old woman who lived in a cottage close to it ; I said to her, " You live in a very pretty place ! " " Yes," she replied, " the water of Tweed is a bonny water." The lines of the hills are flowing and beautiful, the reaches of the vale long ; in some places appear the remains of a forest, in others you will see as lovely a combination of forms as any traveller who goes in search of the picturesque need desire, and yet perhaps without a single tree ; or at least if trees there are, they shall be very few, and he shall not care whether they are there or not.

The road took us through one long village, but I do not recollect any other ; yet I think we never had a mile's length before us without a house, though seldom several cottages together. The loneliness of the scattered dwellings, the more stately edifices decaying or in ruin, or, if inhabited, not in their pride and freshness, aided the general effect of the gently varying scenes, which was that of tender pensiveness ; — no bursting torrents when we were there, but the murmuring of the river was heard distinctly, often blended with the bleating of sheep. In one place we saw a shepherd lying in the midst of a flock upon a sunny knoll, with his face towards the sky, a happy picture of shepherd life.

The transitions of this vale were all gentle except one, a scene of which a gentleman's house was the centre, standing low in the vale, the hills above it covered with gloomy fir plantations, and the appearance of the house itself, though it could scarcely be seen, was gloomy. There was an allegorical air (a person fond of Spenser will understand me) in this unchearful spot, single in such a country,

The house was hearsed about with a black wood.[1]

We have since heard that it was the residence of Lord Traquair, a Roman Catholic nobleman, of a decayed family.

We left the Tweed when we were within about a mile and a half or two miles of Clovenford, where we were to lodge. Turned up the side of a hill, and went along sheep-grounds till we reached the spot ; a single stone house, without a tree near it or to be seen from it. On our mentioning Mr. Scott's name the woman of the house showed us all possible civility, but her slowness was really amusing. I should suppose it is a house little frequented, for there is no appearance of an inn. Mr. Scott, who she told me was a " very clever gentleman ", goes there in the fishing season ; but indeed Mr. Scott is respected everywhere : I believe that by favour of his name one might be hospitably entertained throughout all the borders of Scotland. We dined and drank tea — did not walk out, for there was no temptation ; a confined barren prospect from the window.

At Clovenford, being so near to the Yarrow, we could not but think of the possibility of going thither, but came to the conclusion of reserving the pleasure for some future time, in consequence of which, after our return, Wm. wrote the poem which I shall here transcribe :—

> *From Stirling Castle we had seen*
> *The mazy Forth unravell'd,*
> *Had trod the banks of Clyde and Tay,*
> *And with the Tweed had travell'd.*
> *And when we came to Clovenford,*
> *Then said my winsome Marrow,*
> *" Whate'er betide we'll turn aside*
> *And see the Braes of Yarrow."*

---

[1] Crashaw's *Steps to the Temple ; Sospetto d' Herode*, xliv.

" *Let Yarrow Folk frae Selkirk Town,*
Who have been buying, selling,
Go back to Yarrow :—'tis their own,
Each Maiden to her dwelling.
On Yarrow's banks let herons feed,
Hares couch, and rabbits burrow,
But we will downwards with the Tweed,
Nor turn aside to Yarrow.

" *There's Gala Water, Leader Haughs,*
Both lying right before us ;
And Dryburgh, where with chiming Tweed
The lintwhites sing in chorus.
There's pleasant Tiviot Dale, a land
Made blithe with plough and harrow,
Why throw away a needful day,
To go in search of Yarrow ?

" *What's Yarrow but a river bare,*
That glides the dark hills under ?
There are a thousand such elsewhere,
As worthy of your wonder."
Strange words they seem'd of slight and scorn,
My True-love sigh'd for sorrow,
And look'd me in the face to think
I thus could speak of Yarrow.

" *Oh ! green," said I, " are Yarrow's Holms,*
And sweet is Yarrow flowing,
Fair hangs the apple frae the rock,
But we will leave it growing.
O'er hilly path and open Strath
We'll wander Scotland thorough,
But though so near we will not turn
Into the Dale of Yarrow.

" *Let beeves and home-bred kine partake*
The sweets of Burnmill Meadow,

The swan on still St. Mary's Lake
Float double, swan and shadow.
We will not see them, will not go,
To-day nor yet to-morrow ;
Enough if in our hearts we know
There's such a place as Yarrow.

" Be Yarrow stream unseen, unknown,
It must, or we shall rue it,
We have a vision of our own,
Ah ! why should we undo it ?
The treasured dreams of times long past,
We'll keep them, ' winsome Marrow ',
For when we're there, although 'tis fair,
'Twill be another Yarrow.

" If care with freezing years should come,
And wandering seem but folly,
Should we be loth to stir from home,
And yet be melancholy,
Should life be dull and spirits low,
'Twill soothe us in our sorrow
That earth hath something yet to show —
The bonny Holms of Yarrow."

The next day we were to meet Mr. Scott, and again join the Tweed. I wish I could have given you a better idea of what we saw between Peebles and this place. I have most distinct recollections of the effect of the whole day's journey ; but the objects are mostly melted together in my memory, and though I should recognise them if we revisit the place, I cannot call them out so as to represent them to you with distinctness. Wm., in attempting in verse to describe this part of the Tweed, says of it,

More pensive in sunshine
Than others in moonshine,

which perhaps may give you more power to conceive what it is than all I have said.

393

September 19*th, Monday*. We rose early, and went to
Melrose, six miles, before breakfast. After ascending a hill,
descended, and overlooked a dell, on the opposite side of which
was an old mansion, surrounded with trees and steep gardens,
a curious and pleasing, yet melancholy spot ; for the house and
gardens were evidently going to decay, and the whole of the
small dell, except near the house, was unenclosed and uncultivated, being a sheep-walk to the top of the hills. Descended
to Gala Water, a pretty stream, but much smaller than the
Tweed, into which the brook flows from the glen I have spoken
of. Near the Gala is a large modern house, the situation very
pleasant, but the old building which we had passed put to
shame the fresh colouring and meagre outline of the new one.
Went through a part of the village of Galashiels, pleasantly
situated on the bank of the stream ; a pretty place it once has
been, but a manufactory is established there ; and a townish
bustle and ugly stone houses are fast taking place of the brown-
roofed thatched cottages, of which a great number yet remain,
partly overshadowed by trees. Left the Gala, and, after crossing
the open country, came again to the Tweed, and pursued our
way as before near the river, perhaps for a mile or two, till we
arrived at Melrose. The valley for this short space was not so
pleasing as before, the hills more broken, and though the
cultivation was general, yet the scene was not rich, while it
had lost its pastoral simplicity. At Melrose the vale opens out
wide ; but the hills are high all round, single distinct risings.
After breakfast we went out, intending to go to the Abbey,
and in the street met Mr. Scott, who gave us a cordial greeting,
and conducted us thither himself. He was here on his own
ground, for he is familiar with all that is known of the authentic
history of Melrose and the popular tales connected with it. He
pointed out many pieces of beautiful sculpture in obscure
corners which would have escaped our notice. The Abbey has
been built of a pale red stone ; that part which was first
erected of a very durable kind, the sculptured flowers and
leaves and other minute ornaments being as perfect in many
places as when first wrought. The ruin is of considerable
extent, but unfortunately it is almost surrounded by insignificant

394

houses, so that when you are close to it you see it entirely separated from many rural objects, and even when viewed from a distance the situation does not seem to be particularly happy, for the vale is broken and disturbed, and the Abbey at a distance from the river, so that you do not look upon them as companions of each other. And (surely this is a national barbarism) within these beautiful walls is the ugliest church that was ever beheld ; if it had been hewn out of the side of a hill it could not have been more dismal ; there was no neatness, nor even decency, and it appeared to be so damp, and so completely excluded from fresh air, that it must be dangerous to sit in it ; the floor is unpaved, and very rough. What a contrast to the beautiful and graceful order apparent in every part of the ancient design and workmanship ! Mr. Scott went with us into the gardens and orchards of a Mr. Riddel, from which we had a very sweet view of the Abbey through trees, the town being entirely excluded. Dined with Mr. S. at the inn ; he was now travelling to the assizes at Jedburgh in his character of Sheriff of Selkirk, and on that account, as well as for his own sake, he was treated with great respect, a small part of which was vouchsafed to us as his friends, though I could not persuade the woman to show me the beds, or to make any sort of promise till she was assured from the Sheriff himself that he had no objection to sleep in the same room with Wm.

September 20th, Tuesday. Mr. Scott departed very early for Jedburgh, and we soon followed, intending to go by Dryburgh to Kelso. It was a fine morning. We went without breakfast, being told that there was a publick-house at Dryburgh. The road was very pleasant, seldom out of sight of the Tweed for any length of time, though not often close to it. The valley is not so pleasantly defined as between Peebles and Clovenford, yet so soft and beautiful, and in many parts pastoral, but that peculiar and pensive simplicity which I have spoken of before was wanting, yet there was a fertility chequered with wildness which to many travellers would be more than a compensation. The reaches of the vale were shorter, the turnings more rapid, the banks often clothed with wood. In one place was a lofty scar, at another a green promontory, a small hill skirted by the river, the hill above irregular and green, and scattered over with trees. We wished we could have brought the ruins of Melrose to that spot, and mentioned this to Mr. Scott, who told us that the monks had first fixed their abode there, and raised a temporary building of wood. The monastery of Melrose was founded by a colony from Rievaux Abbey in Yorkshire, which building it happens to resemble in the colour of the stone, and I think partly in the style of architecture, but is much smaller, that is, *has been* much smaller, for there is not at Rievaux any one single part of the ruin so large as the remains of the church at Melrose, though at Rievaux a far more extensive ruin remains. It is also much grander, and the situation at present much more beautiful, that ruin not having suffered like Melrose Abbey from the encroachments of a town. The architecture at Melrose is, I believe, superior in the exactness and taste of some of the minute ornamental parts ; indeed, it is impossible to conceive anything more delicate than the workmanship, especially in the imitations of flowers.

We descended to Dryburgh after having gone a considerable way upon high ground. A heavy rain when we reached the village, and there was no publick-house. A well-dressed, well-spoken woman courteously (shall I say *charitably* ?) invited us into her cottage, and permitted us to make breakfast ; she showed us into a neat parlour, furnished with prints, a mahogany table, and other things which I was surprized to see, for her husband was only a day-labourer, but she had been Lady Buchan's waiting-maid, which accounted for these luxuries and for a noticeable urbanity in her manners. All the cottages in this neighbourhood, if I am not mistaken, were covered with red tiles, and had chimneys. After breakfast we set out in the rain to the ruins of Dryburgh Abbey, which are near Lord Buchan's house, and (like Bothwell Castle) appropriated to the pleasure of the owner. We rang a bell at the gate, and, instead of a porter, an old woman came to open it through a narrow side-alley cut in a thick plantation of evergreens. On entering, saw the thatch of her hut just above the trees, and it looked very pretty, but the poor creature herself was a figure to frighten a child, bowed almost double, having a hooked nose and overhanging eyebrows, a complexion stained brown with smoke, and a cap that might have been worn for months and never washed. No doubt she had been cowering over her peat fire, for if she had emitted smoke by her breath and through every pore, the odour could not have been stronger. This ancient woman, by right of office, attended us to show off the curiosities, and she had her tale as perfect (though it was not quite so long a one) as the gentleman Swiss, whom I remember to have seen at Blenheim with his slender wand and dainty white clothes. The house of Lord Buchan and the Abbey stand upon a large flat peninsula, a green holm almost covered with fruit-trees. The ruins of Dryburgh are much less extensive than those of Melrose, and greatly inferior both in the architecture and stone, which is much mouldered away. Lord B. has trained pear-trees along the walls, which are bordered with flowers and gravel walks, and he has made a pigeon-house, and a fine room in the ruin, ornamented with a curiously-assorted collection of busts of eminent men, in which lately a ball was given ; yet, deducting for all these improvements (which are certainly much less offensive than you could imagine), it is a very sweet ruin, standing so enclosed in wood, which the towers overtop, that you cannot know that it is not in a state of natural desolation till you are close to it. The opposite bank of the Tweed is steep and woody, but unfortunately many of the trees are firs. The old woman followed us after the fashion of other guides, but being slower of foot than a younger person, it was not difficult to slip away from the scent of her poor smoke-dried body. She was sedulous in pointing out the curiosities, which, I doubt not, she had a firm belief were not to be surpassed in England or Scotland.

Having promised us a sight of the largest and oldest yew-tree ever seen, she conducted us to it ; it was a goodly tree, but a mere dwarf compared with several of our own country, not to speak of the giant of Lorton. We returned to the cottage, and waited some time in hopes that the rain would abate ; but it grew worse and worse, and we were obliged to give up our journey, to Kelso, taking the direct road to Jedburgh.

We had to ford the Tweed, a wide river at the crossing-place. It would have been impossible to *drive* the horse through, for he had not forgotten the fright at Connel Ferry, so we hired a man to lead us. After crossing the water, the road goes up the bank, and we had a beautiful view of the ruins of the Abbey, peering above the trees of the woody peninsula, which, in shape, resembles that formed by the Tees at Sockburn, but is considerably smaller. Lord Buchan's house is a very neat, modest building, and almost hidden by trees. It soon began to rain heavily. Crossed the Teviot by a stone bridge — the vale in that part very wide — there was a great deal of ripe corn, but a want of trees, and no appearance of richness. Arrived at Jedburgh half an hour before the Judges were expected out of Court to dinner. We gave in our passport, the name of Mr. Scott, the Sheriff, and were very civilly treated ; but there was no vacant room in the house except the Judge's sitting-room, and we wanted to have a fire, being exceedingly wet and cold. I was conducted into that room, on condition that I would give it up the moment the Judge came from Court. After I had put off my wet clothes I went up into a bedroom, and sate shivering there, till the people of the inn had procured lodgings for us in a private house. We were received with hearty welcome by a good woman, who, though above seventy years old, moved about as briskly as if she was only seventeen. Those parts of the house which we were to occupy were neat and clean ; she showed me every corner, and, before I had been ten minutes in the house, opened her very drawers that I might see what a stock of linen she had ; then asked me how long we should stay, and said she wished we were come for three months. She was a most remarkable person ; the alacrity with which she ran up-stairs when we rung the bell, and guessed at, and strove to prevent, our wants was surprizing ; she had a quick eye, and keen strong features, and a joyousness in her motions, like what used to be in old Molly [1] when she was particularly elated. I found afterwards that she had been subject to fits of dejection and

---

[1] *v. Grasmere Journal.*

ill-health : we then conjectured that her overflowing gaiety and strength might in part be attributed to the same cause as her former dejection. Her husband was deaf and infirm, and sate in a chair with scarcely the power to move a limb — an affecting contrast ! The old woman said they had been a very hard-working pair ; they had wrought like slaves at their trade (her husband had been a currier) and she told me how they had portioned off their daughters with money, and each a feather-bed, and that in their old age they had laid out the little they could spare in building and furnishing that house, and she added with pride that she had lived in her youth in the family of Lady Egerton, who was no high lady, and now was in the habit of coming to her house whenever she was at Jedburgh, and a hundred other things ; for when she once began with Lady Egerton, she did not know how to stop, nor did I wish it, for she was very entertaining. Mr. Scott sate with us an hour or two, and repeated a part of the Lay of the Last Minstrel. When he was gone our hostess came to see if we wanted anything, and to wish us good-night. On all occasions her manners were governed by the same spirit : there was no withdrawing one's attention from her. We were so much interested that Wm., long afterwards, thought it worth while to express in verse the sensations which she had excited, and which then remained as vividly in his mind as at the moment when we lost sight of Jedburgh :—

> *Age ! twine thy brows with fresh spring flowers,*
> *And call a train of laughing Hours ;*
> *And bid them dance, and bid them sing,*
> *And Thou, too, mingle in the Ring !*
> *Take to thy heart a new delight !*
> *If not, make merry in despite*
> *That one should breathe who scorns thy power.*
> *— But dance ! for under Jedborough Tower*
> *A Matron dwells who, tho' she bears*
> *Our mortal complement of years,*
> *Lives in the light of youthful glee,*
> *And she will dance and sing with thee.*

Ee

Nay! start not at that Figure, there,
Him who is rooted to his Chair!
Look at him, look again; for He
Hath long been of thy Family.
With legs that move not, if they can,
And useless arms, a Trunk of Man,
He sits, and with a vacant eye;
A Sight to make a Stranger sigh!
Deaf, drooping, such is now his doom;
His world is in that single room.
Is this a place for mirthful cheer?
Can merry-making enter here?

The joyous Woman is the Mate
Of him in that forlorn estate;
He breathes a subterraneous damp;
But bright as Vesper shines her lamp,
He is as mute as Jedborough Tower,
She jocund as it was of yore
With all its bravery on, in times
When all alive with merry chimes
Upon a sun-bright morn of May
It roused the Vale to holiday.

I praise thee, Matron, and thy due
Is praise, heroic praise and true.
With admiration I behold
Thy gladness unsubdued and bold:
Thy looks, thy gestures, all present
The picture of a life well spent;
This do I see, and something more,
A strength unthought of heretofore.
Delighted am I for thy sake,
And yet a higher joy partake:
Our Human nature throws away
Its second twilight, and looks gay,
A Land of promise and of pride
Unfolding, wide as life is wide.

Ah ! see her helpless Charge, enclos'd
Within himself as seems, compos'd ;
To fear of loss and hope of gain
The strife of happiness and pain
Utterly dead ! yet in the guise
Of little Infants when their eyes
Begin to follow to and fro
The persons that before them go,
He tracks her motions, quick or slow.
Her buoyant spirits can prevail
Where common chearfulness would fail.
She strikes upon him with the heat
Of July Suns, he feels it sweet,
An animal delight, though dim,
'Tis all that now remains for him.

I look'd, I scann'd her o'er and o'er,
And, looking, wonder'd more and more :
When suddenly I seem'd to espy
A trouble in her strong black eye,
A remnant of uneasy light,
A flash of something over-bright !
Not long this mystery did detain
My thoughts.   She told in pensive strain
That she had borne a heavy yoke,
Been stricken by a twofold stroke ;
Ill health of body, and had pin'd
Beneath worse ailments of the mind.

So be it, but let praise ascend
To him who is our Lord and Friend,
Who from disease and suffering
As bad almost as Life can bring,
Hath call'd for thee a second Spring ;
Repaid thee for that sore distress
By no untimely joyousness,
Which makes of thine a blissful state,
And cheers thy melancholy Mate.

September 21st, Wednesday. The house where we lodged was airy, and even chearful, though one of a line of houses bordering on the churchyard, which is the highest part of the town, overlooking a great portion of it to the opposite hills. The kirk is, as at Melrose, within the walls of a conventual church ; but the ruin is much less beautiful, and the church a very neat one. The churchyard was full of graves, and exceedingly slovenly and dirty ; one most indecent practice I observed : several women brought their linen to the flat table-tombstones, and, having spread it upon them, began to batter as hard as they could with a wooden roller, a substitute for a mangle. After Mr. Scott's business in the Courts was over, he walked with us up the Jed, " sylvan Jed " it has been properly called by Thomson, for the banks are yet very woody, though wood in large quantities has been felled within a few years. There are some fine red scars near the river, in one or two of which we saw the entrances to caves, said to have been used as places of refuge in times of insecurity. Walked up to Ferniehurst, an old hall, in a secluded situation, now inhabited by farmers ; the neighbouring ground had the wildness of a forest, being irregularly scattered over with fine old trees. The wind was tossing their branches, and sunshine dancing among the leaves, and I happened to exclaim, " What a life there is in trees ! " on which Mr. Scott observed that the words reminded him of a young lady who had been born and educated on an island of the Orcades, and came to spend a summer at Kelso and in the neighbourhood of Edinburgh. She used to say that in the new world into which she was come nothing had disappointed her so much as trees and woods ; she complained that they were lifeless, silent, and, compared with the grandeur of the ever-changing ocean, even insipid. At first I was surprized, but the next moment I felt that the impression was natural. Mr. Scott said that she was a very sensible young woman, and had read much. She talked with endless rapture and feeling of the power and greatness of the ocean ; and with the same passionate attachment returned to her native island without any probability of quitting it again.

The valley of the Jed is very solitary immediately under

Ferniehurst ; we walked down the river, wading almost up to the knees in fern, which in many parts overspread the forest-ground. It made me think of our walks at Alfoxden, and of *our own* park (though at Ferniehurst is no park at present) and the slim fawns that we used to startle from their couching-places among the fern at the top of the hill. We were accompanied on our walk by a young man from the Braes of Yarrow, an acquaintance of Mr. Scott's,[1] who, having been much delighted with some of Wm.'s poems which he had chanced to see in a newspaper, had wished to be introduced to him ; he lived in the most retired part of the dale of Yarrow, where he had a farm : he was fond of reading, and well-informed, but at first meeting as shy as any of our Grasmere lads, and not less rustic in his appearance. He had been in the Highlands, and gave me such an account of Loch Rannoch as made us regret that we had not persevered in our journey thither, especially as he told us that the bad road ended at a very little distance from the place where we had turned back, and that we should have come into another good road, continued all along the shore of the lake. He also mentioned that there was a very fine view from the steeple at Dunkeld.

The town of Jedburgh, in returning along the road, as it is seen through the gently winding narrow valley, looks exceedingly beautiful on its low eminence, surmounted by the conventual tower, which is arched over, at the summit, by light stone-work resembling a coronet ; the effect at a distance is very graceful. The hills all round are high and rise rapidly from the town, which, though it stands considerably above the river, yet, from every side except that on which we walked, appears to stand in a bottom. We had our dinner sent from the inn, and *a bottle of wine*, that we might not disgrace the Sheriff, who supped with us in the evening, stayed late, and repeated some of his poem.

September 22nd, Thursday. After breakfast, the minister, Dr. Somerville, called upon us with Mr. Scott, and we went to the manse, a very pretty house with pretty gardens, and

---

[1] William Laidlaw.—W. K.

in a beautiful situation, though close to the town. Dr. Somerville and his family complained bitterly of the devastation that had been made among the woods within view from their windows, which looked up the Jed. He conducted us to the church, which under his directions has been lately repaired, and is a very neat place within. Dr. S. spoke of the dirt and other indecencies in the churchyard, and said that he had taken great pains to put a stop to them, but wholly in vain. The business of the assizes closed this day, and we went into Court to hear the Judge pronounce his charge, which was the most curious specimen of old woman's oratory and newspaper-paragraph loyalty that was ever heard. When all was over they returned to the inn in procession, as they had come, to the sound of a trumpet, the Judge first, in his robes of red, the Sheriffs next, in large cocked hats, and inferior officers following, a show not much calculated to awe the beholders. After this we went to the inn. The landlady and her sister inquired if we had been comfortable, and lamented that they had not had it in their power to pay us more attention. I began to talk with them, and found out that they were from Cumberland : they knew Captain and Mrs. Wordsworth, who had frequently been at Jedburgh, Mrs. W.'s sister having married a gentleman of that neighbourhood. They spoke of them with great pleasure. I returned to our lodgings to take leave of the old woman, who told me that I had behaved *very discreetly*, and seemed exceedingly sorry that we were leaving her so soon. She had been out to buy me some pears, saying that *I must* take away some *Jedderd* pears. We learned afterwards that Jedburgh is famous in Scotland for pears, which were first cultivated there in the gardens of the monks.

Mr. Scott was very glad to part from the Judge and his retinue, to travel with us in our car to Hawick ; his servant drove his own gig. The landlady, very kindly, had put up some sandwiches and cheese-cakes for me, and all the family came out to see us depart. Passed the monastery gardens, which are yet gardens, where there are many remarkably large old pear-trees. We soon came into the vale of Teviot, which is open and cultivated, and scattered over with hamlets, villages, and many gentlemen's seats, yet, though there is no inconsiderable quantity of wood, you can never, in the wide and cultivated parts of the Teviot, get rid of the impression of barrenness, and the fir plantations, which in this part are numerous, are for ever at war with simplicity. One beautiful spot I recollect of a different character, which Mr. S. took us to see a few yards from the road. A stone bridge crossed the water at a deep and still place, called Horne's Pool, from a contemplative schoolmaster, who had lived not far from it, and was accustomed to walk thither, and spend much of his leisure near the river. The valley was here narrow and woody. Mr. Scott pointed out to us Ruberslaw, Minto Crags, and every other remarkable object in or near the vale of Teviot, and we scarcely passed a house for which he had not some story. Seeing us look at one, which stood high on the hill on the opposite side of the river, he told us that a gentleman lived there who, while he was in India, had been struck with the fancy of making his fortune by a new speculation, and so set about collecting the Gods of the country, with infinite pains and no little expense, expecting that he might sell them for an enormous price. Accordingly, on his return they were offered for sale, but no purchasers came. On the failure of this scheme, a room was hired in London in which to exhibit them as a show ; but alas ! nobody would come to see ; and this curious assemblage of monsters is now, probably, quietly lodged in the vale of Teviot. The latter part of this gentleman's history is more affecting : — he had an only daughter, whom he had accompanied into Spain two or three years ago for the recovery of her health, and so for a time saved her from a consumption, which now again threatened her, and he was about to leave his pleasant residence, and attend her once more on the same errand, afraid of the coming winter.

We passed through a village, whither Leyden, Scott's intimate friend, the author of " Scenes of Infancy ", was used to walk over several miles of moorland country every day to school, a poor barefooted boy. He is now in India, applying himself to the study of Oriental literature, and, I doubt not, it is his dearest thought that he may come and end his days upon the banks of Teviot, or some other of the Lowland streams, for he is, like Mr. Scott, passionately attached to the district of the Borders. Arrived at Hawick to dinner ; the inn is a large old house with walls above a yard thick, formerly a gentleman's house. Did not go out this evening.

September 23rd, Friday. Before breakfast, walked with Mr. Scott along a high road for about two miles, up a bare hill. Hawick is a small town. From the top of the hill we had an extensive view over the moors of Liddisdale, and saw the Cheviot Hills. We wished we could have gone with Mr. Scott into some of the remote dales of this country, where in almost every house he can find a home and a hearty welcome. But after breakfast we were obliged to part with him, which we did with great regret : he would gladly have gone with us to Langholm, eighteen miles further. Our way was through the vale of Teviot, near the banks of the river.

Passed Branxholm Hall, one of the mansions belonging to the Duke of Buccleuch, which we looked at with particular interest for the sake of the Lay of the Last Minstrel. Only a very small part of the original building remains : it is a large strong house, old, but not *ancient* in its appearance — stands very near the riverside ; the banks covered with plantations. A little further on, met the Edinburgh coach with several passengers, the only stage-coach that had passed us in Scotland. Coleridge had come home by that conveyance only a few days before. The quantity of arable land gradually diminishes, and the plantations become fewer, till at last the river flows open to the sun, mostly through unfenced and untilled grounds, a soft pastoral district, both the hills and the valley being scattered over with sheep : here and there was a single farm-house, or cluster of houses, and near them a portion of land covered with ripe corn. Near the head of the vale of Teviot, where that stream is but a small rivulet, we descended towards another valley, by another small rivulet. Hereabouts Mr. Scott had directed us to look about for some old stumps of trees, said to be the place where Johnny Armstrong was hanged ; but we could not find them out. The valley into which we were descending, though, for aught I know, it is unnamed in song, was to us more interesting than the Teviot itself. Not a spot of tilled ground was there to break in upon its pastoral simplicity; the same soft yellow green spread from the bed of the streamlet to the hill-tops on each side, and sheep were feeding everywhere. It was more close and simple than the upper end of the vale of Teviot, the valley being much narrower, and the hills equally high and not broken into parts, but on each side a long range. The grass, as we had first seen near Crawfordjohn, had been mown in the different places of the open ground, where it might chance to be best; but there was no part of the surface that looked perfectly barren, as in those tracts.

We saw a single stone house a long way before us, which we conjectured to be, as it proved, Moss Paul, the inn where we were to bait. The scene, with this single dwelling, was melancholy and wild, but not dreary, though there was no tree nor shrub — the small streamlet glittered, the hills were populous with sheep; but the gentle bending of the valley, and the correspondent softness in the forms of the hills, were of themselves enough to delight the eye. At Moss Paul we fed our horse; — several travellers were drinking whisky. We neither ate nor drank, for we had, with our usual foresight and frugality in travelling, saved the cheese-cakes and sandwiches which had been given us by our countrywomen at Jedburgh the day before. After Moss Paul, we ascended considerably, then went down other reaches of the valley, much less interesting, stony and barren. The country afterwards not peculiar, I should think, for I scarcely remember it.

Arrived at Langholm at about five o'clock. The town, as we approached, from a hill, looked very pretty, the houses being roofed with blue slates, and standing close to the river Esk, here a large river, that scattered its waters wide over a stony channel. The inn neat and comfortable — exceedingly clean: I could hardly believe we were still in Scotland. After tea walked out; crossed a bridge, and saw, at a little distance up the valley, Langholm House, a villa of the Duke of Buccleuch: it stands upon a level between the river and a steep hill, which is planted with wood. Walked a considerable way up the river, but could not go close to it on account of the Duke's plantations, which are locked up. When they ended, the vale became less cultivated; the view through the vale towards the hills very pleasing, though bare and cold.

September 24th, Saturday. Rose very early and travelled about nine miles to Longtown, before breakfast, along the banks of the Esk. About half a mile from Langholm crossed a bridge. At this part of the vale (which is narrow) the steeps are covered with old oaks and every variety of trees. Our road for some time through the wood, then came to a more open country, exceedingly rich and populous; the banks of the river frequently rocky, and hung with wood — many gentlemen's houses. There was the same rich variety while the river continued to flow through Scottish grounds; but not long after we had passed through the last turnpike gate in Scotland and the first in England (but a few yards asunder) the vale widens, and its aspect was cold, and even dreary, though Sir James Graham's plantations are very extensive. His house, a large building, stands in this open part of the vale. Longtown was before us, and ere long we saw the well-remembered guide-post, where the circuit of our six weeks' travels had begun, and now was ended.

We did not look along the white line of the road to Solway Moss without some melancholy emotion, though we had the fair prospect of the Cumberland mountains full in view, with the certainty, barring accidents, of reaching our own dear home the next day. Breakfasted at the Graham's Arms. The weather had been very fine from the time of our arrival at Jedburgh, and this was a very pleasant day. The sun " shone fair on Carlisle's walls " when we first saw them from the top of the opposite hill. Stopped to look at the place on the sand near the bridge where Hatfield had been executed. Put up at the same inn as before, and were recognised by the woman who had waited on us. Everybody spoke of Hatfield as an injured man. After dinner went to a village six miles further, where we slept.

September 25th, Sunday. A beautiful autumnal day. Breakfasted at a publick-house by the road-side; dined at Threlkeld;

arrived at home between eight and nine o'clock, where we found Mary in perfect health, Joanna Hutchinson with her, and little John asleep in the clothes-basket by the fire.

SONNET

September 25th, 1803

Fly, some kind Spirit, fly to Grasmere Vale !
Say that we come, and come by this day's light,
Glad tidings ! — spread them over field and height,
But, chiefly, let one Cottage hear the tale !
There let a mystery of joy prevail,
The kitten frolic with unruly might,
And Rover whine as at a second sight
Of near-approaching good, that will not fail :
And from that Infant's face let joy appear ;
Yea, let our Mary's one companion child,
That hath her six weeks' solitude beguil'd
With intimations manifold and dear,
While we have wander'd over wood and wild —
Smile on its Mother now with bolder chear !

V

Excursion on
THE BANKS OF ULLSWATER
NOVEMBER 1805

See End-paper map at end of volume

William Wordsworth, 1805
From a tinted drawing by H. Edridge, A.R.A.

EXCURSION ON THE BANKS OF
ULLSWATER NOVEMBER 1805

WILLIAM and Mary returned from Park House [1] by the Patterdale road on Sunday Nov. 4th (along with Mr. and Mrs.
Clarkson), having made a delightful excursion of three days.
They had engaged that Wm. and I should go to Mr. Luff's [2] on
the Wednesday or Thursday if the weather continued favorable.
It was not very promising on Wednesday, but having been fine
for so long a time we thought there would not be an entire
change at once ; therefore, on a damp and gloomy morning
we set forward, Wm. on foot, and I upon the pony, with Wm.'s
greatcoat slung over the saddle crutch, and a wallet containing
our bundle of needments. As we went along the mist gathered
upon the vallies, and it even *rained* all the way to Patterdale ;
but there was never a drop on my habit larger than the smallest
pearls on a lady's ring. The trees on the larger island on Rydale
Lake were of the most gorgeous colours ; the whole Island
reflected in the water, as I remember once in particular to have
seen it with dear Coleridge, when either he or Wm. observed
that the rocky shore, spotted and streaked with purplish brown
heath, and its image in the water were indistinguishably blended,
like an immense caterpillar, such as, when we were children,
we used to call *Woolly Boys*, from their hairy coats. I had
been a little cowardly when we left home, fearing that heavy
rains might detain us at Patterdale ; but, as the mists thickened
our enjoyments increased, and my hopes grew bolder ; and

---

[1] The farm to which Tom Hutchinson had moved from Gallow Hill in
May 1804. It stands on a hill between Dacre and Stainton, 2 m. N. of
Ullswater.

[2] Captain and Mrs. Luff, friends introduced to the W.s by the Clarksons,
lived at Patterdale in a " comfortable cottage most happily situated in the
main vale above the lake of Ullswater " (D. W. to Lady Beaumont, Nov. 7,
1805).

when at the top of Kirkstone (though we could not see fifty yards before us) we were as happy travellers as ever paced side by side on a holiday ramble. At such a time and in such a place every scattered stone the size of one's head becomes a companion. There is a fragment of an old wall at the top of Kirkstone, which, magnified yet obscured as it was by the mist, was scarcely less interesting to us when we cast our eyes upon it, than the view of some noble monument of ancient grandeur — yet this same pile of stones we had never before observed. When we had descended considerably, the fields of Hartsop, below Brotherswater, were first seen like a lake, tinged by the reflection of yellow clouds. I mistook them for the water; but soon after we saw the lake itself gleaming faintly with a steely brightness; then as we descended appeared the brown oaks, and the birches of lovely yellow, and, when we came still nearer to the valley, the cottages and the lowly old Hall of Hartsop with its long roof and elegant chimnies.

We had eaten our dinner under the shelter of a sheep-fold by a bridge near the foot of the mountain, having tethered the pony at the entrance, where it stood without one impatient beating of a foot. I could not but love it for its meekness, and indeed I thought we were selfish to enjoy our meal so much while its poor jaws were confined by the curb bridle. We reached Luff's in the afternoon, about two hours before tea time.

November 8th, Thursday. The next morning incessant rain till eleven o'clock, when it became fair, and William and I walked to Blowick. Luff joined us by the way. The wind blew strong, and drove the clouds forward along the side of the hill above our heads; four or five goats were bounding among the rocks; the sheep moved about more quietly, or cowered in their sheltering-places. The two storm-stiffened black yew-trees on the crag above Luff's house were striking objects, close under or seen through the flying mists. I do not know what to say of Blowick; for to attempt to describe the place would be absurd, when you for whom I write have either been there, or may go there as soon as you like. When we stood upon the naked crag upon the Common, overlooking the woods and bush-besprinkled fields, the lake, clouds, and mists were all in

414

motion to the sound of sweeping winds — the church and cottages of Patterdale scarcely visible from the brightness of the mist. Looking down the Lake, the scene less visionary. Place Fell steady and bold as a lion ; the whole lake driving onward like a great river, waves dancing round the small islands. We walked to the house. The owner was salving sheep in the barn ; an appearance of poverty and decay everywhere. He asked us if we wanted to purchase the Estate. We could not but stop frequently, both in going and returning, to look at the exquisite beauty of the woods on the opposite side of the Lake. The general colour of the trees was brown, rather that of ripe hazel-nuts ; but towards the water there were yet beds of green, and in some of the hollow places in the highest part of the woods the trees were of a yellow colour, and through the glittering light they looked like masses of clouds as you see them gathered together in the west, and tinged with the golden light of the sun. After dinner we walked with Mrs. Luff up the vale ; I had never had an idea of the extent and width of it, in passing through on the other side. We walked along the path which leads from house to house ; two or three times it took us through some of those copses or groves that cover every little hillock in the middle of the lower part of the vale, making an intricate and beautiful intermixture of lawn and woodland. We left William to prolong his walk, and when he came into the house he told us that he had pitched upon the spot where he should like to build a house better than in any other he had yet seen. Mrs. Luff went with him by moonlight to view it. The vale looked as if it were filled with white light when the moon had climbed up to the middle of the sky ; but long before we could see her face, while all the eastern hills were in black shade, those on the opposite side were almost as bright as snow. Mrs. Luff's large white dog lay in the moonshine upon the round knoll under the old yew-tree, a beautiful and romantic image — the dark tree with its dark shadow, and the elegant creature as fair as a Spirit.

November 9th, Friday. It rained till near ten o'clock ; but a little after that time, it being likely for a tolerably fine day, we packed up bread and cold meat, and with Luff's servant to help to row, set forward in the boat. As we advanced the day grew finer, clouds and sunny gleams on the mountains. In the grand bay under Place Fell we saw three fishermen with a boat dragging a net, and rowed up to them. They had just brought the net ashore, and hundreds of fish were leaping in their prison. They were all of one kind, what are called Skellies. After we had left them the fishermen continued their work, a picturesque group under the lofty and bare crags; the whole scene was very grand, a raven croaking on the mountain above our heads. Landed at Sanwick; the man took the boat home, and we pursued our journey towards the Village along a beautiful summer path, at first through a copse by the Lake-side, then through green fields. The Village and brook very pretty, shut out from mountains and lake; it reminded me of Somersetshire. Passed by Harry Hebson's house; I longed to go in for the sake of former times. William went up one side of the vale, and we up the other, and he joined us after having crossed the one-arched bridge above the Church; a beautiful view of the church with its " bare ring of mossy wall " [1] and single yew-tree. At the last house in the dale we were kindly greeted by the master, who was sitting at the door salving sheep. He invited us to go in and see a room built by Mr. Hazel for his accommodation at the yearly Chace of Red Deer in his forests at the head of these dales. The room is fitted up in the sportsman's style, with a single cupboard for bottles and glasses etc., some strong chairs, and a large dining table, and ornamented with the horns of the stags caught at these hunts for many years back, with the length of the last race they ran recorded under each. We ate our dinner there. The good woman treated us with excellent butter and new oaten bread, and after drinking of Mr. Hazel's strong ale we were well prepared to face the mountain, which we began to climb almost immediately. Martindale divides itself into two dales at the head. In one of these (that to the left) there is no house to be seen, nor any building but a cattle-

---

[1] Cf. *The Brothers*, ll. 27, 28:

> *The Parish Chapel stood alone*
> *Girt round with a bare ring of mossy wall.*

shed on the side of a hill which is sprinkled over with wood, evidently the remains of a forest, formerly a very extensive one. At the bottom of the other valley is the house I have mentioned, and beyond the enclosures of this man's farm there are no other. A few old trees remain, relicks of the forest ; a little stream passes in serpentine windings through the uncultivated valley, where many cattle were feeding. The cattle of this country are generally white or light-coloured ; but those were mostly dark-brown or black, which made the scene resemble many parts of Scotland. When we sate on the hillside, though we were well contented with the quiet everyday sounds, the lowing of cattle, bleating of sheep, and the very gentle murmuring of the valley stream, yet we could not but think what a grand effect the sound of the bugle-horn would have among these mountains. It is still heard once a year at the chace — a day of festivity for all the inhabitants of the district, except the poor deer, the most ancient of them all. The ascent, even to the top of the mountain, is very easy. When we had accomplished it we had some exceedingly fine mountain views, some of the mountains being resplendent with sunshine, and others partly hidden by clouds. Ulswater was of a dazzling brightness bordered by black hills, the plain beyond Penrith smooth and bright (or rather *gleamy*) as the sea or sea-sands. Looked down into Boar Dale above Sanwick — deep and bare, a stream winding down it. After having walked a considerable way on the tops of the hills, came in view of Glenridding and the mountains at the head of Grisdale. Luff then took us aside, before we had begun to descend, to a small ruin, which was formerly a Chapel, or place of worship where the inhabitants of Martindale and Patterdale were accustomed to meet on Sabbath days. There are now no traces by which you could distinguish that the building had been different from a common sheepfold ; the loose stones and the few which yet remain piled up are the same as those which lie elsewhere on the mountain ; but the shape of the building being oblong is not that of a common sheepfold, and it stands east and west. Whether it was ever consecrated ground or not I do not know ; but the place may be kept holy in the memory of some now

living in Patterdale ; for it was the means of preserving the
life of a poor old man last summer, who, having gone up the
mountain to gather peats together, had been overtaken by a
storm, and could not find his way down again. He happened
to be near the remains of the old Chapel, and, in a corner of it,
he contrived, by laying turf and ling and stones in a corner of
it from one wall to the other, to make a shelter from the wind,
and there he sate all night. The woman who had sent him on
his errand began to grow uneasy towards night, and the neighbours went out to seek him. At that time the old man had
housed himself in his nest, and he heard the voices of the men,
but could not make himself heard, the wind being so loud, and
he was afraid to leave the spot lest he should not be able to
find it again, so he remained there all night ; and they returned
to their homes, giving him up for lost ; but the next morning
the same persons discovered him huddled up in the sheltered
nook. He was at first stupefied and unable to move ; yet
after he had eaten and drunk, and recollected himself a little,
he walked down the mountain, and did not afterwards seem
to have suffered.[1] As we descend, the vale of Patterdale appears
very simple and grand, with its two heads, Deep Dale, and
Brotherswater or Hartsop. It is remarkable that two pairs of
brothers should have been drowned in that lake. There is a
tradition, at least, that it took its name from two who were
drowned there many years ago, and it is a fact that two others
did meet that melancholy fate about twenty years since. It
was upon a New-Year's-day. Their mother had set them to
thresh some corn, and they (probably thinking it hard to be so
tasked when all others were keeping holiday) stole out to slide
upon the ice, and were both drowned. A neighbour who had
seen them fall through the ice, though not near enough to be
certain, *guessed who* they were and went to the mother to
inquire after her sons. She replied that " they were threshing
in the barn ". " Nay ", said the man, " they are not there, nor
is it likely to-day." The woman went with him to the barn
and the boys were gone. He was then convinced of the truth,

---

[1] Cf. *Excursion*, ii. 730-895, and the I. F. note to *Excursion*.

and told her that they were drowned. It is said that they were found locked in each other's arms. I was exceedingly tired when we reached Mr. Luff's house, owing to the steepness and roughness of the peat track down which we descended. I lay down on the sofa, and was asleep in three minutes. A fine moonlight night — a thick fog in the middle of the vale, which disheartened William respecting the situation of his house. Supped upon some of the fish caught by the fishermen under Place Fell, and thought them excellent.

November 10th, Saturday. A beautiful morning. When we were at breakfast heard the tidings of Lord Nelson's death and the victory of Trafalgar. Went to the inn to make further inquiries. I was shocked to hear that there had been great rejoicings at Penrith. Returned by William's rock and grove, and were so much pleased with the spot that William determined to buy it if possible, therefore we prepared to set off to Park House that Wm. might apply to Thomas Wilkinson [1] to negotiate for him with the owner. We went down that side of the lake opposite to Stybarrow Crag. I dismounted, and we sate some time under the same rock as before, above Blowick. Owing to the brightness of the sunshine the church and other buildings were even more concealed from us than by the mists two days before. It had been a sharp frost in the night, and the grass and trees were yet wet. We observed the lemon-coloured leaves of the birches in the wood below, as the wind turned them to the sun, sparkle, or rather flash, like diamonds. The day continued unclouded to the end. We had a delightful ride and walk, for it was both to both of us. We led the horse under Place Fell, and though I mostly rode when the way was good, William sometimes mounted to rest himself. Called at Eusemere [2]— the Miss Greens not yet settled in their house. Went by Bower Bank, intending to ford the Emont at the Mill, but the pony could not carry us both, so after many attempts, I rode over myself and a girl followed upon another horse to carry back the pony to William. Very cold before we reached

---

[1] v. *E.L.* p. 526.

[2] Eusemere, the house one mile from the foot of Ullswater, previously occupied by the Clarksons, was now rented by the Misses Green.

Park House. Carpets and chairs spread upon the grass, Derwent [1] ran out to meet us. Sate in the kitchen till the parlour fire was lighted, and then enjoyed a comfortable cup of tea. After tea Wm. went to Thomas Wilkinson's and to Brougham.

November 12th, Monday. The morning being fine, we resolved to go to Lowther, and accordingly Sara mounted Tom's horse, I the pony, and William and Miss Green set out on foot, but she had not walked far before she took a seat behind Sara. Crossed the ford at Yanworth. We found Thomas Wilkinson at work in one of his fields ; he chearfully laid down the spade and walked by our side with William. We left our horses at the Mill below Brougham, and walked through the woods till we came to the Quarry, where the road ends — the very place which has been the boundary of some of the happiest of the walks of my youth. The sun did not shine when we were there, and it was mid-day ; therefore, if it *had* shone, the light could not have been the same ; yet so vividly did I call to mind those walks, that, when I was in the wood, I almost seemed to see the same rich light of evening upon the trees which I had seen in those happy hours. At this time the path was scarcely traceable by the eye, all the ground being strewn with withered leaves, which I was very sorry for, William having described the beauty of it with so much delight after having been at Lowther in the summer.

Scrambled along, under the Quarry — then came to T. Wilkinson's new path. We spent three delightful hours by the river-side and in the woods. We were received with much kindness by Richard Bowman and his wife — dinner was presently prepared, and we were officiously [waited] upon by little Hannah, whose light motions and happy looks plainly expressed the hospitality of the house. Went with Miss Green to Penrith — drank tea at Mrs. Ellwood's. Read Collingwood's dispatches. Went to Mr. James's shop, and called upon Miss Monkhouse at Mrs. Coupland's. Mary Monkhouse and Sara mounted at The George. I walked with Wm. through the town

---

[1] *i.e.* Derwent Coleridge, born 1800.

to Mrs. Ellwood's door — the first time I have been in Penrith streets at that time of the night since Mary and her sister Margaret and I used to steal to each other's houses, and when we had had our *talk* over the kitchen fire, to delay the moment of parting, paced up one street and down another by moon or starlight. S. and I stopped at Red Hill, while William went over the ford to T. Wilkinson's — the house untidy and not comfortable — a little girl never ceased rocking a baby in the cradle. We asked if it would not sleep without being rocked, and the mother answered " No, for it was used to it ". Reached Park House at ten o'clock. Joanna had waited dinner and tea for us.

November 13th, Tuesday. A very wet morning ; no hope of being able to return home. William read in a book lent him by Thomas Wilkinson. I read *Castle Rackrent*. The day cleared at one o'clock, and after dinner, at a little before three, we set forward. The pony was bogged in Tom's field, and I was obliged to dismount. Went over Soulby Fell. Before we reached Ulswater the sun shone, and only a few scattered clouds remained on the hills except at the tops of the very highest — the lake perfectly calm. We had a delightful journey. At the beginning of the first Park William got upon the pony, and betwixt a walk and a run, I kept pace with him while he trotted to the next gate — then I mounted again. We were joined by two travellers, like ourselves, with one white horse between them. We went on in company till we came near to Patterdale, trotting all the time. The trees in Gowbarrow Park were very beautiful, the hawthorns leafless, their round heads covered with rich red berries, and adorned with arches of green brambles ; and eglantine hung with glossy hips ; many birches yet tricked out in full foliage of bright yellow ; oaks brown or leafless ; the smooth silver branches of the ashes bare ; most of the alders green as in spring. I think I have more pleasure in looking at deer than any other animals, perhaps chiefly from their living in a more natural state. At the end of Gowbarrow Park a large troop of them were either moving slowly, or standing still, among the fern. I was grieved when our chance companions startled them with a whistle, disturbing a beautiful image of grave simplicity and thoughtful enjoyment, for I could have fancied that even *they* were partaking with me a sensation of the solemnity of the closing day. The sun had been set some time, though we could only just perceive that the daylight was partly gone, and the lake was more brilliant than before. I dismounted again at Stybarrow Crag, and William rode till we came almost to Glenridding. Found the Luffs at tea in the kitchen. After tea we set out again. Luff accompanied me on foot into the lane, and Wm. continued to ride till we came to Brotherswater Bridge — a delightful evening. The Seven Stars close to the hill-tops in Patterdale ; all the stars seemed brighter than usual. The steeps were reflected in Brotherswater, and above the lake appeared like enormous black perpendicular walls. The torrents of Kirkstone had been swollen by the rains, and filled the mountain pass with their roaring, which added greatly to the solemnity of our walk. The stars in succession took their stations on the mountain-tops. Behind us, when we had climbed very high, we saw one light in the vale at a great distance, like a large star, a solitary one, in the gloomy region. All the chearfulness of the scene was in the sky above us.

Reached home an hour before midnight. Found Mary and the children in bed — no fire — luckily Wm. was warm with walking, and I not cold, having wrapped myself up most carefully, and the night being mild. Went to bed immediately after supper.

VI

Excursion up
SCAWFELL PIKE
OCTOBER 7TH, 1818

See End-paper map at end of volume

EXCURSION UP SCAWFELL PIKE

OCTOBER 7TH, 1818[1]

SIR GEORGE and Lady Beaumont spent a few days with us lately, and I accompanied them to Keswick. Mr. and Mrs. Wilberforce and their family happened to be at K. at the same time, and we all dined together in the romantic Vale of Borrowdale, at the house of a female friend, an unmarried Lady, who, bewitched with the charms of the rocks, and streams, and mountains of that secluded spot, has there built herself a house, and though she is admirably fitted for society, and has as much enjoyment when surrounded by her friends as any one *can* have, her chearfulness has never flagged, though she has lived more than the year round alone in Borrowdale, at six miles distance from Keswick, with bad roads between. You will guess that she has resources within herself ; such indeed she has. She is a painter and labours hard in depicting the beauties of her favorite Vale ; she is also fond of music and of reading, and has a reflecting mind ; besides (though before she lived in Borrowdale she was no great walker) she is become an active climber of the hills, and I must tell you of a feat that she and I performed on Wednesday the 7th of this month. I remained in Borrowdale after Sir G. and Lady B. and the Wilberforces were gone, and Miss Barker proposed that the next day she and I should go to Seathwaite beyond the Black lead mines at the head of Borrowdale, and thence up a mountain called at the top *Ash Course*, which we suppose may be a corruption of *Esk Hawes*, as it is a settling between

---

[1] An extract from a letter, now lost, written by D. W. to the Rev. William Johnson, curate at Grasmere 1811–12, and later a schoolmaster in London (*v. M.Y.* p. 445). W. W. printed an adapted version of it in his *Guide to the Lakes* (p. 112 of my reprint, London, 1906). William Wilberforce and his family spent part of September and October of this year at Rydal (*v. M.Y.* pp. 822-8).

the mountains over which the people are accustomed to pass between Eskdale and Borrowdale ; and such settlings are generally called by the name of " the Hawes " — as Grisdale Hawes, Buttermere Hawes, from the German word Hals (neck). At the top of Ash Course Miss Barker had promised that I should see a magnificent prospect ; but we had some miles to travel to the foot of the mountain, and accordingly went thither in a cart — Miss Barker, her maid, and myself. We departed before nine o'clock, the sun shone ; the sky was clear and blue ; and light and shade fell in masses upon the mountains ; the fields below *glittered* with the dew, where the beams of the sun could reach them ; and every little stream tumbling down the hills seemed to add to the chearfulness of the scene.

We left our cart at Seathwaite and proceeded, with a man to carry our provisions, and a kind neighbour of Miss Barker's, a statesman shepherd of the vale, as our companion and guide. We found ourselves at the top of Ash Course without a weary limb, having had the fresh air of autumn to help us up by its invigorating power, and the sweet warmth of the unclouded sun to tempt us to sit and rest by the way. From the top of Ash Course we beheld a prospect which would indeed have amply repaid us for a *toilsome* journey, if such it had been ; and a sense of thankfulness for the continuance of that vigour of body, which enabled me to climb the high mountain, as in the days of my youth, inspiring me with fresh chearfulness, added a delight, a charm to the contemplation of the magnificent scenes before me, which I cannot describe. Still less can I tell you the glories of what we saw. Three views, each distinct in its kind, we saw at once — the vale of Borrowdale, of Keswick, of Bassenthwaite — Skiddaw, Saddleback, Helvellyn, numerous other mountains, and, still beyond, the Solway Frith, and the mountains of Scotland.

Nearer to us, on the other side, and below us, were the Langdale Pikes, then our own Vale below them, Windermere, and far beyond Windermere, after a long distance, Ingleborough in Yorkshire. But how shall I speak of the peculiar deliciousness of the third prospect ? At this time *that* was most favoured by sunshine and shade. The green Vale of Esk — deep and green, with its glittering serpent stream was below us ; and on we looked to the mountains near the sea — Black Combe and others — and still beyond, to the sea itself in dazzling brightness. Turning round we saw the mountains of Wasdale in tumult ; and Great Gavel, though the middle of the mountain was to us as its base, looked very grand.

We had attained the object of our journey ; but our ambition mounted higher. We saw the summit of Scaw Fell, as it seemed, very near to us ; we were indeed, three parts up that mountain, and thither we determined to go. We found the distance greater than it had appeared to us, but our courage did not fail ; however, when we came nearer we perceived that in order to attain that summit we must make a great dip, and that the ascent afterwards would be exceedingly steep and difficult, so that we might have been benighted if we had attempted it ; therefore, unwillingly, we gave it up, and resolved, instead, to ascend another point of the same mountain, called *the Pikes*, and which, I have since found, the measurers of the mountains estimate as higher than the larger summit which bears the name of Scaw Fell, and where the Stone Man is built which we, at the time, considered as the point of highest honour. The sun had never once been overshadowed by a cloud during the whole of our progress from the centre of Borrowdale ; at the summit of the Pike there was not a breath of air to stir even the papers which we spread out containing our food. There we ate our dinner in summer warmth ; and the stillness seemed to be not of this world. We paused, and kept silence to listen, and not a sound of any kind was to be heard. We were far above the reach of the cataracts of Scaw Fell ; and not an insect was there to hum in the air. The Vales before described lay in view, and side by side with Eskdale, we now saw the sister Vale of Donnerdale terminated by the Duddon Sands. But the majesty of the mountains below and close to us, is not to be conceived. We now beheld the whole mass of Great Gavel from its base, the Den of Wasdale at our feet, the gulph immeasurable, Grasmere [1] and

---

[1] D. W. means *Grasmoor*.

427

the other mountains of Crummock, Ennerdale and *its* mountains, and the sea beyond.

While we were looking round after dinner our Guide said that we must not linger long, for we should have a storm. We looked in vain to espy the traces of it ; for mountains, vales, and the sea were all touched with the clear light of the sun. " It is there ", he said, pointing to the sea beyond Whitehaven, and, sure enough, we there perceived a light cloud, or mist, unnoticeable but by a shepherd, accustomed to watch all mountain bodings. We gazed around again and yet again, fearful to lose the remembrance of what lay before us in that lofty solitude ; and then prepared to depart. Meanwhile the air changed to cold, and we saw the tiny vapour swelled into mighty masses of cloud which came boiling over the mountains. Great Gavel, Helvellyn, and Skiddaw were wrapped in storm ; yet Langdale and the mountains in that quarter were all bright with sunshine. Soon the storm reached us ; we sheltered under a crag, and almost as rapidly as it had come, it passed away, and left us free to observe the goings-on of storm and sunshine in other quarters — Langdale had now its share, and the Pikes were decorated by two splendid rainbows ; Skiddaw also had its own rainbows, but we were glad to see them and the clouds disappear from that mountain, as we knew that Mr. and Mrs. Wilberforce and the family (if they kept the intention which they had formed when they parted from us the night before) must certainly be upon Skiddaw at that very time — and so it was. They were there, and had much more rain than we had ; we, indeed, were hardly at all wetted ; and before we found ourselves again upon that part of the mountain called Ash Course every cloud had vanished from every summit.

Do not think we here gave up our spirit of enterprise. No ! I had heard much of the grandeur of the view of Wasdale from Stye Head, the point from which Wasdale is first seen in coming by the road from Borrowdale ; but though I had been in Wasdale I had never entered the dale by that road, and had often lamented that I had not seen what was so much talked of by travellers. Down to that Pass (for we were yet far above it) we bent our course by the side of Ruddle Gill, a very deep red chasm in the mountains which begins at a spring — that spring forms a stream, which must, at times, be a mighty torrent, as is evident from the channel which it has wrought out — thence by Sprinkling Tarn to Stye Head ; and there we sate and looked down into Wasdale. We were now upon Great Gavel which rose high above us. Opposite was Scaw Fell and we heard the roaring of the stream from one of the ravines of that mountain, which, though the bending of Wasdale Head lay between us and Scaw Fell, we could look into, as it were, and the depth of the ravine appeared tremendous ; it was black and the crags were awful.

We now proceeded homewards by Stye head Tarn along the road into Borrowdale. Before we reached Stonethwaite a few stars had appeared, and we travelled home in our cart by moonlight.

I ought to have described the last part of our ascent to Scaw Fell Pike. There, not a blade of grass was to be seen — hardly a cushion of moss, and that was parched and brown ; and only growing rarely between the huge blocks and stones which cover the summit and lie in heaps all round to a great distance, like skeletons or bones of the earth not wanted at the creation, and there left to be covered with never-dying lichens, which the clouds and dews nourish ; and adorn with colours of the most vivid and exquisite beauty, and endless in variety. No gems or flowers can surpass in colouring the beauty of some of these masses of stone which no human eye beholds except the shepherd led thither by chance or traveller by curiosity ; and how seldom must this happen ! The other eminence is that which is visited by the adventurous traveller, and the shepherd has no temptation to go thither in quest of his sheep ; for on the Pike there is no food to tempt them. We certainly were singularly fortunate in the day ; for when we were seated on the summit our Guide, turning his eyes thoughtfully round, said to us, " I do not know that in my whole life I was ever at any season of the year so high up on the mountains on so calm a day ". Afterwards, you know, we had the storm which exhibited to us the grandeur of earth and heaven commingled, yet without terror; for we knew that the storm would pass away; for so our prophetic guide assured us. I forget to tell you that I espied a ship upon the glittering sea while we were looking over Eskdale. " Is it a ship ? " replied the Guide. " A ship, yes, it can be nothing else, don't you see the shape of it ? " Miss Barker interposed, " It is a ship, of that I am certain. I cannot be mistaken, I am so accustomed to the appearance of ships at sea. The Guide dropped the argument; but a moment was scarce gone when he quietly said, " Now look at your ship, it is now a horse ". So indeed it was — a horse with a gallant neck and head. We laughed heartily, and, I hope, when again inclined to positiveness, I may remember the ship and the horse upon the glittering sea; and the calm confidence, yet submissiveness, of our wise Man of the Mountains, who certainly had more knowledge of clouds than we, whatever might be our knowledge of ships. To add to our uncommon performance on that day Miss Barker and I each wrote a letter from the top of the Pike to our far distant friend in S. Wales, Miss Hutchinson.

October 21st, 1818.

APPENDICES

Appendix I

NOTES ON SOME OF THE PERSONS MENTIONED IN
THE GRASMERE JOURNAL

By the late GORDON GRAHAM WORDSWORTH

ASHBURNER

To none of her Town End neighbours does D. W. refer so frequently, or with such affectionate intimacy, as to the family of Thomas Ashburner, who was a small statesman living in the reduced circumstances described on November 24, 1801, and worked up by W. into his poem *Repentance*. He inhabited the cottage now rebuilt with a small shop, just across the road slightly north-west of Dove Cottage. The " lasses clean and rosy " were constantly in and out, taking messages, learning to mark, weeding, helping with the linen, etc. etc.

Thomas A., son of George A., junior, of Grasmere, was baptized June 10, 1754. His first marriage is not recorded, but his children, all born at Town End, were baptized on the following dates : Agnes, November 15, 1781 ; Anne, December 7, 1783 ; Jane, February 5, 1786 ; Mary, March 30, 1788 ; Sara, February 7, 1790. On January 20, 1791, Anne, wife of Thomas A. of Town End, was buried, and on December 10 of the same year Thomas A., widower, and Margaret Lancaster, both of Grasmere, were married. Margaret's delicate health and racking cough are referred to in the *Journals*, and in 1802 she must have left Grasmere for a time, as letters were more than once exchanged with her.

It seems probable that Thomas A. was the widower described in *The Excursion*, vi. 111-91, though there he is given six daughters instead of five, and no mention is made of his second wife ; but the picture may have been drawn during " Peggy " 's absence in 1802. Sara A. married Charles Stuart of Windermere on November 20, 1809 ; Mary A. married James Fleming of Knott Houses, Grasmere, on June 18, 1810. Mrs. Fletcher in her *Autobiography* speaks of her as " our favourite neighbour ", and her daughter-in-law relates that their home was " like a second home " to W. ; he was " for ever there " in his later life.

The carts of coal which Thomas A. so often brought the W.s were carted from Keswick.

FISHER

The Parish Register gives the following particulars relating to the family of Fishers mentioned in the *Journals* :—

Robert Fisher and Anne Dawson, married May 6, 1740.
Mary, daughter of Robert F., baptized March 25, 1741.
John, son of Robert F., baptized July 8, 1746.
John F., cordwainer, and Agnes Mackereth, married April 5, 1774.
John, son of John F., baptized November 9, 1778.
Agnes, wife of John F., buried April 23, 1804.
Mary F., of Town End, spinster, buried June 3, 1808.
John F., of Town End, aged 70, buried April 3, 1820.

John F. lived with his wife Agnes and his sister Mary, known as Molly, at Sykeside, the house across the road from Dove Cottage, slightly to the south-west (the house of which the adjacent barn is now the Wordsworth Museum). There is no doubt but that Agnes is the woman referred to in *The Excursion*, vi. 675-777 : " Tall was her stature, her complexion dark and saturnine ". Her son John is referred to in the *Journal* on June 21, 1802, as well as her power of conversation, and her " avaricious thrift " is hinted at on May 16, 1800. John F. figures constantly in the *Journal* as giving help in the garden, etc. The mention of his " intake " on June 6, 1802, confirms the restoration of his fortune mentioned in *The Excursion*. In 1810 he was employed in the garden at Allan Bank.

Mary F. (Molly), whose surname is never given in either D. W.'s *Journals* or *Letters*, was the loyal servant whose racy dialect gave Dorothy such pleasure. On December 24, 1799, four days after his arrival at Dove Cottage, W. writes to Coleridge : " We have agreed to give a woman who lives in one of the adjoining cottages two shillings a week for attending two or three hours a day to light the fires, wash dishes, etc." On September 10, 1800, D. W. writes to Mrs. Marshall : " Our servant is an old woman 60 years of age. She sleeps at her own home which is so near that it is a great convenience in our small house. She is much attached to us, and honest and good as ever was a human being." In August 1802 Coleridge called at the house in the absence of the W.s, but would not go beyond the kitchen : " I was very wet, and my boots very dirty, and Molly had set the Pride of her Heart on the neatness " of the house. On May 25, 1804, D. W. wrote to Lady Beaumont : " Our old servant whom you may have heard Coleridge speak of as a drollery belonging to the cottage has left us " six weeks ago, a date which corresponds to the illness and death of her sister-in-law Agnes, and the account given thereof in *The Excursion*. On May 7, 1805, Mary Lamb wrote to D. W. : " Pray remember us to old Molly. How well I remember her old friendly face." At the end of March 1808, D. W. writes to De Quincey, " Old Molly talks with chearfulness of dying except when she turns to poor John's melancholy condition ", and two months later the loyal friend and servant had passed away, bequeathing her best gown to D. W.

John Fisher, junior, seems, after a wild youth (*v. The Excursion*, vi. 710-15), to have settled down as a cobbler in his father's house at Sykeside, and was buried thence on April 23, 1827. On November 8, 1817, he had married Mary Dawson, who had been in the service of the W.s at Dove Cottage and of the Lloyds at Old Brathay before becoming factotum to De Quincey on his entry into Dove Cottage in 1809. In 1814 she was cook at Rydal Mount. As a widow she resided at Sykeside till her death in 1854, at the age of 76, and as a last remaining link with the old Town End days her house and conversation formed a strong attraction to W. in his old age.

MACKERETH (or MACKARETH)

Gawen, or, as D. W. often spells it, Goan (baptized September 24, 1745), and George (baptized November 18, 1752) were the sons of George M. of Underhowe, who had married Rebecca Rukin of Patterdale : she was buried from Knott Houses on January 20, 1791.

Gawen M., described in the Registers as husbandman, married on January 16, 1783, Mary Wilkinson, servant, of Grasmere, who was buried from Lane End, August 29, 1806. Five of their children are entered in the Register, from William, born at Church Stile (baptized April 5, 1784), to Rebecca (baptized April 16, 1801), whose illness and funeral are mentioned by D. W. on June 3 and 6, 1802. After the birth of his first-born, Gawen's residence is always given as Lane End, which from D. W.'s frequent references to it must have been near either the Swan Inn or Knott Houses, but the name is now lost.

George M., when the first of his numerous family was born in 1780, was living in his father's house at Underhowe, but shortly afterwards he moved to Knott Houses, whither W. and D. W.

often repaired to hire or borrow a saddle horse. The eldest son was baptized George on February 18, 1780, and his return from London is referred to in the *Journal* for June 29, 1802. Ellen (baptized March 1, 1789) and William (baptized February 13, 1791) also figure in the *Journal* as looking after their father's horse (July 9, 1802, and January 2, 1803).

The Mackereths acted as parish clerks for several generations, George M. witnessing signatures in the Register from September 1791 to November 1830.

OLLIFFS

There is frequent allusion in the *Journal* to the wood and field of these kindly neighbours, and of friendly intercourse with them. Their house is now incorporated in the stables of the modern Hollins. The Registers give :—

> George, son of John Olive, Esq. of Hollins, baptized October 19, 1798.
> Sarah, daughter of, etc., February 28, 1802 ; died March 8, 1802.

Immediately after the death of the last-named Mr. and Mrs. Olliff appear to have left Grasmere. In a letter to M. H. of April 16, 1802, D. W. mentions that the Olliffs had had a sale during her recent absence at Eusemere ; the frequent references to them then come to an end (though there is a reference to their grounds on April 17 and June 1), and the Hollins seems to have been taken by Mr. King (*v.* June 4). For Mr. King *v.* De Quincey, *Works*, ed. Masson, ii. 426-31.

SIMPSON (SYMPSON), of the Nab

The family of Park had owned the Nab since 1332, and Mary Park, daughter and heiress of Willy Park, married John Simpson of Windermere in July 1794 ; after their marriage the young couple lived with her parents. Their children were Margaret (March 1796), John (December 1797), William (March 1801), Mary (March 1803), Anne (August 1806), Elizabeth (December 1808). The three eldest only, therefore, were contemporary with the *Journals*, in which D. W.'s entries on January 27, February 28, and March 13, 1802, record her affectionate admiration for them. Margaret married De Quincey on February 15, 1817 ; William subsequently kept the forge at Tongue Gill.

SYMPSONS (SIMPSON), of Broadrain

The Rev. Joseph Sympson, Vicar of Wythburn for more than fifty years, is described at length in *The Excursion*, vii. 31-291. His intercourse and that of his family with Dove Cottage was almost daily throughout the period covered by the *Journals*. The stone that marks his grave records his death, at 92, on June 27, 1807 ; that of his wife Mary, at 81, on January 24, 1806 ; and of Elizabeth Jane, his youngest daughter, 37, on September 11, 1804. In the Grasmere Registers we find :—

> Margaret, daughter of the Rev. Mr. S. of Broadrain, baptized March 14, 1765.
>
> Elizabeth Jane, do., May 7, 1767.
>
> Elizabeth Julia Sympson, daughter of Julius Caesar Ibbetson of Ambleside, baptized July 23, 1804.
>
> Elizabeth Jane, wife of J. C. Ibbetson of Low Broadrain, buried September 17, 1804.
>
> Elizabeth Julia Sympson, daughter of J. C. Ibbetson, buried December 23, 1804.
>
> Mary, wife of Rev. Joseph S. of Broadrain, buried January 27, 1806.
>
> Rev. Joseph Sympson, curate of Wythburn, buried July 2, 1807.
>
> Bartholomew Sympson of Wray, Grasmere, aged 75, buried January 1, 1832.

The Ambleside Registers contain the entry :—

> John Ibbetson, artist, of the parish of Grasmere, and Elizabeth Sympson of same parish, were married by licence, December 26, 1803.

In a passage of *The Excursion*, cancelled in 1820, W. states that the youngest daughter had married when no longer young, and " dwelt with her mate beneath her Father's roof ". *The Excursion* speaks of five graves, those of the Sire, his Partner, his son, his daughter and his grandchild, but only four burials are recorded in the Register, and only three names given on the tombstone. The omitted passage says that three of the children went out to try their fortune in the open world and that one returned to " humbly till his father's glebe ". This would probably be Bartholomew, to whom there are occasional references throughout the *Journal*. Robert is once mentioned ; whilst the eldest son, who, like his father, was a Joseph and a clergyman, was a poet of no mean skill (*v.* I. F. note to *Excursion* and to *Duddon Sonnets*, vi.). Of the daughters

D. W. mentions Mary and Jenny ; and Mrs. Jameson may have been a third. Little " Tommy " (June 3 and 7, 1800) is probably a grandson.

Mr. Sympson's engraving and drawing, referred to on February 22 and June 10, 1800, are not alluded to in the account of his accomplishments given in *The Excursion*, but general mention is made of his versatility and " hands apt for all ingenious arts " ; and the I. F. note states that there was much talent in the family. It is noticeable that there is no reference in the *Journal*, however indirect, to his clerical ministrations. *The Excursion* mentions his " punctual labour in his sacred charge ", and calls him " a constant preacher to the poor ", but is somewhat qualified in praise of his visiting (*Excursion*, vii. 140-53). His house and garden across the road, where " Death fell upon him like a shadow thrown softly and lightly from a passing cloud ", remain remarkably little changed to this day (1912).

Appendix II

NOTES WRITTEN BY D. W. AT THE END OF HER TRANSCRIPT OF *RECOLLECTIONS OF A SCOTCH TOUR*

MEMORANDUMS

[See *Recollections*, p. 336, end of Sept. 3.] Journal resumed February 2nd, 1804. Nothing written since the beginning of December, the time when Coleridge and Derwent were with us, before C.'s departure for Malta.

[See *Recollections*, end of Second Part, p. 343.] Now I resume my work (after a long pause) on Saturday June 23rd, 1804. I have been ten days in solitude, namely since last Thursday sennight, when William, Mary, and little John went to Park House, and now, having finished my needle-work, letters, etc., I shall endeavour to recollect the latter part of our journey. I feel I shall often be deceived ; a long time and many thoughts have passed between, and always, except a few places or tracts of country, as, for instance, Edinburgh, the Tweed, the Tiviot, and the Esk, the character of the different places was less distinguishable, one place more resembling another, and differing less from what we had seen in England than the space between Loch Lomond and Tyndrum.

So far the 23rd of June. It is now the 23rd of July and I take the pen, more heartless, even, than before, for my recollections must needs be fainter and fainter. The little incidents of our journey are many of them forgotten, or will now hardly seem worth recording, such as this day's good or bad dinner, a kind welcome, gentle or sour looks from the landlady, etc. etc.

[Memorandum at the end of the Third Part, p. 409.] Finished this Journal May 31st, 1805, in the Moss Hut at the top of the orchard. William, Mary and I finished the Moss Hut on the afternoon of June 6th, 1805. After the work was ended we all sate down in the middle of the seat, looking at the clouds in the west, — a very beautiful evening, as it had been a fine sunny day.

Memorandum. The first part of this Journal, and the second,

as far as page 336, were written before the end of the year 1803. I do not know when I concluded the *remainder* of the second part ; but it was resumed on the 2nd of February 1804. The third part was begun at the end of the month of April 1805, and finished on the 31st of May.

The transcript finished in February 1806.

October 4th, 1832. I find that this Tour was both begun and ended on a Sunday. I am sorry that it should have been so, though I hope and trust that our thoughts and feelings were not seldom as pious and serious as if we had attended a place devoted to public worship. My sentiments have undergone a great change since 1803 respecting the absolute necessity of keeping the Sabbath by a regular attendance at Church. D. W.

Appendix III

SPECIMENS OF D. W.'S LATER REVISION OF HER
RECOLLECTIONS OF A SCOTCH TOUR

[p. 195.] On Monday the 15th August 1803, I left Keswick with two companions — our vehicle a jaunting-car, of the kind which is jestingly called an Irish *vis-à-vis*, the Parties sitting back to back. We chose it for the convenience of alighting at will, in the rough and mountainous region through which we were about to wander. On quitting the Vale of Keswick, passed on our right hand the well-known druidical circle, and, soon after, the village of Threlkeld, where formerly stood one of the Mansions of Sir Launcelot Threlkeld, in a domain which he was proud of for being so well stocked with Tenantry to follow him to the wars. Here also he protected his Son-in-law, Lord Clifford, when the Youth was obliged to hide himself in Shepherd's Garb to avoid the power of the revengeful Yorkists. Crossed, in travelling under Saddle-back (formerly called Blencathara) several ravines almost choked up in places with rubbish brought down by the waters from the mountain-side and spread upon the road and adjoining fields. These formidable inundations are principally caused by the bursting of thunder-clouds ; and Blencathara (allow me to give the mountain its ancient appellation) shews in a remarkable degree with what perseverance the fountains of the sky are wearing away the bodies of these giants of earth. At no very great elevation from the road, though entirely hidden from it, on the side of this mountain, lies a pool or small Tarn of singularly melancholy appearance. It is enclosed by circular rocks very steep and on one side rising to a great height, and you might fancy that the pool had filled up the crater of a volcano, a notion one is disposed to encourage as Blencathara has more the appearance of having undergone the action of fire than any of his brethren. Beyond the 5th mile-stone, turned off from the Penrith road. Passed the foot of Grisedale and Mosedale, both pastoral vallies, narrow, and soon terminating in the mountains — green — with scattered trees and houses, and each a clear brook. Travelled at the base of Carrock Fell, covered with loose stones to a considerable height, and very rocky above. The

441

aspect of the whole recalled that characteristic and laboriously moving verse of Dyer

Huge Bredan's stony summit once I climbed.

Had time allowed, we should have been inclined to ascend this mountain, to visit some vestiges of antiquity of which writers give but a confused account, agreeing, however, that the work must have been of a very remote age. Heaps of stones (some of the stones being of enormous size) are said to be scattered over a large area upon the summit. In what form the architecture had arranged these stones cannot be even conjectured ; but the country people believe in the tradition that some of those heaps are the remains of a church without troubling themselves with a question what sort of a building such masses would compose or with a doubt whether the worship was different from that of their own days. Reached Hesket Newmarket and in the evening walked to Caldbeck Falls, a pleasing spot in which to breathe out a summer's day — lime-stone rocks — hanging trees — pools and water-breaks — caves and caldrons, which have been honoured with fairy names, and no doubt continue, in the fancy of the neighbourhood, to resound with fairy revels.

[p. 216.] Such a Boy, thought I, *he* once was; and such an old man will this child become ; and how much have they now in common ! — dress — occupation — mode of life — grave movement of body and of mind ! — So begins, here, and so ends human life ; and the intermediate space might seem to have so little variety that the whole presents itself to meditation with the simplicity of a circle.

[p. 330.] Shall I be forgiven when I add, that we were but little affected by recollections, on the spot, of the barbarous massacre of Glen Coe ? — which William the third neglected to punish, and by so doing, left an indelible stain upon his memory. One reads and thinks with indignation and sorrow of similar events ; but here, in presence of such sublime objects, intimating the power of the creator to confer durability in what manner he chuses, yet affording undeniable evidences of the revolutions to which this planet has been subject, the mind sinks under the pressure of time ; — the crimes and sufferings of individuals, or of this or that generation are lost in a feeling of the great mystery of decay and renovation, of life, and of death.

[p. 343.] I hardly know why we did not go to visit the turf, which is said to cover the grave of Fingal : — The tradition is in unison with the romantic character of the mountainous recesses at the head of Loch Tay, and probably we did not expect to have our faith strengthened by seeing with our own eyes (what we had been told) that there was no *visible* monument on the spot ; besides, the situation of the village is so very interesting that we were satisfied after our walk along the banks of the silent stream with strolling about and lingering not two hundred yards from the houses.

[p. 359.] We both laughed heartily, which no doubt the gardener considered as high commendation, and probably he would have been well satisfied if we had cast but a slight regard upon the living waters of the Bran, or regarded them as merely illustrative of the skill and taste of the contriver of this, to us, ludicrous exhibition : but we soon fixed our eyes only on the breezy dinning cataract — the fretted stones, overhanging crags, and pendant, or stately trees — yet such is the injurious effect of this conceited interposition of artifice, that, grand as are the accompaniments of that mountain torrent, my recollections are very indistinct except of the first over-coming sensation of oddness and surprize ; and this, I believe from repeated experience, is the universal effect of obtrusive attempts to illustrate or adorn nature in places such as this, where submissiveness to her power seems to be the only legitimate homage.

[p. 408.] After sunset we bent our course up the vale — poetic ground ! for Mickle, the translator of *The Lusiad*, was born at L. and has celebrated several of the brooks tributary to the Esk. We thought of him, and with the more interest, evening being the time in which his fancy seems most to have delighted. My companion repeated with pleasure some of his verses — the beautiful description of evening and the approach of night, in the beginning of his elegy on the death of his Brother, and that exquisitely musical stanza at the opening of his Poem of Sir Martyn,

> *Awake, ye west winds, through the lovely dale*
> *And Fancy to thy faery bower betake* etc.;

nor could we forget that other equally appropriate, and still more beautiful stanza,

> *Now bright behind the Cambrian mountains hoar* etc.

END OF VOL. I